The Island Edge
of America

Palace telephotoed against Capitol (2002). Photo by Tom Coffman

The Island Edge of America

A Political History of Hawai'i

Tom Coffman

A Latitude 20 Book
University of Hawai'i Press
Honolulu

Printed in the United States of America

08 07 06 05 04 03   6 5 4 3 2 1

Library of Congress Cataloging-in-Publication Data

Coffman, Tom.
    The island edge of America: a political history of Hawaii / Tom Coffman.
      p. cm.
    "A latitude 20 book."
    Includes bibliographical references and index.
    ISBN 0-8248-2625-6 (cloth: alk. paper) — ISBN 0-8248-2662-0 (paper: alk. paper)
      1. Hawaii—Politics and government—1900–1959. 2. Hawaii—Politics and government—
1959–. 3. Hawaii—Politics and government. I. Title.

DU627.5 .C64 2003
996.9'03--dc21
                                      2002074240

Designed by Argosy

Printed by Thomson-Shore, Inc.

For Nate and Makena

Contents

Preface

I arrived in the new state of Hawai'i in 1965 as a young reporter and was almost instantly immersed in covering politics. Having experienced the civil rights movement in mainland America, I was eager to believe—as were many people—that Hawai'i was the ideal society in the potentially ideal nation. To my shock, the celebration ended with the development of the Vietnam War and the bitterly contested gubernatorial election of 1970, an event I attempted to capture in my first book, *Catch A Wave*.

Thereafter, I stole away from a newspaper industry that I had enjoyed but with which I was increasingly at odds. Drawn by impulses that I could not support financially, I opened a community-based writing business out of a brown backpack. While I wondered whether I could pay the telephone bill, others imagined I was living from royalties. Only slowly did I grasp that the extensive readership of *Catch A Wave* had given me a gift of another sort, which was access to an ever-evolving course of research, interviewing, tape-recording, writing, and eventually, photographing, videotaping, directing, and producing.

Almost by definition I was involved in new things, but with each step forward, I encountered people who craved retrieving something from the past. One vivid example was the editing and presentation of *Culture Plan/Draft One* for the early Office of Hawaiian Affairs, in which vague images of the Hawaiian past cried out for definition. A second was the development of the Japanese Cultural Center of Hawai'i, in which the heroics of the nisei soldier demanded an intergenerational context. Through such experiences I returned to my own origins in research and writing.

Accordingly, the purpose of *The Island Edge of America* became not only to extend Hawai'i's written history (from approximately 1959 to 1990), but to redraw the trajectory of the entire century. While I return to some of the characters of *Catch A Wave*, I have added previously unknown individuals who preceded them and otherwise unexamined individuals who followed them. Because so many who populated this stage were of Japanese ancestry, some readers may insist this is a Japanese American history. It is true that, if anything, Japanese Americans played an even greater role in developing modern Hawai'i than previously has been portrayed. But I nonetheless resist the idea that Hawai'i's contemporary history is mostly about Japanese Americans and the Democratic Party. Rather, it is about the mixing of people, and about a looping progression of changes that sometimes overlap and sometimes diverge. As I wrote my second book, *Nation Within, The Story of America's Annexation of Hawai'i,* these events and trends are not so much parochial history as history that has been parochialized by America's mistaken belief that change moves constantly to the West. To the contrary, the process of change in Hawai'i has contributed to changes in the United States. It has influenced other island societies and it has touched Asia more deeply than is usually appreciated. A more open Hawai'i has begun to redefine itself. This process is tentative and partial. A uniquely island society struggles for breath within the crush of the continental superpower and there, for now, the arc stops, suspended in midair.

Acknowledgments

The writing of this book was made possible by a grant from the Pacific Rim Society.

Without Lawrence S. Fuchs of Brandeis University, there would be no point of departure for Hawai'i's post-statehood history. My friend Edward Crapol of William and Mary College helped me digest the largely hidden narrative of America's expansion into the Pacific. The framework of America's clash with Japan relies on two great American historians, Akira Iriye of Harvard and Walter LaFeber of Cornell. Eileen Tamura expanded the definitions of Americanization and acculturation. Masayo Duus defined the importance of the 1920 strike to both Hawai'i and to United States–Japan relations. Attorney Ted T. Tsukiyama has constantly expanded people's understanding of the nisei fighting units. Jane Komeiji's research on the early Japanese experience in Hawai'i helped in many ways. Dan Boylan's biography of John A. Burns created a much-needed baseline portrait, and Sheenagh Burns provided a compelling interpretation of her father. Two scholars have deepened the understanding of statehood, Roger Bell of the University of New South Wales, Australia, in his treatment of civil rights, and John Whitehead of the University of Georgia, in his simultaneous study of Hawai'i and Alaska. At a crucial point, Noenoe Silva of the University of Hawai'i helped me work out the idea of the single narrative of statehood giving way to multiple narratives. Wendall Marumoto brought a challenging conservative dimension to research of Japanese American community development. The writing of Gary Okihiro of Columbia University constantly and brilliantly challenged from the left. Japan-based scholars of Japanese American Studies—prominently including George Oshiro, Noriko Shimada, and Hiromi Monobe—have added both new information and cultural nuance to the Hawai'i story.

Library finds were unearthed by Makena K. Coffman, as well as Shelley O'Brien and Ashley Langworthy. Joy Doucette searched out all the original newspaper files on the 1970s and 1980s. Chris Conybeare guided me to the three-volume Hawai'i Political History Documentation Project, in which he played a leadership role through Hawai'i Public Television in conjunction with the Center for Oral History, Social Science Research Institute, University of Hawai'i at Manoa.

I am indebted to Masako Ikeda at the University of Hawai'i Press for taking hold of the edit and moving forward energetically. Noe Arista ably searched out and edited photographs. Adriana Lavergne of Argosy directed production and editing of the manuscript. Kathy Reimers gave the manuscript a final editorial reading.

A grant for preproduction of a companion documentary from Gerbode Foundation also contributed to analyzing and simplifying years of research that preceded the writing. Storyline and film production work performed for the Japanese Cultural Center of Hawai'i in the early 1990s also contributed to preparation for this project. For the moral support and wry wisdom that helped keep all of this on track, a special thanks goes to Hideo Murakami.

Voices of those who are gone still inform my thinking, particularly the pioneering ombudsman of Hawai'i, Herman S. Doi; Sakae Takahashi, an innovator in both finance and politics; and John Dominis Holt, the great Hawaiian writer of his time.

Timeline

1875	Under pressure from white planters, Hawaiian crown trades access to Pearl Harbor for duty-free access to the American sugar market (Treaty of Reciprocity)
1885	With sugar cultivation spreading rapidly, planters invest in the massive migration of Japanese workers
1893	Supported by American diplomats and American troops, American-descended citizens of Hawai'i take over the nation of Hawai'i
1896	Native Hawaiians petition U.S. Congress to oppose annexation; America divided over Pacific expansionism
1898	American government annexes Hawai'i on a wave of jingoistic fervor accompanying the Spanish American War; becomes a pan-Pacific power
1909	Japanese workers stage first major sugar strike
1920	Japanese workers stage second major strike, triggering fears of "Japanization" of Hawai'i
1924	Congress passes Japanese Exclusion Act, causing major crisis in U.S.-Japan relations
1939–1941	Japanese American support networks form in anticipation of war with Japan
December 7, 1941	The crisis of the Japanese Americans in Hawai'i becomes manifest
1942	Japanese American support network resists mass internment; nisei 100th Battalion is sent to training
1943	Anti-Japanese movement is thwarted; events in Hawai'i lead new national policy of including AJA in U.S. military; 442nd RCT formed
1946	Labor radicals organize plantation workers, lead strike

1949	Labor shuts down Hawai'i waterfront, consolidates power
1954	Hawai'i Democratic Party sweeps local elections
1959	Hawai'i statehood granted
1962	John A. Burns elected governor of Hawai'i, Democratic Party consolidates power
1964–1968	Hawai'i congressional delegation participates in historic Great Society legislation covering civil rights, Medicare, open housing, War on Poverty, and color-blind immigration
1970	Burns–Tom Gill confrontation imperils Democratic Party, Burns victory confirms centrist positioning
1974	George R. Ariyoshi elected first Japanese American governor and first nonwhite governor of American state; governs twelve years
1986	John D. Waihe'e III, first native Hawaiian governor, succeeds Ariyoshi
1994	Benjamin J. Cayetano, first Filipino American governor, succeeds Waihe'e

From the source in the slime was the earth formed
From the source in the dark was darkness formed
From the depths of the darkness, darkness so deep
Darkness of day, darkness of night
Of night alone
Did night give birth

—Hawaiian chant of creation

. . . the United States should control the
Hawaiian Group as being the western outpost
of Anglo Saxon civilization and a vantage ground of
American commerce in the Pacific.

—Sanford Dole, President of the Republic of Hawai'i (1897)

Hawai'i is what the United States is striving to be.

—John F. Kennedy, President of the United States,
regarding civil rights

Hawai'i is at the hub of the Great Wheel of the Pacific.

—John A. Burns, Governor, State of Hawai'i

Chapter 1

The Edge

When the sun is high in the central Pacific, visitors often wander near downtown Honolulu along the mountain side of 'Iolani Palace, past the iron fence, past the statue of the queen, and into the open-air rotunda of the capitol of the State of Hawai'i. These landmarks say that Hawai'i once was a kingdom, and now it is a state of the United States. If the visitor were to return for a long night of storytelling, he or she might acquire a more intense feeling for their significance, because in Hawai'i there is a story for every niche, stream, stone, and passage. Through storytelling, a sense of the past lives, even as details are lost.

There are many stories about the spirit of the last queen and about the dance of candlelight beneath the closed door of her upstairs room in the Palace, where she was imprisoned by her usurpers. A more recent story of the Palace is about its degenerate condition in the last days of the American territorial government, when rattling air conditioners hung from the arched windows and plywood partitions jutted from the Victorian porches. Members of the Territorial House huddled at tiny desks in the royal throne room, and senators met in the royal dining room. The appointed governor labored in the personal office of the monarch, and the territorial secretary held forth in the royal bedroom. With the approaching transformation to statehood, the people of Hawai'i agreed on at least one thing: The need to build a new capitol.

WHEN THE ARCHITECT John Carl Warnecke uttered the word *symbol*, the "s" whistled like a sharp wind through his imagined structures. Of all the designers who clamored for the commission, Warnecke likely won because of his passion for designing buildings that symbolized a time and place. In American society he was soon to become known as John F. Kennedy's

1

favorite architect and then as the designer of the fallen president's grave site, but when he was awarded the commission to design Hawai'i's new capitol he was not yet burdened by celebrity. He opened an office in Honolulu and immersed himself in what for him was a wonderful, new place. After studying the pre-Western society of Hawai'i, he attempted to organize his design entirely around the rectangular stone platforms of the native Hawaiian temple. Failing to perfect that idea, he pursued a temple of another sort, a synthesis of the Hawaiian world with East and West.

When the Democrat John A. Burns was elected governor of the State of Hawai'i in 1962, Warnecke wondered if Burns would support the continuation of the capitol project. It was elaborate for a small state, and it had been started under a Republican administration. Burns was known for peering sternly at even the smallest budget items, but he had an expansive side. On the playing field, he had been the little boy who demanded the ball, and in his maturity he was driven by the idea that everything in Hawai'i be first class. Warnecke told Burns that the new state needed a symbol the way Notre Dame needed a great football team, and with that he returned to his work.

During the period that John F. Kennedy was calling his administration the New Frontier, the Burns regime in Honolulu was the New Hawai'i. In ways that transcended slogans, the story of Hawai'i seemed not merely to blend in with the evolution of American society but also to influence its development. When Kennedy visited, America was passing into its conflict over civil rights. Inspired by the multiracial community that he saw at work, Kennedy said, "Hawai'i is what the United States is striving to be." In 1961, Dr. Lawrence Fuchs published his widely read social and political history, titled *Hawai'i Pono,* which means Hawai'i the good or Hawai'i the righteous. The people of Hawai'i, he believed, "present the world's best example of dynamic social democracy."[1] It was a utopian moment, in which policymakers talked seriously of curing the problems not only of race but of ignorance, poverty, disease, and oppression. If there was a party with a live band, someone was almost certain to belt out "Impossible Dream," from *Man of La Mancha.*

Not only Burns but many others spoke unselfconsciously of the dream of Hawai'i. James Michener, who was peripherally involved with Burns in creating the modern Hawaiian Democratic Party, described a Golden People in his novel *Hawaii.* The U.S. State Department was pleased by the propaganda value of Hawai'i, because more than half of its people originated from Asia, where much of the Cold War was occurring. At its best, America was determined to compete internationally by improving on itself, and a multiracial state in the Pacific manifested America's claim to being a special nation. Hawai'i was not merely a state but an idea.

At the capitol's dedication, the orchestra played "The Age of Aquarius." Courtesy of The Honolulu Advertiser

Governor John A. Burns often inspected construction of Hawai'i's new capitol. Courtesy of The Honolulu Advertiser

As part of the euphoria, there was a widespread perception that the issues of Hawai'i's history had been resolved. The power of Hawai'i's business oligarchy had been tempered by the organization of labor. The strong showing of the Democratic Party suggested a viable two-party system far into the future. As a sovereign state, Hawai'i would elect its own governor, as well as two senators and as many representatives as its small but enthusiastic population warranted.

THE CAPITOL DESIGN that grew from this environment was pagoda-like in the roofline, neoclassical in the supporting columns, and Hawaiian in the interior. To the left and right, huge volcano-like forms rose from a reflecting pool, one creating a chamber for the House of Representatives and one for the Senate. In the middle was a courtyard, open to the trade winds that blow down from Punchbowl National Cemetery.

During construction, Warnecke often escorted the widow Jacqueline Kennedy, who appreciated Hawai'i in part for the privacy accorded to her and her children. One night over dinner at the governor's mansion, Mrs. Kennedy remarked to Burns that his new chambers might benefit from a higher ceiling. When Burns stopped work on the fifth floor, the press created a storm. By this time, Burns was renowned for reorganizing the Hawai'i Democratic Party, for standing up against the plantation oligarchy, for guiding the statehood bill through congress, and for winning election to a position more akin to the presidency of a small country than the governorship of a small state. Raising the ceiling was a minor problem.

Legislators who had previously labored in plywood shacks on the porch of the Palace now occupied ample offices on the second, third, and fourth floors of the new capitol. None had back doors; all were accessible to the visiting public. The fifth floor was organized around blue mosaic arms that reached upward, creating an opening in the center that allowed sun and rain to fall on the courtyard. On one side of the portal was the office of the governor, and on the other side the office of the lieutenant governor.

When the capitol was dedicated in 1969, Burns pulled aside a billowing white canvas in the middle of the courtyard, revealing the signature art: A large mosaic circle of mysteriously overlapping blue, aqua, and green, representing stone, sea, and sky. The band played "The Age of Aquarius" from the rock opera *Hair,* as if to summon once more the idea of a new age, but in truth the moment of harmony and understanding, in which Hawai'i and enveloping America seemed one, was passing. Between 1965 and 1968, Lyndon Johnson had come to or passed through Hawai'i repeatedly, attempting to make the war in Vietnam work. "Each time that I return from your lovely island," he wrote to Burns, "I wonder how I can ever repay your hospitality.

Happily, I will have many years to try. I look forward to the long and good days of friendship that wait ahead for both of us."[2] Together he and Burns had strategized the statehood bill and construction of the East West Center at the University of Hawai'i. As the presidential champion of civil rights and the new social legislation, Johnson had appeared to be invincible. When he fell politically, he took the national Democratic Party down with him, and it seemed possible and moreover likely that the spreading turmoil might deal Burns the same fate.

Why this did not happen had to do with Hawai'i's separate history. While obviously Hawai'i was an extension of national trends, it was also a place unto itself. It was both periphery and center. In the electoral campaign of 1970, the glow of statehood was displaced by allusions to earlier times in Hawai'i that were, if partially forgotten, sufficiently remembered by an effective majority of the voting public.

The most consistent reminder of history emerged from the campaign of a then relatively obscure candidate for lieutenant governor named George Ryoichi Ariyoshi. At forty-four years old, he was the youngest of the Japanese American political figures who had transformed the postwar period. Week after week, month after month, Ariyoshi painted a picture of Hawai'i as a place where his three children could share fully in society's opportunities, for which he was uniquely obligated to Burns. In this discourse, Burns reemerged not as one trapped in the turmoil of the moment, but as the extraordinary figure of history. In the excitement of the campaign, Daniel K. Inouye, by then one of the better-known senators in the United States, claimed that Burns was the *only* person in Hawai'i—meaning the only white person—who had stood up for the Japanese community when Pearl Harbor was bombed.

The past was not merely the past, but a dynamic force that could be reworked. The purpose of statehood, Burns had always argued, was to create a more open society. The purpose of politics, in its "widest, almost Aristotelian sense," was to secure for each citizen the opportunity to develop to the best of his or her abilities. An open system would lead to an "aristocracy of talent," as described by Thomas Jefferson. If statehood fulfilled people's hopes, it was also "only the first step toward realizing those hopes." If statehood reflected the emergence of Hawai'i's people, "it signified also their first real opportunity for full, genuine emergence."[3]

In retrospect, 1970 was the moment when Burns' conception of history—described most clearly on the passage of statehood—began to be realized more visibly. Where the essential story of the New Hawai'i had been about how neatly the islands fit inside 1960s America, the rising tide of events and feelings had to do with Hawai'i's self-discovery in the statehood period.

It had to do with Hawai'i being different. What was past became prologue not merely to Burns' re-election but also to what followed across the twentieth century—the continuous unfolding of a multiracial, multicultural regime without parallel in an American setting. In partisan terms, Hawai'i continued to be uniformly Democratic, despite the national resurgence of the Republican Party. In the vague terminology of *-ism,* Hawai'i remained a bastion of traditional liberalism. In the description of *Forbes Magazine,* it was the People's Republic of Hawai'i, while in the racially loaded words of *The Wall Street Journal,* the politics of Hawai'i was conducted behind a Bamboo Curtain.

Although statehood had created a kind of end-of-history sensation, it clearly was not the end of history, but was rather, as Burns had said, the end of a long struggle and the beginning of a new openness, the possibilities of which were by definition unknown.

Chapter 2

The Tensions of Annexation

Like springs bubbling up from the back of a wet valley, the renewed inquiry into the nature of Hawai'i was fed by many sources. In the raw, it was developed not so often by academic historians as by celebrations, protests, re-enactments, exhibits, slide shows, and videos. Oral history became important. Genealogies and chants were revived. Novels about the Hawai'i experience began to flourish, along with poetry and public art. Again, the early 1970s were the point of acceleration. Where the writing produced at the time of statehood was about the whole, the new writing was about the parts. Literatures of the Chinese experience, the Japanese experience, and the native Hawaiian experience—all developed rapidly.[1] "No longer were only outsiders looking in," Eileen Tamura would write, "but now insiders, too, were writing the histories of their own ethnic groups."[2] It was as if the diverse society of Hawai'i had absorbed the full blast of America's might, glamour, and wealth but still wanted to understand and express its own unique nature.

As the inquiry reached back in time, the root political question—the question shared by all other questions—concerned the nature of America's annexation of Hawai'i. Among the profusion of propaganda surrounding this event, the notes of a congressional hearing in 1898 survived to summarize the most important political tensions of annexation. The hearing was held in Washington D.C. on May 10, 1898, by the House Foreign Relations Committee. America had entered into its little-understood war with Spain, and the attention of the country was on Cuba, Spain's colony in the Caribbean. The explosion of the USS *Maine* and the assembly of Theodore Roosevelt's Rough Riders obscured the fact that the war had started with America's destruction of the Spanish fleet in the Philippines, nearly half the globe away. With no predetermined plan as to whether America was liberating the Philippines from Spain or capturing the Philippines for itself, an expeditionary army was mobilized on the West Coast to support the U.S. Navy. The needs of this army for logistical support across the breadth of the Pacific tipped the scales of American opinion—slightly—in favor of annexing the midway islands of Hawai'i.

A previously classified reconnaissance of Hawaiian waters was released at the congressional hearing, extolling the unique virtues of Pearl Harbor, on the leeward side of O'ahu. Pearl Harbor, it was said, was large enough to anchor a great fleet outside the range of enemy fire. Its mouth was narrow and therefore defensible. It was a good place to provision and refuel the ships that were carrying thousands of troops to the Philippines. Pearl Harbor was not only the best but also the most strategically located natural harbor in the vast Pacific Ocean. The original author of this opinion was a crinkly-bearded army officer named John Schofield, whose name would survive in Schofield Barracks. As a witness before Congress, he warned darkly that unless America acted, Spain might take Hawai'i and use it as a base for attacking the West Coast (a preposterous contention, given that America sank the Spanish fleet in Manila harbor in a morning without losing a man).[3]

Schofield persisted: The many Japanese plantation workers in Hawai'i were really soldiers, an underground reserve that might rise up and plunge American interests into ruin. "In a very few years," he contended, "Japan can get physical and political control of the islands."

The chairman of the committee, Francis Newlands of Nevada, took a last look back. He asked, might it not be wiser merely to create a military protectorate through America's control of Pearl Harbor? Schofield replied that the entire country must be brought under direct American control because so many Japanese were living around Pearl Harbor. Once under the American flag, the people of Hawai'i might be developed into a trustworthy "reserve militia," so that troops from North America would not have to be garrisoned in large numbers to defend the islands.

From such thinking, the American version of the Territory of Hawai'i was begun, and from this cradle Hawai'i's modern political culture began to develop, in which the island archipelago functioned as a submerged nation, colonial outpost, and aspiring state.

THE INDIGENOUS PARTY

In the last decade of the nineteenth century, a wide range of political societies were organized, reflecting the diverse and often conflicting trends at work in the Kingdom of Hawai'i.[4] The Hawaiian monarchy's struggle to maintain power found expression in overlapping societies and parties that were loyal to the crown, such as Hui Kalai ʻĀina and the Hawaiian Patriotic League, also known as Hui Aloha ʻĀina. The American missionary descendants Sanford Dole, W. O. Smith, and Lorrin Thurston created an imaginary moral high ground for themselves by calling themselves the Reform Party. As tension increased, Queen Liliʻuokalani referred to the Reform Party as the Missionary Party. Less privileged whites formed the Mechanics and Workingmen's Political Protective Union, which subsequently joined with certain Hawaiian elements to form the National Reform Party. There was also a Liberal Party made up of prominent Hawaiians (such as John E. Bush and Robert Wilcox) who sought to develop a democratic republic but maintain native control of the archipelago. Their antimonarchial beliefs were muted by the pressure to protect the existing native Hawaiian government, a constitutionally bounded monarchy.

Although the native Hawaiian electorate was effectively barred from voting between the 1893 overthrow of the constitutional monarchy and the 1898 annexation, it reasserted itself after America's annexation. In the first American election held in the Territory of Hawaiʻi, in 1900, the native Hawaiian patriotic leagues that had opposed annexation merged. The Hui Aloha ʻĀina and the Hui Kalai ʻĀina formed the Home Rule Party. For the office of delegate to Congress, the Home Rule Party elected a person who symbolized Hawaiian resistance to annexation—Robert Wilcox. Because Wilcox's reputation was derived from his having taken up arms against the annexationists, his election was the most pointed statement of protest then available to the Hawaiians through the American political system. During his two-year term of office, Wilcox wandered the cold swamps of Washington with no place to warm his hands. For most of his life, he had been a citizen of the independent nation of Hawaiʻi. He was neither a Republican nor a Democrat but a Hawaiian.

THE OLIGARCHY PARTY

As a group, the families of the American-descended Caucasian elite had been cut loose by the American Board of Foreign Missions in the midnineteenth century. Lacking the subsidies that had supported their mission, they fended for themselves. In general, they were highly educated, domineering, self-assured, and close-knit. They addressed one another as Father, Mother, Sister, Brother, and Cousin. They believed in the Puritan doctrine that earthly wealth was a sign of God's favor. In the transition from God to business, Mother and Father Cooke closed the Chief's Children's School and formed a company with Father Castle, who had handled the supplies of the mission. The result was the famous and enduring Castle and Cooke. Brother

Baldwin married Sister Alexander, then went into business with his new brother-in-law, Cousin Alexander, giving birth to Alexander and Baldwin, Inc.

Such connections were intricately woven. For example, the original partners of the first plantation (Kōloa on Kaua'i) and the founder of the first missionary school (Punahou) all came from the same small town in Maine, as did the first American minister to advocate annexation, Luther Severance; as did Minister John Stevens (who became notorious for his role in the overthrow); as did U.S. Secretary of State James G. Blaine, Steven's benefactor and onetime business partner.[5] In the process, the dynamics of America's expansionist movement, the self-assurance deriving from the Darwinist theory of Anglo-Saxon superiority, and the insecurities of island-based business all merged into a new social, political, and economic order.

With their goal of annexation achieved, the American-descended annexationists logically regrouped themselves as Republicans under the American political system. In so doing, they were following through on contacts they had made with their principal annexationist counterparts in Washington, most of whom were Republicans (such as President William McKinley, the future president Theodore Roosevelt, and an influential senator, Henry Cabot Lodge).

At the onset of the American system, these American-descended Republicans were an extremely small sliver of the population of the Hawaiian Islands—only 2 to 3 percent. They nonetheless retained the essential controls they needed for perpetuation of their closely knit economic oligarchy. Further study of how they did so should begin with the political alliance they struck with a majority of the native Hawaiian electorate. The effect of this alliance was to submerge the indigenous political organizations of Hawai'i inside American political forms. The first task of the Republican Party was to defeat the Hawaiian nationalist Robert Wilcox, so that they could have a direct, effective conduit to Washington.

This occurred in the second territorial election in 1902. The pivotal figure in the story was Prince Jonah Kūhiō Kalaniana'ole, who was to have become the king of Hawai'i in the succession scheme of the monarchy. Kūhiō was the twentieth-century extension of the Polynesian system of ruling chiefs, which was based substantially on inherited rank. In the tradition of the pre-Western system, bad chiefs were scorned and sometimes killed. Good chiefs were loved with a fealty and adulation that is generally beyond the comprehension of Westerners. From a Polynesian point of view, Kūhiō was a good chief, seemingly second in popularity only to the deposed Lili'uokalani.

Because Kūhiō's life extended so far into the twentieth century, there is a tendency for him to be understood merely as a crowd-pleaser of aristocratic origins. This fails to explain why he agreed to make a deal with the conspirators who had dispossessed his people, overthrown his queen, and destroyed his nation. One explanation of his behavior lies in the fact that his brother, David Kawānanakoa, was the candidate of the Democratic Party. It seems plausible that Kūhiō and Kawānanakoa together—as people of chiefly rank—were attempting to reassert as much political control as they could under the circumstances. In effect, they adapted to the two-party American system by allying the most prominent member of the royal family with the Republican Party and the second most prominent member with the Democratic Party.

The 1902 election was close, but the result was Polynesian, a victory for the highest-ranking chief. It was the first of Kūhiō's ten election victories, covering the years 1902 to 1922. With the American-Hawaiian alliance in place, a long slumber descended, during which the white elite extended its control of the territorial political institutions as well as the territorial economy. What mattered most was who was appointed governor of the Territory of Hawai'i by the president of the United States. Through the combined efforts of business and the Republican Party, labor was routinely defeated. To be a Democrat was to risk being regarded as quixotic, and even as a fool. Although the native nationalist Home Rule Party withered, by virtue of numbers and organization Hawaiians continued to be the main voting force in both the Republican and Democratic parties. As a sop to home rule, county governments were organized throughout the territory, and through them Hawaiians secured additional government patronage jobs but considerably less than controlling political power, let alone economic power.

For at least forty years the oligarchic system, reinforced by the colonial control of the executive branch of government and the enormous influence of the U.S. Navy, maintained an astounding level of privilege. The sugar and pineapple plantations together covered all of the arable islands—Hawai'i, Maui, Moloka'i, Lāna'i, O'ahu, and Kaua'i. White men drove the countryside in black sedans. Their apparel was accented by little neckties, high-topped boots, and even the *pincé nez* ("nose-pincher") eyepiece in the style of Theodore Roosevelt.

Housing of this essentially feudal order maintained a perfect hierarchy of architecture and construction. The domain of the lord might be sequestered artfully, but the manager's house was as visible on the top of hills as the temples of the Hawaiians once had been. In descending size down the slope were the homes of the overseers, who were at that time usually Portuguese immigrants, and below them were the ever-smaller homes of the nonwhites by date of arrival, meaning the Chinese, Japanese, Koreans, and Filipinos.

Citizens of the transitional Republic of Hawai'i were given voting rights in the Territory of Hawai'i, meaning essentially that haole, Hawaiian, and Portuguese were allowed to vote, while the immigrant Asians were not. Hawai'i's legislature was made up initially of haole and Hawaiians, a circle from which Asians were at first excluded. The governor's office was the paramount place of control. Its occupant was appointed by the president of the United States, and the business and political forces surrounding the office were interwoven.

The annexationist Sanford Dole was not only president of the Republic in 1893 but also its first appointed governor in 1898. He was succeeded by George R. Carter (grandson of the seafaring Joseph Carter of the same small community in Maine) and then by Walter F. Frear, the law partner of the most famous—to Hawaiians, the most notorious—of all annexationists, Lorrin Thurston. All were Republicans. These were followed by two appointees of the Democrat Woodrow Wilson, Lucius Pinkham and Charles McCarthy.

Like Dole, the next territorial governor, Wallace Rider Farrington (1921–1929), was from Maine.[6] He was educated at Maine State College in Bangor and worked briefly for the *Kennebec Journal,* following in the footsteps of Severance, Blaine, and Stevens. He then moved to New York City, where he made the acquaintance of Henry Northrup Castle, son of the missionary-turned-businessman Samuel Castle and brother of the annexationist W. R. Castle. In New York he was recruited to work for the news and propaganda organ of the annexationist movement, *The Pacific Commercial Advertiser* (the precursor of today's *Honolulu Advertiser*).

Farrington arrived in Hawai'i in the fall of 1894 in the aftermath of the American-backed overthrow of the Hawaiian monarchy. In January 1895, Hawaiian nationalists—realizing after careful inquiry that the U.S. government would never restore the native government—took up arms against the Republic. Farrington described the only annexationist casualty as "a martyr to the cause." He castigated Lili'uokalani for allegedly knowing about the uprising but not disclosing it to the Dole government (a crime called misprision of treason, for which she was convicted by a martial law court and imprisoned).

Thereafter Farrington moved to the evening *Star,* which became the *Honolulu Star-Bulletin,* Hawai'i's main afternoon newspaper. There he became the champion of agricultural education. A photograph recorded Farrington in a three-piece suit flanked by seven barefooted boys of apparently Hawaiian, mixed, and Asian ancestries. The boys were in their early teens. One held a rake, two held hoes, two held shovels, one held a pick, and the seventh held a stick.

In 1915, Farrington organized the Honolulu Ad Club. In that capacity he invited a visiting Republican senator from Ohio as a guest speaker. Farrington introduced Warren Harding as a "future president of the United States." Harding said if Farrington was ever proven correct, he would name Farrington governor of the territory of Hawai'i. In 1920, Harding became the twenty-ninth and possibly most inept president of the United States. Farrington stirred, apparently in competition with Prince Kūhiō for the governorship. He wrote a friend in Washington that the "larger businessmen" of Honolulu were behind him. Lorrin Thurston was behind him, as well as "an inside circle that ought to bring considerable influence to bear."

Former governor Frear supported him. Former governor Carter, reached in San Francisco, telegraphed, "Hooray for Farrington!" Over dinner, the seventy-six-year-old Dole said he too supported Farrington's candidacy. "This, of course, was very gratifying," Farrington wrote, "since it completes the list of Ex-Governors who have endorsed me." Above all, the leading men wanted, in Farrington's words, someone who could be "depended on to think first, last, and always for the United States of America and its interests"— a slur presumably aimed at Kūhiō. Harding appointed Farrington the sixth territorial governor of Hawai'i.

Unlike his predecessors, Farrington served not one but two terms. His most sustained effort, spanning his days as both editor and governor, was lecturing the Japanese immigrants on their behavior and beliefs while professing his profound admiration for them as a people. He argued for closing the Japanese language schools. He charged that the "alien spirit" behind the schools was the "greatest stumbling block in our pathway to statehood." He advocated English Standard schools, contending that children who spoke proper English had a right to be educated without associating with children who spoke pidgin. "It is not necessarily a race problem that is here presented," he wrote, "but a mere inability to talk English."

To see photographs of Farrington in his tailed morning coat and his nose-pinching glasses is to see the illusion of the territory as a genteel outpost of Anglo-Saxon civilization. But to accept the image of tranquility is to ignore the significant number of Hawaiians who dissented from the system as backers of the Home Rule Party and subsequently the Democratic Party, which together might be more accurately described as the antioligarchy party.

THE ANTIOLIGARCHY PARTY

For many years, the task of the Democratic Party was not to represent the common man in the American sense but rather to carry on the essential task of the Home Rule Party, which was to represent the disinherited Hawaiian. The most effective early-day Democrat was the part-Hawaiian John H. Wilson, who followed in the footsteps of David Kawānanakoa. John H. Wilson lived so long that few remembered he was a member of the royal circle. His father was the marshal of the kingdom. His mother was a lady in waiting to the queen. As a child, he played at the queen's feet along with Kūhiō and

Kawānanakoa. In 1892, he was studying engineering at Stanford University, supported by a stipend from Liliʻuokalani. He also happened to play in the Stanford band, and as a band member he attended a political rally in which he heard Republicans preaching America's "manifest destiny" in the Pacific.[7] This sounded to Wilson like code for an American takeover of Hawaiʻi, so he decided that he would *not* be a Republican. After the overthrow, his stipend from the queen stopped coming and of necessity he abandoned his studies at Stanford. Wilson's biographer, Bob Krauss, assembled convincing evidence that Wilson participated in the 1895 Hawaiian revolt against the Republic.[8]

In contrast to the governors of the territory, who were appointed by the president, mayors in territorial Hawaiʻi were elected outright by the voting public. Campaigning against the Republican Party as the party of privilege, Wilson repeatedly won election as mayor of the city and county of Honolulu. His vision of helping the commoner combined with the creation of government employment. In an economy that generated few paying jobs other than at the plantations, it was no small thing to be a policeman, fireman, refuse collector, or clerk.

In addition to Wilson, other Hawaiians gained prominence as mayors, council members, and territorial legislators. Among the most important were leaders of large political families, such as the Heens, Trasks, and Kauhanes. They were patriotic Hawaiians but as the decades passed their connections to Hawaiian patriotism were to lose currency with the general public. For example, Ernest Kai, one of the most prominent Chinese Hawaiian figures, was descended from the Hawaiian patriot Joseph Nāwahī, who had given his life fighting annexation. By the time Ernest Kai's oral history was taken down in the 1980s the interviewers rushed past his reference to Nāwahī, apparently not knowing who Nāwahī was.

While the roles of the Republican Kūhiō and the Democrat Kawānanakoa may have seemed a clever way of acquiring leverage in a new electoral system, it was clever only as long as Hawaiians made up a majority of the voters. The underlying demographics worked against this. A census by the Hawaiian Kingdom in 1853 provided a benchmark for this tumultuous change. In that census, Hawaiians made up 96 percent of the population. By 1884 Hawaiians made up only half of Hawaiʻi's population, and by 1896 barely a fourth. Soon the remaining Hawaiians—living in a sea of immigrants who had been brought in by the planters—were to become a minority not only of the resident population but also of the electorate. As a result, the division between the Republican Kūhiō and the Democrat Kawānanakoa was politically disastrous for native interests, as Hawaiians were to divide their votes over the entire twentieth century between the two American parties.

Chapter 3

The Japanese Migration

The mass migration of Japanese to Hawai'i eventually was to become the single most important factor in the development of the State of Hawai'i and also the making of Hawai'i's unique contribution to America. If a single object could be lifted from its box at the Bishop Museum to symbolize the origins of the Japanese in America, it might be a coral-colored brocade pouch that arrived in Hawai'i in 1886. The pouch contained an agreement that had been worked out between the governments of Hawai'i and Japan covering standards of pay, health care, and housing on the plantations, and access by Japanese labor inspectors to the immigrant workers. The agreement reflected Japan as an awakened, autonomous nation that was actively concerned with its citizens abroad. Japan's representation of its citizenry was in contrast to China, which was in danger of being dissected by the European powers; the Philippines, then a colony of Spain; and Korea, which was in disarray and increasingly vulnerable to domination by Japan.

Several contemporary writers, in their eagerness to portray the planters simply as exploiters and the Japanese simply as victims, have suggested that the workers were lured to Hawai'i by false promises. A broader inquiry suggests otherwise. The scholars who have conducted original research in Japan begin with the enthusiasm of the Japanese for Hawai'i, and also with Japan's determination to connect itself to the wider world.[1] Out-migration was a part of Japan's modernization strategy, and the Kingdom of Hawai'i was Japan's first, largest, and most important experiment with migrating outside of Asia.

The excitement that swept Japan was given a name: "Hawai'i *netsu*" (the Hawai'i fever). The first recruitment drive called for six hundred workers, for which twenty-eight thousand people signed up. In his study of the immigration, *Imingaisha*, Alan Takeo Moriyama wrote, "What attracted almost all of the Japanese to work in Hawai'i was the $15 a month they could earn."[2]

While fifteen dollars may seem like a ridiculous figure, Moriyama provides the context: The wage of the common laborer in rural Japan at the time was nine yen, or roughly half of fifteen dollars. Most of the emigrants were from farming families that had been temporarily impoverished by Japan's pursuit of modernization and urbanization. Typically they planned to make money, send home what they could to their families, and then return home.

The Japan that had carefully decided to allow emigration was otherwise transforming itself. In 1889, the emperor gave Japan its first constitution. In 1890 the emperor proclaimed the Imperial Rescript on Education, which said in part: "The entire nation is mobilized behind children and their education." The immigrants often have been described as illiterate, sometimes to enlarge the nature of their struggle. In fact, virtually all could read and write, reflecting the minimum sixth-grade educational standard set by Meiji Japan. In the early days of the migration, more than a dozen Japanese language newspapers sprang up to fill the demand of a literate population for information.

Even though most of the Japanese came as laborers, they brought vibrant traditions and strong ideas about themselves. They were imbued with the Confucian doctrines of East Asia and animated by the legendary stories of the unification of Japan. The most exciting stories were of the samurai and the value system of the Japanese warrior, *bushidō*, which had been codified in the sixteenth century and then widely disseminated as a set of exemplary attitudes for the Japanese people. *Bushidō* taught several core concepts: bravery, loyalty, and filial obligation to one's parents and one's lord.

While the immigrants must have been affected to some degree by the modernization movement in Japan, they nonetheless were immensely parochial. Most were villagers from four southern and western prefectures: Hiroshima and Yamaguchi, on the southern tip of Honshu (the largest of the Japanese islands), and Fukuoka and Kumamoto, across the inland sea on the southern island of Kyushu.

The scholar Moriyama mapped the apparent route of a labor recruiter who traveled from village to village along the tip of Ōshima island in Yamaguchi: He recruited eight workers from the village of Ihota, thirty-five workers from the next village, three from the next, ten from the next, and eighteen from the last. In all, seventy-four people were recruited in one pass from a single byway on the tip of a small island. Once in Hawai'i, people from the same locale tended to be assigned to the same plantations. From one ship in 1885, forty-nine people from Hiroshima went to a plantation at Kohala on the island of Hawai'i, while thirty-one people from Yamaguchi went to another plantation on the same island, Hāmākua.

As a group they were chosen because they were "young, able bodied, healthy, agricultural laborers . . . habitually engaged in agricultural pursuits," according to the standards of the Hawai'i Immigration Bureau. Under no circumstances were they to be recruited from towns or cities or to have training in anything other than farming. While they were often stereotyped as submissive, a more careful examination shows they were consistently ready to stand up and defend their interests. Again Moriyama provides the original, convincing detail: Sixteen workers, arriving at Pāpaʻikou plantation on the Big Island in February 1885, complained of being forced to work longer hours than stipulated and also of being forced to work if they were sick. Within less than two months, they went on strike. Theirs was the beginning of innumerable wildcat strikes and confrontations that the Japanese labor inspectors were hard-pressed to monitor and the plantations were hard-pressed to put down.

Initially a high percentage of workers returned to Japan after the fulfillment of contracts, but this percentage declined over time. Many emigrants went on to the American mainland in search of higher wages. Those who stayed in Hawai'i formed an ever-larger population.[3] It seems safe to generalize that over time about a third returned to Japan, and nearly a third reached the mainland, leaving something less than half to accumulate and build the history-making community in Hawai'i. As it became apparent that many would stay, more resources went into community-building. To provide men with wives and stable families, the tradition of arranged marriage was adapted to the emigration of picture brides. Japan maintained a highly visible consulate in Honolulu, and dozens of capable, strong-willed individuals arrived from Japan to help bring a proper Japanese order to a frontier environment. Many were Christian, Buddhist, or Shinto missionaries, whose life stories provided revealing glimpses into the development of the Japanese community. One was the Reverend Shiro Sokabe, who became known as the samurai missionary.[4] Sokabe's grandfather was a samurai, as was his father, who dutifully attempted to instill samurai virtues in young Sokabe. Finding his father's disciplinary regime unbearable, Sokabe ran away. He roamed the countryside, begged for food and slept in barns, wandering through Kyushu and western Honshu and then across the Inland Sea to Shikoku, where at the age of eighteen he was taken in by a Christian minister. Deeply moved by the man's kindness, Sokabe dedicated himself to helping others. He studied in Kyoto, the center of Japanese culture, then migrated to the island of Hawai'i in 1894.

Sokabe was appalled by what he perceived as a breakdown of personal standards among the Japanese in Hawai'i. Again he set off on foot, crossing the Big Island, begging for contributions to a shelter for abused women and neglected or out-of-control children. To his humble following he preached the discipline of *bushidō* and the love of Jesus. Everyone ate the same fare from the communal garden—vegetables boiled in a pot with a piece of chicken. His mission continued for forty-eight years, until he was curtailed by the combined effects of the Pacific war and old age.

Yemyo Imamura migrated to Honolulu as a highly educated Buddhist priest. Soon thereafter he became bishop of the Honpa Hongwanji Buddhist mission, which established temples and Japanese language schools throughout the islands. As an alternative to the YMCA and YWCA, Imamura started the Young Buddhist Association.

The Reverend Chinpei Goto originally was known as one of the best early-day Japanese baseball players in Honolulu. As a young man he converted from Buddhism to Christianity and adopted John Wesley and Billy Sunday as his heroes. He pedalled a bicycle throughout Windward Oʻahu, engaging the young with bat, baseball, and Bible.

AFTER THE COMMENCEMENT of large-scale migration in 1885, Japanese immigrants quickly came to make up 40 percent of Hawaiʻi's population (and at one point were 42 percent). As such they were the largest of Hawaiʻi's many ethnic groups. Although they fell short of being a majority, by working with others they might break the grip of oligarchic society. Accompanied by the rise of Japan on the world stage, the sheer size of the Japanese community was to be a source of endless drama and tension. The Japanese became an obsession of society not only in Hawaiʻi, but also America and even, at times, Japan. The story requires extraordinary attention because it is at the core of the creation of modern Hawaiʻi.

SOURCES OF FRICTION

The first generation issei (from *ichi,* or one) were born in Japan and were barred from U.S. citizenship, yet increasingly settled into lifelong residency. The second generation nisei (from *ni,* or two) were born on U.S. soil and therefore became U.S. citizens. Issei and nisei were distinct from succeeding generations in that both were citizens of Japan, a fact that was fundamental to the crisis that would engulf them.

It was a mark of Japan's active interest in the migration that it originally perpetuated the tradition of dual citizenship. The names of the second generation were often recorded on a village register—let us say, on the register of the village of Ihota on the island of Ōshima. Japan's interest in the *imin* (immigrants) was intertwined with its most essential goals: modernizing and gaining acceptance on an equal basis with the Western powers, meaning Britain, France, Germany, Russia, and the United States. In this respect, the status (or treatment) of Japanese immigrants became a test of Japan's status. Japan consciously balked at the Western assumption of superiority. As a result, the younger son of an impoverished farm family might have become a field laborer in Hawai'i, but he was entitled to the respect due a citizen of Japan.

While the years 1893 to 1898 were obviously fateful for native Hawaiians, in less obvious ways they were fateful for the Japanese as well. The rising military power of Japan, combined with the potential influence of Japanese immigrants in Hawai'i, precipitated profound suspicion not only of the planters in Hawai'i but of the Anglo-Saxon friends of the planters in Washington, D.C. When the diplomatic historian Akira Iriye of Harvard studied the archives of Japan and the United States as a single effort, he focused on the fact that the two nations were engaged in virtually simultaneous drives toward national expansion. Two years after America's support of the 1893 overthrow, Japan defeated China in war in 1895. In the process it gained increasing dominance over Korea, which it reduced to a protectorate in 1905 and annexed outright in 1910, at which point it attempted to obliterate the identity of the Korean nation. Japan also took over Taiwan and various Pacific islands, and it became poised to make its fateful thrust into Manchuria and China. The United States meanwhile had taken over the Philippines, Guam, and various other Pacific islands, in addition to Hawai'i, and in 1902 acquired control of the deep-water harbor at Pago Pago, Samoa. These nearly simultaneous movements of national expansion by Japan and America fed on one another. Each stimulated and rationalized the other.

It was the beginning of an international conflict in which the Japanese immigrants to Hawai'i (and ultimately to America), would be caught. The writer Masayo Duus, who spanned the two cultures, would say the immigrants were at once the symbol and victim of the relationship. "What happened to the Japanese immigrants and their children in the United States very much affected how the two nations saw each other," she wrote, "and in turn the vicissitudes of U.S.-Japan relations had a profound impact on the Japanese American community."[5]

In the 1880s and 1890s, the growth of the sugar industry was so rapid and the pace of migration was so intense that in a short time Hawai'i became a way station of Japanese culture. People dined at Japanese restaurants, attended Japanese films, and worshipped in Japanese temples. The single men were followed by picture brides, Buddhist priests, Christian missionaries of Japanese ancestry, Japanese businessmen, and occasionally a Japanese intellectual or labor organizer. While all of this would be interpreted as the planter's immense appetite for low-cost labor, it also reflected Japan's new interest in the wider world.

AS PART OF THE ANNEXATION STRATEGY, the government of the Republic of Hawai'i had initiated a campaign of harassing selected Japanese immigrants and insulting the government of Japan. In this clandestine effort they were encouraged by their expansionist allies in Washington D.C. At a private audience in mid-February 1896, the chairman of the U.S. Senate Foreign Relations Committee, John T. Morgan of Alabama, suggested to Hawai'i's ambassador to the United States, Francis Hatch, that the number of Japanese arriving in Hawai'i was threatening the goal of annexation.[6] In response, the members of the oligarchy began to talk about a "peaceful invasion" by the Japanese immigrants—a gross hypocrisy, insofar as the Japanese were an economic necessity of the plantation system.

The Republic of Hawai'i baited Japan with a series of calculated insults, by detaining and turning back to Japan a total of thirteen hundred immigrants.[7] To mollify an angry Japanese public, Japan responded by dispatching a warship to join the U.S. warships that constantly lay at anchor in Honolulu Harbor, setting off a reaction within the U.S. government. Theodore Roosevelt, then effectively the acting Secretary of the Navy, pressured a weak American president, William McKinley, into deploying more ships to Honolulu. Of his friend from Hawai'i, Lorrin Thurston, he inquired eagerly whether Japan might make a fight of it in Honolulu. To his friend Alfred Mahan, a navy captain who became the American evangelist of seapower, Roosevelt predicted that the deadlock over annexation of Hawai'i soon would be broken. Three days later, McKinley sent a draft treaty of annexation to the U.S. Senate. Japan protested. Roosevelt responded with a belligerent speech, announcing that Japan would not tell America what to do.

When Senator Morgan subsequently came to Hawai'i to promote annexation, he told native Hawaiians that America intended to protect them from the aggression of Asian powers. "It makes very little difference whether you are smothered by a landslide or by an influx of Asiatics," he warned darkly. "The result is the same."[8] When Japan had filled the islands with her people, Morgan went on, the Hawaiians would disappear like raindrops into Hawaiian soil.

Although the white elite of Honolulu formulated crude strategies for keeping the immigrant community in its place (such as denial of naturalization and denial of the vote), they imported workers by the tens of thousands. The *Pacific Commercial Advertiser* said the government of the Republic of Hawai'i was riding "the stream of prosperity even if it carries us into the Asiatic sea." Within the missionary-descended inner circle, Lorrin Thurston immediately fell into representing Japanese immigration companies as an attorney even as he spread the allegation of their "peaceful invasion." His former law partner, W. O. Smith, wrote with furrowed brow that the Japanese were intelligent and ambitious. A group of young whites convened to analyze the traits of Hawai'i's numerous racial groups and concluded that the Japanese were possibly a superior breed.

All of this occurred in parallel with a vein of thinking in mainland America that was represented most effectively by Alfred Mahan and his disciple, Theodore Roosevelt. More than any others, these two men—both avid Social Darwinists—set the stage for America's imperial thrust into the Pacific. Because Darwinism was often used to justify white supremacist thinking, both would eventually be widely portrayed as racists. However, neither believed that the survival of the fittest was merely a matter of race or ethnicity. In the words of a recent historical study, "TR considered the Japanese substantially equal to whites in their level of civilization, and he in fact believed that Japan had much to teach the West."[9] In fact, Roosevelt's respect for Japan's success in war lay at the heart of his desire to stop Japanese immigration to the West Coast.[10]

THE ANNEXATION OF THE JAPANESE

Because native Hawaiians dramatically and tragically lost their homeland in the annexation, little attention has been paid to the fact that annexation also resulted in America acquiring a large number of Japanese as well as Korean and Chinese immigrants. This was the beginning of a large presence of Japanese descendants in America.

In the exchange prior to annexation between Schofield, who had surveyed Hawai'i, and the House Foreign Affairs Committee, Schofield insisted that Hawai'i must be annexed outright and not merely controlled as a protectorate. His reason was the presence of so many Japanese in the islands. The people of Hawai'i were to be won to the American flag and were also to become a "reserve militia" who would serve as defenders of Hawai'i.

The first U.S. Army garrison in Hawai'i was part of the contingent en route to the Philippines. Troops were left behind in Kapi'olani Park at the base of Diamond Head. Following annexation, the army immediately began devising plans by which it hoped to defend Hawai'i from attack. How the resident population was to become a reserve militia in this effort quickly became a much more pointed question. In 1905, Japan shocked the Western world, and America in particular, by defeating Russia and demolishing its fleet. According to U.S. Army war planners, Japan had moved a hundred thousand troops by sea, undetected. How America would defend itself if faced with a similar attack, and how the Japanese population of Hawai'i would respond, became the questions that haunted the Japanese community in Hawai'i, as well as the larger society, for the next forty years. Tensions heightened in 1907, in the wake of an attempt by the San Francisco school board to send immigrant Japanese children to a racially segregated school.

That this attempt to segregate the Japanese was not a parochial but a major international issue was illustrated by the intervention of Theodore Roosevelt, by then president, when he pressured San Francisco into backing down from its plan.[11] During this crisis, America formulated its first Orange Plan, its blueprint for war with Japan. Roosevelt also issued an executive order stopping the movement of Japanese residents of the U.S. Territory of Hawai'i to the U.S. mainland. Japanese immigration to America was limited informally by what became known as the Gentleman's Agreement. As a result, the Japanese of Hawai'i—both resident aliens and American-born citizens—became a special category of semiseparate people, barred not only from U.S. citizenship but from free movement to the U.S. mainland. If they were going to get ahead in America, they would have to do so, for the time being, in island Hawai'i.

JAPANESE BUSINESS

Rapid, vigorous development of businesses was one of the early foundations of a strong, enduring Japanese community in Hawai'i. A few businesses were transplants from Japan, but most were started from the bottom up. For example, in the earliest days of the migration, a man named Sanshichi Ozaki began to peddle food through the streets of Honolulu. In 1891, he opened the first independently owned Japanese store, S. Ozaki Shoten. In the next several years, fifteen more locally owned Japanese stores followed, and several merchandising firms from Japan opened stores as well. With the encouragement of the Japanese consulate, a Japanese Merchants Union was formed in 1895, for which Ozaki served as president.[12]

The organization dissolved as a result of economic and regional rivalries, but the need for cooperation became painfully apparent when bubonic plague was detected along the Honolulu waterfront.[13] On January 18, 1900, the Japanese merchants gathered at Ozaki's store on North King Street to discuss the territorial government's plan to burn all goods imported from Asia. Arbitrarily the government announced it would reimburse the owners at two-thirds of the goods' value. The fact that the activities of the territory's Health Department were guided by the annexationist Henry Cooper, who in 1897 had turned back the thirteen hundred Japanese to Japan, must surely have increased the feelings of mistrust. On January 20, the government lit a fire to raze the house of a plague victim and instead razed the entire district. That this disastrous event became known as the Chinatown Fire obscured the fact that of the seven thousand people who were burned out, more than half were Japanese.[14]

At an assembly of fire victims, Ozaki was elected chairman of a group to pursue claims against the government, by which several hundred thousand dollars were recouped. Ozaki also joined the newly organized Emergency Japanese Association, which soon was renamed the Honolulu Japanese Merchants Association. According to a Japanese Chamber of Commerce history, they were stirred by the spirit of *ganbare:* "I refuse to give up!" Most of the Japanese merchants reopened, including Ozaki, who prospered and eventually built a two-story house in Waikīkī to be near the ocean.

Ozaki is a symbol of the many immigrant Japanese who almost immediately began building a business base throughout the Hawaiian Islands. Their stories reflect the diversity of the first immigrants. As people who created or capitalized on opportunities, their experience runs counter to the overwhelming image that has been developed of the first generation—the image summarized by the phrase *kodomo no tame ni* ("for the sake of the children").

Along with clergy, editors, and scholars, Japanese businessmen quickly knocked on the door of a white-dominated world. In 1904, they organized their first annual celebration of the emperor's birthday, to which they invited members of the haole business community, as well as government officials, judges, and customs agents.[15] In the process the Japanese businessmen became an elite of a sort, interacting with haole in many ways that Japanese workers did not.

Skilled craftsmen also were among the earliest businessmen, transforming themselves in a few years from independent workmen to contractors. Reflecting this development, a Honolulu Japanese Contractors Association was formed in 1911 that eventually merged with the Japanese Chamber of Commerce (of Honolulu).

In a 1912 report, the Japanese consulate took note of business associations not only in Honolulu but in Hilo and North Kona on Hawai'i Island, as well as Kahului, Maui. Hawai'i had three Japanese banks, most prominently including a branch of the Yokohama Specie Bank, which opened in 1892. In the work force of Honolulu, seventy people were employed by the banks; nearly three hundred people were barbers; more than two hundred were tailors or seamstresses; and more than five hundred worked as carpenters. The Honolulu of 1912 also had forty geisha, eighteen Shinto priests, nineteen Buddhist priests, seventy-seven bathhouse employees, thirty-eight

Japanese missionaries, and eighteen Japanese photographers. The Japanese fishing fleet was well established, and more than five hundred Japanese on Oʻahu were engaged in hog and poultry farming.[16]

A Japanese pineapple plantation operated on Maui, and a large-scale cooperative of Japanese farmers cultivated seven thousand acres of pineapple on Oʻahu.[17] The number of Japanese working as contract growers of sugar cane on Oʻahu nearly rivaled the number of Japanese working as employees of the plantations.[18] While landless tenants have a dubious claim to autonomy, the fact that nearly five thousand Japanese were working as contract growers by 1911 says something about a serious change in the immigrant relationship with plantation society. Around this time, the number of nisei births began to increase sharply, creating a rapidly expanding population of American citizens.

THE JAPANESE WORKERS' MOVEMENT

From the first wildcat strike in 1885, the immigrant Japanese worker had shown an inclination to stand up and be counted. The result was a long stream of protests, confrontations, work stoppages, and wildcat strikes. Eventually, these rolled into the mass strike of 1909.

The leadership of the 1909 strike came from a Japanese language newspaper called *Nippu Jiji,* owned and edited by an urbane man named Yasutaro Soga. Soga shared leadership of the strike with a pugnacious store owner of half-Caucasian, half-Japanese ancestry, Kinzaburo Fred Makino, who subsequently would become a famous editor in his own right. That two city dwellers would lead a strike suggests that many Japanese labor issues already were well developed, and that the catalyst for coordinated action was communication. The strikers congregated in the Japanese community in Honolulu for support, but support was far from uniform.

The Japanese merchants announced a position of "strict neutrality" and advocated a "speedy solution so that the peaceful interests of the general public may be enhanced."[19] The long, bitter strike was, on the surface, won by the planters but it resulted belatedly in improved rewards, benefits, working conditions, and living conditions. It was the beginning of a protracted period in which a combination of racial and citizenship issues was never far from the center of public life in Hawaiʻi.

All the while, the first generation of Japanese was treated by the federal government as resident aliens. In 1919, after the conclusion of the First World War, Japan appealed to America for support of a clause in the League of Nations charter declaring all races inherently equal. America refused, in what was arguably its last clear-cut opportunity to set aside its tradition of white supremacy and create a positive relationship with Japan prior to World War II.

The next step in the deterioration of U.S.-Japan relations occurred in 1920 in Hawai'i, when Japanese plantation workers again went on strike. John H. Wilson had been appointed mayor of Honolulu, and Wallace Farrington was maneuvering to be appointed governor. Where the strike of 1909 had been led by editors, the strike of 1920 was led by a coordinating committee of men who saw themselves as men of labor, the Federation of Japanese Workers. The leader of the committee was a man named Takashi Tsutsumi.[20]

In response to the strike, the territorial government devised a variation of the "peaceful invasion" story that had been concocted with such success before annexation. The Territory contended that the strike was an international plot by which the imperial government of Japan sought to control the economy of Hawai'i.[21] Allegedly the Federation, under the sway of Tokyo, would achieve this control by monopolizing the work force. From Honolulu to Washington the strike was described as a Japanese conspiracy.

During the strike, the living room of the house of a Japanese interpreter on the Big Island (who worked closely with plantation management) was blown up with dynamite. The interpreter was named Juzaburo Sakamaki. He had been born in a fortified town on the northern tip of Honshu, the main island of Japan, in the year Meiji Two (1869),[22] the son of a samurai of modest rank. After learning English in San Francisco, he had worked for Ōla'a Plantation on the island of Hawai'i, where he raised his children as patriotic and Christian Americans even though he himself was denied American citizenship. In the prosecution of strike leaders, government lawyers alleged that the strikers had conspired to intimidate opponents of the strike by dynamiting Sakamaki's house.

Despite shameful plea bargaining by key witnesses, who tended to have demonstrable records of lying, the strike leaders were convicted and imprisoned. After several years they were freed, at which point they returned to Japan. Thereafter they were never to be seen in the Territory of Hawai'i again, nor were they a part of written history until Masayo Duus published a remarkable book about them—first in Japanese, then in English—in 1991.[23]

Duus captured a world of Japanese men who moved from island to island, congregating in Japanese hotels and boarding houses. When they agitated for improvements in wages and working conditions, they were accused of racial plotting and beaten down. Even with the publication of Duus' book, their story was ignored. On the surface the strike of 1920 was a failure, but it further changed the relationship between the Japanese community and the dominant haole elite. Many Japanese left the plantations during the strike and settled in the towns. In Honolulu, the neighborhoods of Mō'ili'ili, McCully, and Kapahulu became the heartland of a growing Japanese community, which was becoming ever more intricate and potentially powerful in not only economic but also political terms.

A MEETING IN TOKYO

Recent historical research increasingly reveals a pattern in which the 1920 strike was a turning point not only in Hawai'i but nationally and internationally as well. It set off trends that are easily traceable for several decades. The most obvious reaction to the strike was a growing certitude that Hawai'i had a Japanese problem—a code of alarm that influential people accepted and used as an article of faith. While many interesting details of recent research are about Japan, the context is an America caught up in a wave of jingoism. As the scholar Tamura wrote,

> The national movement to Americanize immigrants and their children began at the turn of the twentieth century. It escalated into a feverish crusade even before America entered the First World War, producing a frenzy of xenophobia between 1915 and 1921.[24]

The Americanization crusade in Hawai'i, Tamura argued, differed from the national movement in two ways: First, it was aimed at the Japanese immigrant; second, it continued until World War II, long after the mainland movement had dissipated.[25] Visitors often wrote about the Japanese problem, and residents talked about it as well. Likewise so did key individuals in the highest reaches of Japanese society, such as Eiichi Shibusawa, one of Japan's foremost internationalists. Shibusawa was one of the great modernizers of Japan. Born in 1840, he claimed to have swam out to Commodore Matthew Perry's great black ships as a fourteen-year-old, a knife clenched in his teeth. He was credited with having financed five hundred businesses and was to soon be one of Japan's several representatives at the Washington Conference on Naval Armaments of 1921.

In Shibusawa's lifetime, America had become a principal trading partner of Japan, which then (as now) depended on importing commodities and exporting products.[26] Militarily, America had emerged as a major world power on a par with Britain. Japan had allied itself to both during World War I and in the aftermath, Japan's empire had expanded in the western and southern Pacific islands at the expense of defeated Germany.

Paradoxically, President Woodrow Wilson had stimulated a wave of new internationalist thinking during the early interwar period, only to have the

United States Senate reject participation in the League of Nations. Within the white elite of Hawai'i, a group of internationalists had developed who resonated with both Wilson's ideals and their own unique observations of interracial relations. Foremost was Frank Atherton, a major force in the corporate world of Hawai'i, including in the *Honolulu Star-Bulletin* and the sugar-based Castle and Cooke, Inc. As internationalist ideas were alternately advanced and rejected, Atherton wrote to Shibusawa in the wake of the 1920 strike. He said if the American-born children of the Japanese immigrants planned to live in Hawai'i, they "should rightly seek to imbibe our American ideals and customs and become loyal Americans."[27]

He urged Shibusawa's support of a campaign for the assimilation of the new generation into American society, a plan then being presented by the Reverend Takie Okumura of Hawai'i to Shibusawa as a "Campaign to Remove Causes of Friction Between the American People and Japanese."[28] Okumura tended to synthesize everything he encountered. On the one hand, he believed passionately in the code of *bushidō*. On the other, he was a convert to Christianity. After studying at Doshisha University, he migrated to Hawai'i as a missionary in 1894, the second year of the Republic of Hawai'i. While Shiro Sokabe was making his lonely trek through the Big Island searching for orphans and abused spouses, Okumura cut a path through Honolulu. In quick succession he organized kindergartens for working Japanese mothers, the first language schools for the teaching of Japanese, and dormitories for boarding young Japanese Americans who came in from the plantations to study. Thereafter, he founded Makiki Christian Church, famous to this day for its replication of a medieval Japanese castle.

In 1920, Okumura offended many of his fellow Japanese by refusing to support the strike. He argued that while the capitalist and laboring classes were both American on the mainland, in Hawai'i the capitalists were Americans and the laborers were Japanese. "Strikes may not end as capital-labor conflicts," Okumura concluded, "but occur between Americans and Japanese and turn into a race war."[29] By such reasoning he skirted the class issues of wages and working conditions and essentially gave credibility to the planters' complaints.

Along the way, Okumura talked with Atherton about his idea of promoting the Americanization of the nisei generation, then departed for Tokyo. In Japan he appeared before an organization founded by Shibusawa called the Japanese American Relations Committee.

Okumura argued that assimilation of the nisei into American life was in the best interests of America, Japan, and the nisei themselves.[30] Shibusawa and his colleagues endorsed Okumura's campaign. The scholar Noriko Shimada believes that Shibusawa was deeply alarmed by the anti-Japanese movement in California, and that he "heartily agreed to Okumura's proposal to prevent Hawai'i from becoming another California."[31] Shibusawa's organization provided Okumura with financial support, and Shibusawa introduced Okumura to the highest levels of Japan's government, including the prime minister and the minister of foreign affairs, who specifically gave their blessing to nisei in Hawai'i renouncing dual citizenship and becoming exclusively American citizens.[32] Shibusawa gave Okumura a message for the young: "They should observe the U.S. institutions and civilization, share the joys and the sorrows of the American people, and cultivate the good custom of 'when in Rome, do as Romans do.'"[33]

When Okumura returned to Hawai'i, he set out with his son, Umetaro, to proselytize on all the islands, visiting each plantation twice a year for six years. In 1925, he incorporated renunciation of Japanese citizenship into his campaign. In 1927, he organized the New American Conference, which was held each year until 1941, bringing together many of the brightest nisei to promote devotion to America. How much of Okumura's budget was supported by Hawai'i's white elite and how much was supported by sources in Japan is unclear.[34] But documentation of Japan's involvement adds a new level of complexity to the historical interpretation of Okumura's New American movement. "Though this campaign appeared to have been conducted solely by one tenacious Issei man," a Japanese scholar has written, "Okumura was part of a transnational/trans-Pacific social mechanism."[35]

THE NEW AMERICAN CONFERENCE

The first speaker of the first New American Conference was Governor Farrington, then in his second term. Although people of Japanese ancestry were "one of the very serious problems of this part of the world," Farrington nonetheless pronounced himself a "blind optimist" regarding their future. He said their situation was not unlike that of the Irish in his home state of Maine whose fathers had dug the ditches—"the heavy and hard work that has been done by immigrants ever since the beginning of our country." Farrington reminisced:

> We used to draw some very sharp lines and called them some very evil names, and they reciprocated in kind. There were fist fights.[36]

But, like the Irish, the Japanese could join in the cause of nation-building:

> We have to prove that American principles and ideals and institutions will operate as successfully in this part of the United States, and that

*the elements centering here in this outpost will operate as successfully
as they have done in any other part of the United States. . . .*[37]

However condescending, Farrington reinforced Okumura's essential theme
of assimilation. The endorsement of assimilation takes on added meaning
in light of the then-prevailing American view that Japanese immigrants could
never be assimilated. For example, Theodore Roosevelt believed that "large-
scale immigration of Japanese was not possible because the two populations
could not be merged."[38] Mahan similarly argued that "virile qualities" made
Japanese unassimilable in America.[39] The most essential line of attack in
California was that Japanese could not be assimilated. That opinion, in the
vein of Mahan and Roosevelt, seemed initially to be out of fear of their hard
work and acumen, and not because Japanese were alleged to be inferior.
Therefore Farrington was stating an important belief that even at this early
stage distinguished Hawai'i from the West Coast: Nonwhite people in Hawai'i,
and Japanese in particular, could and would be assimilated by the dominant society.

Following Farrington's opening remarks, Okumura deployed a combination of issei and Caucasian leaders, editors, businessmen, educators, and
finally, high-ranking military officers to lecture the young nisei on how to
conduct their lives. The president of the University of Hawai'i, David Crawford, said, "Do not count on education to do too much for you, do not take
it too seriously."[40] A white business leader warned against the evils of a world
populated by too many "highbrows." Nisei offered testimony on the stability
of the sugar industry, as well as its opportunities for promotion and recreation programs. The chairman of the territorial board of education said work
on the plantations was like having "diamonds in our own yards."

Some of the speakers ascribed fixed characteristics to the Japanese. The
director of the territory's agricultural extension service said Japanese were
"ideally suited" to farm work. Okumura said farming was "inborn" in
Japanese.

While the composite message was not to entertain dangerous dreams,
the educator Miles Carey articulated a contrary viewpoint that excited the
young. As a practitioner of John Dewey's philosophy of progressive education at McKinley High School in midtown Honolulu, he was popular with
the mostly nisei student body. "Instead of criticizing our young people for
looking for the so-called 'white collar' jobs," Carey said, "we should com-
pliment them for wanting to improve their present state." He was never
invited to speak to the conference again.

The most devastating critique of the New American Conference was that
it was not so much about being American, but about calming the waters

and returning nisei to the plantations. It speaks of the orchestrated, semi-feudal nature of island society in the 1930s. Viewed in the longer context of the Japanese migration, the conference may be understood more accurately as an evolutionary step in what had begun as a top-down, government-to-government agreement to supply and regulate workers in three-year increments. In other words, the suffocating nature of the New American Conference descended from an even more tightly controlled set of circumstances.

About fifty to eighty delegates attended the conference each year, many of them the brightest young nisei in Hawai'i. Many nisei seem to have experienced these gatherings as the world changing but not changing fast enough. Earl Nishimura, who eventually became an attorney, was an early-day nisei who participated in the first conferences. Born in 1906, he remembered out-of-work relatives living with his family for several months during the 1920 strike. He interpreted the strike as the Japanese community on one side and the dominating Big Five companies of Hawai'i on the other. He thought of Okumura as motivated by the fact "that we were not recognized and given job opportunities and that we were mistrusted." The issue of trust he saw as going to the core question of who would control Hawai'i, those in charge or "the Japanese." He thought of the conference as productive. He particularly liked a resolution that was passed and sent to the president of the United States informing him "that here we're trying to become good Americans."[41]

TASUKU HARADA AND JAPANESE STUDIES

Like the New American Conference, Japanese studies at the University of Hawai'i started in the 1920s, similarly suggesting a new respect for Japan among the oligarchy and a concern for harmonizing the interests of Japan and the United States. The founding scholar was Tasuku Harada. Born in 1863 in Kumamoto, Harada converted to Christianity in 1881, studied theology in Japan, ministered to a church in Kobe, then earned a divinity degree from Yale in 1890.[42] From 1907 to 1919, he served as president of Doshisha University in Kyoto, a university that appears repeatedly in the story of Hawai'i, presumably because of its Christian origins. During this period, he lectured widely throughout the United States, including Honolulu.

In 1909 he was visited at Doshisha by William R. Castle, an immediate descendant of the founders of Castle and Cooke, Inc., who donated money to the college. Like Atherton, Cooke had acquired an international perspective, and his son was to become an influential assistant secretary of state for Far Eastern affairs. In 1920, Castle chaired a centennial celebration on the arrival of the missionaries in Hawai'i, at which Harada was the only non-white asked to speak. At the time, the sugar plantations were mired in the 1920 strike, so those who assembled for Harada's address must have been starkly aware of their need for a better relationship with the Japanese.

While in Honolulu, Harada was asked by the president of the University of Hawai'i to start a program of Japanese language, literature, and history. Harada returned to Japan to consider the offer seriously. In the meantime, he was summoned to Tokyo by Shibusawa, who was deeply concerned with the anti-Japanese prejudice that again had flared in California and throughout the western states. Japanese were reacting to the fact that most of the western states had adopted California's Alien Land Law—aimed primarily at prohibiting immigrant Japanese farmers from buying land—and also reacting to talk in California of stripping American-born nisei of their U.S. citizenship. It is probably more than coincidence that Harada was at the Tokyo meeting where Okumura promoted the New American Conference. At Shibusawa's direction, Harada departed on a four-month fact-finding trip on behalf of the Japan America Relations Committee, inquiring into the anti-Japanese movement in mainland America.[43]

Harada then relocated in 1921 to Honolulu, where he began twelve years of pioneering academic and community work. One of his closest friends and collaborators was the editor Yasutaro Soga, who had been jailed for his leadership of the 1909 strike but had opposed the 1920 strike for reasons much like Okumura's. Breaking the usual barriers between student and professor, Harada founded a Japanese Language Research Club in concert with Soga, and once a month they held meetings for dozens of students in their homes.

Together Okumura, Soga, and Harada orchestrated a course of caution and accommodation for the Japanese community, with a focus on the assimilation of the new generation into American society. Like Okumura, Harada received expense money from the Japanese government to support his "campaign of education," as did Soga.[44]

MAKINO AND THE LANGUAGE SCHOOLS

Anglo-American chauvinism fueled by World War I—and also by the 1920 strike—found expression in legislative proposals for the government of the territory to take over the Japanese language schools and test and license their teachers. In response, Okumura and his supporters maneuvered for a compromise in which the Japanese language would continue to be taught, with assurances to the territorial government that pro-Japan views would not be taught. In opposition to this accomodationist approach, the editor Fred

Makino—whose *Hawaii Hochi* was by then the main competitor to Soga's *Hawaii Times (Nippu Jiji)*—campaigned against the legislation as an exercise in intolerance. Makino led the move to challenge the law as unconstitutional, eventually succeeding in appeals to the U.S. Supreme Court. It was a victory for which he would be remembered kindly by liberal historians concerned with civil liberties and civil rights, which is to say, most of the historians concerned with Japanese Americans.

THE JAPANESE EXCLUSION ACT

Just as the New American movement and the language school controversy flowed from the 1920 strike, so too did Hawai'i's contribution to passage of the Japanese Exclusion Act. The author Masayo Duus has ably described how the tycoon Walter Dillingham and others were propelled by the strike to lobby in Washington for ways to control the Japanese population. Jonah Kūhiō, in his twenty-year sojourn through the American congressional system, had become an anti-Japanese bigot who participated vigorously in the propaganda campaigns of the oligarchy. In the committee rooms of the American congress, Kūhiō explained to his colleagues that the long-standing goal of the Japanese was to take over Hawai'i.[45]

The efforts of Dillingham and Kūhiō were swept along on the jingoistic wave that followed World War I and led to Congress setting immigration quotas in 1924 proportionate to the composition of the American population.[46] Under this white-weighted formula, Japan would have been allowed only a handful of entry permits, but Congress added insult to the injury by banning Japanese immigration to America altogether.

As a result, the 1924 immigration law became known as the Japanese Exclusion Act—an act singling out the Japanese for especially insulting treatment. Japan, having prided itself in its relationship with the United States, had been subjected to the same treatment as disorganized China. In response, people rioted in the streets of Tokyo. One person committed seppuku in front of the American embassy. The internationalist Shibusawa, then eighty-four, said, "By the passage of this bill, Japan lost face."[47] From then on, Japanese political figures who were inclined to work with America were effectively restrained by Japanese public opinion from doing so, and the stage was set for the downward spiral that led to Pearl Harbor.[48]

Despite the deterioration of U.S.-Japan relations, or possibly because of it, Honolulu became a focal point for attempts to hold things together. Just as Japanese immigration and U.S.-Japan friction were intertwined, attempts to build international goodwill were likewise intertwined with attempts to build mutual understanding within the territory.

INTERNATIONALISM AS A BRIDGE BETWEEN CAUCASIANS AND JAPANESE

In 1911, a group was organized in Hawai'i called Hands Around the Pacific. It and its successor groups were led by an energetic if quixotic man, Alexander Hume Ford. Hands Around the Pacific had an idealistic, international focus with an underlying concern for interracial relations in Hawai'i. The latter was reflected in a subgroup called the 12-12-12 Club, which brought together a dozen representatives of several racial groups periodically for dinner and discussion. The historian Paul Hooper, who conducted pathfinding research on the international movement in Hawai'i, described the meetings as covering "points of racial grievance and misunderstanding in much the same fashion employed in contemporary encounter therapy."[49]

In 1917, Hands Around the Pacific was transformed into the Pan Pacific Union, which eventually organized chapters and sponsored conferences around the Pacific. Nearly coinciding with America's entry into World War I, the Pan Pacific Union served as a cradle for a Hawai'i variant of Wilsonian internationalism.[50] In 1925, the Pan Pacific Union was followed by a more focused organization called the Institute of Pacific Relations (IPR). While the IPR attracted participants from around the Pacific, leading haole citizens of Hawai'i such as Frank Atherton and William Castle played prominent roles, as did such Japanese luminaries as Tasuku Harada and Yasutaro Soga.[51]

Civic organizations with seemingly similar ideals were spawned in this same period. In 1926, a combination of issei business leaders and the earliest nisei leaders joined together in an organization called the Hawaiian Japanese Civic Association, which was devoted to dealing with issues of the Japanese community in context of the wider community. As described in the Pan Pacific Union's magazine, the Hawaiian Japanese Civic Association was organized "under the happy auspices" of Ford.[52] Its original significance lay in its involvement of nisei, in contrast to the Japanese Chamber of Commerce, which was dominated by issei. Secondly, the Hawaiian Japanese Civic Association—unlike previous civic groups—was not organized under the auspices of the Japanese consulate.[53] In a real sense, this was to become the root organization of post-statehood Hawai'i.

The same year, 1926, again with Ford's involvement, a chapter of Lions International was formed in Honolulu "with broad and understanding interracial policies."[54] There were Lions clubs for various ethnic groups, and one club was explicitly interracial. The Lions territorial president wrote, "It has fulfilled the hope of the many racial groups for an organization in which they could work together for the advancement of common interests without thought of race, creed or color." Lions clubs quickly spread around the territory, including Kailua, O'ahu, where the club attracted the participation of young John A. Burns.

While no one has documented the overlapping of these organizations, there is an apparent recurrence of participation by the haole community on one hand and influential members of the Japanese community on the other. Although the IPR failed to avert war between Japan and America, it and its companion efforts are important, because they nurtured the possibility of a multiracial society. Such efforts helped define the idealism that hovered over the nisei as they completed their studies at the high school level and went on to the university.

ASSIMILATION

In the constant reworking of the issues of immigration and ethnicity, the acculturation and assimilation of the nisei in Hawai'i remain an issue of scholarly dispute. For many nisei, assimilation was and is an important ideal, and for many white people it is a comforting idea that reinforces their assumptions about creating the American mold. In contrast, the research of various contemporary scholars of ethnicity has linked the idea of assimilation to a larger context of white racism, and for some the idea of assimilation has become virtually synonymous with cultural genocide.

As used before World War II, assimilation was for a time more clearly connected to gaining acceptance by learning American culture while not abandoning the culture of Japan (as Japanese Americans would be pressured to abandon things Japanese in 1941). Okumura himself advocated "absorbing fundamental American ideals and values while retaining certain Japanese characteristics that meshed with American culture . . . such as diligence, perseverance and strong sense of loyalty."[55]

Harada wrote that neither American moral standards nor the way of the samurai would prevail among the nisei, but the best of the two views.[56] The new generation, he believed, was "going through one of the most interesting experiments in the history of mankind."[57] One of the most prominent early nisei was Shunzo Sakamaki, a student of Harada and an offspring of the interpreter Juzaburo Sakamaki, whose house had been dynamited during the 1920 strike.

In 1927, Sakamaki was president of the University of Hawai'i (UH) Japanese Students' Association. There he told his fellows that to simply break with Japan would cause them to "float helplessly, cut adrift from the ancient moorings."[58] Instead, with "the noble traditions and history of our race underlying our every action, we have been born to be citizens of a great democracy." Young Japanese Americans must therefore embrace a great mission: "Let each of us resolve to be as good an American citizen as our ancestors were good

Japanese citizens." It was a perfect extension of the ideas shared by Shibusawa and Okumura.

Sakamaki won a speech contest by addressing *The Second Generation Problem*, in which he argued that young Japanese Americans could free themselves from the "'sickening sense of inferiority' which overtakes most of us at times." He argued that in contrast to materialism (implicitly, the materialism of the West), the Japanese culture gloried in spiritual and cultural achievement. "The shining blossom of *Yamatodamashii!*" Sakamaki exclaimed, "The sublime magnificence of *bushidō*, the spirit of the samurai!" Sakamaki echoed Harada in arguing that the American-born generation draw on the best of both traditions, with the goal of making a special contribution to mutual understanding between Japan and America.[59] Sakamaki went on to study at Doshisha University in Kyoto, earn a doctorate from Columbia University in New York City, and return to teach at the UH campus. There he played a key role in the prewar period and subsequently played a prominent role in UH administration.

Regardless of how the concept of assimilation is interpreted, it seems indisputable that Japan sought the "assimilation" of the nisei by America, and so did many nisei. The impact of the New American movement and of Okumura as an individual was considerable, and yet Okumura's reputation was always to be tainted by the suspicion—the allegation—that he was a pawn of the plantation interests. His accommodations to American pressure suffered particularly in accounts that celebrated the organization of labor and the civil rights movement while, in contrast, Fred Makino was lionized in the 1960s and 1970s for his more direct, confrontational approach.

With greater distance, it seems apparent that this polarity between accommodation and confrontation reflects an overly simplistic view of a highly charged, constantly changing course of events, in which international and local issues were interwoven, often in confusing ways. In the 1909 strike, Soga and Makino clearly provided the leadership. During the 1920 strike, Takashi Tsutsumi held sway. In Okumura's opposition to the 1920 strike, Okumura presented a strong but unpopular point of view. No sooner had Okumura's assimilation campaign begun than he faced the language school controversy, in which his opponent Makino carried the day. Nonetheless Okumura persisted year after year over two decades, weaving relationships among issei and nisei, as well as the haole establishment. His work, along with that of Harada, Soga, and Makino, probably provided the most consistent nourishment to the new American generation over the years.

The eventual performance of the nisei was to suggest that more than any other single person, Okumura prevailed. That is, the main current of nisei in Hawai'i embraced their identity as Americans and tended to downplay America's shortcomings in the interest of creating a multiracial society, in which all would be equal.

After World War II, Okumura wrote General Douglas MacArthur to offer the opinion that what Japan needed most was mass conversion to Christianity. MacArthur declined Okumura's proposal to lead the effort. In old age, Okumura was photographed in his Japanese robe, looking for all the world like his samurai ancestors. He died in 1951 at the age of eighty-six.

Chapter 4

Prewar Change

If the sugar industry and the Big Five corporations could have seen further into the future, they might have opted for institutionalizing their relationships with the mostly Japanese leadership of the 1920 strike through collective bargaining. Had they done so, it seems plausible they could have benefited from the willingness of immigrants to work hard and get ahead. A Japanese-led system of collective bargaining might have evolved that included Filipino workers as well as the small number of Koreans and Chinese. By resisting the strikers, the companies delayed the organization of labor. This eventually left them face to face with labor radicals who for a time thought not only of gaining greater benefits from the system but revolutionizing it.

While plantation strikes recurred, the focus of labor activity shifted from the fields to the waterfront. The transitional figure was a handsome young Japanese American named Jack Kawano, who was in some respects an inheritor of the locally based traditions developed in the 1909 and 1920 strikes. Kawano was born on the Big Island and worked on its plantations, then moved to Honolulu, where he worked as a stevedore. On the waterfront Kawano joined a fledgling chapter of the International Longshoremen's Association (ILA). Animated by the possibilities of union organization, he began to question the companies and voice grievances. He was fired often, then blacklisted. Thereafter he lived for years in a shack, trying to build up the ILA.

With the economic depression of 1929, conditions on the waterfront worsened. While it often has been said that America's prolonged depression did not affect Hawai'i as it did many places, this observation refers to the relative market stability of plantation agriculture and ignores the plight of unorganized working people. The writer Sanford Zalburg's description of the Honolulu waterfront in the early 1930s reveals another reality—a crowd of men gathering every morning, hoping to get a day's work. A company man would look over the crowd, where men would "mill around, yelling, shouting, kicking, punching, trying to attract attention." The company man would pick the day's work gang out of the crowd, and the rest would be turned away.

This scene reflected the fact that Hawai'i had a bloated working class resulting from the annexation of a large native population, the importations of Asian immigrants, and the barriers erected by the 1907 Gentleman's Agreement with Japan—which prohibited immigrant relocation to more lucrative mainland labor markets. Kawano estimated that half of the longshoremen were native Hawaiians. Most of the remaining half, Kawano believed, were Japanese. To recruit a worker into the union, Kawano would knock on the man's door after work and present his case for the union. The worker who agreed to join would pay a month's dues. Because there was no collective bargaining agreement, there was no system of dues check-off from the company payrolls. The next month, the new member would forget to pay. Kawano would recall: "By the time you signed up this bunch, that bunch quit."[1]

When Kawano saw longshoremen coming down the street, they would cross to the other side, then call out, "Hi, Jack." Kawano would begin anew, knocking on doors. Sailors off the ships told him about the improved wages and working conditions on the West Coast and about the radical union leader, Harry Bridges. Kawano pleaded repeatedly with Bridges to send money for an organizing drive in Hawai'i, but Bridges was battling the old-line leadership of the ILA and begged off by saying he already was spread too thin.

In 1938, a strike began with inland boatmen and spread to Kawano's longshoremen, then to metal tradesmen. On the Big Island, in the port of Hilo, longshoremen attempted to block the unloading of "hot"—or nonunion—cargo. The police wounded fifty people with buckshot. After that Bert Nakano, a union man in Hilo, walked with a limp. It was for events such as this that a report of the National Labor Relations Board described Hawai'i in the 1930s as a "picture of fascism" and its people "more slaves than free."

While Kawano waged his lonely struggle, he was at first influenced then joined by Caucasian union men who nursed ideas of creating a class-based rather than ethnically based labor movement in Hawai'i. Their arrival coincided with the congressional passage of the Wagner Act in 1935, which created a framework for the collective bargaining of labor with management. Among these men, Jack Hall would eventually displace Kawano and come to be remembered as the great figure in Hawai'i's labor history.

JACK HALL

As described by his able biographer Zalburg,[2] Jack Hall was a man of extraordinary intelligence who grew up in nightmarish circumstances. His mother committed suicide when he was four, leaving him to the belt of his violent father, who loved women and drink. He graduated from high school in Los Angeles at sixteen by skipping grades. Enraged by his father's beatings, he abandoned his plan of studying physics, packed his belongings in a pillow case, and ran away to sea. At seventeen, he sailed through Honolulu, then on to the ports of Asia. "I saw colonialism at work, and poverty," he was to say. "It upset me. I determined which side of the fence I was on."[3]

Returning to the West Coast, Hall became involved in what union literature calls—with capital letters and no quotation marks—the Big Strike of 1934. This strike influenced American working people in the Pacific, because it was a long and all-encompassing strike. In its first phase, the ILA closed down West Coast ports. Against the resistance of the waterfront employers, the strike spread to men who worked the ships.

In San Francisco, the strike spread from the waterfront through the entire city, a development that union men called the "march inland." Teamsters joined the strike. Warehousemen were organized. When the city government tried to force the waterfront open, police injured over a hundred people. Three men were killed. A pamphleteer, Mike Quin, described a scene in which 40,000 workers marched down Market Street behind the bodies of the dead strikers. Mediation collapsed, and unions throughout the city joined in a display of class solidarity.[4] For people who believed in Marx's doctrine of class struggle, it was like a dream coming true: a general strike. "Labor held the life-blood and energy," Quin wrote, "the owners remained in possession of the corpse."

When ILA leadership agreed to a settlement, three thousand members turned out to a mass meeting and voted it down. From amid the turmoil over contract ratification came Harry Bridges, who took his following out of the ILA and formed the International Longshoremen and Warehousemen's Union—the ILWU. In 1949 Bridges wrote a postscript to Quin's book about the strike. The battle, he said, was just beginning: "And if any dues-payer asks, 'When will it end? When can I knock off?' the only answer is, 'Brother, not until we win all the way.'"

In San Francisco, the nineteen-year-old Hall walked the picket lines, ran from the tear gas, and signed a union card with the Sailors' Union of the Pacific. In subsequent months he caught the eye of a business agent for the Marine Cooks and Stewards Union, who raised a small stake to agitate for unionism in Honolulu. Hall arrived in his new home port in 1935, jumped ship, and reported to a shore agent of the Sailors' Union, a haole Hawaiian man named Maxie Kamaka Weisbarth. Shortly thereafter Hall went to work for a labor publication—first mimeographed, later printed—called *The Voice of Labor*.

At this early stage, union organizers doubled as propagandists. A man named Corby Paxton had written that Hawai'i was a boss's paradise and a workers' hell. "The future strike," Paxton prophesied, "will be of the working class and not of any particular nationality." Young Hall was in demand because he could write better and faster than most people. He could even type. If he were disturbed while pounding on the newspaper's one typewriter, he yelled at people to shut up and leave him alone. When he was hungry, he made the price of a meal by selling the *Voice* in the bars along the waterfront.

In 1936 Hall signed on to a ship that sailed around the earth, and during the trip he joined the Communist Party. He returned to Hawai'i just as another maritime strike was starting on the West Coast. This time the strike extended to Honolulu Harbor, shutting down a dozen ships, including Hall's, which he represented on a strike committee.

His friend Maxie Weisbarth is said to have knocked Hall down a flight of stairs when he found out that he had joined the Communist Party, but nonetheless introduced Hall to "another Commie" named Big Bill Bailey, who arrived in Honolulu in response to the maritime strike. Bailey put up a Communist Party flag in his room and called together a handful of the most militant unionists. He said that when everyone else had turned their backs on strikers, the Communist Party U.S.A. would be there to help. Membership cost a dime. Thereafter Hall and Bailey went to Maui to pursue the unrest of plantation workers, and at close range Hall saw the closed, hierarchical, and race-based nature of the plantations.

He also saw the futility of ethnically based labor organizing. Hall and Bailey implored one of the Filipino leaders to organize all the sugar workers, not just Filipino workers. The man's name was Antonio Fagel, a follower of Pablo Manlapit, who had led the Filipinos in the 1920 strike. Fagel replied that he would organize the Filipinos first. Three thousand Filipino workers struck on Maui but again failed to gain union recognition and bargaining rights. Nonetheless something like San Francisco's march inland was beginning to occur in Hawai'i. Starting in the maritime and longshore unions, a new and militant unionism was spreading to the plantations.

DURING THE 1938 STRIKE, Jack Hall had been confronted on the Honolulu waterfront by a policeman who took him into the station house. Hall knew that in matters of union organizing, due process of law did not apply. The police stopped the elevator between floors and beat him. Around the same time, a policeman sauntered up to Bill Bailey on the dock and gave him a friendly tip: If Bailey would take the next ship out, he could avoid arrest. Bailey talked with Jack Kawano, who reassured him that he had made a mark: If Bailey was thrown in jail, they had no lawyer to get him out. Bailey caught a ship, but Hall and Kawano clung to Hawai'i.

When not in Honolulu, Hall was on Kaua'i, the most geographically separate of the four main Hawaiian islands. There, from 1937 to 1941, Hall worked out his organizational and political strategies. Kaua'i was the wettest island and had the most naturally perfect terrain and growing conditions for sugar. Socially and politically, it was the most thoroughly dominated by plantations. The prototype of the sugar industry, Kōloa Plantation, had been developed on Kaua'i. It was as if Hall, fulfilling his childhood ambition of being a physicist, had wandered into an unused laboratory.

Sugar and other goods were shipped out through two docks on the island's east side. One was Ahukini Landing to the north, where most of the workers were Filipino, and Port Allen to the south, where most of the workers were Japanese. Against Hall's advice, the Filipinos went on strike. He nonetheless stuck with them. When ships attempted to unload through Port Allen, the mostly Japanese work force refused to handle the cargo. Hall believed that through such interracial cooperation, the day was dawning that Corby Paxton had envisioned—all-encompassing strikes by the working class "and not of any particular nationality."

With *The Voice of Labor* out of print for lack of funds, Hall started a union newspaper on Kaua'i called *The Kauai Herald*. He also founded a political action group dedicated to electing candidates friendly to unionism, called the Kauai Progressive League. Hall targeted the Territorial Senate seat of a Republican plantation manager named Lindsey Faye. In his place, the Kauai Progressive League elected a Democrat, J. B. Fernandes. Zalburg delineated the laws Hall wanted the territorial legislature to change: an antipicketing law, a trespass law, a criminal syndicalism law, and a law that allowed police to arrest anyone they thought might commit a crime.

More than anything, labor in the Territory needed a collective bargaining law that would prescribe procedures for voting on union representation, bargaining, and mediation and in general level the playing field between labor and management. Jack Hall went down to 'Iolani Palace in blue jeans to work as J. B. Fernandes' clerk, pounding out legislative programs on the typewriter. He quickly assessed the committees that counted most: the money committees, which handled government spending and taxation, and the judiciary committees, which handled the writing of new labor laws. Thereafter the smartest politicians who represented labor went straight for the money committees.

What Hall achieved on Kaua'i before the war signaled a trend. More and more labor organizers arrived, working people became more determined, and there were more strikes. On September 1, 1940, more than seven thousand people marched in a Labor Day parade in Honolulu.

THE AGENDA OF STATEHOOD

For reasons almost entirely different from the issues of labor, an additional force for change in prewar Hawai'i emerged almost simultaneously, in 1934, when the Republican Party decided to pursue statehood actively. The reason was a new development in political regulation of the sugar market involving the tradeoff that Hawai'i's oligarchy had made in return for annexation. This tradeoff dated to the 1860s, when the oligarchy had first sought duty-free access to the American sugar market. Pursuit of duty-free access had led to the treaty of 1876, inaccurately named the Treaty of Reciprocity.

When the 1876 treaty came up for renewal ten years later, American expansionists in the United States Senate pushed for a greater advantage by demanding permanent rights to develop Pearl Harbor. Hawaiian nationalists objected. By 1887, conflict between planters and native Hawaiians over the terms of renewal of the treaty led to the first of the armed coups by white people against the monarchy. The coup produced not an outright takeover but the Bayonet Constitution of the Hawaiian Kingdom—that is, a constitution thrust onto King David Kalākaua at the point of a bayonet. Under it, the white government forced the Hawaiian Kingdom to accede to the demand of expansionists in the U.S. Senate for the exclusive right to develop Pearl Harbor.

American access to Pearl Harbor continued to function as payment for Hawai'i's access to the American sugar market—at the expense of the real sovereignty of the Hawaiian nation. In 1893, when the planters again were threatened by higher sugar tariffs, the American and American-descended enclave overthrew the native government of Hawai'i.

With duty-free access achieved in 1898, a marginally profitable sugar industry became highly profitable. In light of this history, the sugar industry of Hawai'i was more a function of ruthless political maneuvering than of supply and demand. The sugar industry of Hawai'i was reminded of this essential fact in 1934 by congressional passage of a bill setting quotas on sugar production, known as the Jones-Costigan Act. Hawai'i's quota reduced the total volume of the industry. The oligarchy cried that Hawai'i was being treated as less than fully American. The only remedy to Jones-Costigan was for Hawai'i to achieve full representation in the halls of government, which meant that Hawai'i must become a state.

It is one of the ironies of Hawai'i's history that the oligarchy, which depended for its privileged existence on Hawai'i being a backwater, was thrust ever further into the arms of America's democratic political culture by its need for market security. Its materialism would be its undoing.

With statehood seriously on the agenda by 1935, the otherwise conflicting interests of the sugar industry and the American-born citizens of Japanese ancestry modestly converged. Both agreed on statehood. The political problem, which the oligarchy had figured heavily in creating, was the erroneous impression that the Japanese Americans of Hawai'i were not to be trusted—most particularly in the event of war between Japan and the United States. It is at this point that the obscure history of the territory began to converge with the question of how the Japanese community might survive such a war.

THE QUESTION OF LOYALTY

The crisis that was to define the future of Hawai'i approached with a slow-motion kind of certainty. The issei, the nisei, the FBI, the military intelligence agencies in Hawai'i, the White House, and the old-time internationalists in Japan all had agonized at length over the identity and loyalties of the Japanese community in Hawai'i in the event of war between Japan and the United States. For the nisei, the question, "Who are we?" had been asked over and over, and it would be fundamental to Hawai'i's political history that John A. Burns was part of the inquiry.

By the time John Burns became a policeman, he was aware of an unwritten rule against too many Japanese going up the police department ladder too quickly. By the time he competed for promotion to captain, everyone was talking about the possibility of war with Japan. As war became a more obvious threat, Chief William Gabrielson called Burns into his office and said he had a new job that would make Burns an *acting* captain. Burns' new job was to form an espionage unit and to work cooperatively with the Federal Bureau of Investigation.

On the first day of 1941, Burns, then thirty-two, reported to Robert L. Shivers, special agent in charge of the Honolulu office of the FBI. Burns was given to understand that he had been handpicked by Shivers, who had arrived in Honolulu in August 1939 to re-establish the presence of the FBI. The bureau had maintained an office during the 1920s, when fears of foreigners and socialism ran high, and now Shivers had arrived on the scene with a mandate from the director of the bureau, J. Edgar Hoover, to seize control of internal security in Hawai'i. The focus of this effort was to determine what America should do with the Japanese community in the event of war with Japan.

Shivers is of far more importance to Hawai'i's history than has been recognized, partly for his direct contributions and partly for his relationship
with Burns and, through Burns, events to come. Shivers was born in Ten-
nessee in 1894, the year after the overthrow of the Hawaiian monarchy. In
1941 he was forty-six, a small and seemingly unathletic man who parted
his shiny black hair in the middle. In many ways he was an antecedent to
Burns. He possessed a powerful will to control whatever situation he was
in without flaunting his power too visibly. He was a tough-minded investi-
gator of few words and deep convictions. People who worked with him sometimes saw him as domineering. Beneath the calculated exterior, they found
a person of emotion and empathy.[5]

More than any other person during the years 1939 to 1941, Shivers held
the future of Hawai'i's unique society in his hands. At Hoover's direction,
he achieved considerable control of the federal agents, spies, and intelligence
officers swarming around the issue of Japanese loyalty. This was no small
task, because it required asserting authority over Army Intelligence (G-2)
and the Office of Naval Intelligence (ONI). ONI was a particular problem,
because the navy had been influential in the annexation and had then built
out Pearl Harbor as its headquarters in the central Pacific. High-level navy
people not only saw Hawai'i as their base for projecting American force in
the Pacific, but thought of themselves as practically owning Hawai'i.

The army followed Shivers' lead more readily. It had been on the ground
in Hawai'i since 1898, when the first contingent had passed through on its
way to war in the Philippines and a smaller contingent had stayed back to
begin fortifying the new territory. When the American Congress eventually
wanted to know why things had gone so awry at Pearl Harbor, it would
become apparent that the navy and army regarded one another with suspicion and jealousy.

In this rift between the military services lay Hoover's opportunity to take
charge of internal security in the United States. In 1940, the FBI was still
an unblemished institution in the eyes of the press and the movie industry,
and Hoover was regarded as the great crime fighter. After a bruising struggle, President Franklin Delano Roosevelt named the FBI to take charge of
internal security relative to the loyalty question, and the FBI became the
lead agency in examining the lives of the 40 percent of the population who
traced their ancestry to Japan.

FDR AND TR

While Franklin Roosevelt would come to be regarded as a great progressive, he clung to a nineteenth-century view in which the issues of Japan and

the Japanese-ancestry population in Hawai'i were inseparable. In that regard he was the spiritual and policy heir of his cousin Theodore, who as assistant secretary of the navy had advanced the cause of annexing the Hawaiian Islands by exploiting friction with Japan over Hawai'i. Theodore Roosevelt had been acutely aware of Japan's victory over China in 1895. When the Republic of Hawai'i had delivered its calculated insults to Japanese immigrants, provoking Japan's dispatch of a battleship to Honolulu, Theodore had inquired of Lorrin Thurston, "Do you think, Thurston, the Japanese really intend to fight in Honolulu? If so, I hope they will do so now, and we certainly will give them a bellyful." He watched with growing respect as Japan defeated Russia in 1905. In the aftermath, having ascended to the presidency, he brokered a peace treaty in which America turned its back on Japan's takeover of Korea in return for Japan's acceptance of America's occupation of the Philippines.

When *Bushidō: The Soul of Japan*[6] was published in 1905, Roosevelt bought sixty copies.[7] He saw in Japan's code of the warrior a cultural variation of his own devotion to fitness, guns, horses, ships, new territory, and war. By 1907, near the end of his tenure, the city of San Francisco had developed a Japanese community, most of whom had arrived in North America by way of Hawai'i. Early showing the colors of California, the San Francisco school district attempted to segregate this new population in separate schools. Japan protested, and Theodore—now worried about a war with Japan—intervened. He pressured the San Francisco politicians into abandoning their plan while arriving at the so-called Gentlemen's Agreement with Japan to minimize further migration. As a result, the migration of Japanese immigrants to California grew slowly, while a consistently large part of Hawai'i's population was of Japanese ancestry.

HOW TO DEFEND THE COLONIES?

Thanks significantly to Theodore Roosevelt, the United States had acquired not only Hawai'i but a series of stepping stones across the Pacific, including Guam and the Philippines. In the aftermath, it wanted neither to acknowledge the imperial nature of its expansion nor to do what was necessary to defend its new possessions.[8] After military studies of how to defend the Philippines, Roosevelt announced that it was like the heel of Achilles, but he failed to extricate America from its colony in the far western reach of the Pacific.

Military planning for Hawai'i's defense was interrelated with the Philippines and was nearly as uncertain. In an American war game in 1907–1908, a Hawai'i garrison of fifteen thousand was attacked by an imaginary army of fifty thousand from Japan. In the exercise, the Japanese army landed on O'ahu's north shore and rolled down the plain between the Ko'olau and Wai'anae mountains. In three weeks it overcame the resistance above Pearl Harbor and took over the island.[9] A lecturer at the War College observed that America had become like Spain, which had collapsed pathetically in 1898 under American fire in the battle of Manila. That is, the United States held distant outposts that it was not prepared to defend against attack by a strong regional power, such as Japan.

As military strategists mapped O'ahu, they relearned what the warring chiefs of old Hawai'i had experienced firsthand: Namely, that because of the islands' long, irregular coastlines, a fast-moving amphibious force could land at an undefended place and attack at will. O'ahu itself has nearly 150 miles of coast. One plan fortified only the space of the two major harbors, from Diamond Head to Pear Harbor. Reinforcing the lessons of the 1907 war games, a 1924 exercise determined that O'ahu's defense required a garrison of 94,000 men, nearly ten times more than America had on the ground.

A grossly undermanned U.S. military was responsible for defending an archipelago that not only lay halfway to Japan but was heavily populated by Japanese aliens and their American-born children. As a result, wrote the historian Brian M. Linn, "Nowhere was the connection between external threat and internal security more apparent than in Hawai'i."[10]

Not being given the manpower and material to defend Hawai'i from an all-out attack, the U.S. military was in a constant quandary: Could it recruit and train a trustworthy territorial guard from the island population? While racial prejudice colored analysis over time, serious attempts were made at rational planning. The initial assumption was that the Japanese immigrant would come to the aid of a Japanese army. Therefore the original war plans called for putting the Japanese in concentration camps. A plan of the Army War College written in 1907 envisioned making Japanese, "so far as possible, hostages to secure immunity from attack."[11] A 1912 plan envisioned pushing all the immigrants outside the defensive perimeter, forcing the invaders to feed, house, and transport them. When a future war hero, George Patton, was stationed in Hawai'i in the mid-1930s, he revived the hostage idea, going so far as to draw up a list of people who he imagined would be bartered to Japan. Since by Patton's time the idea of using hostages was more transparently fantastic, the story of Patton's plan tends to obscure the beginnings of a more reasoned approach to the nisei in Hawai'i.

The attitudes of the military were partially reflected in the policies of the Hawai'i National Guard, which was originally inherited from the Republic of Hawai'i. The Guard expanded several times over during World War I to compensate for the removal of U.S. troops to Europe. Of five thousand men in the Guard, only sixteen were of Japanese ancestry during this period.[12]

MILITARY ATTITUDES BEGIN TO CHANGE

In the aftermath of the 1920 Japanese workers' strike, Governor Wallace Farrington argued for increasing nisei participation in the National Guard as a step toward Americanization—a thought that ran parallel to the New American Conference. The army opened an ROTC program at the heavily nisei McKinley High School. Verbalizing an idea that would reverberate across time in Hawai'i, the army's Hawaiian Department commander said, "There is no better way of securing the loyalty of such people than to incorporate them in our military forces."[13]

Admiration of the nisei, or at least an admiration of the Japanese cult of the warrior, influenced the military's thinking not only about the army of Japan but also about Japanese Americans. A U.S. Army study in 1910 concluded the Japanese soldier possessed a "fine physique, agility, initiative, pertinacity, valor and intense patriotism, with contempt of death."[14] It contended that the Japanese fighting man had no equal. By 1924, the commander of the Hawaiian Department, while contemptuous of other nonwhites, described the Japanese of Hawai'i as "energetic and ambitious, aggressive, shrewd, cunning, secretive, persistent, clannish, and astute."[15] While military policymakers tried to sort through the teachings of Social Darwinism, they simultaneously struggled with letting Japanese Americans into the Guard. In effect, the historic preoccupation with racial superiority and inferiority was becoming confused with issues of American citizenship—a confusion that would haunt Japanese Americans in eerie and frightening ways throughout the interwar period.

The closer that war came, the more ambivalent the American military became. During the 1930s, army officers on the ground in Hawai'i began to diverge from, and conflict with, war planners in Washington. In 1931 and again in 1934, the Hawaiian Department recommended using young Japanese Americans, at first seeking to commission Japanese American officers and subsequently recommending formation of a racially separate Japanese American unit. Washington not only rejected both of these steps but reduced the number of Japanese American guardsmen—from 188 to 72.[16]

In 1938, a new commander of the Hawaiian Department, after talking with community leaders, again took up the issue of involving Japanese Americans. His recommendations received more support in Washington than previous attempts, but were vetoed by the chief of staff. However, a bright young army intelligence officer, Moses Pettigrew, was stationed in Hawai'i during this period of changing attitudes, and he absorbed a new view of the nisei that was to be significant in Washington at a crucial moment in midwar.

Although the army headquarters in Washington did not agree to a more open policy, a small number of nisei were nonetheless being commissioned as officers through the University of Hawai'i ROTC program. With resumption of the draft, nisei were also being drafted. So while the front door was closed, the back door was ajar. In early 1941, the activation of Hawai'i reservists included a large number of nisei. At that time the Hawaiian Department commander was the ill-fated Lieutenant General Walter C. Short, who would take the blame for Japan's raid on Pearl Harbor. Short was the fourth Hawaiian commander in ten years to hold a considerably more positive view of the nisei than the view of the War Department in Washington. When Short included nisei in the newly activated reserve units, he said, "If we expect loyalty from a second generation citizen we must show the same loyalty to him."[17]

As war approached, the army was still of two minds. Officers who became acquainted with nisei in Hawai'i increasingly leaned toward including and incorporating the nisei, with a presumption of loyalty. At least two influential officers in the ONI in Honolulu also had become convinced that most nisei were loyal. But in Washington, decisions of record consistently came down on the side of suspicion and rejection, even though opinion in Washington was becoming divided.

INTELLIGENCE INTENSIFIES

By 1939, new intelligence investigations of the Japanese community in Hawai'i again asked whether, in the event of war with Japan, the Japanese Americans would be loyal to the United States. The massive scope of this investigation contrasted sharply with the military's lack of intelligence on the Japanese community on the West Coast.

The most suspect figures were the first-generation immigrants, who had been barred from citizenship by U.S. immigration law. Many members of the first generation had maintained kinship, regional, religious, and cultural ties with Japanese groups and many took pride in Japan's new status as a first-class nation and a first-class military power.

With that said, the most crucial decision made by anyone was the decision of the first generation to nurture a sense of loyalty to America in their children, even though the first generation had themselves been denied the opportunity of becoming naturalized citizens. H. S. Kawakami, who became the merchant prince of Kaua'i, had been brought to Hawai'i from Japan at the age of twelve. He quoted a Japanese saying that he translated into English as follows: "When you have had two mothers, one who brought you

into this world and one who brought you up, you owe much more obligation and respect toward the mother who brought you up." By virtue of the
long Japanese presence in Hawai'i, America was the mother "who brought
you up."[18]

All of this was far from Washington, where vague thoughts of distant
Asian markets and distant threats to Pacific peace comingled. When Franklin
Roosevelt became president in 1933, he shocked his aide, H. Rexford Tug-
well, by remarking that war with Japan was likely. Therefore, he said, the
United States might as well be done with it. He was sufficiently interested
in the intelligence reports coming out of Hawai'i that by 1936 he wrote a
memorandum directing the development of concentration camps for anyone of Japanese ancestry who had been in contact with Japanese training
ships. Since these ships regularly called in Hawai'i, and since contact with
the ships provided an exciting piece of entertainment, a great many people
were involved. This approach revealed Franklin Roosevelt's intense suspicion of Japanese aliens (who had been prohibited from becoming naturalized U.S. citizens) as well as his inability to distinguish them from their
American-born children, who were U.S. citizens. It further reflected, early
on, Roosevelt's willingness to violate the civil and legal rights of both aliens
and citizens.

ONI took up the nisei loyalty question more actively during the late 1930s
than it had previously, although its activities were virtually unknown then
and generally have remained so. ONI formed a group of nisei advisers numbering at least 100 people, and possibly as many as 150.[19] How the intelligence files of ONI related to other intelligence work is not completely clear,
but ONI's work was to have a crucial impact on later policy.

More visible activity centered around FBI special agent Shivers, who was
to say that on his arrival he was bombarded by the view that the Japanese
community was not to be trusted. Nonetheless Shivers was determined to
address personally the question of his assignment: In the event of a war with
Japan, which side would the Japanese of Hawai'i be on?

EVENTUALLY SHIVERS WOULD TELL a congressional committee that no
one wanted to talk with him. The elite members of the Caucasian population, who traditionally had an intimate relationship with the navy, were
"utterly cold" toward the FBI. "They felt we were not needed here," he said,
"and were completely disinterested." Orientals, he said, were "most reticent"
and wanted above all to avoid contact with his office.

Shivers was convinced that behind this veil of silence was a disastrous
potential. Not only was Shivers concerned the Japanese community was so
large and so much the object of suspicion, he was also preoccupied with the

several other ethnic communities whose countries of origin had suffered, or were likely to suffer, at the hands of Japan. Foremost were the Chinese, who had preceded the Japanese in their migration to Hawai'i. China was the main battlefield of the war in the Far East. In 1937, the Japanese army had murdered tens of thousands of people in the city of Nanjing, an event that would become a code word of history—the rape of Nanjing. Shivers was convinced that enmity between Chinese and Japanese immigrants alone could seriously compound Hawai'i's problems in the event of a war with Japan.

Korean immigrants also posed a serious issue relative to Japan, because their homeland had been annexed and colonized by Japan, and Koreans had struggled for thirty years to restore its sovereignty through a Korean independence movement. As the possibility of war increased, hopes rose in the Korean community that at long last Japan might be driven out of Korea.

The large population of Filipinos was an issue as well, since the American territory of the Philippines lay in the path of Japan's expansion into resource-rich Southeast Asia. As Theodore Roosevelt had belatedly concluded, the Philippines was an Achilles heel. If Japan were to invade the Philippines, as it could easily do, the Filipinos of Hawai'i would likely be inflamed.

Shivers took it upon himself to learn about this mixture of people and issues in a remarkably short period of time. On arrival, he and his wife were urged to take in a young Japanese woman named Shizue Kobotake, from the island of Maui, as a student-boarder. In spare moments, Shivers sat with Shizue in the living room of his home and engaged her in long conversations. What was her family life? Who were her friends? What were their interests? What was school like? What was Japanese language school like? Saying he would never be capable of pronouncing her name correctly, he renamed her Sue.

As part of his inquiry, Shivers went to see a person of considerable reputation in the community named Charles Hemenway. Hemenway had migrated from Vermont to Honolulu in 1899 and had initially taught at Punahou School. He then became an attorney for the big corporations and was a favorite to sit on the interlocking boards of the sugar companies. He was also a director of a railroad company, a steamship company, and the Hawaiian Trust Company, which managed the assets of the well-to-do.

In Hemenway's special niche, one needed only to play by the small-town rules to maintain one's status, but a desire to do right gnawed at him. Apart from his corporate tasks, Hemenway was living a second life at the University of Hawai'i, where he fashioned an astonishing record of service. In 1907 he helped draft the university's original documents of incorporation, then was named to the Board of Regents, which he served for thirty years. A professor of German extraction, Marie Heur, was fired by the Regents for her refusal to sign an oath of exclusive loyalty to America but alone among the board members, Hemenway protested, arguing that in the absence of subversive activity, foreign citizenship was an insufficient and discriminatory ground for dismissal.

In 1922, Hemenway's only son, Charles Jr., died, and Hemenway intensified his work with the Regents. He had an office on campus and watched every football practice of the season. He became acquainted with hundreds of young students of varied racial backgrounds. He quietly paid tuitions of the needy out of his own pocket, arranged for students' entry into graduate schools, and invited students into his home. Those who came would sometimes remember his place as the first white person's home they had ever been in. They ate, talked, told stories, and relived athletic events.

Although Hemenway had grown up in a world in which the intellectual argument for white supremacy was essentially unchallenged, he would write, "The old notion of superior and inferior races has been proved wrong and must be discarded in the thinking of all of us."

Shivers set up his meeting with Hemenway at FBI headquarters, which he had located on the third floor of the Dillingham Transportation Building, an ornate five-story structure of red stone at the corner of Bishop and Merchant Streets, within view of Honolulu Harbor. It was at that meeting, Shivers said, that he began to see the racial situation in Hawai'i in a new light. He acquired from Hemenway a list of Japanese Americans to work with on the proposition that a great deal could be done to avert disaster in the event of a war.

Whether Shivers also got from Hemenway the idea of working in groups is not clear. Teamwork was so much a part of nonwhite culture in Hawai'i that working in groups might have been assumed. At any rate, Shivers began to create a labyrinth of councils and working groups. The councils were public, but the working groups were closed circles. "They had several groups under the FBI, unknown to each other," Mitsuyuki Kido, then a teacher, would recall. "We didn't know how many groups there were." He described his own as "a small group they could trust, whose loyalty was not in question."[20] He listed subjects of discussion as the Japanese language schools, Shintoism, the Japanese Chamber of Commerce (and prominent Japanese businessmen by name), the Japanese consulate, and the United Japanese Society. An FBI agent, Tex Hughes, once called Kido specifically to ask if the Shinto priests were loyal above all to the emperor of Japan. Another participant, Shigeo Yoshida, was explicit in saying that names of people were never discussed, only ideas and forces within society.[21] In any case, these groups were a significant factor in creating a sense of confidence among intelligence agencies that the nisei were loyal to America.

IT CAN BE ARGUED that after Shivers set the scene, Burns' role was the most crucial to what happened next, because Burns was assigned to generate a new and deeper layer of firsthand information on the loyalty question. He was to speak with those who were, in Shivers' words, "most reticent" to speak.

Burns recruited a team of four people from the police department. One was Kanemi Kanazawa, a tall, handsome young man with a university education who spoke Japanese. A person of mixed Japanese Caucasian ancestry named Miller also spoke Japanese, as did a Korean named Chung. The fourth, Bill Kaina, a Hawaiian who had worked with Burns on the vice squad, did not speak Japanese. Thirty-five years later, Burns would say of his investigators, "The FBI couldn't compete with us, in capacity and ability to reach the people."

Despite the passage of time, Burns could recite verbatim the FBI's wording of its requests for investigation: "We received information that (name) has a relative who is a member of the general staff of the Japanese navy and that he has further links with the imperial government. Will you investigate his background, general reputation, and activities to ascertain whether in the event of hostilities between this country and Japan his interests would be inimical to those of the United States?"[22]

Burns and his four men worked for eleven months investigating the same points over and over—the background of the person in question, as well as his or her reputation, activities, and likely loyalty to America in the event of war. The results were the raw data of the FBI's internal security inquiry.

As political history, the investigation is remarkable as a massive and systematic contact with the Japanese-ancestry population. If one wanted to learn about people of Japanese ancestry, or communicate with them, the investigation was perfect practice. While Burns almost certainly was predisposed to think that most of the Japanese community was loyal to America, his experience moved him to start developing his voice in the community.

A reporter and friend on the *Honolulu Star-Bulletin* named Harry Frederickson encouraged Burns to write an article, which appeared on November 18, 1941, under the headline "Why Attack the People of Hawai'i?"

Burns wrote flatly that the investigations had found no evidence of disloyalty. "Let's be American" should mean equal justice to all, he argued.[23] "Our pride in ourselves and our ability to fulfill our obligations as Americans dictates that we also be jealous of our rights—that we should not allow ourselves to be condemned or our people condemned without proper reason." At the bottom were his initials, JB.

Japan's attack on Pearl Harbor was then nineteen days away. Given the possibility that a small number of saboteurs might cause a great deal of harm, as the military feared, Burns' column was a courageous public act that would be specifically remembered by a handful of the young nisei generation. It was as if his attitudes were fully formed, even if his plans were not.

ON OR AROUND the first of December, Shivers called Burns into his office and asked him to close the door. For someone who had created an image of staying cool and being in command, Shivers was in an emotional state. Late in life Burns quoted him as saying, with tears in his eyes, "I'm not telling my men this but I'm telling you. We're going to be attacked before the week is out."[24]

Shivers assigned Burns to intensify his search in the Japanese community for hints of possible espionage or sabotage. Burns told his men to visit with at least ten or fifteen people a day, to listen for any allusion to pending catastrophe, and to give him reports with names. If each of the four investigators spoke to seventy-five people, they would have spoken to more than three hundred people in that week alone. They found nothing. On December 7, Burns was at church when he heard a distant rumbling of explosions, and he initially mistook them for blasting at a quarry.

The Japanese migration to Hawai'i intersected historically with annexation. Courtesy of Hawai'i Archives

After America's annexation of Hawai'i, the military question was how to defend the territory. Could America trust Japanese immigrants as soldiers? Courtesy of Bishop Museum

While he took pride in his Japanese heritage, Reverend Takie Okumura was the voice of Americanization and assimilation. Courtesy of Hawai'i Archives

Editor Yasutaro Soga promoted both accommodation to American society and pride in Japanese tradition, for which he would eventually be interned. Courtesy of Bishop Museum

Eiichi Shibusawa, the great internationalist of Japan, supported Americanization of the nisei. From Shibusawa Eiichiden *by Kōda Rohan (Tokyo: Iwanami Shoten, 1939)*

Wallace R. Farrington,
appointed governor from 1921 to
1929, was a voice for
Americanization of the nisei.
Courtesy of Hawai'i Archives

Editor Fred Makino
fought closure of the
Japanese language
schools, for which he
was remembered fondly
in the civil rights era.
Courtesy of Bishop
Museum

Liliʻuokalani (1838–1917), center, the last monarch of Hawaiʻi, lived nineteen years under American rule. Courtesy of Hawaiʻi Archives

Chapter 5

When Time Began

It is often said that Americans from all over connected with one another through their stories of December 7, 1941. The question, "Where were you?" was like resetting a clock. Everything that happened before Pearl Harbor was old news, and everything that happened after Pearl Harbor was charged with meaning.

Daniel K. Inouye was seventeen. He rushed into the streets, shook his fist at the sky, and said, "You dirty Japs." George Ryoichi Ariyoshi was fourteen. He had gone to the Buddhist temple on Fort Street early that morning to play ping pong in the basement. As the ball bounced, the attacks began. Excited by the immediacy of the midrange pongs, he missed the distant, bass rumble of explosions. Sakae Takahashi had already graduated from college and was staying all night with a friend at a house overlooking Pearl Harbor. He watched the bombing with a sense of outrage, then took off in a Model-T Ford to report to his National Guard unit, in which he served as one of the few nisei officers commissioned through the ROTC. John Burns drove home from church. His wife was on the West Coast receiving treatment for her paralysis. A live-in couple was caring for his children. To make room for the couple, Burns was living in the garage between his home and his mother's home.

While Burns ate his breakfast, he saw airplanes with the big red sun of Japan circling against the mountains, lining up for a second strike. He called Shivers. Shivers asked him to look at the Kaneohe Marine Corps Air Base on his way in. It was Burns' daughter Sheenagh's seventh birthday, and she thought he was leaving to buy the ice cream. The airplanes at Kaneohe made a perfect target, because they had been ganged together as a precaution against sabotage by people of Japanese ancestry. The fires that raged on the airstrip were a symbol of the price that America was paying—and would continue to pay—for its misplaced fears of espionage and sabotage.

Downtown, key individuals were converging on Shivers' office, including the chief and deputy chief of Army Intelligence. Shivers had been eating breakfast at home with a group of Japanese American advisers when the telephone call informing him of the bombing was answered by the live-in Japanese American student, Sue Kobotake. Shivers and his wife—who were childless—had become so attached to her that they now introduced her as their daughter. Shivers finished his breakfast and said he would probably be gone for days. To his wife he said, "Don't let Sue out of your sight." At headquarters, Shivers reached J. Edgar Hoover. To convince an incredulous Hoover, Shivers held the telephone out the window so Hoover could hear the explosions.

Twenty-four hundred people died as a result of the raid. Pearl Harbor was on fire. Antiaircraft shells fell on Honolulu, killing civilians, starting fires, and wrecking buildings. Tens of thousands of people on Oʻahu reported to military units or otherwise adapted their lives to the reality of war. Suddenly the world was focused on America's overseas territory in the mid-Pacific. Rumors started in Hawaiʻi and spread quickly around the world that people of Japanese ancestry had engaged in spying and sabotage, materially contributing to Japan's stunning military success. For some, the story explained how the great American nation could be so devastated by an Asian nation the size of California. It was a perfect climate for sowing the story of the enemy within, better even than Communism, because the subjects of the story all shared certain indelible physiologies, surnames, and migration histories.

THE FBI ARRESTS

The aim of the arrests on December 7 was to foreclose the possibility of espionage or sabotage. Not to be confused with the subsequent, much better known internment, these arrests were supervised by the FBI, which was under the U.S. Justice Department. While no one of Japanese ancestry was ever charged or convicted of a crime, let alone of spying or sabotage, the arrests were grounded in a constitutional idea that the government had a right to preserve itself when presented with a clear and present danger. The arrests were not racial per se and included persons of Japanese, German, and Italian ancestry, although they were obviously weighted toward people of Japanese ancestry. The only two arrestees in Hawaiʻi ever convicted of spying were of German origin and were in the employ of the government of Japan.

By noon of December 7, Shivers, Burns, and Col. George Bicknell, deputy chief of Army Intelligence in the army's Hawaiian Department, were going through the files of people who had been categorized as high-risk.[1] The idea of this "A" list was to round up people who were associated with Japan by virtue of business, religion, cultural practice, language instruction, or overt interest in the Japanese military (such as visiting Japanese naval vessels).

With the passage of time, and Burns' rise to political prominence, the roundup that day become only a whisper among older Japanese and virtually unknown to others. I stumbled across the events of December 7 while researching *Catch A Wave*. At a certain point in my research, I was granted an interview with Burns at Washington Place. It began over breakfast and went on for nearly six hours. When I asked Burns where he was on December 7, 1941, Burns did not relish the story but neither did he shrink from telling, matter-of-factly, how he had headed the Police Espionage Unit. He emphasized the FBI not communicating well with local people, where his men did. The file cards reflected not only the thousands of interviews conducted by the Espionage Unit, but many more notes and files previously assembled by the FBI, Army Intelligence and—it is presumed—Navy Intelligence. Each person's card was taken out and reviewed. Then the three voted. If all three voted yes, the person was put on an arrest list. If two voted yes, the dissenting person presented reasons why the other two might change their minds. If two voted no, then the person in question was taken off the arrest list. While people could avoid detainment on Shivers' say-so alone, Burns' intimate knowledge of the notes and the people almost certainly carried a great deal of weight. Bicknell was sympathetic to the plight of Japanese Americans but was the least knowledgeable of the three.

Burns said the process reduced the size of the arrest list: "I'd come to a name of a person I knew and I would say, 'I think he's a damned fine American through and through.' Shivers would generally be in agreement with me."[2] Names were taken off the "A" list, but how many will probably never be known. A second and also unknown number of people were arrested, then released when their loyalty to America was vouched for by a trusted person—essentially persons close to the FBI agent Robert Shivers, such as the attorney Masaji Marumoto, the YMCA executive Hung Wai Ching, or Burns.

Most of those arrested were the nucleus of the traditional leadership of the Japanese community. Most were of the first generation. They usually belonged to one or more of several categories of people: Volunteer workers for the Japanese Consul (often referred to ominously as "consular agents");

students who had spent part of their lives in Japan (*kibei*); principals of the Japanese language schools; the leadership of traditional Japanese religions (the indigenous Shintoism and long-practiced import, Buddhism); and the leadership of the business community (particularly the Japanese Chamber of Commerce).

Obviously, this was a deeply flawed process that led to profound abuses of civil and human rights. It resulted in injustices and hardship that have never been forgotten. Several people have recounted, with great bitterness, the abuse of their fathers as arrestees. For example, one man was ordered to spit on the Japanese flag; his refusal was counted against him.[3] Despite the gravity of these injustices, they have never been catalogued and have been substantially ignored in Hawai'i and throughout the country to this day.[4]

The FBI was free to do whatever it deemed necessary to maintain internal security. The arresting teams went out in police department squad cars driven by Honolulu Police Department officers. One or more federal agents went for the arrest, from either the FBI or the army's provost marshal office. Burns coordinated HPD's work with the other agencies.

The center of activity began at FBI headquarters and shifted down Merchant Street to the largest Japanese bank, the Yokohama Specie Bank, which was taken over and used for booking and fingerprinting. Those arrested were then shuttled to the Immigration Station located on the harbor, and then temporarily resettled in crude, makeshift conditions on Sand Island, the entrance to the harbor.

A language school teacher wrote a poem about his experience:

The time has come
For my arrest
This dark rainy night.
I calm myself and listen
To the sound of the shoes.

A young nisei police officer drove out the Wai'anae Coast of O'ahu with two uniformed soldiers who carried submachine guns. They arrested a temple priest who was so decrepit that he stooped over as he walked to the squad car. The nisei was mortified and avoided speaking.[5] Most of the arrests were made that week, not only on O'ahu but across the Hawaiian Islands, typically in the same categories of people. Individuals in the city disappeared with less community notice, while on the plantations the absence of a particular figure was more inescapable. Accordingly Daniel Inouye, who grew up in Mō'ili'ili, the Japanese area of Honolulu, threw himself into the work of his Red Cross team and was unaware of the arrests. Sakae Takahashi was unaware of the FBI arrests and subsequent detainment until he arrived in military training camp. In contrast, Patsy Takemoto Mink, then a fourteen-year-old in a small plantation community in Maui, was acutely aware that the language school principal and the priests were missing. She heard whispered conversations that created an atmosphere of intense fear.

Neighbor Island people were initially held in on-island community facilities (such as the Kilauea Military Camp near the volcano, on the Big Island), which served as counterparts to Oʻahuʻs Sand Island. Some were held for the duration of the war at Honouliuli, on the hot, arid plain of leeward Oʻahu, and others were incrementally shipped off for the duration to camps on the mainland.

The consul of Japan was taken over by the American government. For humanitarian purposes, its duties were assumed by the volunteer consul of the Swedish government, which in turn hired a beautiful young Japanese American woman, Shimeiji Ryusaki (now Kanazawa). She met frequently with wives of the internees. As they talked, their pent-up feelings poured out. The wives wept, and in response she wept with them. They would end up holding one another in the office of Japanʻs consulate and weeping, before getting any work done. This happened day after day.[6]

Up to this point, the FBIʻs response in Hawaiʻi was parallel to its response on the West Coast, in which leadership figures with more active ties to Japan were arrested and interned. What distinguished Hawaiʻi from the United States mainland is what happened next: A coalition of widely divergent forces formed to minimize further arrests and to resist a mass internment of the Japanese-ancestry population based on race. This sequence of events was to lay the basis for the political future of Hawaiʻi.

As a young police officer, Jack Burns was far from being the most prestigious person involved in this effort, but he was the most single-minded and persistent haole. Led by Shivers and then by people in the martial law government, Burns became part of a network of people who devised a strategy of affirming the loyalty of Japanese Americans and protecting the Japanese aliens. Their high level of confidence was derived from their extensive contact with people of Japanese ancestry and more particularly from the quality of their relationships with educated nisei.

For Shivers, the most important nisei was Masaji Marumoto, a young attorney who had been recommended to him by Hemenway. Marumoto was one of those nearly perfect people. After perusing the Archives of Hawaiʻi, he could recite that of the 29,069 Japanese immigrants who arrived between 1885 and 1894, his father was the 5,140th. Marumoto had thick black hair that was always combed, a perfectly even smile that he employed at will, and a trim athletic body that he maintained by playing tennis despite his one defect, a twisted foot that resulted from injury as a young child.[7] In any situation, ranging across high school, law school, protection of the Japanese community, or use of the Japanese language in military intelligence, Marumoto always went to the top. Most important, he was a person of character and principles. When the army eventually offered him a commission, he accepted it only on the condition that he take basic military training, which he completed despite his handicap as he neared forty.

Marumoto's father had left the plantation life and acquired a store on the Kona coast of the island of Hawai'i.[8] The store financed Marumoto's schooling on O'ahu, first at Mid-Pacific Institute, then at McKinley High School, where he was the top student in the famous class of 1924. With his father's help, at an expense of two hundred dollars, Marumoto renounced his Japanese citizenship. He graduated from the University of Chicago, then Harvard Law School, where he was the only student of Asian ancestry. He returned to Hawai'i in 1930, and by 1935 was so well established that he made George Patton's list of people who might be held hostage in the event of an attack by Japan. The same year, Marumoto testified before a traveling congressional committee, facing down and discounting the hostile questions regarding "the Japanese problem." As the war approached, Marumoto had a thriving law practice that included many of the leading Japanese businessmen.

A photograph survives of the night that Shivers met Marumoto.[9] They were at a party on board a Japanese luxury liner, the *Tokyo Maru*, which was making its last call in Honolulu. They sat at the same table along with a third person. Marumoto had had several drinks and was beaming at the camera. Shivers was staring at Marumoto as if he were already formulating his question. The next day Shivers invited Marumoto to his office. He said that since his arrival he had heard only why the Japanese community should not be trusted. He said he would like to hear the other side of the story. From this conversation a close personal relationship evolved, in which their wives visited one another and Shivers became acquainted with Marumoto's two children, Wendell and Claire. From their relationship grew the formation of several groups of nisei who worked with Shivers. Although the documentation is not clear, the relationship of Shivers and Marumoto almost surely was at the heart of what would become, under the martial law government, the highly influential Emergency Service Committee (ESC), which Marumoto chaired.

Shivers' network also included Hung Wai Ching from the Council for Interracial Unity, which Shivers had organized to foster good relationships among ethnic groups in the event of war. Shivers had assumed that the Chinese, Korean, and Filipino communities all would despise the Japanese community in Hawai'i for Japan's militarism in Asia. He was surprised to find that this was not necessarily so, that in Hawai'i enduring relationships had formed that transcended the nationality conflicts of East Asia.

Ching, who had served as secretary of the council, was yet another person who came to Shivers from the orbit of Hemenway. Ching was a person of keen wit and great personal warmth. He had come up from the same streets that had produced John Burns and many of the nisei, and he was widely acquainted with students from the Japanese community—first as a 1924 graduate of McKinley High School (he was Marumoto's classmate), then as an outstanding athlete at the University of Hawai'i, and then as director of the university branch of the Young Men's Christian Association (YMCA). Originally trained as an engineer, he then had gone on to Yale Divinity School. Ching was to become ubiquitous during the war, playing an enormous role as a creative and steadfast friend of the nisei. Ching's closest associate was the writer and teacher Shigeo Yoshida, whose plea for statehood in 1937 was memorable for its mixture of personal torment and prophecy. "As much as we would hate to see a war between the United Sates and Japan . . ." he had said, "it would be much easier for us, I think if such an emergency should come."[10] Only then would it be possible for the cloud of suspicion to be lifted.

While Shivers himself was under pressure to make decisions regarding probable loyalty, the networks of people who addressed the issue realized that the loyalty of immigrant groups for their adopted nation was not a fixed thing, like printing a picture. The chemistry was not perfectly stable, as the evolving gulf between Hawai'i and the mainland was to prove. Burns, for example, was keenly aware that the first generation of Japanese settlers had been barred by United States law from becoming naturalized citizens. This reinforced the separateness of the Japanese and limited their participation in the new country, even when they had been lifelong residents. It was from observations such as these that a body of opinion was rapidly evolving: The best way to reinforce the idea of loyalty to America was to treat people like loyal Americans.

Nonetheless this interior debate was a work in progress, and the rumors of espionage and sabotage posed a national issue that was paramount and immediate. In response, again based on investigation, Shivers announced that the rumors of sabotage and espionage were untrue. His agents had directly checked out each rumor, likely pursuing them with not only intensity but suspicion. At the bottom of each rumor lay either hysteria or a logical explanation. As he proceeded with this work, Shivers was reassured by the large aggregation of relationships and information. He had at his fingertips all the military assessments plus all the intelligence inquiries and, most recently, the work of Burns' espionage unit, the most current body of data.

CHAOS AND FEAR

"An extreme degree of fear was present," the sociologist Yukiko Kimura wrote in 1943 from her firsthand observations of the issei.[11] "Their first reaction to a stranger was fear—fear of being questioned, fear of being suspected, fear of being accused of being Japanese." A story circulated that a half-human animal had appeared as an evil omen in Japan. Japanese families cooked their rice with red beans to protect themselves from impending danger. A rumor of mass internment sent people rushing to stores to buy suitcases and warm clothes to protect themselves against the cold of North America. The traditional cultural interpreters of reality had disappeared. Kimura believed that although the issei were prepared to cope with poverty, they were unprepared to deal with the loss of authority figures. "The alien Japanese," she wrote, "feel lost without the domineering guidance of leaders."

When a member of the community died, there was no priest to conduct services or lead the process of grief and condolence. All were in jail. A contrasting image survives in a photograph of a funeral in one of the camps. A single deceased person is ministered to by dozens of priests. Another contrasting pair of photographs is of the board of directors of the Japanese Chamber of Commerce. Just before the war, they sat in fine clothes, with the most prestigious Japanese businessmen in the center. The young attorney Masaji Marumoto stood in the back row. In internment camp they were photographed again, seated in the same configuration, absent their fine clothes and absent Marumoto.

JAPANESE AMERICAN COMMUNITY STRENGTHS

Although anxiety and demoralization featured heavily in the reactions to December 7, the more important determinant of history was the underlying strength of Japanese American community leadership. Its existence reflected the development of a growing urban middle class and the development of an American-educated second generation. This leadership group had depth and breadth. It functioned on a community-wide basis throughout the city of Honolulu, bringing people of Japanese ancestry together across neighborhoods as well as across prefectural and religious lines. It was of crucial importance because government authorities who wanted to reach out to the Japanese community could quickly find established nisei leaders with whom to work.

The regrouping of nisei leadership occurred under the auspices of the martial law government, which had been proclaimed immediately after the bombing. From December 16 forward, this government was presided over by Lieutenant General Delos Emmons. Emmons apparently had come to

Hawai'i sharing the nation's suspicions of the Japanese, regardless of their American citizenship. Once established, he and not Shivers was in the most pivotal position. But where Shivers had been greeted by a prevailing wisdom that the Japanese could not be trusted, Shivers, his data, and the circles of people working in support of the Japanese community, were all in place to vouch for the loyalty of the nisei and their parents as well.

Beneath Emmons (who also commanded army operations in Hawai'i), Army Intelligence was handled by Colonel Kendall Fielder, who laid his career on the line in support of his belief in the loyalty of the Japanese American.

In the short term, the regrouping of the nisei supporters network reflected the organizational work of Shivers, but in a longer time frame it reflected the community-building and sometimes internationalist efforts that had gotten started in Hawai'i in the 1920s.

Hung Wai Ching moved from the Council of Interracial Unity into the Morale Division of the martial law government. Ching had been an enthusiastic participant in the Pan Pacific Union and the East West Philosopher's Conference and by 1940, he was an important figure in the YMCA. Shigeo Yoshida, who had played a prominent role in the Hawaiian Japanese Civic Association, also played an important role in the Morale Division. The third person in the Morale Division was Charles Loomis, who was originally part of the Honolulu YMCA, then served in the secretariat of the internationalist Institute for Pacific Relations.[12]

The Morale Division was the link to the Emergency Service Committee, which specifically addressed the Japanese community. Marumoto, who had served as president of the Hawaiian Japanese Civic Association, was the first chairman of the ESC and, arguably, the nisei who had most influenced Shivers. The young police captain involved in the loyalty issue was John Burns, an eager participant in the interracial service club, Lions International. The enduring acronym AJA—Americans of Japanese Ancestry—also came into widespread use around this time.

THE EMERGENCY SERVICE COMMITTEE

In research until now, the ESC has been described only as an invention of the martial law government. Actually, the roots of the ESC are traceable to the organization of the Hawaiian Japanese Civic Association in 1927.[13] This group was led mainly and then almost exclusively by nisei. One of its early presidents was the pathfinding Marumoto, arguably the most key American of Japanese ancestry in negotiating the problems of the war. Other presidents in the 1930s included Marumoto's one-time law partner, Robert K. Murakami, and Dr. Ernest Murai, a stalwart of the ESC and a founder of the modern Democratic Party. Each was to play key roles in the pending crisis. Lists of officers and committee members published in the late 1930s and early 1940s form a roll call of subsequent wartime leadership for the Japanese community in Hawai'i. They include insurance executive Masatoshi Katagiri (president, 1940); statistician Jack K. Wakayama (president, 1941); the attorney, politician, and eventually Supreme Court justice Wilfred C. Tsukiyama; the university historian Shunzo Sakamaki; the attorney Katsuro Miho; engineer Arthur Y. Akinaka; Dr. Robert S. Komenaka; the educators Mitsuyuki Kido and Stanley M. Miyamoto; and police official Yoshio Hasegawa.[14]

The purposes of the Hawaiian Japanese Civic Association were simultaneously educational, cultural, and political. In 1936, it established a scholarship fund at the University of Hawai'i. The following year it organized a kimono ball, the proceeds of which went to the scholarship fund. By 1940, a photograph of the association president presenting a check to the president of the university was displayed prominently in the *Honolulu Star-Bulletin*. The association also sponsored discussions of "civic and economic problems facing American citizens of Japanese ancestry."[15]

Its most publicized and seemingly most concentrated effort was its campaign against the dual citizenship imposed on nisei by the laws of Japan. Renunciation of Japanese citizenship—known as expatriation—was cumbersome and costly. The association's campaign for expatriation began in 1938 and became an annual event. From less than four hundred in 1937, applications to the Japanese consul for expatriation rose to more than thirty-six hundred in 1941.[16]

In response to the bureaucratic problems of expatriation, the association petitioned U.S. Secretary of State Cordell Hull in November 1940, asking that he negotiate with Japan for a simplified process. The petitioners sought twenty thousand signatures and got thirty thousand.[17] At a rally sponsored by the association, Sakamaki noted that dual citizenship was imposed by governments but that it was often mistaken for dual allegiance. If people of Japanese ancestry did not take action to clarify their position, he warned, "It is not difficult to see how suspicions . . . might lead eventually to terrible conclusions."[18] The Hawaiian Japanese Civic Association also secured the endorsement of the Hawai'i Education Association. Sakamaki was quoted as saying that Japanese Americans needed the moral support of the entire community and all racial groups.[19] While the Hawaiian Japanese Civic Association clearly was predominantly urban, it made traveling presentations on expatriation. Newspaper coverage referred to rural O'ahu civic clubs sponsoring speakers. The association conducted periodic membership drives and by wartime was reported to have eighteen hundred members.[20]

Tracing this group over time is complicated by the fact that it changed its name in 1941 to the Honolulu Civic Club. In mid-1942 it merged with the Emergency Service Committee, an apparently formal process in which six representatives were reported by the *Honolulu Advertiser* to have been chosen from each group for the central committee, with several more chosen at large. Judging from the membership of the ESC, by this time the leadership selection process seems to have been well developed, and the key leaders in the wartime ESC and the prewar Civic Association were nearly one and the same. Of the original six founders of the ESC, three were past presidents of the Hawaiian Japanese Civic Association. Shigeo Yoshida was a spokesman for expatriation from Japan. The other two men, Y. Baron Goto and Dr. Katsumi Kometani, almost certainly had been active in the Civic Association, given their backgrounds and education. With the addition of six new ESC members (actually seven, including Sakamaki) after dissolution of the civic association, the ESC had become a distillation of the long-standing Hawaiian Japanese Civic Association.

The fourteen-year history of the Hawaiian Japanese Civic Association helps give historical definition to the ESC. While Gary Okihiro described the ESC as "a nisei counter-propaganda system directed against ethnic identity and culture,"[21] which is in many respects inarguable, it culminated a long-standing effort at leadership development. As such, the ESC had a legitimacy that transcended Shivers' formation of organizations, as well as the army's. In tandem with the ESC, there were morale committees on the Big Island, Maui, and Kaua'i that functioned as counterparts.

THE POLICE CONTACT GROUP

In all, this labyrinth was the fulfillment of the original vision of Robert Shivers after his meeting with the university regent, Charles Hemenway. It was a world of overlapping networks, agencies, councils, and committees. The organization that most directly overlapped with the ESC was the Police Contact Group, which became the crucible for John Burns' ongoing relationship with the Japanese community after the FBI arrests had been made.

While late in life Burns responded to questions about the Police Contact Group (and the ESC), it was far from being his favorite subject. No adequately informed interviewers existed to pose the questions.[22] Pearl Harbor had become the dawn of history, and only a few people's memory went back that far. Dr. Ernest Murai, a close associate of Burns, would remember that work got done at night only because Burns, as a police officer, could drive through the streets despite the blackout. The attorney Ted Tsukiyama remembered Burns picking him up at Schofield Barracks and driving him through the dirt roads of cane fields to tell immigrants about the work of nisei war volunteers. (Tsukiyama remembered Burns as a stern fellow who was not inclined to chat.)

As in his work before December 7, Burns continued to span the first and second generations of Japanese and to deal with their relationship to the wider community. His wartime role had evolved from a rally in June 1941 in which two thousand people, mostly nisei, had packed the auditorium at McKinley High School. This was an instance of Japanese community activity prior to the war that helped stabilize the community during the war. At the meeting, the head of Army Intelligence made a carefully worded statement saying that the Japanese community would be safe in war, provided it cooperated actively with the American war effort. Although it was a veiled threat, the sense of dread was so heavy by midsummer of 1941 that the statement was regarded as a hopeful sign that the Japanese in Hawai'i could get through a war without a mass removal and internment. In the evolution of American intelligence assessments of the Japanese-ancestry community, the statement at the McKinley rally reflected a shift away from the simple declarations that in the event of war most people of Japanese ancestry would support Japan.

A nisei group had gone from the McKinley rally to the Honolulu Police Department to volunteer their services as reserve officers. They were directed to Burns, but their contribution was delayed. Time was lost, presumably to the FBI investigation, then to a West Coast trip in which Burns met with the FBI in Los Angeles and San Francisco to describe Hawai'i's approach to the Japanese community. Then there was the final week of intense investigative work before the attack on Pearl Harbor. By then the nisei volunteers had been selected and screened and were scheduled to meet with Burns on December 8.

The idea got back on track in January 1942. The group became known as the Police Contact Group. Press announcements appeared in mid-May. *The Hawaii Hochi* described Burns as "the driving force" behind the organization. The stated goal was for representatives in every community on O'ahu to promote "the spirit of Americanism among their fellow Japanese."

The contact group had sixty members. Burns introduced their names in the press announcement by saying, "It is the American way to give credit where credit is due." A James Kushima represented Honouliuli, a plantation town in leeward O'ahu that now is so small it scarcely exists. Clarence T. Toguchi represented the windward town of Kahalu'u, now a suburb, then known as a place where immigrant families raised pigs and farmed pineapple. The town of Wahiawā, next to Schofield Barracks, was represented by a Masao Kanemaru. Honolulu representatives were lumped together. They included Sakae Amano, who would eventually serve in the legislature; Arthur Akinaka, a prominent engineer; and Wallace Amioka, who would eventually be a successful businessman.

The stated objective of the Contact Group was "To contact all persons of the Japanese race, whether citizens of America or Japan, in person." The representatives would point out "that Americanism is not a condition particularly of birth but of choice." Even though a person was not allowed by law to become a citizen "he can still be an American." The group was "to stress to all contacted that at this time all-out Americanism is demanded and necessary to the detriment of personal feelings and comfort." All would be urged to participate in the war effort to the fullest extent possible.

All were to be persuaded "that a definite break should be made from those things and institutions which are, or represent, Japan itself." This statement was qualified to include Shinto but not bushidō "as a philosophy of life." (In other words, Shinto was bad but the bushidō code of the warrior was viewed as good, as—remarkably—it had been treated since the time of Theodore Roosevelt in America.) All would be counseled on reasons for bearing the burden of prejudice and discrimination.

Another purpose of the Police Contact Group was to provide people with "someone to come to with their troubles." This was particularly interesting in light of the fact that the leading figures of the Japanese community— priests and language school teachers, for example—were now unavailable. The last point was, "To stop the spread of rumors and substitute facts," which was how Burns often described the work of his group.

The *Honolulu Star-Bulletin* said that by the time of the announcement, more than six thousand contacts already had been made. The contact group was described as having organized 121 meetings at which Burns or others had spoken. If these meetings were spread over the four months between the January regrouping and the press announcement in May, they would have amounted to a meeting a day. The meetings revolved around Burns and the younger nisei generation talking to the older issei generation about how to get through the war.

To project back over more than half a century into one of the many spare, grim rooms in which these meetings occurred, one may imagine the presentation being undertaken with tact and respect but also with authority. Burns was likely the only white person in these rooms. He was between the ages of the younger and older generation, but he spoke for the nisei to the issei. The Confucian order, in which authority flowed downward through the generations, was stood on its head. Now the young directed the old. The job of the parents was to listen.

Burns experienced the confusion of the "old Japanese" over and over. In his elliptical fashion, he attempted late in life to explain the situation:

> *Military laws and rules, regulations, were coming up one after another. I knew these old Japanese couldn't understand them even when they were printed in Japanese in the Japanese paper. Why, it was probably some haole writing the Japanese. They were getting picked up for having too much money in their pockets or having the Japanese flag stored in an old suitcase.*

"Oh, cripes," he went on, ". . . to explain to them the necessity of some of the things that were done, at least as far as us poor human beings were concerned—maybe not done in a perfect world but in our imperfect world they are going to have to be done—some of these things would have to be done just because of the fears of the majority. If they [the issei] took it in that kind of a spirit, why, they would be a lot better off."[23]

THE WEST COAST ANTI-JAPANESE MOVEMENT

The importance of events in Hawai'i can best be appreciated by contrasting Hawai'i with California, Washington, and Oregon.

The original Japanese immigrants to the West Coast had typically arrived by way of Hawai'i, leaving the plantations for higher wages on the mainland. By 1900 there was a substantial settlement and a venomous reaction. In 1906, the San Francisco school board upset Japan by attempting to segregate Japanese students in separate schools, creating a far-reaching international incident. In 1913, the California state government adopted the Alien Land Law, prohibiting aliens "ineligible for citizenship" from owning farmland. In 1923, the California chapter of the American Legion coalesced with organized labor, the Grange, and the Native Sons and daughters of the Golden West to promote a race-based immigration law, which became the Japanese Exclusion Act of 1924 (the act to which Hawai'i's delegate, Jonah Kūhiō, had contributed). Thereafter a coalition of organizations continued to stir up antagonism toward Japanese immigrants and Japanese Americans and to oppose modification of the Japanese Exclusion Act. By the time Pearl Harbor was bombed, an organization dedicated to suppression of Japanese Americans had long since been firmly in place.

In the first four to six weeks after the bombing, a strange tranquility prevailed on the West Coast.[24] On December 8, 1941, a congressman from the state of Washington, John Coffee, spoke up passionately on the future of Japanese Americans. He had neighbors of Japanese ancestry and commended them for being law-abiding and industrious. He said it was his fervent hope that they "not be made the victim of pogroms directed by self-proclaimed patriots."[25] Coffee was one of several congressmen who talked about maintaining a climate free of recrimination. Then, in February, as the organizations dedicated to supporting the Japanese community in Hawai'i were beginning to function, the atmosphere in California began to unravel, thanks to the strident anti-Japanese coalition in California.

The focal point of anti-Japanese sentiment was an organization that called itself the California Joint Immigration Committee, which brought together various long-time pressure groups to consider the possibilities created by the bombing. "What we want," the executive secretary said, "we ought to get now."[26] A congressman from Los Angeles, Leland Ford, said nothing would be too strict in light of Japanese treachery. He passed along to the U.S. secretary of state a constituent's telegram that proposed moving the truck farmers of Japanese ancestry inland.

The American Legion lobbied for taking extreme security measures against all people of Japanese ancestry, regardless of whether they were American citizens. The United Spanish War Veterans, the Veterans of Foreign Wars, and the Disabled American Veterans of the World War all supported the Legion. The Los Angeles Chamber of Commerce lobbied for evacuation with great effect, as did the Grower-Shipper Vegetable Association, the Western Growers Protective Association, and the California Farm Bureau Federation, all of whom were in competition with the immigrant and Japanese American farmers. Labor groups supported the crusade. When it became apparent that an evacuation would diminish the labor pool, farm and manufacturer organizations proposed conscripting people of Japanese ancestry in an "agricultural division" of the military. In this scheme, all American citizens of Japanese ancestry would become soldiers who were really farm workers, and they would be stationed alongside the interned Japanese aliens.[27]

Irrationality fed on itself. In response to the cry for an evacuation inland, politicians inland protested against Japanese being dumped on their communities. This led in turn to the idea of resettlement in remote places where no one lived, behind barbed wire. According to the systematic study of social scientist Morton Grodzins, the military was at first indifferent to these ideas and the Justice Department, which had oversight of the FBI investigations and arrests, was opposed. Repeatedly, opponents of the various removal-and-internment schemes noted the racial nature of a blanket evacuation and the inherent violation of civil rights in the absence of a clear and present danger. Nonetheless in the face of informed testimony from Hawai'i (including the testimony of Shivers and Burns), proponents of a West Coast internment insisted that Pearl Harbor had been accomplished with the help of espionage and sabotage. Such allegations were circulated and recirculated in the press, which ignored all investigative evidence to the contrary. The propaganda campaign relied on the concept that if one is to tell a lie, one should tell it so boldly and so often that it becomes accepted as truth.

Refrains of propaganda began to converge, taking over realms of the mind in which rational questions were no longer entertained. Proponents of internment insisted that the absence of espionage and sabotage demonstrated not that the Japanese Americans were innocent but rather that they were cunning and disciplined. They would strike later. On February 14, the army's Western Defense Commander, General John DeWitt, agreed to this preposterous thesis, saying, "The very fact that no sabotage has taken place to date is a disturbing and confirming indication that such action will be taken." The attorney general of California, Earl Warren, later lionized as the great liberal of the U.S. Supreme Court, became a channel for internment propaganda. He argued that Japanese Americans lived where they did for conspiratorial reasons. He told the anti-Japanese Joint Immigration Committee they were fighting an "invisible deadline" and the only way to head off a second Pearl Harbor was to seek the protection of the regional military. Warren poured out his thinking in a face-to-face meeting with DeWitt; the next day DeWitt embraced evacuation as a military necessity.

Such opposition as there was came from church groups, academics, the National Association for the Advancement of Colored People (NAACP), and an occasional labor radical, such as Louis Goldblatt, later to become well known in Hawai'i through the ILWU. Goldblatt predicted the internment would be a dark page in American history. The National Association for the Advancement of Colored People argued, "What has happened to these Americans in recent months is of direct concern to the American Negro. For the barbarous treatment of these Americans is the result of the color line."

The stance of the Japanese American Citizen's League (JACL) was a variation on the Japanese theme of mutual obligation: "The greater our cooperation with the government, it can be expected that the greater will be their cooperation with us in the solution of our problems."[28] An occasional person of Japanese ancestry actively dissented. "Has the Gestapo come to America?" asked a James M. Omura. "Have we not risen in righteous anger at Hitler's mistreatment of the Jews? Then is it not incongruous that citizen Americans of Japanese descent should be similarly mistreated and persecuted?"[29]

Grodzins believed that the finding of "military necessity" carried the day even in the absence of credible evidence to support the idea. People

believed that something unknown lay behind the two words "military necessity." Evoking military necessity, he wrote, was "inscrutable and therefore
incontrovertible."[30] After DeWitt fell in line with the chauvinists of California, the War Department fell in line with DeWitt, and the Justice Department fell in line with the War Department. Seventy-four days after the
bombing of Pearl Harbor, on February 19, 1942, President Roosevelt signed
Executive Order 9066, allowing military commanders to exclude any person from any place in the United States. A month later, Congress passed a
law empowering the Secretary of War to levy fines of $5,000 and impris-
onment of one year for anyone who violated a military relocation order.
Debate was brief, and passage was by voice vote, without dissent.

The young scholar Grodzins had endeavored to conduct an objective
study of "the policy-making process" of internment. He peers from his 1940s
photograph as an earnest young man, with his bow tie neatly tied, his pen
and spectacles at the ready. The internment, he wrote, "was predicated on
a racist philosophy, nurtured by regional pressures, and eventually justified
by falsehood."

AT THE TIME, contact between Hawai'i and the West Coast was scant. Shivers was a link through Hoover's office, and early in the war Burns had met
with the FBI on the West Coast. Periodically Hung Wai Ching talked with
supporters of the nisei on the West Coast, to no apparent end.[31] The congressional investigative committees, the Roberts and Tolan committees, created forums that people in Hawai'i and the West Coast shared, with little
apparent result. If there was meaningful communication that influenced people's actions, it is unknown.

However, in a general way DeWitt's order on March 3 for all people of
Japanese ancestry to evacuate the West Coast heightened the pressure for
a program of evacuation and internment in Hawai'i. The secretary of the
navy, Frank Knox, while conceding "little, if any sabotage"[32] at Pearl Harbor, nonetheless advocated a mass internment in Hawai'i. Like DeWitt, he
was to be remembered for saying, "Once a Jap always a Jap." Long afterward a team of elderly nisei researchers, combing the National Archives, found
a memo that was written to Knox by President Roosevelt.

"Like you," Roosevelt said, "I have long felt that most of the Japanese
should be removed from O'ahu to one of the other islands. This involves much
planning, much temporary construction and careful supervision of them when
they get to the new location."[33] Roosevelt was unconcerned about the legal
issues. "I do not worry about the constitutional question—first, because of
my recent order" (presumably Executive Order 9066), "and, second, because
Hawai'i is under martial law. The whole matter is one of immediate and present

war emergency." Roosevelt directed Knox to seek the agreement of the secretary of war, Henry Stimson, and to proceed with the mass internment as a military project. In other words, it was to be handled much as the West Coast relocation was handled—under the veil of military imperative. He directed Knox to speak with the director of the federal budget on how to finance the work. The memorandum was initialed "F.D.R."

Fifteen days after the first FDR memorandum, he sent a memorandum to Emmons saying that the Japanese of the Hawaiian Islands, "either U.S. citizens or aliens" who were considered to be a source of danger were to be transported to concentration camps on the U.S. mainland. Five days later, on March 18, Emmons was directed by yet another memorandum to carry out the order. Emmons stalled. He was being advised by his own intelligence, as well as by Shivers and various community figures, that most of the people in question were totally loyal to America, and that the others were not a danger. If Emmons were to issue the orders for an extensive internment, he might create an embittered population.

A few arrests continued to result from raids by the FBI and the Counterintelligence Division of the army. These were directed at individual homes as well as Japanese religious temples. Agents smashed radios, frightened people, and occasionally took someone into custody. As a device for discovering wrongdoing among members of the Japanese community, these raids continued to draw a complete blank. Shivers had said that there had never been a documented case of espionage or sabotage, and nothing happened to change the minds of anyone in intelligence agencies in Hawai'i.

Society in general and Japanese Americans in particular were tightly controlled by the immediate declaration of martial law. But within the confines of martial law, more than ninety-nine of a hundred people of Japanese ancestry went about their business, albeit heavily regulated. Those living close to harbors and military facilities were forced to move, a variation of the evacuation idea. Long afterward, the Honolulu chapter of the JACL attempted to identify this category of evacuees. Four thousand people were estimated to have moved, practically without public remark of any type. One family relocated to a chicken coop.[34] Workers in defense projects were required to wear badges, and Japanese workers were required to wear black badges declaring their ethnicity.

The workings of anti-Japanese sentiment in Hawai'i is a subject few people have wanted to talk about. It was most carefully described and documented as an element of the new history by the historian Gary Okihiro in his book *Cane Fires, The Anti-Japanese Movement in Hawai'i*. In his view, the controls exerted over the population in a set of disjoined islands served as an alternative to internment.

Through the long reach of the martial law government, people of Japanese ancestry were pressured to be less Japanese in culture. The tight weaving that protected the Japanese community also shaped it. The Morale Office devised cues for the ESC, which in turn devised cues for the masses of Japanese aliens and Japanese Americans. Events typically described in history as spontaneous were actually orchestrated by the ESC under the auspices of the martial law government. The ESC developed the campaign for the issei to "Speak American." Students at McKinley High School gave money to buy "Bombs Over Tokyo." The Japanese communities in Hawai'i broke records for donating blood to the Red Cross. People burned their kimonos and destroyed heirloom swords, as well as portraits of the emperor. The Japanese Americans who held political office were pressured into stepping down for the duration of the war. Not everyone followed orders perfectly: One issei man slipped a photograph of Roosevelt inside a picture frame, covering the countenance of Emperor Hirohito for the duration of the war.

THE RIGHT TO FIGHT

The most basic element of the loyalty issue was debated within the army throughout the 1930s—whether Japanese Americans could or should be allowed to serve in the military. The initial question focused on the nisei who had been drafted starting in late 1940, and who were already in some stage of service. An additional handful of nisei had earned commissions through the ROTC at the University of Hawai'i. On December 7, they were activated into two National Guard units (about half AJA), which guarded the perimeter of the Hawaiian Islands, waiting for an invasion.

ROTC students from the university were also activated on December 7 as the Hawai'i Territorial Guard. This outfit included several hundred AJA. As a result, the perimeter and many strategic facilities of the islands were being guarded by spottily trained forces composed heavily of AJA. This situation continued during the days and weeks when Japan was in the best position to invade Hawai'i.

During the time that AJA stood guard throughout the islands, the possibility of invasion waned. Abruptly, the army dismissed the AJA members of the Hawai'i Territorial Guard, in what some would remember as the most devastating event of their lives. Tears flowed. No explanation was given for the dismissal, which left the nisei feeling mistrusted and dejected. The date, January 19, coincided with the rise of anti-Japanese agitation on the West Coast, so the dismissal could be interpreted as part of a widening pattern of discrimination.

Years later, in an obscure fifteen-page memoir, Emmons wrote that he was actually trying to protect the nisei in the event that Japan invaded Hawai'i.[35] Emmons said he had been informed that Japanese soldiers would first kill Japanese Americans in uniform. "This could not be allowed to happen," said Emmons. For that reason he ordered the dismissal to be made by the adjutant general of Hawai'i, who he blamed for not explaining the dismissal of the nisei. Emmons said his intention was to regroup the nisei into a service battalion. While this explanation may seem of doubtful plausibility, it is consistent with Emmons' overall concern for the nisei.

Although the reservists had been dismissed, the nisei draftees and commissioned officers nonetheless continued to serve. The internment proceeded, and the pressure built on Hawai'i's martial law government to intern people in large numbers. Supporters of the Japanese community maneuvered for breathing room through their labyrinth of organizations, and Emmons stalled.

The sequence of crucial events then shifted to the AJA guardsmen from the university who had been dismissed. Perhaps it was a moment when the weave of history hung by a thread. A small group of nisei from campus went to Hung Wai Ching, who was still executive secretary of the university's YMCA. They were indignant and disgruntled. The nisei asked what they should do. Ching advised them to "go the second mile," to turn the other cheek. If the American government would not let them fight the enemy with bullets, they should fight with shovels. The students wrote a petition that famously began, "Hawai'i is our home, the United States our country. We know but one loyalty, and that is to the Stars and Stripes." One hundred and sixty-nine nisei signed the petition. Buoyed by the support of Army Intelligence and the network of people originally organized by Shivers, Emmons approved formation of a nisei labor battalion on February 23. The fact that this approval occurred four days after Roosevelt signed Executive Order 9066 facilitating the internment underscores the opposing directions that events on the mainland and in Hawai'i were taking. The students became the Varsity Victory Volunteers, the "service battalion" of Emmons' memory. They would become important to history not only for what they did but for who they were. Although few in number, they included many of the most accomplished of the nisei generation.

DELOS EMMONS

A great deal is known about how Hawai'i's treatment of the Americans of Japanese ancestry under Emmons diverged from the mainland thanks to the nisei veteran Ted T. Tsukiyama, who pursued declassification of the archival record during the 1990s.[36] Tsukiyama was convinced by the comments of Kendall

Fielder of Army Intelligence that Emmons had initially bought into the idea of a large-scale internment and that he would ask Fielder almost daily how many people had been picked up.[37] Jack Burns told of running into Fielder, who said he had been warned, "If anything goes wrong, anything, sabotage or anything like that happens, we'll try you for disobedience of orders." Regardless of the nuance regarding Emmons' evolution, what mattered is that Emmons quickly became the shield of Hawai'i's nisei, constantly citing the need for manpower and the lack of shipping space as reasons for ignoring orders to evacuate and relocate people. An irritated Roosevelt at one point told Marshall that Emmons should be reminded, as a spur to proceed with relocation, "Military and naval safety is absolutely paramount." The labor situation was "not only not a secondary matter but should not be given any consideration whatever."[38]

Emmons' remarkable ability to withstand pressure from the president and the secretary of the navy can be understood only in context of his national stature, which has been essentially lost to history because of his parochial identity as Hawai'i's martial law governor. As a teenager, Emmons had written Orville Wright a letter rejoicing in man's first flight. He was accepted into the Army Air Corps in 1916 and became its seventh trained pilot, joining such flamboyant figures as Billy Mitchell and Hap Arnold. By the late 1920s he was the Army Air Corps man in the War Department, working alongside George Marshall, Dwight Eisenhower, and Douglas MacArthur. He was closeted with Marshall the day after the Pearl Harbor bombing. He was then a three-star general, which, according to his memoir, made him the highest ranking officer of the air corps and the fifth ranking officer of the army. He warned Marshall against the fragmentation of military commands and recommended a principle he called Unity of Command. The following week, Marshall assigned him to take over the Hawaiian Department of the army and to subordinate himself to Admiral Chester W. Nimitz under his Unity of Command principle.[39]

Since competition between the army and the navy had contributed mightily to Pearl Harbor, Emmons' contribution to unity was important, but it was only part of the picture. Emmons had received awards for having the best-run army bases, which qualified him as a good man on the ground. He was also a leading strategist and advocate of the long-range bomber, having worked directly with the British during Germany's blitz bombing of London. In mid-1942, his prestige as a military man grew as a result of the Army Air Corps's contribution to the defeat of Japan in the battle of Midway.[40] Accordingly he was by far the most prominent and influential person among those in Hawai'i who shared positive feelings about Japanese Americans participating in the military.

Circles within circles of people were beginning to think and act along similar lines, more often in concert than before. The Office of Naval Intelligence, Army Intelligence, and the FBI (supported by Burns' espionage unit, and then by Burns' Police Contact Unit) were all working with nisei and encouraging the idea of a nisei fighting force. Naval Intelligence had an advisory group of between 100 and 150 nisei. Shivers had several groups of indeterminate size, as described previously. Burns' Contact Group had sixty members. The definition of a volunteer, adviser, or informant was spongy, but it seems clear that at least several hundred nisei were actively helping the intelligence agencies.[41] As a result of these working relationships, each intelligence agency was secure in the idea that the nisei were loyal Americans. From this base of opinion, the idea of nisei fighting units was gaining momentum in Hawai'i in the early spring following Pearl Harbor, even as people on the West Coast were being herded into detention.

In Washington D.C., at the War Department and the Navy Department, people who had served in Hawai'i or who had other connections with Hawai'i also became conduits for a favorable view of the nisei. One notable example was Col. Moses Pettigrew, who was the intelligence officer for the Far East under the chief of staff, General George Marshall. Pettigrew had served in Hawai'i in 1938 when the Hawaiian Department was trying to expand the military participation of nisei. He conducted a statistical analysis and constantly recommended the formation of nisei units, eventually putting himself forward as prospective commanding officer.[42] Both before and after Pearl Harbor, Pettigrew worked with Fielder, the outspoken enthusiast of the nisei. Fielder in turn relied on Lt. Col. George Bicknell, who had worked closely with Shivers and Burns. By February, Bicknell had been reassigned to Washington and continued working with Army Intelligence. On the navy side, the connection that ran between Honolulu and Washington was even more important, thanks to the extraordinary ability of one particular officer to convince himself and others that when he talked about the Japanese issue in Hawai'i, he knew whereof he spoke.

CECIL COGGINS

Cecil Coggins was the son of a preacher, an adventurer, and a self-made spy. He became a medical doctor in the Depression and joined the navy. He also read a hundred books on intelligence, which he categorized and indexed. Bored with delivering babies in Long Beach, California, he studied the Japanese fishing boats that worked the West Coast fisheries and read books predicting war with Japan. Wanting urgently to catch a spy, he provoked enough suspicion of the fishing fleet to attract the attention of the Office of Naval

Intelligence (ONI). Of that moment, he was to say, "I realized the depth of the ignorance in Washington."[43]

Reassigned to ONI in Hawai'i, he continued his search for evidence of Japanese espionage. People told him there wasn't any. "They said they were just too darn loyal," Coggins would explain. Within ONI, he recruited and trained a group of nisei to watch for suspicious activity in the Japanese community. "They were just itching to prove that they were good Americans," Coggins said. "They'd go anywhere and do anything you asked them." From this experience, Coggins acquired a cause, which was to explain how and why nisei felt the way they did.

His role model as a self-made expert was likely his superior officer, Captain Ellis M. Zacharias, who had been sent to Japan by the navy in 1920 to learn the Japanese language. Zacharias read everything he could about Japanese character, which he tested in conversation "like a collector of butterflies with a little green net."[44] Zacharias was fascinated by the seminal generalizations of a Japanese writer in 1890, who had catalogued the four leading characteristics of Japanese as extreme aversion to disgrace, extraordinary regard for unblemished honor, intense loyalty to superiors, and a deep sense of duty to one's parents. Seemingly inspired by Japan's obsession with national character, Zacharias unabashedly engaged in generalizing about Japanese psychology.

Coggins was similarly bold in generalizing about the character of the Japanese American. In this process he was aided by a young naval intelligence officer named Kenneth Ringle, who recruited Japanese Americans to the navy network and became a voice of reason on behalf of the nisei.

SOMETIME IN THE SPRING after Pearl Harbor Coggins met with the executive board of what he understood to be the Honolulu Civic Association, previously the Hawaiian Japanese Civic Association. He remembered the presence of a lawyer, a merchant, an editor, a salesman, and a business executive. They discussed the West Coast internment and explored ways to express their loyalty to America. They said they wanted to appeal to someone to be given an opportunity to prove themselves in the war effort. Coggins said they should appeal to the president of the United States. Together they drafted a petition, which presented a heart-wrenching statement of allegiance. It acknowledged that AJA participation in guarding Hawai'i "has caused a sense of insecurity among other Americans," which they sought to remove by forming combat units to serve outside the Pacific theater— in other words, combat units to fight the Axis powers in Europe. While the petition talked about American rights and privileges, a clause set Hawai'i apart. It said: "Hawai'i is our homeland, and will be the homeland of our children." It asked for "the opportunity to fight for our country, and to give our lives in its defense."[45]

Coggins took the petition to the aging Walter Dillingham,[46] whom Coggins considered to still be the most influential person in Hawai'i. In Dillingham's office in the O'ahu Land and Railroad building, he handed it to Dillingham to read. Coggins said that tears came to Dillingham's eyes, and his hands shook. "What can I do?" he asked. Coggins replied, "We want to ramrod this through to the top." Dillingham organized a luncheon to which he invited Emmons; Admiral Chester W. Nimitz, the commander in chief of the Pacific fleet; and a variety of other high-ranking generals and admirals.[47]

At lunch, the petition was read aloud. The listeners applauded. General Emmons promised his assistance, as did Admiral Nimitz. At the time Emmons was under pressure from the national government—most vocally from Navy Secretary Knox—to go beyond the FBI arrests to a general roundup and relocation of anyone who was of Japanese ancestry. However, the reasons for doing so were being made more and more obviously irrational, based on the demeanor and attitudes of both the AJA and aliens, as well as the work of the Morale Division, the FBI, the Emergency Service Committee, the Neighbor Island morale committees, and Burns' contact group, which all continued to do their work.

Emmons ordered a massive review of the existing intelligence files on people of Japanese ancestry in Hawai'i. Coggins would later write that 100,000 files were reviewed. While this may sound outlandish, it is credible in light of the hundreds of people in Hawai'i engaged in assessing, and spying on, Japanese aliens and citizens of Japanese ancestry in Hawai'i. What was Emmons to do? With the signing of Executive Order 9066 and Roosevelt's order to evacuate all who were "a source of danger," it was within his power to relocate the 157,000 people of Japanese ancestry from Hawai'i.

THE 100TH BATTALION

Meanwhile, 1,400 nisei draftees continued to stand guard in the fortifications around Hawai'i, and another 160 labored at Schofield Barracks with pick and shovel, hammer and saw. Thousands more worked in civilian defense jobs, albeit with the requirement of the black badge.

On April 26, 1942, less than five months after the attack on Pearl Harbor, Emmons acted. As the American navy headed for a decisive battle at Midway Island, in the western reach of the Hawaiian archipelago, he recommended that the War Department reorganize the draftees into an AJA battalion. Given the time frame in which Emmons' recommendation occurred, this was a highly important decision, if less dramatic than subsequent events surrounding the 442nd Regimental Combat Team. An initial negative response came quickly. It was written by the future president, Dwight D. Eisenhower, then the assistant chief of staff of the army. Eisenhower directed that nisei in Hawai'i be dispersed to service units "where they cannot gain valuable information, or be in a position to execute damage to important installations."[48] Anyone left over could be transferred to the United States interior.

A month later, Eisenhower's position was reversed. The idea of transforming the nisei draftees into a fighting unit was approved in Washington as "the result of previous recommendations of Admiral Nimitz and General Emmons,"[49] which means a great deal of credit must be given to the petitioning nisei of the Honolulu Civic Association and their friend Coggins.

The pivotal person in the national government was John J. McCloy, the undersecretary of the War Department (the predecessor of today's Department of Defense). McCloy was then considered a bright young man of the government and was to advise American presidents for the next half century. In response to the pressures from California, he had helped facilitate the internment. Now, presented with a countervailing pressure from Hawai'i, he twisted and turned pragmatically and relocated himself on the side of the nisei. So did Eisenhower's superior, General George Marshall, who in late May sent orders to Emmons to ship the unit of nisei guardsmen to the mainland for training. Marshall wanted secrecy without creating a "feeling that soldiers are being disarmed and sent to mainland for internment." With no word of farewell, more than twelve hundred AJA soldiers were shipped from Hawai'i to the West Coast.

"No one waved goodbye to us," wrote one of the veterans, Raymond Nosaka. "No band music to bid us aloha. I felt very depressed thinking that I would never again return to Hawai'i Nei."[50] With the blinds closed, they were taken by train over three different routes to Camp McCoy, Wisconsin. McCoy was nearly deserted, except for a compound that held detainees of German, Italian, and Japanese ancestry. Understandably fear was aroused, and years later veterans still debated whether the army's original intent was to relocate and intern them (decidedly, it was not).

Navy Admiral Zacharias reported to the Joint Chiefs of Staff that these fears also circulated in Hawai'i, causing Marshall to issue an additional order publicizing the formation of the new unit, which was designated the 100th Battalion. Marshall's order was the first step in a propaganda campaign of massive proportion that the United States government would wring from the faithfulness and sacrifices of the Japanese Americans. "Close-up pictures, with names of individuals who are popular or well known in Hawai'i should be featured," the order read. "Good health and living conditions of troops should be indicated."

The 100th Battalion was trained to be ready for battle in September 1942. The unit quickly attracted favorable attention. Trainees set up machine guns in an average of five seconds, compared to an army standard of sixteen seconds. In eight-hour hikes in full gear, carrying machine guns, they covered 3.3 miles an hour, compared to an army standard of 2.5 miles.[51] Nonetheless the training deadline for commitment to battle came and went. Instead of shipping out to the battlefield, the 100th was shipped to Camp Shelby, Mississippi, nominally for further training but actually because it now figured into much larger issues of national policy.

INTERNMENT OR INCLUSION?

On one side of the subterranean national debate lay the strategy of internment, which had been generated in California, and on the other side was the strategy of inclusion, which had largely been generated in Hawai'i. Even with the 100th Battalion in training camp, the pressure on Emmons to systematically relocate large numbers of people continued. In June 1942 the order to move people to concentration camps was revised. Emmons was directed by McCloy to dispense with the idea of interning up to fifteen thousand "dangerous" people, but instead to resettle the same number through the War Relocation Authority (WRA).

The reason given by McCloy makes no apparent sense. It was that Hawai'i evacuees, after arriving on the mainland, could free themselves by filing a writ of habeas corpus, demanding that the government show cause why they were being held. In contrast, the suspension of habeas corpus under martial law would preclude such a thing happening in Hawai'i, McCloy was saying. At one point, War Department memoranda went so far as to portray Roosevelt as unwilling to suspend habeas corpus on the mainland to solve the problem. The fact was, there was no such barrier to internment on the mainland, because habeas corpus was not restored to Americans of Japanese ancestry in court rulings until 1945.[52] That being so, it seems possible that McCloy was stalling for time by leading people in circles. McCloy's main focus had become the formation of nisei fighting forces, and it seems likely that he was working with Emmons on how to remold the thinking of the War Department and the president.

In any event, someone at a high level was looking out for Emmons, because his resistance to national policy flirted with insubordination. Marshall's staff assistant concluded that the policy regarding evacuations from Hawai'i needed to be clarified because Emmons' lack of action was "at variance with the policy approved by the Joint Chiefs of Staff and . . . the President."[53] In response to the new pressure to resettle up to fifteen thousand people, Emmons again did essentially nothing. The only further shipment of civilians from Hawai'i to the mainland was humanitarian. It consisted of reuniting the families of internees. All moved willingly (at least as willingly as one might under the circumstances). The journeys of wives and children to internment were supervised by nisei from Hawai'i, including Shimeiji Ryusaki, who was attached to the Swiss consulate, and Dr. Ernest Murai of the ESC. Emmons later testified that the arrests already had resulted in innocent people being incarcerated. "We leaned over backward," he recalled, "in order to achieve as much security as we possibly could."[54]

While Emmons ignored Washington, a military board convened at the War Department in late summer to again consider the idea of AJA fighting units. From Army Intelligence, both Pettigrew and his superior, Col. Rufus Bratton, supported fighting units, as did the War Relocation Authority, including Eisenhower's brother, Dr. Milton Eisenhower. As the agency in charge of the internment, the Relocation Authority seemed to have understood quickly that the detention camps were a fiasco from almost any point of view.

In opposition to expanding the military role of the nisei, Navy Secretary Knox spoke up against having Japanese Americans in the navy. General DeWitt wanted to isolate nisei in army service units within the continental United States—unarmed. On September 14, the board recommended against nisei fighting units. Their reason was "the universal distrust in which they [AJA] are held."[55]

McCloy held up the recommendation. Again, history seems to have hung by a thread—in this instance, on the maneuvering of McCloy. On the same day as the board decision, a document arrived from a young scholar at Harvard University in support of McCloy's sentiments. It was written by Edwin O. Reischauer, then an instructor in Far Eastern Language at Harvard and later a principal architect of American policy toward postwar Japan (and, under John Kennedy, ambassador to Japan).[56] Reischauer argued that in Germany and Italy, people would recoil against Nazism and align themselves with a new postwar order, but Japan would not as readily reject its past and embrace a new future. Reischauer argued that Japan had partially succeeded in portraying the war as a struggle against the dominance of the white race, a view to which America had "unwittingly contributed" through the West Coast internment. Up to that point, Reischauer argued, the AJA—presenting both security and propaganda problems—had been a "sheer liability to our cause."

"We should reverse this situation," Reischauer said, "and make of these American citizens a major asset in our ideological war in Asia. Their sincere and enthusiastic support of the United States at this time would be the best possible proof that this is not a racial war to preserve white supremacy in Asia, but a war to establish a better world order for all, regardless of race." He predicted that once the war was won, AJA would be "an opening wedge into the hearts and minds of the Japanese people." Through the AJA, Japan's people could realize the war was not fought against them but "to crush the wild schemes of their military clique."

On October 2, 1942, this view was embraced by a powerful figure, Elmer Davis, director of the Office of War Information. Davis warned Roosevelt that internees should not be treated as enemies, but instead be allowed to volunteer for military service. "Japanese propaganda to the Philippines, Burma, and elsewhere insists that this is a racial war," Davis said. "We can combat this effectively with counterpropaganda only if our deeds permit us to tell the truth." He said Naval Intelligence—surely meaning the intelligence officers Zacharias, Coggins, and Ringle—were certain that 85 percent of the nisei were loyal Americans and that it was "possible to distinguish the sheep from the goats," a crude figure of speech that echoed through government jargon.

Back stage at the White House, Eleanor Roosevelt, appalled by the internment, was pressuring the president to close the internment camps. Roosevelt refused, but inched his way toward a new policy. Over lunch he told Elmer Davis that perhaps AJA could enlist for restricted duty—in essence becoming Varsity Victory Volunteers (VVV) with uniforms.[57] Henry Stimson—surely with McCloy working in tandem—took an opposing position to the effect that service units were "a faint-hearted compromise which would not fail to rob the plan of most of its value."[58] Stimson agreed that AJA fighting soldiers might cause people in Japan to doubt their cause. Further, when the war was over, AJA would return with pride "instead of being released like lepers." Stimson wrote Marshall a note in his own hand: "I don't think you can permanently proscribe a lot of American citizens because of their racial origin. We have gone to the full limit in evacuating them."

As the debate neared a conclusion, McCloy was reinforced in his views by a visit to Hawai'i late in 1942. At Fielder's direction, Hung Wai Ching took McCloy to Schofield Barracks, where they found what the VVV called the Quarry Gang—a group who broke rocks in a crusher in the Wai'anae Mountains. Ching was a great storyteller. With the crusher punctuating his words, he told the story of the VVV abandoning college to work with their hands as a demonstration of loyalty. Surely he must have quoted himself on the virtues of turning the other cheek and going a second mile.

THE OPPONENTS OF NISEI MOBILIZATION gave in grudgingly and with misgivings. The order written on December 17, 1942, for formation of an all-AJA volunteer unit cited a paper trail of six documents supporting the reversal of policy. But when Roosevelt came around, he did so by giving his "full approval," describing it as a logical step toward normalizing Selective Service procedures that had been temporarily disrupted by the West Coast evacuation. So great was his prestige that his great hypocrisy was ignored. In words that nisei would cling to, he wrote, " . . . Americanism is a matter of the mind and heart. Americanism is not, and never was, a matter of race or ancestry." When Ted Tsukiyama located the original draft of Roosevelt's statement in the national archives, he found that the stirring sentence on the nature of Americanism was inserted into a draft in the handwriting of Elmer Davis.

Just as the future definition of the word American was being negotiated, so too was the future health of society in Hawai'i. With the declassification of these documents, it now can also be seen that this was a two-way proposition. The nisei of Hawai'i and their supporters had significantly affected national policy. What happened thereafter underscores this point.

MOBILIZATION

On the fourth day of 1943, McCloy convened a meeting in the War Department. There he announced the decision to commit Japanese American troops to combat.[59] He cited their fighting qualifications, reflecting what he had seen of the 100th Battalion and also the widely current belief, as Stimson had put it, "that in their anxiety to show their loyalty to the United States, they would display a willingness and a bravery of a high order." McCloy's second reason was propaganda value and its impact on the war in Asia.

The room was filled largely with army officers, but McCloy pointedly turned the meeting over to Captain Zacharias, who was by then the acting head of Naval Intelligence, and to Coggins, who had been summoned from Hawai'i to Washington as someone who knew about "the Japanese." Coggins had met privately with McCloy and now he was being put on wider display.

Zacharias began by insulting the army for poor intelligence on the Japanese communities on the West Coast, and for not getting into the field and understanding who they were dealing with. It was an idea that Zacharias had derived from Coggins, who liked to recall an army officer in San Francisco telling him, "Look at me. I am Army Intelligence for the West Coast. There ain't any more of us." From such impressions, Coggins had concluded that DeWitt, not being acquainted with the AJA, had no choice but to evacuate and intern them.

Coggins had an infectious faith in himself that was bolstered by the moment he had realized "the depth of the ignorance in Washington." He began by saying that the majority of nisei wanted to be loyal citizens but that their loyalty might be impaired if it was not acknowledged in the near future. The men of the 100th Battalion felt double-crossed because they had not been committed to the field, Coggins said, and they "felt something was wrong which they could not quite discern." He described his counterintelligence network in Hawai'i and the petition of the Hawaiian Japanese Civic Association for an opportunity to serve the country by bearing arms. He said that by not being allowed to fight, the AJA had "lost face" and Washington had failed to help them recover. He urged that the new combat units be given "lots of publicity so as to erase the impression that the army was discriminating against this racial group."

The proposal apparently on the table was to commit the 100th Battalion to combat in North Africa and Europe, and also to train a new fighting regiment. Discussion then turned to using "Hawaiian Japanese," such as Sakae Takahashi and Jack Mizuha, as officers. McCloy agreed this could be done, but added that several colonels had asked to command the new outfit. One was the high-ranking Army Intelligence officer Moses Pettigrew. Dissenting, Coggins said the nisei who had been commissioned through the ROTC at the University of Hawai'i probably would like to be in command.

A long, muddled discussion ensued about how to get nisei out of the relocation camps, clear them as security risks, and get them into the army. The representative of Army Intelligence said repeatedly that the army had inadequate information, confirming the judgment of Zacharias and Coggins, whose prestige seemed to be soaring.

Viewed at a distance, the meeting provides a stunning contrast between the West Coast internment fiasco and the strategy that came out of Hawai'i of including Japanese Americans. The 100th Battalion was virtually an all-Hawai'i outfit. The petition for inclusion had come from a broad-based citizen group in Hawai'i. Emmons' recommendation obviously carried considerable weight, particularly because he had in midyear played a role in defeating Japan at the battle of Midway Island. The Army Intelligence officers who favored the idea were in constant touch with Hawai'i. In the back of McCloy's mind was the image from his trip to Hawai'i of the VVV laboring in the sun at Schofield Barracks. Finally, when Coggins spoke with such self-assuredness about the nisei, he referred to the people he had come to know in Hawai'i.

The fact was that the estimates of the nisei were derived entirely from Hawai'i (actually from a small elite in Honolulu), and a projection was being made that the nisei of the mainland more or less fit the Hawai'i mold. A background paper stressed that a volunteer unit would make a more powerful propaganda statement than a unit of draftees: "However," the paper said, "it must be assured that a voluntary recruitment program will not fail."

To an amazing extent, the recruitment of volunteers from the internment camps rested on the well-meaning Coggins, who was walking proof of the adage that a little knowledge is a dangerous thing. Coggins was put in charge of training four-man recruitment teams to go into each of the ten detention camps. A team was led by a low-ranking Caucasian officer, two Caucasian enlisted men, and a Japanese American enlisted man. Coggins almost surely was the primary author of the loyalty questionnaire that was administered to internees, which became the subject of intense controversy. ("This questionnaire," according to a January 8 directive, "will be based chiefly upon the experience of the Office of Naval Intelligence.")[60]

A training session for recruitment teams was held on January 26, three weeks after McCloy's meeting. Assuming four-man teams for ten internment camps, there were forty students, plus staff. Coggins was introduced as an expert who was going to talk about Japanese psychology. He said it was a mistake to assume that a person of Japanese ancestry thought like a Japanese. "A nisei thinks like any other American boy who has lived in the same environment exactly," he went on. If the feelings of a real Japanese were hurt, he would smile, Coggins said, but a nisei would likely sock you in the eye, like a good American. In Coggins' telling, the complexities of family and cultural tradition were blithely ignored, resulting in jumping from one simplistic, prejudicial perception to another in which history and culture instantly evaporated. As for his group in Hawai'i, they were boys with whom he would go "to hell and back." The problem was the camps, he said. Trying to resolve the issues of mainland nisei without closing the camps was "like sitting on a pile of manure with a fly swatter." Coggins suggested the recruiters acknowledge that mistakes had been made in the heat of the moment, but now the message was, "We want to give everybody here in the camp a chance to prove that he is pro-American, that he is loyal, no matter what has gone on before, the water is over the dam."

In Hawai'i, Naval Intelligence had gathered a vast amount of information on "the things they said, the clubs they belong to, the contributions they made, the guests they entertained, the efforts they made to maintain contact (with Japan)," etc. From the sum of people's lives, they had concluded most were loyal. Now that entire process was to be foreshortened into presentations and questionnaires for people who had been imprisoned or witnessed the imprisonment of their families.

RECRUITMENT FROM THE CAMPS

On January 28, 1943, the War Department issued a call for three thousand volunteers from the mainland and fifteen hundred volunteers from Hawai'i.

Since the army estimated that the nisei manpower pools in Hawai'i and the mainland were of nearly equal size, the anticipated number of mainland volunteers obviously reflected the propaganda goal of a fighting unit made up mostly of internees. By February 11, McCloy remarked that more than four thousand nisei in Hawai'i had volunteered, while less enthusiasm was evident from the camps. Two days later, Emmons revised the Hawai'i number upward to seventy-four hundred. Meanwhile, only three hundred had volunteered from inside the camps, and a small handful from the interior of the continent. By March 8, Hawai'i was past nine thousand volunteers while the mainland number was still under one thousand. A week later, the War Department was warning that instead of three thousand mainland volunteers, there would be fewer than a thousand.

Within a sea of problems created by the internment, the questionnaire was a problem. It asked about education, religion, language, foreign investment, newspaper and magazine readership, and dual citizenship. It asked if the respondent had ever applied for repatriation to Japan. Question 27 asked, "Are you willing to serve in the armed forces of the United States on combat duty, wherever ordered?" Question 28 asked, "Will you swear unqualified allegiance to the United States of America and faithfully defend the United States from any or all attack by foreign or domestic forces, and forswear any form of allegiance or obedience to the Japanese emperor, or any other foreign government, power or organization?" Those who answered no, or who qualified their answers, were told that these were the crucial questions. The recruitment teams were instructed to allow several opportunities for "yes" answers before dismissing the respondent as one of what were variously referred to as "goats" or rotten apples.

Dillon Myers of the War Relocation Authority blamed the low turnout from the camps on issei and *kibei* (nisei who had studied in Japan) who "did everything known to man to prevail upon the youngsters not to volunteer. In some cases, mothers committed suicide and parents disowned their sons."[61] He said 45 to 50 percent answered no or qualified their answers to Questions 27 and 28. A report from the Manzanar camp said more than 40 percent of the respondents either answered in the negative or qualified their answers with the notation, "Yes, if my constitutional rights are guaranteed in writing."

As the recruitment plan went sour in the mainland camps, the romance between the War Department and Naval Intelligence soured as well. The army reminded McCloy of the meeting in which Coggins had claimed that loyalty could be determined by a questionnaire, adding, "It was later determined that all the representatives of the navy meant was that assuming you have a complete investigation of Americans of Japanese Ancestry, you can make some reasonable determination of loyalty."[62] As misunderstandings go, it was another big one.

A chasm lay between the War Department's goals and the actual turnout from the internment camps. The resulting fallout was apparent as early as February 8, when Davis's Office of War Information (OWI) attempted to capitalize on the recruitment of internees. OWI issued a bulletin stressing that Japanese Americans would be fully trained and armed with modern weapons in contrast to non-Japanese troops used by Japan who were used as "cannon fodder" and put into the field only when Japanese were at their backs with machine guns and artillery. General George Marshall passed the word from on high to wait the production of trained nisei troops before using them for propaganda.[63]

By the second week of March, it was apparent that the idea of recruiting a majority of the fighting regiment from the internment camps had failed. The answer was Hawai'i. Army Intelligence recommended that the number from Hawai'i be revised upward "to the necessary number." The Japanese American community of Hawai'i had become the recruitment pool of last resort. It had become America's way of saving face.

Where the initial goal was to recruit three thousand from the mainland and fifteen hundred from Hawai'i, the actual pool for selecting men was overwhelmingly from Hawai'i—apparently by a ratio of ten or eleven to one. The revised quota for Hawai'i became twenty-five hundred. With encouragement from Emmons, the number crept higher, so that 2,925 officers and enlisted men were shipped in the first group in early April. Seven thousand Hawai'i volunteers were turned away, which kept the imbalance from being even more extreme.

WRA administrator Dillon Myers concluded that, rather than seeking volunteers, it would have been better to draft nisei from the camps to free them from the influence of their parents. After the initial mobilization, nisei were reclassified from enemy alien (4-C) to draft-eligible, which meant that as the draft continued the disparity between Hawai'i and the mainland was not so obvious.

During the war, the army's reliance on the nisei of Hawai'i was covered in secrecy. After the war, AJA turned away from the pain of internment for several decades. The rest of society ignored the internment as something that corroded America's definition of itself. Hawai'i's nisei forged ahead on their development of a new society in Hawai'i, without ever publicly noting that they had carried the main burden of the war. In thirty-five years of intermittent conversations and interviews with Hawai'i nisei, I never encountered this idea. After initial conflicts between the Hawai'i nisei and the mainland nisei, the feelings and contribution of the mainland nisei were treated with profound respect by people from Hawai'i. In response to the congressional hearings on reparation of internees, no less a figure than Senator Inouye was to say that if his family had been interned, he did not know whether he would have volunteered.

THE RECRUITMENT FROM HAWAI'I

As the war went into its second year, a certain amount of confusion and contradiction persisted in Hawai'i about relocating the Japanese community, even though the issue was effectively settled in Washington. In all, about fifteen hundred people of Japanese ancestry had been arrested. Nearly half had been sent to mainland camps, some joined later by relatives, while the rest stayed in a camp on the 'Ewa plain of O'ahu, at a place called Honouliuli. The decision about who was arrested varied according to broad, vague criteria and depended on who was known to whom. The fighting editor Fred Makino, a friend of Shivers, was not arrested, while Makino's competitor, the more gentlemanly Yasutaro Soga, was. Several hundred people were arrested then released. The idea of interning five thousand people as a starting point for a large-scale internment gave way to interning five thousand people as a sort of end point. As late as the fall of 1942, Emmons was told during a trip to Washington D.C. that the War Relocation Authority had five thousand slots set aside for Hawai'i's people.[64] In the beginning of 1943, telephone company executive John Balch published a widely distributed pamphlet entitled *Shall the Japanese Be Allowed to Dominate Hawai'i?* It echoed the most essential line of anti-Japanese thinking and was to be long remembered by coming generations, but in truth the matter had become moot. Inspired by people and events in Hawai'i, the United States government had set a new course.

Although there were no recruitment teams in Hawai'i comparable to those on the mainland, volunteering for the new fighting unit was far from the spontaneous act that so often has been portrayed. It is true that a great deal of fervor was at work, but the enormous turnout was the result of a carefully orchestrated campaign conducted by the same support network of people who had helped ward off an internment. Again, there was a contrast between people in Hawai'i, who essentially knew what they were doing based on a myriad of trusting relationships, and people on the mainland, who were confused and disorganized, based on mistrust, bigotry, and greed.

Shivers himself made presentations to volunteers. The Emergency Service Committee held forty-two meetings on the mobilization and talked to 3,331 people.[65] The ESC distributed Roosevelt's statement, along with that of Emmons and Stimson. It also distributed its own statement, titled "We

Will Not Fail." ESC speakers went to schools and clubs. Posters were put up throughout the islands. Leslie Hicks, president of Hawaiian Electric Company, went to Maui to help spread the word. Dr. Murai went to the Big Island. Although there was no morale group on tiny Moloka'i, Dr. Robert Komenaka and attorney Katsuro Miho went there to encourage volunteers.

Burns, with the ESC's assistance, spoke to men working in defense projects, according to the ESC's summary. Apparently these were defense installations for which Burns, but not ESC members, held a security clearance. Burns recalled holding meetings "all over the place." He paraphrased some of the more pungent lines: "Okay, Uncle Sam has kicked you in the ass. You're entirely right that you be mad about it. . . . The question is, 'Are you an American? Are you willing to give your life for your country? Do you believe in your country?' If you don't, if you're not willing to die for your country, don't volunteer, please." Not everyone in the audience was enamored with his approach. A nisei named Ron Oba was working at an army ammunition depot but went to a meeting in the gymnasium of his hometown, 'Aiea, then a plantation settlement over Pearl Harbor. He remembered Burns repeatedly pointing his finger and saying, "You must volunteer to prove your loyalty." Oba thought, "Hey, you're talking to an American. Loyalty is a given." For several days Oba refused to sign up, then decided to do so based on the fact that so many others were.[66]

Nisei lined up at draft boards and schools. There weren't enough typewriters to type the required forms, so the ESC borrowed typewriters from private business schools to keep the lines moving. When Daniel Inouye attempted to sign up, he was told he had become indispensable to his Red Cross first aid team. He raced to the Red Cross and resigned, raced back, and announced that now he must be taken in. Attorneys and notaries volunteered their services to write wills and powers of attorney for the soldiers-to-be.

Inouye told a story about the day of departure, in which he described his father riding with him on a bus across town. For a while they were silent. Finally his father said that he must bring honor to the family name, that if he were to dishonor the family name it was better that he not return. Many others told similar stories. No shame could be brought to the family name. If shame resulted from cowardice in battle, it was better that the person should die. In its intensity, in its preoccupation with *haji* (shame), the story is undistilled Japanese culture. It referred to what Zacharias had read about an extreme aversion to disgrace.

While writers have described the many kimono that were burned, no one has described a photograph taken of the 442nd Regimental Combat Team as it was pulling away from the downtown train station for Schofield

Barracks. It is a street scene flooded with families, in which some of the women are wearing kimono.

The ESC took up a collection so Hung Wai Ching could go to the mainland to watch over the treatment of the 442nd. He stopped at the army fort in San Francisco, the Presidio, and argued with General DeWitt over terms of the transfer from ship to train. He then went to Camp Shelby, Mississippi, to lecture the local newspaper editors on how to welcome the nisei.

Hung Wai Ching went on to Washington D.C., where he called the White House and asked for Mrs. Roosevelt, whom he had escorted in Hawai'i during her earlier visit. Mrs. Roosevelt returned his telephone call and told him to come right over. She ushered him in to see FDR, then left them to talk. Roosevelt said his grandfather on the Delano side had been in the China trade, a factor that underlay FDR's hostility for the Japanese.

Ching told Roosevelt that things were going well in Hawai'i, that an FBI agent named Bob Shivers was on top of everything, and that an internment of the Japanese population was entirely the wrong idea. He found Roosevelt to be immensely charming. Roosevelt lit Ching's cigarette. When Mrs. Roosevelt appeared in the doorway to signal the end of the audience, Ching stuffed his cigarette in his jacket pocket without first snuffing it out.

At the training camp in Mississippi, the gamblers in the 442nd developed a code for betting everything, "Go For Broke," a slogan that was to become a national legend. The young men from Hawai'i regarded themselves as high-spirited and friendly, while their mainland counterparts were stereotyped as somber and aloof. Young Inouye was told that unless the initial conflicts between the Hawai'i and mainland elements were not somehow bridged, the unit might be disbanded. A delegation of noncommissioned officers, including Inouye, was bused to the internment camp in Jerome, Arkansas.[67] They drove through the barbed wire to learn firsthand about the lives of internees. In shocked silence, they drove home to repair their relationships.

When the nisei went on pass in the racially segregated South, they were typically directed to the white line or the white facilities. One day Mike Tokunaga was on pass with some of his friends, riding a bus. A young black soldier boarded the bus and sat down midway toward the back. The bus driver said, "You, black boy, get to the back of the bus." The soldier was said to reply, "You see this uniform? I am an American soldier, and you're not going to put me in the back." The white driver grabbed the young black man by the shirt. Tokunaga and his friends disengaged the driver, threw him from the bus, and drove off with the black soldier. Outside New Orleans, they abandoned the bus.[68]

The sociologist Yukiko Kimura believed that after the mobilization, life got better for the older generation. A report written by the ESC in February 1943 agreed, citing the inner security derived from the mobilization. The YWCA created service organizations for the issei women. Kimura says that forty to fifty years after their arrival in Hawai'i, they became acquainted with Caucasians "as friends who are interested in them as persons." White soldiers from the mainland were invited into their homes, where they shared the food, helped with yard work, and sometimes referred to their hosts as their "mom and pop" in Hawai'i. Simultaneously nisei were being welcomed on the mainland as U.S. soldiers, and sometimes the issei were striking up correspondence with these mainland host families. Dr. Kimura's paper was presented to the YWCA in Honolulu in 1943. Regarding the Japanese aliens it concluded, "The experiences they have had since December 7 have helped solve a great part of the so-called Japanese problem in Hawai'i, a problem which the previous half century had not solved."

HAWAI'I AND THE WEST COAST

The combination of martial law and the FBI arrests are ample evidence that what happened in Hawai'i was not diametrically opposite the West Coast but nonetheless substantially different, with profoundly different results. At the time, the contradiction of interning 110,000 West Coast residents while allowing 160,000 people of Japanese ancestry to live independently in Hawai'i was strangely ignored. It has been generally overlooked in history and usually comes as a surprise to Americans today. The fact is that people of Japanese ancestry could indeed have threatened the security of Hawai'i, by sheer force of numbers and access to strategic facilities, while their West Coast counterparts were swallowed up in a sea of Caucasians. Where historians have remarked on these facts, their comments have centered on the contention that if the Japanese-ancestry community in Hawai'i had been interned en masse, the Hawaiian economy would have collapsed.

While it is true that labor was an important factor, this assertion in isolation does not stand the test of reason or of facts contained in declassified documents. When Roosevelt and Knox expected to evacuate everyone of Japanese ancestry, they did so believing there was no manpower problem too big for America to solve. In Roosevelt's view, security was paramount and manpower was not to "be given any consideration whatsoever." Further, the idea of "the economy of Hawai'i" had no real meaning in the context of the war. The federal government controlled work, created jobs, and relocated, trained, and housed people on an enormous scale. That the government was willing to engage in the self-defeating behavior of internment had been vividly illustrated on the West Coast. That it was capable of doing so in Hawai'i was illustrated by the government's movement of both civilian and military personnel into or through the islands. Ninety thousand civilians were added to the population of O'ahu. A quarter million troops were assembled by the army at one point, another 60,000 by the marines, and another 137,000 by the navy—which at its peak effort had another half million men at sea in the Pacific, many coming for shore leave in Hawai'i.[69] Seen in this light, the idea of relocating 160,000 people and replacing the able-bodied workers among them was merely another task of the great war, daunting but achievable.

In this light, the issue of manpower is but one of several factors. Most important, prejudice against people of Japanese ancestry in Hawai'i was not comparable in depth or respectability to that of the West Coast. Influential elements in Hawai'i offered active, effective support for the Japanese community, ranging from Walter Dillingham to Samuel Wilder King, Republican delegate to Congress, from Republican party boss Roy Vitousek, who chaired a Honolulu Citizens Committee, to Charles Hemenway and the network around Shivers, including ONI, Army Intelligence, and Burns.

In California, proponents of the evacuation often alleged that the nisei did nothing to assist the intelligence community. In contrast, the doors of intelligence agencies were open in Hawai'i, and hundreds of nisei collaborated with them on maintaining morale and mobilizing support for the war.

Over and over Californians contended that neither Japanese immigrants nor Japanese Americans could be assimilated. In Hawai'i, the idea of assimilation had been widely if condescendingly embraced from the late 1920s on through the annual New American Conference. The concept of assimilation was supported by a wide range of institutions, from the YMCA to the territorial legislature.

In California the dual citizenship of the nisei was held up as evidence of their potential treachery, even though dual citizenship was imposed by the laws of Japan and had no effect on American soil. However unfair the stigma of dual citizenship (the American president Herbert Hoover was a dual citizen of America and Switzerland, and millions of Americans were dual citizens of European nations), a movement to renounce Japanese citizenship had taken place in the late 1930s and early 1940s in Hawai'i.

Finally, Californians isolated their victims by insisting that race, culture, and national origin were one and the same, unchanging. Rational distinctions among American citizens of Japanese ancestry, aliens, Japan's military, and the government of Japan crumbled in the American discourse under the weight of relentless propaganda, fear, and prejudice. Congressman John Rankin of Mississippi explained that "once a Jap, always a Jap," as did DeWitt, who told Congress, "It makes no difference whether he is an American citizen, he is still Japanese."[70] In Hawai'i the nomenclature Americans of Japanese Ancestry and its acronym, AJA, were nurtured and observed.

While Japanese Americans of the mainland were not completely despairing and disorganized, they lived in scattered settlements. Lacking audiences, their voices were muted. In comparison, the nisei of Hawai'i had sufficient security, cohesion, and foresight to state their views effectively. On the plantations the Japanese had almost immediately organized wildcat strikes, then big strikes. As early as 1919, an organization called the American-Japanese Association of Hawai'i had simultaneously petitioned the government of Japan and President Woodrow Wilson for easy access to expatriation.[71] The 1940 petition of the Hawaiian Japanese Civic Association to Cordell Hull and the 1941 petition to the War Department and the navy were in that tradition.

Not long after Emmons' arrival in Hawai'i, a group of nisei met with him to talk about the right to serve in the military. Emmons asked who they represented. Reflecting the confidence that comes from a well-developed voice, Dr. Ernest Murai responded, "We are talking for the people of Japanese ancestry in the territory of Hawai'i." In contrast to the reassurances given to Emmons, DeWitt was the object of intense anti-Japanese complaints until he took up the racist cause of internment. The American Legion told a California congressman, "Please build a fire under him."

Emmons' open-mindedness compares favorably to DeWitt's lack of reason and backbone, to put it mildly. When Emmons was eventually reassigned to DeWitt's job, he recommended, to no avail, that the evacuees be allowed to return to the West Coast. But Emmons was the beneficiary of the intelligence agencies in Hawai'i, as well as strong elements of the community. Emmons' fears were eased, where DeWitt's were inflamed. In hindsight we may say that the military mirrored the surrounding community in Hawai'i and that it also did so in California. In each instance, California and Hawai'i influenced what became national policies that were essentially at odds. The contradiction was heightened further by the occasional person who operated in both arenas, such as Ringle and Coggins.

The most contradictory figure of all—with the possible exception of Roosevelt—was John J. McCloy, the undersecretary of war. Having played a key role in the internment, he would eventually say that he wanted his support for the nisei soldier carved on his tombstone.

How Hawai'i dealt with the crisis induced by December 7 had everything to do with determining its future. By virtue of the fact that a mass internment was averted in Hawai'i, the practice of interracial cordiality was, for most people, preserved. The interracial aspects of life in Hawai'i were given time to evolve, accelerated by the urgencies of war. The Japanese American community was changed, but in broad terms this community remained intact. The older, more conservative Japanese elite was cut off. The young generation got what Shigeo Yoshida had described in 1937, the chance to settle the issue of their status as Americans, once and for all.

The American narrative and the realities of Hawai'i are at odds. The effectiveness of nisei leadership in the crisis of World War II is about the strengths of a rapidly evolving community in Hawai'i, the history of which has been overshadowed by an overall American narrative that is understandably about the gross injustices of the internment.

FAME

Franklin and Eleanor Roosevelt, the Justice Department, General Marshall, the Secretary of War, McCloy, the Office of War Information, the top generals in Washington and Europe, even such people as Nimitz—all had sooner or later gone down the path of allowing nisei to exercise their right to fight. All watched. A stream of headlines, close-up photographs, and moving film emanated from the brutal cold, the injuries, and the disproportionate number of deaths of nisei that resulted. The battles of the 100th Battalion and 442nd Regimental Combat Team in Italy, France, and Germany are a roll call of strategic breakthroughs on the road to America's World War II victory: Salerno, Anzio Beach, Volturno River, Cassino, Biffontaine, Bruyeres, the Voges Mountains, and—of greatest political importance to the future of Hawai'i—the rescue of the lost battalion of Texas guardsmen.

Total participation in nisei units constantly grew as the military saw more ways to use them. The draftees of the 100th took such horrendous casualties that a large number of trainees from the 442nd had to be brought in as replacements. Thereafter the 100th became a battalion of the regimental combat team. Slowly the history has deepened. During the 1970s the story began to percolate that bilingual individuals had been lifted from training camp and put into the Military Intelligence Japanese Language School. As interpreters, interrogators, and code breakers, they were credited by General Douglas MacArthur's intelligence officer with shortening the war by two years and saving a million lives. From Hawai'i, Masaji Marumoto led a signup for the military intelligence language service.

Most recently, stories have surfaced about training companies, combat engineers, and the 522nd Artillery Battalion, which was one of the units to open the door on the German Nazi death camp, Dachau. There, firsthand, Japanese Americans who had been interned looked in the face of the internees of the German Reich.

As has been said so many times, the combined force of the 100th and 442nd was the most decorated unit in American military history for its size and time in battle. The stoicism of the participants was such that people ever since have leaned forward to learn more about them, and to elicit their story. Initially they were given seven Presidential Unit Citations. President Truman personally greeted them on their return and delivered his prophetic statement: "You fought not only the enemy, you fought prejudice—and you won. Keep up that fight . . . make this great Republic stand for what the Constitution says it stands for: the welfare of all the people all the time." Immediately they were the subject of a motion picture, *Go For Broke*, a book, and thereafter a stream of books and documentary films. Because of their reticence, each new layer of the story becomes more intriguing. An army review of war records, at the insistence of United States Senator Daniel Akaka, resulted in giving twenty-one Congressional Medals of Honor, twenty of them to men from Hawai'i. The recipients were men who, other than Inouye, had lived their lives in anonymity.

From conversation and interviews, what endures most painfully is the memory of fallen comrades. In the 442nd's 50th anniversary booklet, Raymond Nosaka told about first seeing his friends die: "When we pulled back for our first rest period, I knelt down and just cried like a baby, asking, 'Why? Why?'"[72]

Moving film survives in early-day color of the 100th Battalion and 442nd Regiment returning home. As their ship enters Honolulu Harbor, they crowd the deck. Hula girls dance for them. They hoist their gear and stride down the ramp, young and strong. They march past cheering crowds to the grounds of 'Iolani Palace. After being dismissed, they wander in the bright sunlight on the Palace grounds, covered with flowers and smiling sweetly. Family, friends, and beautiful girls swarm around them. To see them in this film is to think that while their battle for equality on the homefront had not yet begun, they had become an invincible force.

A contrasting image is of the returning internees, who populate photographic prints in black and white. They had spent five years being shuttled through various detention camps, the names of which live on in an infamy of a sort: Heart Mountain, Jerome, Rowher, Manzanar, Tule Lake. They had experienced death in other venues. One wrote:

A fellow prisoner
Takes his life with poison.
In the evening darkness,
Streaks of black blood
Stain the camp road.[73]

To greet this returning ship, a crowd also gathers, but on a much smaller wharf. People who greeted them were criticized in the press. The returnees are dressed in suits and sometimes in fedora hats. Most are single men, but some are with families. Singly, or in small groups, they look at the camera with a grim determination.

WHEN IT SEEMED that an American victory was only a matter of time, the Emergency Service Committee turned its attention to what people of Japanese ancestry in Hawai'i would do when the war ended. In 1944, the ESC's full-time staff person, Mitsuyuki Kido, analyzed the status of Japanese Americans for a conference of social workers.[74]

"In colonial possessions, there is an axiom," Kido said. "'The white man's floor is the colored man's ceiling.'" Kido cited a Japanese foreman who had worked many years and was given to understand that when the superintendent of the workplace died, he would be superintendent. The superintendent died. The foreman took over his duties. The company then brought in a mainland haole to fill the job. Kido said the most urgently needed change was in job opportunities. If prejudice could be eliminated in employment, prejudice in all other areas would immediately lessen. "For instance," he said, "if I were vice president of the Bank of Hawai'i, there is a possibility that I might be admitted to the Commercial Club and that I might be permitted, without too much protest, to live in Dowsett Tract or other restricted residential areas."

Few if any AJAs were in managerial positions on the plantations or in the white banks and corporations. Vacancies were filled by haole from the mainland.

Kido was particularly shocked that the Republican caucus of the territorial senate had stated publicly in 1943 that no AJAs were to be hired— this occurring after the call for army volunteers had been made. Only a few AJAs were listed as appointees of the territorial and county governments, and fewer still were in higher-level, better-paying jobs.

At the time, AJA were barred from working at Pearl Harbor and military installations as well. Neither were they employed by the telephone company. "Americans of Japanese ancestry, like other late immigrant groups," said Kido, "are the last to be hired and the first to be fired." Regarding wages, Kido cited a journeyman electrician who was paid as a third-class electrician until he proved himself. After proving himself, his pay was not adjusted. He quit and was hired onto another job site as a journeyman. Even the YMCA paid different salaries to different racial groups, despite comparable positions.

The English standard schools created predominantly haole student bodies, Kido said, and an insidious form of de facto segregation. Most of the city's social clubs barred AJAs. He specifically mentioned the Pacific Club, Outrigger Club, Rotary Club, and Waiʻalae Golf Club. He said there was a real need for a place like the Pacific Club to open up so businessmen could communicate freely across racial barriers. "We hope that some farsighted leaders will start such an interracial club," he said, "because this method seems better than to fight one's way into places where he is not wanted."

Kido acknowledged that change already was in the air, particularly in employment opportunities created by the war. Like the researcher Yukiko Kimura, he described ways in which the war had brought about an intermingling of races. Suddenly not all whites were bosses, but some worked with their hands. Interracial marriage was increasing rapidly, despite the opposition of issei.

The ESC held a conference in early 1945 anticipating the postwar period.[75] The opening remarks were made by Masa Katagiri, an ESC member who had been intimately involved in the loyalty issue. The keynote presentation, "The Job Ahead," was by Shigeo Yoshida, the writer and educator who worked with Hung Wai Ching to coordinate the relationship between the ESC and the martial law government.

Yoshida was a lean, energetic man with handsome, chiseled features, a wide smile, and a bald dome. Like Ching, he seemed omnipresent during the war years. Friends called him "the samurai." He had a poetic side, but he was also a vigorous thinker and expressive writer. He contended that AJA problems were "so closely interrelated with the larger problems of the Territory as to be inseparable from them."[76]

He challenged the audience to project themselves outward. "There must be," he said, "a continued change for the better in the relationship among people of all races in Hawaiʻi, and in the place that each shall occupy in relation to the others." He called for people of Japanese ancestry to eliminate "all vestiges of alien influences" inconsistent with American ideas.

Kido posed the issue of total assimilation versus cultural pluralism. The introduction of this subject provoked an agonizing discussion of everything from Japanese funeral practices to calligraphy and ikebana. One person said they could refute the racial stereotypes ascribed to Japanese but "as fast as we break one of these stereotypes down . . . new ones will be devised and promoted against us." Among the conferees, there was widespread support for liquidating the assets of the Japanese language schools and putting the money into a fund for the support of veterans.

At the end of the day, a participant named Stanley Miyamoto offered a resolution embracing Yoshida's theme—"all problems need to be solved within the framework of the good of the whole community." It proposed "an interracial organization whose purpose will be to work towards social progress and more democracy in Hawai'i." Miyamoto argued that as Hawai'i sought more real democracy, "we need to establish an interracial basis for our lives after the war ends."[77]

The respected attorney Robert Murakami, the renowned Marumoto's partner, suggested the resolution be withdrawn. He cautioned against formal action "which might mark out any such moves in the future as emanating from the ESC." Dr. Murai said he was appointing a committee within the ESC to address interracial community action. Even though "there seemed to be overwhelming approval" for the resolution, it was withdrawn as Murakami had suggested, with the understanding that the ESC would deal with the substance of it.

However arcane the exchange was, it was extraordinary, reflecting a self-consciousness that had been drummed into the AJA community over the preceding quarter century: In renewing their attempts to work with others, they must even be careful not to appear to be leading such initiatives. This incessant concern became a fundamental part of the postwar political culture of Hawai'i, in which most AJA—despite their wartime achievements, educational credentials, numbers, and organization—proceeded with restraint, giving credit, votes, and leadership positions to friends in other ethnic groups.

Chapter 6
The ESC and the Modern Democratic Party

While the nisei soldier has become a staple of Hawai'i's story, the overall pattern of self-imposed AJA restraint has obscured the extent to which the contemporary state of Hawai'i grew out of the effort to get Hawai'i's Japanese community through World War II.

The first recorded vignette of a heightened nisei determination to pursue social and economic change through the democratic process was in the training camp of the 100th Battalion, where a group of young nisei officers stayed back from weekend passes to discuss, over and over, how Hawai'i must be transformed after the war.[1] The debate centered on whether priority should be placed on economic or political means. Sakae Takahashi, who was to be a pathfinder in both realms, carried the day by arguing that AJA could achieve across-the-board change rapidly by participating in the political process. Young Oak Kim, unique as a Korean American in the 100th (and also a mainlander), participated in these discussions, which he described as occurring over a period of five or six weekends and involving close to a dozen individuals. Kim believed that the determination to change Hawai'i in the postwar period became firmly held as a result of these discussions and eventually was disseminated throughout the ranks.[2] In later years Takahashi would modestly downplay the significance of this event by saying that everyone he knew felt the same way he did.

A more systematic discussion grew out of the ESC in Honolulu. As the war progressed, ESC affairs were increasingly managed by its full-time staff, former teacher Mitsuyuki Kido. The ESC was housed at the Nu'uanu YMCA, which had been organized as the first racially integrated YMCA in 1917.[3] The ESC was never a mass organization but a coordinating committee, usually made up of fourteen members, as previously described. All were of Japanese ancestry, although John A. Burns not only attended ESC meetings, but during a given week would drop by the ESC office to drink coffee. At first Kido thought of Burns as curt and unsmiling, but by working with Burns on the recruitment of volunteers to the 442nd he began to see Burns in a new light.[4]

As part of its morale effort, the ESC corresponded with the nisei overseas, and Kido began to receive letters from soldiers asking how they were to be recognized as first-class Americans. Kido particularly remembered a letter from Jack Mizuha, also an officer in the 100th, who asked, "How long are we going to be second-class citizens?" Kido recalled saying to Burns, "Here we've got these boys to volunteer to serve, and they're coming back, some of them broken in spirit and body. What the hell are we going to do?" Burns replied that they must get involved in politics and, in the process, "change some of the rules."

Although Burns would come to be credited with the visionary quality of their subsequent effort, both the scale and the specifics of it were generated by the ESC, which is to say they were generated by the AJA community. The political conversation quickly included Dr. Murai, a key man on the ESC board, and Jack Kawano, who had been included in the ESC because of his ties to labor.[5] Seeking political expertise, they eventually added a Democratic member of the Honolulu Board of Supervisors, the Chinese American Chuck Mau.

MITSUYUKI KIDO

Kido was the fifth of nine children born to a plantation family on Maui in 1906. A disability reduced his father to running a Japanese *furo* (bath) for the plantation workers, and as a boy Kido washed the *furo,* gathered wood, and stoked the fire. From that he learned, "It's pretty hard to be poor."[6]

Despite the family's poverty, Kido went to Honolulu to study at the University of Hawai'i. He first lived in a tenement, then a Young Buddhist Association dormitory. He paid ten dollars a month for room and board and did yard work, graduating in four years with a degree in political science. Having no money for law school, he began teaching. He began to question why Hawai'i was controlled by such a small group of people, and he began to think that the structure of Hawai'i conflicted with a truly free, democratic society. He had an impressive list of students at Farrington High School in Kalihi, including the future scholar George Akita, the labor leader Ah Quon MacElrath, and legislators Won Bae Chang, Stanley I. Hara, and Vincent Yano.

Interestingly, Kido felt isolated from Japanese culture, having attended neither Japanese language school nor Japanese temple. "So I don't think I was considered a good Japanese at the time,"[7] he would say in his old age. "I think I was an outcast."

Prior to the war, he was a member of one of Shivers' several groups. After the war started, he went from ESC membership to full-time staff director, abandoning his teaching career. Kido ran an exemplary organization. He kept excellent records and made incisive and passionate presentations on issues of concern to Japanese Americans. He also acted on the ESC's conviction that AJAs must get involved in politics after the war. In light of an AJA record of involvement in the Republican Party, it is significant that Kido was attracted to FDR. He was impressed by Roosevelt's liberalism and was seemingly oblivious to Roosevelt's suspicious, chauvinistic side. His liking for FDR worked against the many pressures to be Republican. On hearing that Kido had become a Democrat, Charles Hemenway said: "Where did I go wrong?"

Although Burns had joined the Democratic Party on his brief trip to California with Beatrice, Kido was not initially convinced that Burns was an impassioned Democrat. He was aware that brother Edward Burns was a Republican and that Jack himself was, as he saw it, "very close to the Republican Party," because of his friendship with the Republican House Speaker and party boss, Roy Vitousek. Some of the older, most respected nisei soldiers were Republican, such as "Doc" Kometani, the dentist from Mōʻiliʻili who was the morale officer of the 100th Battalion. The two most quoted letter writers from the battlefront, Mizuha and Joe Itagaki, were both to run for office as Republicans. Hung Wai Ching was a Republican. Dr. Murai had campaigned for Republican candidates and it would be rumored that he was more a Republican than a Democrat. Many of the ESC and the Police Contact Group were doctors, dentists, and lawyers—scarcely fertile ground from which to create a new, liberal party.

As Mitsuyuki Kido looked around in 1945, the future partisan affiliation of the war veterans simply could not be predicted. What was dramatically apparent was not the inclinations of the veterans but the meteoric rise of organized labor, and in the early days of 1945, no one symbolized labor as clearly as the third member of the ESC-based group, Jack Kawano, who was the link to the International Longshoremen and Warehousemen's Union (ILWU).

KAWANO AND THE ILWU

Although the war had inhibited labor organizing, it created excellent preconditions for the labor battle that was to come. The army's takeover of government power diminished the influence of the oligarchy's paternal system.

Almost overnight the war doubled the population of Hawaiʻi. With the war came opportunities for working people to make money, either in small businesses or fast-track construction projects. Nonetheless, the hope of sharing in the new flow of income was dashed by the martial law government, which put a freeze on wages and job mobility. As a result of the freeze, plantation workers got forty-one cents an hour while others made a dollar or a dollar and a quarter. Plantations even contracted their workers to the military with a markup. For absenteeism, let alone any other protest, workers could be fined two hundred dollars and jailed for two months by the military. The actual conditions of work were much like those under the Masters and Servants Act of the nineteenth century, yet existed in a political environment drenched by antifascism and the celebration of democratic ideals. Frustration and aspirations rose simultaneously.

Toward the end of 1943, Jack Kawano—after repeated appeals for help to the ILWU's Harry Bridges on the West Coast—set off on a campaign to organize the plantations. He picked eight longshoremen, gave them a brief training session, and sent them to the Island of Hawaiʻi. Dodging plantation managers, sometimes dodging representatives of the martial law government, they rolled up pledge cards for union organization by the thousands. From Hawaiʻi they went to Maui, and then to leeward Oʻahu. Along the way they organized pledges of support from a majority of the workers in many of the plantations.

Kawano explained: "We're gonna organize the sugar workers and the pineapple workers. We're gonna lock the ports. If they bring it to the waterfront, we got them. If they break us down there, we block them on the mainland." Kawano understood the strategic advantage of Hawaiʻi being a set of islands where almost everything came and went by ship. By the spring of 1944, Kawano had convinced the ILWU on the West Coast that labor was going to become widely organized in Hawaiʻi, and that if the ILWU wanted to lead it had better do so. Martial law was ending in 1944, although many of its regulations lived on, including labor regulations. Territorial government resumed and, with it, the ripe possibility of organizing working people into unions, through which they could bargain collectively for improved wages and conditions of work.

The West Coast ILWU addressed the question of Hawaiʻi in earnest. Harry Bridges sent a scout named Matt Meehan to recommend a regional director of the ILWU. Meehan looked carefully at Jack Kawano. He conceded that Kawano was highly capable and the spearhead of labor in Hawaiʻi. However, Meehan complained bitterly that Kawano was uncommunicative. He said Kawano would "sit there like Buddha" and say nothing. It was partly a matter of the loquacious haole versus the reserved AJA, but Meehan also dwelled on Kawano not being allowed on the waterfront by the martial law government. Kawano was severely handicapped, Meehan said, "because he is of Japanese ancestry." It was a description so tinged with racial and cultural stereotypes that today it would be attacked as racism, but in the environment of the war, it seems to have gone unchallenged. What Kawano needed, according to Meehan, was a white man "to front for him."

THIS WAS PROBABLY THE FIRST AND LAST time anyone ever alluded to Jack Hall as a front man, but at the time Hall's reputation was probably at something of an ebb. In the early days of the war, according to Hall, men from the corporations had given Robert Shivers a dossier portraying Hall as a security risk. Would Shivers not detain Hall as a dangerous person who was disloyal to America? Shivers said no. Shivers' closest associate in Army Intelligence, Lt. Col George Bicknell, helped clear the way for Hall to apply for a job as a labor inspector in the army's martial law government, where he spent most of the war. It is tantalizing to wonder if Jack Burns was involved in Shivers' decision, since it was he and not Shivers and Bicknell who knew of Jack Hall before the war. (In fact, he knew of Hall being beaten in an elevator, between floors, by police strong-arms.)

When Meehan presented Hall's name as ILWU regional director to Kawano's local, Kawano resisted. He had always had in mind getting organizers from the West Coast to support what he and others were already doing. Kawano said the ILWU should send someone "to show the local boys the tricks." Now he was being passed over in favor of a newcomer haole who had settled in Hawai'i, a person who excelled in speaking and writing English. Further, although Hall had married a woman of Japanese ancestry, Yoshiko Ogawa, he believed that most first-generation aliens and many Japanese Americans were emotionally bonded to the emperor.[8]

For being only twenty-nine, Hall had a wealth of labor experience. He was a proven political organizer, writer, agitator, and negotiator. He knew about writing legislation and electing people to office. During the war, he had learned about the government side of labor relations. Best of all, he was regarded as courageous and incorruptible.

Hall was also autocratic and had a disturbing tendency to drink enormous amounts of alcohol. Louis Goldblatt, who came and went from ILWU headquarters on the West Coast, was concerned that Hall did not try to help other people develop leadership skills, but tended instead to "monopolize all the thinking and direction" of the union. Goldblatt saw instances where Hall and the other ILWU leaders sat down to drink and local people would break out a bottle but not drink themselves. Goldblatt suspected they were withholding their approval.

Under Hall's direction, the ILWU formed a territory-wide political action committee to accumulate political power in the 1944 legislative election. The union promised to support any candidate who agreed with its objectives, regardless of party. It registered voters and educated them on who had been endorsed and why. Fifteen of nineteen ILWU-endorsed candidates won House seats and six of eight won Senate seats. Two ILWU business agents were elected—an accomplishment that the union would repeat systematically over the coming decades. The now-obscure 1944 election was the beginning of the voter revolt against oligarchic control. The community structure preserved in 1941 by the Shivers network—the continued existence of the Japanese community, and the continued presence of labor organizers—made a significant difference at the polls by 1944. The lead element was not the Democratic Party but radical labor, which had consciously sought to span ethnic lines and organize diverse ethnic groups into a single force. The next step would be the return of the Japanese community to active participation in the political process.

In the meantime, with the ILWU's new base of legislative strength, Hall won passage of a collective bargaining law that encompassed agricultural workers, who were by far the largest element in the peace-time economy. From less than a thousand members in early 1944, ILWU membership rose in a year to more than six thousand and during the next year to more than thirty thousand. Although the legislature was Republican, it passed legislation the ILWU needed to organize the working class in a way unparalleled in America—that is, horizontally. In 1945, the union negotiated a short-term raise with the sugar industry, buying time to further prepare its resources. In the summer of 1946 so much rice was bought up by union members in anticipation of a strike that a black market developed in Honolulu.

As a countermeasure, in the last gasp of importing Asian labor, the planters brought in six thousand workers from the Philippines. The influx occurred at the last moment of America's imperial hold on the Philippine Islands, just prior to America finally granting the Philippines its independence. The importation of Filipinos was a classic attempt to flood the labor market and, potentially, pit one group against another. The ILWU was enraged, and the Marine Cooks and Stewards Union placed organizers inside the crew on board the immigrant ships to preach the gospel of unionism. In the midst of their anticipation and excitement, the Filipinos must have wondered what they were getting into.

The sugar contract lapsed in the election season, on the last day of August 1946, and the ILWU immediately went on strike, shutting down the plantations. In the scale of turmoil, it was a revisiting of the great strikes of 1909, 1920, and 1924, except that now the issue of racial solidarity had been resolved. The ILWU adhered rigidly to the concept of abandoning the old ethnic approach to labor organization. Stop-work meetings were sometimes trilingual. They were conducted in English, Ilocano (the main dialect of the Philippines), and Japanese. People had changed. Through long, bitter strikes—the sugar industry in 1946, the pineapple industry in 1947, the waterfront industries in 1949—the ILWU would make its slogan, One Big Union, a working reality.

When stripped of inflammatory words and viewed as a social organism, the ILWU can be seen as emerging from the shipping industry of the West Coast of the United States, making its way across the Pacific to the strategically located mid-Pacific U.S. territory, taking hold on a new set of docks, then spreading across the landscape. In the sense that the ILWU followed the American flag, it was not a radical but a colonial operation.

Rather than creating more and more units, the ILWU worked assiduously—sometimes ruthlessly, it was contended—to simplify its structures into industry-wide units. It was an industrial approach to unionizing that was powerfully responsive to the situation. It was oriented to transforming the status of an entire class of people. In the socialist view, the actual organization had been accomplished by the capitalists, who had aggregated the workers into highly productive industrial settings. Work already had been socialized; now rewards if not ownership were to be socialized as well.

The industrial approach was the underlying reason that radicals were succeeding in Hawai'i where organizers of the American Federation of Labor moved forward more slowly. The AFL was an extension of the ancient guilds, which were organized with a strong vertical rather than horizontal reference. At the bottom of the guild was the apprentice; at the top was the master, or journeyman. The AFL had made a conscious decision to go after wages and working conditions, but not to challenge the social, political, and economic structure. In Hawai'i the structure was so archaic that a democratizing union was needed to go after change on all fronts. It was in this climate that the postwar Democratic Party of Hawai'i started down a winding path through the extreme uncertainties of the postwar period.

By 1945, Hall as ILWU regional director was on his way to eclipsing Kawano in the labor movement, but Kawano was still president of the union and a respected figure. He had fought his fight, brought in the ILWU, and gone on his rampage through the plantations. Through Kawano's participation in the ESC, he was part of the inner circle of what was to become the new Democratic Party. Like Kido, he did not initially like Burns but gradually came to see Burns as a caring person. "If you cry," Kawano was to say, "he will comfort you." Kawano said Burns would sometimes come to his door at midnight and talk until three or three-thirty in the morning.

THE 1946 ELECTION

From the ESC, Mitsuyuki Kido was the litmus test of the immediate post-war for what might happen if an AJA Democrat and the ILWU got together. Because Kido had left his teaching position, he reluctantly agreed to run for the territorial house of representatives. The east half of Oʻahu was (and still is) made up of the comfortable and the well-to-do. The west half was made up of the working class and the poor. The old Fifth House District was the west half, encompassing the neighborhoods of Jack Burns' youth as well as the rural areas of Oʻahu, including the sugar and pineapple plantations of the leeward side.

Kido put up five hundred dollars of his own money for campaign expenses. Contributions came from the ESC members in amounts of five, ten, and twenty-five dollars. Kido bought a few newspaper ads and some radio time. He printed a card that had his platform on one side and a little biography on the other. There was no television and therefore no need to raise a large sum of money. In all he spent less than two thousand dollars.

Kido stated his priorities as supporting returning war veterans, equal job opportunity, free public education, a higher standard of living for all (including an increase in the minimum wage), protection for workers through unemployment compensation, reforming taxation on the basis of ability to pay, and putting land to its highest and best use.[9]

The businessmen of the Japanese Chamber of Commerce refused to endorse him. Kido believed it was because of his support for increasing the minimum wage. A group of first-generation Japanese who could not believe that Japan lost the war insisted that Kido was *inu,* a dog, by which betrayal was implied. Kido was defended against that charge by a white man from Mississippi named Earl Finch, who had become acquainted with the nisei generation as they trained at Camp Shelby, Mississippi. Finch had moved to Hawaiʻi and in response to the whisper that Kido had betrayed his own people he took out a full-page advertisement extolling Kido's virtues.

Kawano was Kido's most important supporter. Kido campaigned in Honolulu and relied on Kawano to deliver the ILWU precincts in the plantation countryside—places that previously had been off limits to Democratic candidates. Suddenly a lot of workers were listening. Wherever the ILWU held meetings, Kawano would work Kido in to give a talk. To Kido's surprise he not only won but led the ticket.

While the ILWU tried to remain beyond partisanship, its proclivity to support Democrats became more visible in 1946. With ILWU support, Democrats actually elected a one-person majority in the House, setting off a barrage of charges that the ILWU was a communist organization. One of the Democrats crumbled under the pressure, which allowed the Republicans to maintain control.

The most interesting Republican to be elected in 1946 in light of the subsequent mythology of the Democratic party was Joseph Itagaki, who was elected in Kido's West O'ahu district. Itagaki had volunteered for the 442nd at the age of thirty-six. He was a prolific and thoughtful letter writer from the battlefront, urging a social transformation in the post war. A key aspect of the modern Democratic story—in not only Burns' but Kido's telling of the story—was the importance of such letters. However, Itagaki had engaged Joe Farrington and Charles Hemenway in correspondence,[10] and in the postwar Itagaki was a Republican.

Of the six AJA elected in 1946, only two were Democrats, Kido and Steere Noda, a star baseball player and self-educated legal practitioner. The fact that most of the successful AJA candidates were Republican is further evidence that the changes of 1946 were not yet of the ILWU's making, but the AJAs'.

If anything, the relationship between labor and the AJAs was in jeopardy in 1946. Not only were two-thirds of the successful AJA candidates Republican, but the Japanese role in the ILWU was being diminished. When Jack Hall was named regional director, it was the beginning of the end for Kawano. Throughout the union, second-tier leadership positions held disproportionately by Japanese Americans were being redistributed to multiracial slates made up of Filipinos, Hawaiians, and Portuguese.[11] Although the ILWU's success would be widely credited with creating a class-based multiracial union, its core leadership was white and would remain so for another quarter century.

In light of the inconclusive results of the 1946 election, the political evolution of the AJA became an even more urgent question for the future of Hawai'i. It was here that the subterranean events of the prewar and early wartime began to take hold politically. Burns resigned from the police force in late summer of 1945. With a major assist from Beatrice, he ran a liquor store in Kailua and devoted himself to the Democratic Party. As the election of 1946 neared, with the ILWU sugar strike in full swing, Burns, Kido, Murai, Kawano, and Mau turned to their old networks—the overlapping memberships of the ESC and Police Contact Group—urging as many people as possible to hold party meetings in their home precincts.[12]

The condition of the Democratic precinct organizations on O'ahu would become a staple of the Burns legend, which held that the Democratic Party was at a low ebb when Burns went to work. The reality was that thanks largely to the ILWU the Democratic Party was on an upswing, despite the fact that precinct offices on O'ahu were not systematically filled. Nonetheless it is true there was something of a vacuum, in which Burns, Mau, Kido,

Kawano, and Murai quickly became a force in the Democratic central committee. Almost unnoticed (either then or later), Burns also ran for the Honolulu Board of Supervisors. With six of seven candidates to be nominated in the Democratic primary, he ran seventh. Burns was a failed candidate, but he had found a media at which he excelled—the conversation of small groups, the development of core thoughts, and the inner workings of the grassroots Democratic Party. If he had a perceptible political future during this period, it was as a backroom party man. In the immediate postwar period, the most prominent figure was not Burns but a person who would be all but forgotten, Chuck Mau.

CHUCK MAU

Mau might have disappeared into the new, moneyed Chinese community in Hawai'i had he not remembered so vividly what it was like to be poor. His immigrant father worked on the plantation, cooked in the houses of rich haole, then started a small store. Mau's mother died in the influenza epidemic of 1918. As a child Mau sold newspapers and shined shoes. He joined a gang on Vineyard Street who fought with the boys from Kalihi on one side and Kaka'ako on the other.[13]

A minister, Theodore Richards, asked Mau's father if he would like a scholarship to send his sons to Mid-Pacific Institute, a missionary boarding school. By this time young Mau was shooting dice, and his father thought missionary school was a good idea. While Mau was at Mid-Pacific, he maintained contact with one of his most faithful newspaper buyers, Judge James Banks, a Democratic appointee to the bench, who urged him to attend the University of Colorado. By 1933, Mau was back in Hawai'i with a law degree.

He first worked as Judge Banks' law clerk, then was appointed deputy attorney general (and was thought of as the first Asian American, as opposed to Hawaiian, attorney general). Thereafter he went to see Roy Vitousek about running for office. He remembered Vitousek saying, "The Republican Party has controlled the legislature since we became a territory. We'll control it for another hundred years." There were no openings. In 1940, a member of the powerful Chinese Hawaiian Heen family, Ernest Heen, asked Mau to run as a Democrat for the Board of Supervisors, so Mau became a Democrat. When he tried to solicit the vote of plantation workers, he was shocked to find he was not allowed entry to campaign at 'Ewa Plantation. He nonetheless won. When the war started, rents rose along with the rapidly swelling population. Even though propertied Chinese Americans were among those prominently reaping the benefits, Mau introduced a rent-control bill. Despite warnings of political disaster, he got his bill passed. He had become a rent-control liberal. Mau believed that he was easily re-elected every two years because poor people appreciated what he had done.

When he was approached to meet with Burns, Kido, and Kawano after the war, the intermediary was an old friend, Kats Kometani, who had left his dental practice to serve as a morale officer with the 100th Battalion. Kometani was one of those centrist Republicans who was friends with everyone—Mau, Burns, Dr. Murai, Kido, and Kawano on one side, Hung Wai Ching, Marumoto, and the delegate to Congress Joe Farrington on the other.[14]

Mau remembered the group holding its first several meetings at his house on Nuʻuanu Avenue. Believing that Kawano was "the spark plug" of the group, Mau moved the meetings to Japanese teahouses, where Kawano would be at his most relaxed. He then began feeding Kawano a mixed plate of U.S. history, constitutional law, economics, and the history of communist Russia. Obviously Mau was concerned that Kawano knew little about the wider world and leaned far to the left, but he had no idea that his new friend was a member of the Communist Party.

Meanwhile there was considerably less happening between Mau and Burns. Mau decided Burns was less than knowledgeable about politics, government, and economics. Further, Burns was not as educated or articulate as Kido, and he did not have a strong speaking voice.

Mau credited himself as most consistently articulating a philosophy of government, but Burns "did not quite state that philosophy . . . as clearly as we would have liked to have him state it." Nonetheless Mau wanted a haole to succeed in the Democratic party. "We were looking for all kinds to come in because we didn't want it slanted just to the Japanese," Mau was to say. "That would have made it a Japanese party rather than a Democratic Party. . . . The wider the racial group, the better it was for us. So we were constantly looking, and particularly for Caucasians because the Caucasians at that time—you know, if they belonged to the Democratic Party they were ostracized just like we were."

The combination of Mau, Kido, and Burns reached its peak of effectiveness in 1948. Kido and Burns tended to the affairs of a bruising local convention while Mau represented Hawaiʻi at the National Democratic Convention. Their goal was to seize the initiative on statehood and thereby attract young people to the Democratic Party. The immediate agenda was to make the transition from "eventual statehood" (the traditional phrasing of both the Democratic and Republican national platforms) to "immediate statehood."

Mau lurked outside the office of the platform committee chairman, a Senator Francis Myers, hoping for a moment to promote the immediate-statehood amendment to the national Democratic platform. The secretary said everyone wanted to see the senator. Mau said he had traveled six thousand miles for this one little conversation. The secretary told Mau to wait outside the back door at nine the next morning. Mau arrived at seven. At nine the senator walked out his back door, and Mau introduced himself on the move. He said he wanted to address the platform committee. The senator said to see his aide, who was trailing them. Mau made friends with the aide, then sat through three days of meetings, afraid even to go to the bathroom. At two o'clock in the morning of the third day, he was called to speak. Given five minutes, he spoke for twenty.

Kometani had described to him the nisei rescue of the "Lost Battalion" of Texas National Guardsmen, and Mau spoke of those who had given their lives. The governor of Texas stood up and said, "We will support you 100 percent." Further, he promised to lobby for support among Southerners who otherwise would fight immediate statehood because of Hawai'i's Japanese population. The immediate-statehood plank passed in a moment that announced a coming change in America. It was the same year that Truman integrated the armed forces by executive order, causing a walkout from the convention by delegates from the Old South.

Chuck Mau was riding high. On his way home, he got a call from Kido congratulating him for being elected chairman of the Hawai'i Democratic Party. Burns had chaired the convention and had been elected chairman of the O'ahu County committee. Kido was a member of the party's central committee, while Murai and Kawano were precinct officers. Less than four years after their first discussion, and just two years after Mau's first involvement, the group of five had taken over the top offices in the Democratic Party.

Despite their apparent success, problems abounded. If Democrats were to succeed in Hawai'i, they needed to pursue credibly the "immediate statehood" that they now promised, yet they faced a deeply entrenched opposition from Southern Democrats, who equated Hawai'i with civil rights legislation. Hawai'i was in a rising panic over communism, and the Democratic Party of Hawai'i already was split—and soon the group of five would be split—over how to respond. All the major Democratic Party figures who were eventually to dominate the postwar era had to deal with the question of how to wend their way through this conflict. In the process, relationships came undone, commitments came unstuck, and hatreds developed that were to last through lifetimes.

THE COLD WAR

As the most important outpost of America, Hawai'i existed in a special relationship to international tensions and wars. Annexation had resulted from the Spanish-American War. Pearl Harbor was the culmination of tensions between Japan and America that had begun with annexation. World War II was followed almost immediately by the Cold War, and probably no place in America was so affected by the Cold War as Hawai'i.

Events between 1946 and 1954 seemed to move at an ever-accelerating pace. From one angle they were local, but from another they were national and international. Time after time, the old political, economic, and social orders were threatened, then attempts were made to restore the status quo as it had perilously existed before the war. Only in hindsight was it apparent who would succeed and who would fail.

THE ILWU AND ANTICOMMUNISM

Cold War tensions in Hawai'i occurred against the background of the ILWU's dramatic rise to power and the thirty-fold increase in its membership. When the sugar workers went on strike in 1946, they forced all the Big Five plantations to the bargaining table at once, achieving a goal of industry-wide bargaining. The strike ran for seventy-six days, extending through the political campaign season. Two weeks after the 1946 territorial elections, union and management reached agreement.

The Republican contention that the Democratic Party was infected with communism caused one Democratic House member to change parties, which allowed the Republicans to maintain control of the 1947 legislature. Nationally, President Truman—fearing the perception that the Democratic Party was "soft on communism"—required loyalty oaths of all federal employees, including the employees of the Territory of Hawai'i. On November 11, the governor of the territory, Ingram Stainback, alleged that the Communist Party had a detailed plan to take over the Hawaiian Islands. He contended Hawai'i was "the most fertile field for communism in the whole nation."

Within days, the schoolteachers John and Aiko Reinecke were fired from their jobs for refusing to sign a loyalty oath as territorial employees. John Reinecke was a soft-spoken man from Kansas who possessed a doctoral degree and wrote an enduring basic work on Hawaiian pidgin English. Aiko Reinecke was a warm, angelic-looking woman with a round face and round spectacles.

Within months, there were several highly publicized defections from the ILWU. The most celebrated was Ichiro Izuka, an early-day leader from Kaua'i. A pamphlet containing an exposé of the Communist Party was published in his name and distributed by business interests throughout the territory. The next most prominent defector was the head of the Big Island unit, a man named Amos Ignacio, whom the ILWU had elected to the legislature in 1944 and 1946. Yet another man who had built the union from the bottom up, Bert Nakano, who had been crippled by buckshot in the Hilo waterfront strike, left the ILWU in 1947.

The wave of defections was partly a matter of the ILWU's West Coast origins returning to plague the union in a time of crisis. When Robert Mookini, the leader of the pineapple workers, defected, he called on native Hawaiians to "throw off the yoke of false mainland leadership."

Why the ILWU next tried to take over the grassroots structure of the Democratic Party has never been explained, only that it was, in retrospect, a mistake. The anticommunist crusade was a threat that required a defense, perhaps a defensive fortress, such as a political party. What Jack Hall had been building since the Kauai Progressive League of 1940 was in danger of slipping away. Surely the desertions were a factor. In the increasingly hysterical atmosphere, the Republican Party was dividing between those who understood that organized labor must be accommodated and those who believed that revolutionaries lurked behind every tree. A voice of Republican reason, Roy Vitousek, had died in 1947. It seems plausible that Jack Hall could see that with Republican control waning, the ILWU might seize the political system through the Democratic Party and have things its way.

Much has been written about the 1948 and 1950 Democratic conventions, essentially about prewar Democrats colliding with the ILWU.[15] Burns distinguished himself by holding to a centrist course even when there was no apparent middle ground. He resisted ILWU control of the party but also refused to renounce the ILWU. Within the Oʻahu Democratic committee, Burns tabled a resolution for the expulsion of communists and instead substituted a condemnation of "witch-hunting and name calling by which persons are branded."[16] At Jack Hall's urging and the ILWU's expense, Burns went to Washington during the 1949 dock strike to head off federal intervention, convincing the U.S. Labor Department that the strike was essentially economic in nature.[17] After Governor Stainback's faction walked out of the Democratic convention in 1948, Burns stayed behind and served as convention chairman.

All of this amounted to an elaborate negotiation. The political gains of the 1944 and 1946 elections could not be defended against the ferocity of the anticommunist movement. Where Democrats had won half of the House of Representatives in 1946, they won only a third in 1948. Hall was forced to fall back incrementally in the arena of elective politics, leaving the Democratic Party to the Burns group; Burns in turn supported the ILWU in the realm of trade unionism.

In *John A. Burns: The Man and His Times,* Boylan and Holmes focused on a statement by Burns in 1948 that described a New Deal type of middle ground between the contending forces. "The era of selfishness and unfettered greed is and must remain dead," Burns wrote. "There must be some retreat from the economic individualism of our fathers." He said that while the Democratic Party did not want a collectivist state, failure to solve society's problems would lead to one.[18] It was a perilously complicated position in a time of increasingly simplistic thinking. The Soviet Union had developed the atom bomb with the help of information provided by American spies. The Communist Party of the People's Republic of China had prevailed in 1949, causing the fantasy of an Open Door to China to evaporate. In mid-1950, the army of North Korea invaded South Korea.

Tension over communism and anticommunism reached directly into Burns' original group of five. In 1950, Kawano revealed that he had been, until a few months earlier, a member of the Communist Party. He sat up all night with Mau before telling a U.S. House Un-American Activities Committee hearing in Honolulu that he was *not* a member of the Communist Party, in contrast to thirty-eight other subpoenaed witnesses who took the Fifth Amendment against self-incrimination. By 1951, Kawano was being led by Mau to testify to HUAC in Washington D.C. Jack Hall asked him to not go. Two years had passed since Kawano had last served as president of the ILWU local. Kawano called Hall a traitor to America; Hall called Kawano a traitor to their cause.[19]

After Kawano's detailed testimony to HUAC, he thanked his friends in the Democratic Party, including Burns, Murai, Kido, and Mau, for teaching him to be a good American. He was asked in a 1975 oral history interview if he felt he had been used by them and then discarded. He said no, that he had fallen in battle so that Burns and the rest could fight another day. On the Washington trip, Mau went to the Justice Department and argued that the communists of Hawai'i were in the top tier of the Communist Party U.S.A. As a result, the federal government immediately pushed ahead with prosecuting Hall and six others under the Smith Act, alleging a conspiracy to overthrow the government. Burns offered to testify as a character witness for Hall, but Hall told him to preserve himself as a potentially electable political figure. The convictions were overturned on the grounds that the law was unconstitutional.

In 1952, Mau was passed over for a new term as chairman of the Democratic central committee and was succeeded by Burns. Kawano was dropped by the ILWU. He ran a liquor store in the old downtown, then moved to Los Angeles. His divided allegiance had cost him a large place in the history of Hawai'i. Less obviously, Mau's anticommunism cost him similarly. The two men had admired one another, and their combined political capital burned up in the same fire.

COMMUNISM AND THE DEMOCRATIC PARTY

Several writers have ably documented both the communist movement in Hawai'i and the anticommunist movement that followed, prominently including Sanford Zalburg's biography of Hall and T. Michael Holmes' *The Specter of Communism in Hawai'i*. With Lawrence Fuchs, they more or less concurred that as the ILWU succeeded, the influence of the Communist Party waned, and most importantly the zeal of Hall waned.

In this popular view, emphasis rested on the idea that communism never posed a serious internal threat to the American system in Hawai'i, and that the cure of anticommunism was worse than the disease. As proof it was often said that communists were few in number, and their numbers were actually in constant decline. Burns would eventually recite FBI reports on the Hawai'i party's declining numbers—down from a peak of 160 members in 1946 to 36 in 1952—with the reassuring suggestion that communist influence in Hawai'i was declining. Holmes quoted an attorney of the American Civil Liberties Union as saying the Communist Party in America was led by "confused, futile men who have been able to get nowhere in all these years."

While there is apparent truth that various Marxists such as Hall likely were dedicated unionists, this line of thought diminishes the accomplishments of radical unionism in Hawai'i. It obscures the fact that in no other place did such a far-reaching, class-based type of labor organizing succeed, apparently because plantation Hawai'i was such a class-ridden society.

The success of the ILWU in organizing the plantations on a horizontal, industry-wide basis, as well as organizing the related waterfronts, with backup lines of defense at sea and also on the docks of the West Coast—and nearly taking over the legislature as well—is ample testimony to a working class craving for redress. Harriet Bouslog, who was to become the ILWU's lawyer, said there was "something about the oppression of people here that turned me from what you might call 'parlor liberal' to radicalism."[20] A reactionary U.S. senator, Pat McCarran, saw accurately what liberals were loathe to see. McCarran said, "About the most complete Communist organization I have yet encountered, I found to exist in the Hawaiian Islands."[21]

As a student of history, Burns might have flinched at the political expediency of his own analysis, knowing that small groups had repeatedly shaped large events. Kamehameha had won his war with the commitments of his four Kona uncles. Sanford Dole's original Reform Party had five members, and Lorrin Thurston's committee of annexation had thirteen. Even in the fattest days of the Big Five, its interlocking directorates likely had nowhere near the 160 purported members of the Communist Party in Hawai'i in 1946.

The number in a leadership group was largely irrelevant to Hawai'i's history. What mattered was clarity of thinking. There is something about the so obviously tangible boundaries of the Hawaiian Islands that inspires small groups to think they can prevail in a volatile situation, and occasionally they do.

The December 7 crisis of Japanese Americans, resulting from Japan's bombing of Pearl Harbor, came to define modern Hawaiʻi.

FBI agent Robert Shivers nurtured the networks that averted a mass internment of Japanese Americans in Hawai'i.

The brilliant nisei attorney, Masaji Marumoto (right), surrounded Shivers (left) with patriotic nisei who were determined to secure their place in America. Courtesy of the Marumoto family

Marumoto in later years became a justice of the Supreme Court. Courtesy of The Honolulu Advertiser

Navy Intelligence Officer Cecil Coggins. Courtesy of Dr. Cecil Coggins Jr.

Charles Hemenway. Courtesy of Hawai'i Archives

YMCA executive Hung Wai Ching emerged as the godfather of the Varsity Victory Volunteers. Courtesy of The Honolulu Advertiser

Young John A. Burns courageously vouched for the loyalty of the Japanese community. Courtesy of Hawai'i Archives

General Delos Emmons, military governor of Hawai'i. Courtesy of Hawai'i Archives/Pan Pacific Press Bureau

John J. McCloy, assistant secretary of war. Courtesy of Amherst College Archives

First Lady Eleanor Roosevelt opposed internment. Courtesy of Franklin D. Roosevelt Library

President Franklin Delano Roosevelt agreed reluctantly to the nisei fighting units. Courtesy of Franklin D. Roosevelt Library

Detainee camp at Honouliuli, Oʻahu.

Varsity Victory Volunteers with picks and shovels. Courtesy of the U.S. Army Signal Corps

Eleanor Roosevelt visited internees at the Gila River camp. Courtesy of Franklin D. Roosevelt Library

Nisei in Hawai'i lined up to volunteer for the army, in contrast to interned Japanese Americans on the mainland. Courtesy of Hawai'i Archives

The 442nd Regimental Combat Team was celebrated at 'Iolani Palace before leaving for training. Courtesy of Hawai'i Archives

ILWU membership rose from six hundred to twenty-nine thousand at the close of World War II. Courtesy of the ILWU

Sakae Takahashi was at the center of a training camp dialog on the future of Japanese Americans in Hawai'i. Courtesy of the Takahashi family

Mitsuyuki Kido managed the home front Emergency Service Committee, then organized the new Democratic Party with Burns. Courtesy of The Honolulu Advertiser

Union leader Jack Kawano generated ILWU votes for Democratic candidates. Courtesy of The Honolulu Advertiser

*Attorney Chuck Mau,
Burns' predecessor as
Democratic Party
chairman. Courtesy of*
The Honolulu Advertiser

Returning war heroes. Courtesy of the 442nd Club

A returning internee. Courtesy of Hawai'i Archives

Joe Farrington, Republican delegate to Congress. Courtesy of Hawaiʻi Archives

Jack Hall, Hawaiʻi leader of the ILWU. Courtesy of The Honolulu Advertiser

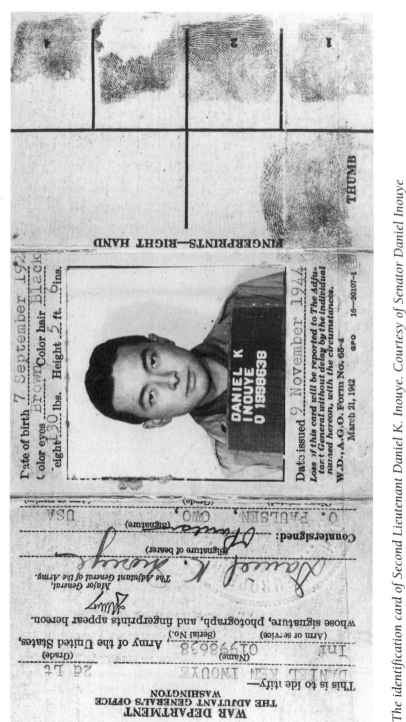

The identification card of Second Lieutenant Daniel K. Inouye. Courtesy of Senator Daniel Inouye

Chapter 7

The Island Democratic Party

The story of Burns' formative years has a striking parallel to the story of Hawai'i in the first half of the twentieth century: It is wrapped in vague generalizations that present a mythic outline but conceal a great deal of pain. Burns was the oldest of four children born to Harry Jacob Burns and Anne Scally Burns, a military family whose lives were shaped by how America came to be a Pacific power. Harry was a veteran of the Spanish-American War, as were two of his brothers-in-law, Jack and Elmer Scally. John Burns was born in 1909 at a remote army fort, Fort Assineboine, Montana, only a generation after the closing of the American frontier. Harry Burns had been reassigned to the Pacific, not knowing whether he was to be stationed in Hawai'i or the Philippines. From Hawai'i, Harry sent a picture of himself on an all-star baseball team that Burns would keep his entire life. Burns thought of his father as a fine barroom fighter. Harry was such a good rifleman that he was once part of a national army rifle team. After Harry clarified that he would have a long-term assignment in Hawai'i, he moved his family to Fort Shafter, O'ahu. The way other people remember birthdays, Jack Burns remembered his date of arrival, May 30, 1913. He was four years old. Queen Lili'uokalani was to live another four years and Sanford Dole another thirteen years. Initially the Burns family was billeted at Shafter in a tent with a wooden floor, then rented a house in the nearby neighborhood of Kalihi.

While the Hawai'i of Burns' childhood had only a fifth of today's population, it was growing rapidly and had a startling number of children. In the census of 1920, 40 percent of the people were under the age of fourteen.

His sense of intimacy with local people was derived from close proximity. He lived across the street from an Auntie Josephine Maunakea. Burns' mother became a godmother of the Kupau children. When Filipino workers went on strike, they set up a camp across the street and cooked their meals on an open fire. Burns' mother took them food. The Portuguese, who shared the Burns' devout Catholicism, lived up Kalihi Valley. Two Japanese appear in his childhood stories, both storekeepers.

"Our Kalihi," as Burns called it, was on the west side of Kalihi Stream near Fern Park, which was named for the first Hawaiian mayor of Honolulu. As a boy Burns listened to Prince Jonah Kūhiō speak at a rally in the park, in one of Kūhiō's ten successful campaigns for the office of delegate to Congress. When Burns' family temporarily relocated across town, he ran away from school to Waikīkī Beach, passing the shacks of native Hawaiians. They called out to him, *"E komo mai, haole"* (come in, foreign boy). Why was he not in school? Young Jack would sit and talk, eating their fish and poi.

In 1990, fifteen years after his death, Burns' daughter, Dr. Sheenagh Burns, a psychologist, published an article in *The Hawaiian Journal of History* that addressed the psychology of her family. It was studiously ignored, perhaps reflecting the lethargy of the public media, but perhaps also reflecting the extent to which Burns had been elevated to the realm of mythology. Her orphaned piece described Harry Burns as dashingly handsome, intelligent, and fun-loving. He could have captured any number of beautiful girls but instead chose Anne, a plain, deeply religious woman who Burns would come to describe as a saint. Sheenagh's interpretation of Harry's behavior echoed Jack's: "The rigors of family life with four young children soon proved to be too much for Harry." He became "more irresponsible" and at times abusive. Jack Burns said Harry "liked to gaddy and party," while his mother did not. Harry was let out of the army,[1] lost one civilian job, then another. Then he announced he was going to the West Coast to find work. When he did, the family was to join him. After being hired by a munitions plant, he wrote that he was planning to send money, which was the last Jack Burns—at age ten—heard from him.

Remarkably, Anne Scalley Burns never retreated to the support of her family on the U.S. mainland. At first she washed diapers for Tripler Army Hospital, and Jack delivered them in a wagon.[2] Her brother, Jack Scally, was stationed at Fort Shafter. He tutored Anne in arithmetic so she could pass the Postal Service exam, which led to her being the postmistress of Fort Shafter. In a portrait of Anne and her four children taken two years after Harry's departure, she appears tired to the bone. She is stooped but determined. Jack is in the foreground, with his high cheeks pulled up to his eyes, barely smiling. His black hair is combed back and there is more than a hint of the charismatic but tension-ridden man he would become.

He was suddenly the man of the family. He attempted to exercise responsibility for the three younger children but they balked at his assertion of authority. In response, Sheenagh Burns believed, "he became willful, autocratic, and more headstrong and forceful than ever." His brother Edward, two years his junior, was an expert on the strong-willed Jack. "He bullied a little . . . as an older brother does a younger brother . . . and I resented it, as the younger brothers always do, I suspect."

His habit of resisting authority colored his life as a student. Burns said that as early as the first grade at Saint Louis School he had been instructed in the "going-along theory." In the fourth grade he found a teacher he liked and scored one hundred on nearly everything. Thereafter he quickly slipped back into the bottom third of the class: "I could always get by and never mind opening the book." In the eighth grade he played hooky fifty-eight days.

Edward told a story of the eleven-year-old Jack: A club formed in a vacant garage in the neighborhood, but Jack had a falling out with the leaders and stopped going. The members indicted him for not participating. They went to Burns' house to arrest him for a mock trial, with little Ed trailing. The leader hollered, "Jack, come out, you're under arrest." Jack came out with his father's twelve-gauge shotgun. "Don't come any nearer," he said, "or I'll blast this thing." The boys thought he must be joking. They took a step. Jack fired. The gun exploding over their heads "sounded like a cannon," as Edward remembered it. "This was the kind of guy Jack was: 'You don't make me do anything I don't want to do, no siree.' He was tough. He wasn't the biggest and he wasn't the strongest, but 'You don't bully me.'"

Jack experimented with the habits of his father. He smoked cigarettes and drank beer with his friends. Sheenagh believed he was seriously divided over what sort of person to be. He could fail his mother, or he could abandon the image of the star baseball player in the photograph.

At birth he had been christened Harry John Burns. At his Catholic confirmation at age thirteen, he changed his name to John Anthony Burns. Harry's name was gone, but the turmoil wrought by Harry had a life of its own. Jack's behavior caused Anne to call in the parish priest, Father Alphonsus, as an alternative role model. Next Mrs. Burns sent Jack to live with her brother, Jack Scally, by then reassigned to Fort Leavenworth, Kansas. He started out playing quarterback for one Catholic school. When they lost to another school, he was so determined to be on a winning team that he transferred— a breach of the code of loyalty that in retrospect horrified him: "I don't know how I could be so selfish."

In the summer he approached two men who were harvesting wheat. He got a job feeding wheat into their thrashing machine, following the two men from field to field and job to job, sleeping in barns. In his junior year, his uncle Jack Scally was reassigned to the East Coast. Things were, in Burns' words, "going a little broke." Without completing high school, he enlisted in the peacetime reserve army at nearby Fort Leavenworth, Kansas. As he was telling this story he said, without any prior reference to drinking, "I still drank like hell . . . and I didn't study too damn much."

At Leavenworth he saw people with "the jakes" from drinking Jamaican rum. He hung out in a Negro bar and admired the girls. One night a fight started, and he dove out the window. Along the way he booted his chance to become an army officer. He then struck out for the East Coast, hitchhiking. In Pennsylvania he came down with pneumonia. He found an aunt who nursed him through what he reported to be a temperature of 107. He then shipped out on an ocean liner, working as a mess boy, surrounded by Filipino shiphands, and finally he returned to Hawai'i.

His North American sojourn evokes the feelings of a Thomas Hart Benton mural—the rawness of the country and the juxtaposition of strangers. There are no comparable images of the Hawai'i to which Jack Burns returned, because the territorial period is a sort of black hole, in which the essential matter is lost to sight. We have instead the gloss of menu art from the early ocean liners and the art from sheet music that was popularized by Tin Pan Alley. There are images of an island paradise, peopled by gorgeous, welcoming natives. In groups they offer up vast trays of fruit or singly they offer themselves—there are always women in this image, propped against palm trees in the moonlight, revealing the curves of their breasts.

Reality lay in a semiclosed system that had flowed from the question posed in 1894 by the annexationist W. O. Smith: How could the elite white group create the appearance of democracy while preserving an essentially oligarchic society? On Burns' return to Hawai'i, brother Edward fell ill. Burns took Edward's place at Saint Louis High School. The man in charge of the boarding school said to him, "Aren't you Jack Burns?" "Yes, sir," he replied. "You're not gonna' be a boarder, are you?" "No, sir." "Well," the man said, "thank god for little favors." At the age of twenty-one, Burns graduated from high school.

In telling his story Burns often engaged in a ritual modesty, but beneath the controlled surface flowed a powerful conception of himself. In football he played quarterback. In the army he played on a team of "high school kids" who took on one of the top amateur teams in the country. Burns was nearly ejected for rough play, but "somebody had to make the rest of the guys remember that they were just as good as the other guy was."

Burns remembered a girlfriend telling him, "To want impossibility is to be dissatisfied." He struggled with that idea then rejected it—determined as he was to entertain powerful dreams and to undertake the seemingly impossible. Burns' sister would tell his biographer, Dan Boylan, "Jack thought he could do anything."[3]

When he attended the University of Hawai'i, he thought he would become a newspaper journalist. He did not complete a single class. It was his only formal higher education. During this period Burns worked part-time as a switchboard operator at the afternoon daily, the *Honolulu Star-Bulletin*. One day a man called identifying himself as Frank Atherton, president of the financial giant Castle and Cooke and also an owner of the newspaper. He had a message for Wallace Rider Farrington, publisher of the newspaper and by then the former governor of the territory. Atherton said, "Will you tell the governor to come see me." Burns then witnessed Governor Farrington trotting across Merchant Street to see Atherton. He inferred that in territorial Hawai'i, business ruled and the politicians obeyed.

THE YEAR OF HIS HIGH SCHOOL GRADUATION, Burns met Beatrice Van Fleet, an army nurse. Burns was twenty-one and she was twenty-five, a person of will and warmth who would turn out to be nearly as saintly in his eyes as Anne Scally Burns. Jack and Beatrice married a year later, in 1932, in the bottom of the Great Depression. Job openings were virtually nonexistent. He and Beatrice moved to California, where he worked on her father's fruit farm. While there, he joined the Democratic Party, for no apparently compelling reason, then—conflicting with his father-in-law over how to run the farm—returned to Hawai'i.

He thought he might get a job on a plantation. He would remember all his life that the questions began with, did he go to Punahou School? No. And then, "As soon as they found out I was a local born haole that lived in Kalihi, they found every excuse in the world" not to give him a job. He drove a truck, delivering milk. Drivers reported to work about ten o'clock at night, loaded their trucks, finished their deliveries by seven o'clock in the morning, ate breakfast, then hit the road to collect on their accounts and find new customers.

From the hopelessness of the private sector, he turned to the Honolulu Police Department (HPD). Burns said he joined the HPD because it offered the hope of rising through a merit-based system under the civil service. On his entry exams, he remembered taking a test of IQ that yielded an astronomical, genius-level number. Assuming the test was even vaguely accurate, it is a clue to his future capacity. It also provides a ready explanation for his rise through the ranks of the police department. By 1940, after seven years on the force, he was in contention for the rank of captain. He scored well on the civil service exams for further advancement, but his career stalled.

There was tension between young Burns and the chief of police. People would ask him why he was being passed over for promotion to the top reaches of the department, and he would say it was the chief's business, not his.

From his subsequent performance, one can imagine the younger man in context of the HPD. He was an athlete. He was impeccably groomed. Even if his clothes were frayed, he wore suits, jackets, and ties. Because of his much-remarked posture, clothes fell on him perfectly. He could speak pidgin. He could toss down a drink. He could unwind and talk intimately with someone for hours.

A SON, JOHN, was born to Jack and Beatrice, followed by Sheenagh. Looking back, Sheenagh believed that in the early years of the marriage, Burns' wild, erratic side persisted. As a psychologist, she saw him alternately embracing and rejecting his father, while struggling to get distance from a mother whom he essentially idolized. Sheenagh says he continued to drink heavily (at a time when heavy drinking was rampant).

Beatrice was seven months pregnant with their third child when she was struck by polio. The terror of the disease cannot be readily understood now, after the development of a vaccine: Polio was thought to pass during heat waves; it sometimes killed; it often crippled its victims for life. Beatrice was paralyzed. The child she had carried was delivered but lived only a few hours. Burns was determined that Beatrice walk again. He took her for treatment on the mainland, even though he could ill afford the cost. He kept crutches at the ready. He pulled her up to exercise, and she cried out in pain.

Sheenagh believed that the paralysis of Beatrice was Burns' defining moment. Burns' biographer, Dan Boylan, focused on an incident in which Burns was caught drinking on the job. His mother pleaded for leniency from the chief of police, then confronted her son in a three-hour conversation. Boylan and Holmes believed Burns quit drinking at that moment.[4] He vowed to go to Mass and to care for Beatrice and his children with a renewed diligence.

"The Mass became his AA meeting," according to Sheenagh. As he reconciled himself to the fact that Beatrice would not walk, he let go of his father's behavior and, in Sheenagh's words, "combined the two most powerful influences for good in his life—his mother and his religion, the latter personified by the nurturant figure of Father Alphonsus. . . ." She went further: "In a sense, he achieved his own priesthood." Boylan used the same image: Burns was a priest.[5] The issues of his powerful drive to dominate and his underutilized intelligence were sealed beneath the surface. He became a creation of his own resolve and of his mother's determination that he be self-controlled.

He dedicated himself to a rigid code of discipline. He demanded this discipline of himself and of everyone around him—of Sheenagh to an obviously uncomfortable degree. A child's accident could provoke rage. An irritant could cause him to leave the house seething, struggling to bottle up his anger. Sheenagh believed he wrestled with demons. When he returned to the house, his inner discipline would be restored. Through this agonizing process, which in her view comprised the entire first phase of his life, she believed he developed "the seeds of his greatness."

Sheenagh's biographical analysis of her father struck some people as invasive. Since he had created an impression of near perfection in public life, why did her interpretation matter? People who objected to the probing of the inner person—people who saw Burns as the perfectly clear-minded individual who lived by clear-cut guideposts—might have been surprised to read his own words in the 1959 Congressional Record.

In the opening passages of "Statehood and Hawai'i's People," he wrote: "The search for identity, which characterizes most of our individual lives, is one of the great problems of modern life." While the search for identity is an age-old problem, it is "potently and primarily" an issue of modern life. "The great question—for individuals, as for larger groups—is 'Who am I?'"[6]

The story of Burns' inner life matters because his life was an allegory. Most people who were devoted to him only glimpsed the inner person, or sensed it, but nonetheless on some level understood it, because in Burns they found some part of themselves. It was an allegory of adversity and frustration offset by extremes of discipline. The discipline was channeled by powerful codes. These codes translated passions, dreams, and events into understandable terms and prescribed how to deal with them.

NEVER GIVE UP

In the Japanese language, the word for determination is *ganbare*. "Never give up." The intended result is a way of being. Regardless of circumstance, one is to keep going. The importance attached to the word lies at the heart of the Japanese reputation for determination and stubbornness, including stubbornness to a fault.

By 1952, what was left of the little group—Burns, Kido, and Murai—had reasons to be discouraged. The Republicans again controlled the legislature. Most of the AJA legislators continued to be Republican, making Kido a minority not only in political party but also within his own ethnic group. The labor movement was on the defensive. Along with the haole, many Hawaiians, Japanese, Chinese, and Koreans continued to vote for Republican candidates. The appointed Democratic governor Ingram Stainback had turned out to be the Democrats' worst enemy. Neither was the quest for statehood helping Democrats. Delegate Joe Farrington was popular in part because he had gotten statehood bills through the U.S. House of Representatives in 1947 and 1950. In 1948 Burns had run against Farrington and received only a quarter of the vote. Coupled with Burns' previous failed race for the Honolulu board of supervisors, this defeat would have discouraged most people from again standing for public office. Contrary to later stereotypes of being political monoliths on behalf of the Democratic Party, the nisei war veterans' clubs, the 442nd Club and the Club 100, adopted policies of remaining detached from partisan politics.

Nonetheless Burns determinedly followed through on the plan to recruit nisei veterans into the political process. According to Kido, the job fell to Burns because Burns was the only one with the time to do it. It would become a standard aspect of political legend that the 442nd Club made Burns an honorary member, apparently in 1948.[7] The context and connotation of Burns' membership are elemental to an accurate understanding of the position of the nisei veterans. Judging from the way others were similarly honored, the Club did not single out Burns as a political figure, but instead thanked him as part of the network that had helped them get organized. The other honorary members were from either the Morale Office of the Martial Law government (Hung Wai Ching and Shigeo Yoshida) or the Emergency Service Committee (Dr. Ernest Murai, Katsuro Miho, Jack Kawano, and Mitsuyuki Kido). One other person so honored was Earl Finch, the Mississippian who had so avidly supported the nisei in training camp and thereafter.[8] "We of the younger group were aware of the work being done, the effort that they [nisei supporters] were making," Inouye would recall. "When the war was over, they were hailed as our patron saints." For Burns, this honor was especially important, because it was a powerful nisei statement that stamped him in the wider community as one who helped, and not *inu*—as some of the older generation had said.

One of the first veterans associated with Burns was Sakae Takahashi, an FDR Democrat who had decided in training camp on a course of political action. Takahashi was one of the AJA officers in the original 100th Battalion. He had studied military strategy while his comrades were out on weekend pass, and in battle he became known for his courage and sound judgment. Wounded, he recuperated in an army hospital with Inouye, and he was credited by Inouye with inspiring Inouye's determination to run for public office. Their conversation in the veterans' ward about postwar politics became famous, as did Inouye's telephone call to Burns volunteering to help in his 1948 campaign. This was also the year that Dan Aoki came onto the scene. Aoki was a burly man whose fierce presence harkened up thoughts of samurai warriors. Aoki had been a first sergeant in the 442nd Regiment and would be, for all time, the first sergeant of Burns' political organization.

Aoki subsequently recruited Mike Tokunaga from Club 100, giving Burns a campaign manager in both clubs. After graduating from high school, Tokunaga had gone to work as a cane cutter. One day he was kicked in the pants by an assistant manager of the plantation for loafing on the job. He responded by saying that if he were kicked again, "I'll wrap this cane knife around your neck." In the war, he was wounded three times.

When Aoki first took Mike Tokunaga to see Burns, Burns asked Tokunaga if he was a plantation boy. "Yeah," Tokunaga replied. Burns asked, "You feel you're getting equal treatment in this community?" "No," said Tokunaga. "If you want to get treated like a first-class citizen," Burns said, "play politics."[9]

As a local haole, Burns presented a hopeful contrast to Governor Stainback, who not only ratcheted up the communist hysteria but also told the Young Buddhist Association, "I regret to say that the most numerous converts (to communism) in the Territory are the Japanese Americans."[10] After all that people like Aoki and Tokunaga had given in the war, it was a cruel suggestion that they still could not be trusted.

AN EARLY SEARCH FOR A GOVERNOR

In complete frustration with Stainback, Burns and Kido embarked on an effort to topple him from office and secure the appointment of a new governor. Their original alternate was none other than Robert Shivers, one of many indications of how rooted their group was in the prewar efforts to protect the Japanese community. In 1943 the Emergency Service Committee had written to Shivers saying that a mass internment had been avoided "largely through the thorough groundwork that you laid . . . and your influence and good judgment since then."[11] Midway through the war, Shivers had been reassigned to the mainland, but longed for Hawai'i. His friends had taken up a collection to send Hung Wai Ching to Washington to again see Roosevelt, and Ching had successfully pleaded for Shivers to be named collector of U.S. customs in Honolulu.

Jack Hall was one of many who were indebted to Shivers for keeping him out of jail during the war, and in anger with Stainback he too had written the Secretary of the Interior proposing Shivers as governor. Speculation in late 1949 that Shivers might be named governor led to a denial on his part in the local press.[12] The campaign nonetheless continued. In January 1950 Burns spent nearly two months in Washington lobbying against the reappointment of Stainback and promoting Shivers for governor.[13]

The idea likely would have gained momentum had Shivers been in better health. He suffered from heart disease and in midsummer of 1950, he died at age fifty-six. His obituary described him as a casualty of the war. Among the public, Shivers was forgotten, but for a circle of people who understood how Hawai'i had gotten through the war years, he remained a heroic figure.[14] His adopted daughter, Sue Isonaga, continues to place flowers on his grave. When Burns became governor, she took Shivers' brother, visiting from the mainland, to see him. Burns said if things had gone differently, it would have been Robert Shivers who sat in the governor's chair.

AFTER SHIVERS, THE CHINESE HAWAIIAN attorney Ernest Kai was seriously considered for the appointed governorship. Burns, along with his two key associates, Aoki and Tokunaga, went to see Kai, seeking assurances that he would consult with the local Democratic Party on federal appointments, including territorial cabinet officers and judgeships. Kai refused. On the day that Kai was to have been appointed, Burns again arrived in Washington and argued successfully for an alternative candidate, Oren Long. Kai blamed Burns, probably correctly, for his not being appointed governor.[15]

Oren Long was a newcomer to Hawai'i who had served as the head of the Department of Public Instruction, and he was more Kido's candidate than Burns'. Kido's wife, as a student, had worked in Long's house as a domestic, and Kido had taught in the schools under Long's administration. In the initial meeting with Burns, Long seemed distinctly amenable to cutting local Democrats in on patronage. He said that Kido should be Secretary of the Territory, a position equivalent to lieutenant governor. Chuck Mau was to be attorney general, and Burns was to be appointed to the cabinet. However, after Long met with the U.S. Interior Department in Washington, Long said that Mau was unacceptable and that Kido could not be appointed because he had invested money in the ILWU-aligned newspaper, the *Honolulu Record*. Long said Burns could have the largely ceremonial job of territorial sheriff, an offer that must have appalled Burns.[16]

Long said it would be acceptable to appoint one person of Japanese ancestry to the cabinet. Burns and Kido proposed Takahashi, who in 1950 had won election to the Board of Supervisors. After Long was appointed governor by President Truman in 1951, Takahashi was appointed treasurer of the territory. In context the gains were agonizingly modest, underscoring the inadequacy of territorial politics. Power emanated from Washington, nearly six thousand miles away, and try as the Democratic party might, it had scant influence over who was appointed to high office. The campaign through which Long replaced Stainback was a case study in why people in Hawai'i wanted statehood.

THE HAWAIIAN ALLIANCE

From an inner circle that had grown out of the wartime AJA movement, Burns was determined to build a political coalition with native Hawaiians. It was an idea that flowed not merely from political calculation but from his experience. He had grown up among many more Hawaiians in Kalihi than Japanese. His mother was an "auntie" to Hawaiian families in Kalihi. His brother Edward was married to a Hawaiian, as was his sister Helen. The Hawaiians who had called out to him as a teenager on his way to the beach—"*E komo mai, haole*"—were people who elected Hawaiian mayors and hoped their offspring could get paying jobs through City Hall, a realm Burns understood as a policeman and candidate, and later as a civil defense administrator.

In conversation, Burns repeatedly stressed the need to combine AJA and Hawaiian votes. Kido quoted Burns as saying: "If this Democratic Party is going to be a success, you've got to get the Hawaiians and the Japanese together." It was an idea that Burns expressed privately to many people, over and over. In Kido's recollection, Burns added, "You can't depend on the haoles to come in. They'll gravitate to the Republican Party because of economic reasons. So concentrate on . . . the Hawaiians."[17]

The initial Hawaiian additions to Burns' circle were William S. Richardson, a young attorney, and Herman Lemke, an accountant. Richardson was the grandson of John Richardson, who had gone to Washington D.C. in 1897 as part of a native delegation petitioning for restoration of the Hawaiian nation. Since Bill Richardson was the foremost Hawaiian insider in the early 1950s, his participation was crucial, and other Hawaiians played important roles as the years went on.

To some, Burns' cultivation of an alliance between AJA and Hawaiians was evidence that he was a crude broker of ethnic politics, but for others it was evidence that Burns acted on the world as it was in his effort to transform it. In a more historical vein, his strategy can be more accurately understood as an attempt of the postwar antioligarchy party—the Democrats—to incorporate the key element of the postannexation antioligarchy party—the more disaffected native Hawaiians, with whom Burns was both comfortable and familiar.

Burns' on-again, off-again relationship with the Chinese Hawaiian Heen family reflected his preoccupation with Hawaiians. Senator William Heen was one of the most influential figures of the 1920s, 1930s, and 1940s. If Hawai'i then had been a state, Heen's popularity would have made him a top contender for governor or congressman. His brother, Ernest Heen, also had a following, and behind them was another generation of Heens preparing themselves for politics (such as Walter Heen, Marion Heen Shim, Marion's husband, Alvin Shim, and Ernest Heen Jr.) Although William Heen had supported the collective bargaining law for labor, he was among those who would be described in the late 1940s as a conservative. He had parted ways with the new Democrats over the Red Scare, subscribing to the anticommunist movement even as Burns maneuvered to maintain his relationship with the ILWU.[18] Despite his party-based conflicts, Burns was to support the candidacy of William Heen to the U.S. Senate in the first statehood election at the expense of his protégé Inouye. (After two weeks of being nagged by Aoki to let Heen have a clear shot at the U.S. Senate, Inouye reluctantly complied, running successfully for the U.S. House instead, only to see Heen lose in the primary.)

The slate-making maneuvers by Burns can be interpreted readily as concern for maintaining ethnic balance in the party, but they were more subtly an extension of what Burns had been doing since 1941: negotiating a balance between AJA and the rest of the community. For AJAs to be elected to too many offices ran against a long, deep tradition of the public not being "ready"—a widely used rationale. The restraint on AJAs had been internalized as self-restraint or self-policing. In terms of Japanese folk wisdom, collectively AJAs did not want to be the nail that stuck out too far from other ethnic groups. The nail that sticks out gets pounded down.

While the burden of history restrained AJAs from asserting their maximum potential influence, sheer numbers and the Japanese encounter with adversity propelled them to act decisively. Arguably AJAs would have led the reformation of the Democratic Party even had they been a smaller group. Their parents had been animated by the emergence of Japan onto the world scene. The entire Japanese community had been put on trial by the war. They had been pushed together—in a general way by plantation society, in a specific way by the War Department. Nisei soldiers had suffered and sacrificed together in their military achievements, and individual veterans often had pursued higher education together and run for office together.

WITH THE ADDITION to his circle of such people as Inouye and Richardson, Burns had become, unambiguously, the leader of a major faction within the Democratic Party. Zalburg described him as a simple man. Fuchs pictured him driving around Honolulu in an old car. In fact, Burns was always a work in progress. After the Pearl Harbor scare, he had been assigned to not only continue his FBI work but also run the vice squad for the second time. He policed the wartime trade of the *madames*. His days were mired in the problems of prostitutes while his work with the Japanese community exposed him to great issues of history.

After leaving the police force, he searched for a new way to make a living. He secured a real estate license, forming something called Burns & Co., with the idea of developing a building in his hometown of Kailua. In early

1951, Mayor Johnny Wilson appointed him administrator of disaster relief for Oʻahu. After hours, he held political meetings in a storage room in the basement of City Hall.

As a moment of transition from the old to the new, Burns' meetings at Johnny Wilson's City Hall with the inner circle of the new Democratic Party forms a perfect historical image. The modest accommodations made for Hawaiian patronage at City Hall were giving way to the rising political influence of Asian Americans. The essential goal was not the revival of the Democratic Party per se, but serious and immediate movement toward economic and social equality of opportunity, regardless of race. Mau's critique of the early Burns as not stating a philosophy adequately illustrates the pressure that Burns was under to do so. A handful of Caucasians were needed to articulate in philosophical terms the political changes that nonwhites sought. A philosophically referenced approach served to focus the basic ideals of America, which could not be attacked as mere self-interest.

It was in this environment that Burns applied himself to a program of disciplined reading. Once a week, he went to the University of Hawaiʻi to see a professor of political science, Alan Saunders, an influential teacher who spawned the postwar involvement of university faculty in Democratic Party politics. One of Saunders' academic recruits was Dan W. Tuttle, a political scientist who introduced sophisticated public polling to Hawaiʻi. Saunders had told Tuttle, "Burns may not impress you so much, but I have a hunch he's going to be fairly prominent in Hawaiian politics."[19] Every week at Saunders' office, which was across from Tuttle's, Burns would stop to chat and borrow new books from Saunders' personal collection. This self-education process was to distinguish him from others who were much better educated in the conventional sense. He knew what he didn't know and through a determined effort filled in the pages. As a result, people would describe Burns as a man of the street who quoted from Aristotle and Aquinas, Jefferson and Jackson. This practice continued. His daughter observed him reading the periodic theological tracts of the Pope—papal encyclicals—over and over, in their entirety. She also was aware of his consulting friends in Washington on ideas for reading, including Lyndon Johnson and U.S. Senator Mike Mansfield of Montana.[20]

THE MAKING OF '54

Perhaps myths are made when history takes a new direction. Like the New Deal in American politics, the 1954 Democratic revolution is something that long-time residents in Hawaiʻi know about, even though remarkably little has been written about the details.

As we have seen, 1954 was the culmination of change that originated not in the postwar but the prewar period. The most identifiable drive for change came from the determination to ward off a mass internment of alien Japanese and AJA, and then to mobilize a display of AJA devotion to America. The organization of workers was led by the most radical strains of the American labor movement, which found fertile soil in the economic backwardness that labor radicals effectively addressed. The Red Scare had peaked in 1950. Ingram Stainback was no longer governor. The House Un-American Activities Committee and the Smith Act Trials had come and gone, but the labor movement had survived. The meanest internal battles had been at least temporarily settled within the Democratic Party, and all factions focused on defeating Republicans at the polls.

Nonetheless there was no apparent great expectation of a lasting, decisive political change prior to the election. No dramatic prophesies survive to be quoted. No master plan, no backroom strategy, explains the outcome. Contrary to the belief that the 442nd Club was an extension of the Democratic Party, the club was officially neutral, partly out of concern for its tax-exempt status.[21] A young veteran, Masato Doi, was president of the 442nd Club that year. He was asked to appear on the ILWU's weekly radio program. Despite reservations, he said he would do so, provided he would be referred to as an individual, and not as president of the club. Nonetheless a newspaper advertisement referred to the 442nd Club. Doi's friend and mentor, the Republican Hung Wai Ching, an honorary member, was irate. He refused to speak to Doi and even suggested that he step down as president. In the 1954 election, Masato Doi was a member of the Burns group but not of Burns' immediate circle. He ran for the legislature as a response to the times, but not at Burns' urging. He was one of the attractive new candidates, a graduate of the Columbia University school of law, whose central concern was faithfulness to the U.S. Constitution.

Many Democrats were like Masato Doi. They were people of the center, who knew several Republicans well—the names of Ching, Marumoto, and Kometani come up repeatedly—but did not know the ILWU well, nor were they comfortable in their dealings with the union.

Clearly Burns recruited legislative candidates in 1954, but how many is not known. The impression that he recruited a field of candidates is heightened by the fact that Burns' two best-known protégés, Daniel Inouye and George Ariyoshi, both told of conversations in which Burns urged them to run for the legislature in 1954. The fact that Democratic candidates had gotten educations with the GI Bill and could now appeal to voters as well-educated individuals undoubtedly was of great importance, as it has always been portrayed.

Mismanagement by Republican legislators also played in to Democratic hands. After promising government workers a pay increase, the Republican administration reneged, claiming lack of revenue. The traditionally cautious Hawai'i Government Employees Association—then an in-house group—took on greater energy, abandoning Republican candidates and backing Democrats.

Not only the temper but the composition of the electorate was changing. In 1952, the U.S. Congress amended the immigration and naturalization law to facilitate the naturalization of resident aliens. The naturalization law (but not the immigration law) was finally color-blind. This change was, in the view of scholar Roger Daniels, "a fruit of the Cold War,"[22] yet another way that tensions in Asia influenced the development of Hawai'i. The new law meant that immigrants from China, Japan, and Korea could now become naturalized citizens of the United States. Because of Hawai'i's settlement history, the amendment affected a far higher proportion of the population of Hawai'i than of any other place in America. Thousands studied for their tests and proudly became naturalized citizens. A clue to the readiness of Democrats to pick up these votes lies in Burns' recorded lobbying for changes in the law as early as 1941, and in his Kailua chapter of the Lions International Club passing a resolution asking that any legal immigrant be accorded the right to become a naturalized citizen. To maximize the effect of the new citizens, Democratic party workers were assigned to Japanese prefectural organizations—*kenjinkai*—as a way of systematically combing the older generation of new citizens for support at the polls.[23]

FINALLY, THERE WAS a Joe Farrington factor. Farrington was the son of Wallace R. Farrington, who had served two terms as an appointed governor of the territory. In 1933, Joe Farrington had succeeded his father as publisher of the afternoon *Honolulu Star-Bulletin,* where Jack Burns had once answered the telephone. Joe had become involved directly in territorial government in the aftermath of the infamous Massey case, in which a white woman had allegedly been raped by a group of young local men. The woman's husband and mother killed one of the young men. On the conviction of the husband and mother, the appointed governor of the territory, Lawrence M. Judd, under pressure from the U.S. Navy, commuted their sentence to an hour's detention in the governor's office in 'Iolani Palace. Various American politicians, far from being sated by this travesty of justice, clamored to impose a commission form of government on Hawai'i that would be dispatched directly from Washington.

Young Joe was among those who intervened, serving as secretary of a commission that preserved the system under which his father had been appointed—that is, by presidential selection of a resident of Hawai'i. After a stint in the legislature, Joe was elected in 1943 to serve as delegate to Congress.

In spite of his elite origins, the younger Farrington tried to attune his party to the postwar era. He was approachable by people of all races. He cultivated relationships with the attorney Marumoto and with the circles around Ching and Kometani. (For example, when Ching went to see Roosevelt, he called the White House from Farrington's office.) While the morning *Honolulu Advertiser* continued to perpetuate images of a yellow peril, Farrington's newspaper adopted the acronym AJA—Americans of Japanese Ancestry. When communist-baiting was at its most vicious, Farrington accepted the endorsement of the ILWU and as a consequence was reviled by the anticommunist movement. He convincingly worked for statehood. In 1947 and again in 1950, he managed statehood bills through the Republican-controlled House of Representatives, only to see them die in the Senate under the threat of filibuster. He defeated Burns by a margin of three to one in the 1948 Congressional race, after which Burns said, "I know of no one to whom I would rather lose." He also supported the color-blind naturalization feature of the 1952 amendment to the naturalization law.

Farrington died in office in 1954 and was succeeded by his wife, Elizabeth, who was not nearly as well liked. If in hindsight the Republicans were headed for oblivion—again, few if any seemed to have thought this at the time—the impact of Farrington's death in the summer of 1954 was both literal and symbolic. In filing to run against Mrs. Farrington in the fall election, Burns again was thought to be taking on a hopeless task. Although filing at the last moment with little preparation, as before, the outcome was entirely different. Against Farrington's widow, Burns received more than 49 percent of the vote. The usual strong showing of Joe Farrington at the top of the ticket was gone, and the effect rippled through the House and Senate races.

The first Japanese Americans had been elected to the territorial legislature in 1930. Seven of the eight AJA elected in the 1930s were Republicans. The largest number elected at one time was three, which left AJA badly underrepresented (in a then thirty-member House and fifteen-member Senate). In 1940, the number of AJA in the legislature rose to seven, all Republican. In 1946, four of six were Republican, including Thomas Sakakihara of Hilo, who had served before the war and then had been interned.

In 1948, the number of AJA rose to twelve, two-thirds of them Republican, including the 442nd veteran Joe Itagaki and the 100th veteran Toshio Ansai. Noboru Miyake of the Kaua'i Morale Committee was elected to the

House as a Republican. By 1952, AJA were experiencing even greater success, filling sixteen of the legislature's forty-five seats. Eleven were Republican.

In other words, by 1952 AJA had attained a level of legislative office-holding nearly proportionate to the Japanese-ancestry population and probably disproportionately large compared to citizenship, since amendment of the naturalization law had not yet affected the composition of Hawai'i's electorate.

The drama of the Democratic story, combined with errors in written history, have obscured this trend of increasing AJA success within the Republican party prior to 1954. (For example, Burns' biography, describing the oppressive atmosphere for AJA in 1941, says, "None served in the territorial legislature.")[24] In 1954, when twenty-one AJA were elected, sixteen were Democrats. Given the fact that most ILWU-influenced voters long since had gone over to the Democratic Party, the most likely explanation of 1954 was AJA voters migrating from the Republican to the Democratic Party. As such, this was not an uprising or a "revolution," as it is often called, but an evolutionary shift that was mostly centrist and moderate in nature. The Democratic Party's search for votes within the *kenjinkai* (prefectural clubs), for example, is not likely to have turned up many radicals. Nor were other campaign tactics, such as the concentration by Aoki and Tokunaga on the Parent Teacher Associations and the service clubs, such as Lions and Rotary.

The most consistent force on the left, creating a counterweight to this strong centrist tendency, were union communities controlled by the ILWU (which often elected ILWU business agents). Further tension was introduced into this coalition by the gradual development of the trade and craft unions—the carpenters, electricians, laborers, hotel workers, and so on—who were becoming more a part of the urban and town mix. However, as members of conservative unions, they and their proxies held the ILWU in particular suspicion.

Nonetheless there was a broad scenario of change that was common to all of these elements: A process of compromise and accommodation had begun before the war and many elements of society in Hawai'i had helped sustain both the Japanese-ancestry community and the larger community through the war. The process of social and political change resumed immediately after the war and continued at an accelerating rate. The animating goal was equality.

With a few notable exceptions on the left of the labor movement, AJA sought not to overturn but to participate fully through hard work in an evolving community. The margin of the Democratic "revolution" had to do with a relatively slower pace of change associated with the Republican party and the extent to which the AJA continued to be frustrated by the existence of both visible and invisible ceilings, and with a relative lack of opportunity. For example, practically every one of the young AJA attorneys, from Marumoto to Masato Doi and Robert Oshiro, would tell stories of interviewing with the old white Republican law firms, to no avail. Doi was given fifteen minutes and told he would get a call, but never heard a word. Young, energetic AJA in many cases simply did not have enough to do. Before either was elected to the legislature, Doi got to know George Ariyoshi by playing pool with him during lunch hour. Not only the law firms but also executive offices, board rooms, the upper reaches of management, the race-based social clubs, and neighborhoods in which ownership was for whites only—all remained closed to AJA.

The Democratic Party had the edge where it counted—in its active, unequivocal concern for openness, acceptance, and the development of opportunity. It unleashed a pent-up energy and enthusiasm that underlay the process of change across the board—not only around Burns, but in all factions of the Democratic Party.

Finally—in some ways most amazingly—the Democratic Party managed to seize the initiative on the overriding issue of statehood, even though the principal barriers to statehood lay not with old guard Republicans in Hawai'i (as Burns so vigorously argued) but with the national Democratic Party as it was represented in the U.S. Senate.

THE STATEHOOD STRATEGY

The Democratic victory of 1954 in Hawai'i was widely ignored on the national scene. Hawai'i had always been Republican. Surely the combined influence of a Republican national administration, Mrs. Farrington (who had hung on by a few votes), and the appointed Republican governor (Sam King), could return Hawai'i's legislature to the Republican fold. A view along these lines was held by much of congress, by leading members of the national press, and by Eisenhower himself, with serious consequences for the issue of statehood.

The national confusion over Hawai'i's political leanings has been compounded by the Hawai'i Democratic Party's mythological story of gaining statehood, to the detriment of developing a better understanding of the significance of Hawai'i as a state. Again, the underlying story begins with the fact that a mass internment of the Japanese community was averted in Hawai'i, thus preserving a society with the potential to function as a state.

For the shorter term, a more accurate interpretation begins with the fact that after World War II, statehood for Hawai'i had the support of both the Republican and Democratic national party organizations, as well as

Democratic President Harry S. Truman (1945–1952) and then Republican President Dwight D. Eisenhower (1952–1960). A majority of the American people supported statehood, overwhelmingly so outside the white supremacist states of the Old South.

When Farrington managed a statehood bill onto the floor of the House in 1947, Republicans voted for it by a margin of three to one, while a majority of Democrats voted against it. This was an opportunity for the Republican Party to consolidate its position in Hawai'i and gain the long-term loyalty of Hawai'i's people, but the Hawai'i bill died in a Senate committee in 1948 at the hands of conservative Republicans.

The Red Scare notwithstanding, the House in 1950 again approved statehood for Hawai'i. This time Republican congressmen voted for statehood by nearly *four* to one. With Truman actively supporting statehood, Democratic congressmen voted for it by a margin of two to one. This bill died in the Senate under threat of a filibuster by Southern Democrats.

The House again voted for Hawaiian statehood in 1953. With the communist hysteria waning, Republicans supported this bill by nearly *five* to one. Without Truman in the White House, a slight majority of Democrats voted against the bill. In the Senate, a bill joining simultaneous statehood for Alaska and Hawai'i passed by a vote of fifty-seven to twenty-eight. The erroneous political presumption underlying this bill was that Hawai'i would elect Republican senators and Alaska would elect Democratic senators. Republicans voted for the Alaska-Hawai'i bill by thirty-three to nine, while Democrats were split, twenty-three to nineteen. In other words, at the last moment before the 1954 election in Hawai'i, when political analysts in Washington might have rationally believed—based on previous voting patterns— that two Republican and two Democratic votes would be added to the Senate by Hawai'i and Alaska respectively, both political parties approved of statehood for Hawai'i. The problem was that the two houses had passed different bills, with no intention of reconciling their differences before Congress adjourned. However, with Republicans leading the way over eight postwar years (1947–1954), the House had approved statehood for Hawai'i three times and the Senate once.

The context for the passage of the statehood bills was not merely the persistence of Hawai'i's people, but also the agonizing events of the era— the Cold War in Asia, the domestic Red Scare, and above all the struggle to redefine America as a political ideal and not merely a white man's country. Where this larger story was mostly lost in Hawai'i, it was retrieved by the scholarship of an Australian political scientist, Dr. Roger Bell, and detailed in a little-read book, *Last Among Equals, Hawaiian Statehood and American Politics*. By linking events in Honolulu with events in Washington, and by putting these in context with America's relationship to Asia, the book tends to correct for the tenacious parochialism of the political dialog in Hawai'i.

Bell credits Truman with defining statehood as a civil rights issue. It was Truman who had saluted the nisei fighting units on their return to America, Truman who had integrated the armed forces by executive order in 1948, and Truman who stood fast on the civil rights plank in the Democratic platform. When his civil rights initiatives were frustrated by the southern bloc of his own party, Truman accused them of living eighty years behind the times. Despite a lack of congressional action on civil rights, the definition of American society changed dramatically in 1954 when the U.S. Supreme Court ruled that "separate but equal" public schools were a fiction. "Separate educational facilities," it held, "are inherently unequal."

The future of Hawai'i's hopes for statehood now lay inescapably with the nineteen Democratic senators who had voted against the Alaska-Hawai'i bill of 1953. All these senators were from the Old South, which had become engaged in its last desperate, sometimes violent defense of racial segregation and white supremacy. Hawaiian statehood, Bell wrote,

was an important aspect of the divisive and bitter struggle over civil rights after World War II. Unless a compromise could be reached on civil rights generally, there was little prospect of a successful compromise on statehood.[25]

The Republican Party had displayed its support for Hawaiian statehood, but it had failed to put the pieces together. Within Hawai'i, the rear-guard battle against statehood did in fact—as Burns so often said—emanate from a handful of adherents to the Republican Party.

Of greater specific importance, the Democratic majority in the 1955–1956 territorial legislature had passed a raft of progressive legislation regarding labor, education, and taxation, only to have it vetoed by the appointed Republican governor. Never had it been so clear that Hawai'i was a distant, second-class appendage of America. As the 1956 election approached, Elizabeth Farrington pleaded with Eisenhower to do something dramatic for statehood so that she might be re-elected delegate.

When Burns defeated Mrs. Farrington in 1956, an extraordinary situation was created. A politically progressive element from a small community in the mid-Pacific had been joined to the national Democratic Party, which still harbored the most obstructionist racists in the country. Statehood had followed such a twisting path that many people now despaired of reaching its end. Popular support for statehood was actually declining, both in Hawai'i and across the country.[26] In the Senate, Lyndon Johnson of

Texas remained unconvinced. Behind him stood the segregationists, ready to filibuster, as they had threatened to do in 1954. House Speaker Sam Rayburn was opposed to statehood for Hawai'i, as was the chairman of the nearly dictatorial House Rules Committee, Howard Smith.

As Bell said, "Hawai'i's future rested on developments within the Democratic party."[27] Burns picked up where Chuck Mau had left off. While both Johnson and Rayburn were Southerners, they were also Texans who had become national figures. To a correspondent in Hawai'i Burns confided, "I am going to see if I cannot work on our 'Southern Brethren.'"[28] Burns' biographers, Boylan and Holmes, superbly painted a picture of Burns as he pursued his invasion of the South through Texas. Burns frequently insisted that Southerners were not necessarily the real problem, but that the oligarchy of Hawai'i had poisoned the well for statehood. He distributed photocopies from the proclamation of the 442nd Regiment's honorary citizenship in Texas, which had been extended in recognition of their rescue of the Lost Battalion.

He courted Rayburn, who incessantly referred to Japanese Americans as "Japs." Burns poured bourbon for the drinkers in Rayburn's entourage, and there he met the mercurial Lyndon Johnson and his famous aide, Bobby Baker. Rayburn had grown up under the tutelage of Johnson's father, and Johnson had risen to power under Rayburn's guidance. These were ingrown relationships that an islander could understand without pause. Life was about relationships.

Johnson called Burns "Johnny," which likely made him the first person in a long while to address Burns with a familiar diminutive. Johnson was becoming famous for his slogan, "Come, let us reason together," and for his saying that if you could not get a whole loaf take half, and if not half then two slices.

Burns composed a litany of praise for Southerners who had supported statehood for Hawai'i. In some instances he ignored a great deal of stench, as when he praised the rabidly anti-Japanese senator from Alabama, John T. Morgan, for advocating statehood as part of the 1898 annexation. Yet there was an inner core of truth to the way Hawai'i had touched certain Southerners, stretching from Shivers and Earl Finch to the congressman Henry Lacarde of Louisiana, who had supported the 1947 bill, and finally to Johnson himself.

The courage and shrewdness of Burns has always been defined by his active agreement with a strategy to let Alaska become a state before Hawai'i. Over and over the story has been repeated that by risking his political career, he created a situation in which Hawai'i could not fail. In response to the earlier failure of the combined Alaska-Hawai'i statehood bill, supporters of the two new states agreed to separate bills in 1957—a tactic to which Burns clearly subscribed.[29] During this period, Johnson and various other influential Democrats warmed to the idea of Alaska being a state. Although less developed than Hawai'i, it was mostly white and of Democratic leaning. While Alaska was not contiguous to the existing forty-eight states, it was on the North American continent.

A meeting involving Burns, Johnson, and Rayburn in early 1958 clarified an Alaska-first strategy, in which Johnson promised Burns that Hawai'i would be brought up early in the next session of Congress. When the Eisenhower Administration pushed a statehood bill for Hawai'i, Burns took a dramatic step, moving to shelve the bill for the remainder of the session. When the Alaska bill finally cleared both the House and the Senate, Burns once again agreed to hold up action on a Hawai'i statehood bill on Johnson's advice, and on Johnson's continued assurance that the Hawai'i bill would be a priority in the first session of the new Congress. The problem was not mustering a majority vote (it had existed for a long time), but the threat of a filibuster by Southern Democrats in the U.S. Senate, precipitated by antagonism for Hawai'i changing the chemistry of the civil rights issue in America.

As Bell stresses, the key people who contemplated a mid-Pacific, multiracial state were carried along on currents of social and geopolitical change, in which Hawai'i was the leading edge. What mattered was agreement that if Alaska could go first, the Democratic congressional leadership—most importantly Johnson and Rayburn—would guide Hawai'i past the obstructionist tactics of the Southern segregationists in the next session of Congress.

Alaska passed, Congress adjourned, and Burns won re-election by saying that if Hawai'i did not become a state in the next congress, he would never run for office again. His campaign was a wink and a nod that could be summarized in two words: *Trust me*. When he returned to Washington he collected on the promise made by Johnson and Rayburn. According to one of Johnson's biographers, "Johnson threw himself into the Hawai'i statehood enterprise with his usual manic energy." To Johnson, Hawai'i offered an example of racial harmony and "its example could help the South with its own racial problems." Further, the admission of Hawai'i would offer proof to the world that America was committed to multiracial equality. The passage of the statehood bill was the high point of Johnson's year.[30]

The Alaska-first story was one layer of a more complex story. The second layer was the depth of relationship that Burns formed with Johnson and Rayburn and the subsequent personal and political determination of Johnson to make good on his behind-the-scenes promise. Third was the subterranean change in the national Democratic Party's stance toward civil rights. Fourth was the context of the Cold War.

The actual vote in the Senate on statehood for Hawai'i was seventy-six to fifteen.[31] Fourteen of the nay votes were Democrats of the Old South, which meant that a crucial eight votes had defected from the Southern bloc to Hawai'i. In the House, the vote was 323 to 89. The margin for Hawai'i among Republicans was wider than among Democrats, as it always had been, but politically it was nonetheless a victory for the Democratic Party in Hawai'i.

As one who stood by his prior utterances (and convincingly believed them with all his heart), Burns continued to praise the South and disparage the white elite in Hawai'i. In his article, "Statehood and Hawai'i's People," Burns said, "The reasons why Hawai'i did not achieve statehood, say 10 years ago—and one could without much exaggeration say 60 years ago—lie not in Congress but in Hawai'i." The most effective opposition, he went on, was always in Hawai'i. "For the most part it has remained under cover and has marched under other banners."[32] He outlined the evolution of the white oligarchy from annexation forward, but neglected to say that after 1935 the Big Five companies had favored statehood as protection of their sugar quota, and that thereafter Republican opposition to statehood had dwindled.

Contradicting Burns by name, the historian Bell concluded that after 1945 the reactionary element in Hawai'i did not "influence decisively the fate of any legislation before Congress."[33] Rather, the Republicans served as "a convenient political whipping boy" for the Hawai'i Democratic Party. "Failure to appreciate the relationships between statehood and the Southern position on civil rights," wrote Bell, "has obscured from most observers . . . the real obstacles to admission."

The Alaska-first narrative also tends to obscure an understanding of Hawai'i's contribution to civil rights and to a more egalitarian America. Hawai'i's identity in Congress was muted by the alliance with the South. After the first statehood election, Burns guided Daniel Inouye into the waiting embrace of the Texans. When Inouye arrived in Washington to be sworn into the U.S. House, the mighty House Speaker greeted him by name. Inouye said he was grateful to be recognized. Rayburn replied that Inouye was the "only one-armed Jap" in Washington—this from the same courtly person who said, "God bless you," to Beatrice Burns whenever he saw her.

The man who called Burns "Johnny," Lyndon B. Johnson, ran for president the year after the statehood vote. An out-of-work Burns spent much of 1960 traveling the country with the title of National Representative of the Johnson campaign, appearing for Johnson in thirteen states. After Johnson was forced to settle for the vice presidency, he succeeded to the presidency on November 22, 1963, on the death of President Kennedy. By this time, the country was seething with nonviolent protest against racial segregation. Rather than join his fellow Southerners in obstruction, Johnson threw his support behind the civil rights movement. The national Democratic Party became the progressive party on the issues of race.

It should be asked to what extent a significant number of more enlightened Southerners, such as Johnson, looked to Hawai'i as a step toward reconfiguring racial relationships in America. Truman's decree in 1948 ending racial segregation in the military was a step. The civil rights act of 1957, although criticized as a weak piece of legislation, was the first civil rights legislation to pass Congress since Reconstruction, and it too was a step. Hawai'i in 1959 was a step. Within five years, Johnson would be, among American presidents, the most impassioned and effective advocate of civil rights in history, presiding over passage of both the 1964 Civil Rights Act and the 1967 Voting Rights Act. With four new senators from Alaska and Hawai'i, Southern obstruction of civil rights legislation was no longer a real possibility.[34]

After 1959 the question for Burns was whether to stay in Washington D.C. by taking a virtually certain seat in the Senate or risk a losing campaign for governor of the new state. His answer would not only shed light on Hawai'i's past but foreshadow its future. As he debated, he wrote his treatise on the movement for statehood, in which one could glimpse a rare understanding that Hawai'i was truly the sum of its history, which was distinctly not a state history, in the sense that forty-nine other states could recite state histories. Rather, it was a history of two nations, Hawai'i and America, with other blue water naval powers, including Russia, Britain, France, and Japan, hovering close at hand. It was a history of the suppression of the Hawaiian nation, of the ensuing long period of imposed American tutelage, and finally the surge of optimism generated by Hawai'i's admittance to the Union. "Hawai'i occupies the central, preeminent position in the Pacific Ocean," said Burns. "Hawai'i is America's bridge." All was but a beginning. The optimism was like a dip in the ocean on a sunny day. Perhaps it would go on forever.

Chapter 8

A State Like No Other

If the only clue to Hawai'i's political culture was a map, the viewer might be struck by the wide dispersal of the islands. They are separated by imposing channels, which are usually wider than the islands themselves. Although the land mass of the archipelago is only a little larger than Connecticut, it is spread across a space the size of Kansas.

The islands were formed by an outpouring of lava from a fissure in the earth's tectonic plates. Over millennia, the fountain of lava has remained in place, but the plates themselves have migrated, carrying islands to the northwest. As a result, the most western inhabited island, Kaua'i, is many times older than the easternmost island, Hawai'i. Because of an extreme difference in age, the topography of each island differs, as do soil erosion, coral formation, and differentiation of species. Island by island, nature differs. In varying patterns, islands are subdivided by dramatic mountain ranges, and even adjoining valleys are separated by high, steep ridges.

The extent of this diversity resulted in the early settlements of Hawai'i being highly decentralized. The Hawaiian historian Samuel Kamakau wrote of an idyllic time "when no man was chief over another." As the population grew, this idyll of a folk culture was displaced by progressively more complex and powerful chiefdoms.

At the time of the first Western contact, four supreme chiefs ruled four kingdoms: the Hawai'i Island kingdom; the Maui kingdom (made of the interrelated islands of Maui, Lāna'i, Moloka'i, and Kaho'olawe); the O'ahu kingdom (which sometimes included Moloka'i); and the Kaua'i kingdom, which included the island of Ni'ihau. Centers of power shifted from Hilo and Waipi'o on the Big Island to Hāna and Wailuku in Maui, Waikīkī and Kualoa on O'ahu, and Waimea and Waialua on Kaua'i. In the ebb and flow of powerful chiefly lines, island kingdoms alternately attempted to achieve dominance.

Oʻahu dominated Molokaʻi. Maui dominated Lānaʻi, then Molokaʻi as well. This cluster—of Oʻahu, Molokaʻi, Maui and Lānaʻi—formed a central core, which was in some ways best positioned to achieve eventual control of the others.

When the British arrived in 1778, they stayed longest on the inner or Kona coast of Hawaiʻi Island and would often return to a protected leeward bay, Kealakekua. Contact with the West led to trading for firepower, which accelerated the process of interisland warfare. Hawaiʻi Island was bigger than all the other islands combined. Its strategic resources—such as food, weapons, and ocean craft—could be developed to support extended campaigns of warfare. Further, Hawaiʻi Island derived a certain protection from the fact that it was upwind. Opposing armies struggled to sail to Hawaiʻi, but the Hawaiians could easily swoop downwind on the attack. After several centuries of intermittent warfare, the heavily armed Hawaiians came to dominate the archipelago. The strategically situated island of the periphery had conquered the islands of the center, with remote Kauaʻi eventually but reluctantly pledging its loyalty to the newly centralized kingdom.

By 1895, seventeen years after the first sustained Western contact, the supreme chief of the Hawaiian Islands was the man in the golden cloak, Kamehameha. Most important in an agrarian society, he controlled use of the land. Exhibiting a fine understanding of the exercise of power, Kamehameha moved from his original home on the periphery to one of the two islands of the center, Oʻahu. Initially he chose a traditionally Hawaiian place, Waikīkī, which was not unlike his home valley, Waipiʻo, on Hawaiʻi. It was rich in water, taro, and fish. When he observed that the long keels of western ships could clear the reef and find adequate shelter only at the dry, barren village of Kou, he relocated his royal compound down the coast to dominate what would become known as the harbor of Honolulu.

During the reign of the third Kamehameha, the centralized powers of the dynasty were tempered by the establishment of a constitutional monarchy, with executive, legislative, and judicial branches. What had begun as a highly ranked chiefdom more and more resembled the organization of the powerful, seagoing nation-states. With the institution of fee simple land ownership, about 45 percent of the land was still controlled by the crown. Part of these enormous land tracts were for the support of the monarch, and part were for support of the government.

As a result of diplomacy in the early 1840s involving Britain, France, and America, constitutional monarchy survived in Hawaiʻi until the American-backed coup d'état of 1893. Thereafter the Republic of Hawaiʻi adopted a constitution that actually expanded the powers of the chief executive. The purpose of the powerful executive was to suppress rebellion and ward off assertions of power by the legislature. The native electorate was effectively disenfranchised by a combination of loyalty oaths and property or income qualifications.

After the 1898 annexation, citizens of the territory were re-enfranchised, but the idea of a strong governor remained, for reasons that were an extension of the constitution of the Republic. Through a powerful governor, appointed by the president of the United States, America could maintain control over its new island colony. "There is a government in the Territory," its attorney general told Congress in 1903, "which is centralized to an extent unknown in the United States and probably almost as centralized as it was in France under Louis XIV."[1] The territorial governor appointed all key administrators. The executive branch maintained control of the 45 percent of the island land base that had been taken over by the oligarchic Republic as a result of the overthrow and annexation. The governor also could veto bills passed by the elected legislature, and his veto could be overridden only by a two-thirds vote of both houses. Even had he been popularly elected, the territorial governor of Hawai'i would have been regarded as an unusually strong governor.

In an attempt to break the congressional stalemate over statehood, Hawai'i's people held a constitutional convention in 1950, in the third year of the turmoil over communism. The idea was to prove Hawai'i's worthiness for statehood. In that convention, ratified subsequently by a public referendum, the powers of the governor were further expanded to include the appointment of the entire judiciary. The most serious dispute centered on the ILWU's contention that the draft constitution made the governor too strong.

With statehood, much of the land that had been ceded to the United States by the Republic was returned to the State of Hawai'i in the form of a land trust. Lands retained by the U.S. government prominently included the large or strategic tracts taken for military bases and national parks (such as the Volcanoes National Park). However, even with persistent pilfering of the land trust, it still contained more than 40 percent of all the land in the Hawaiian Islands. Had the admission act treated Hawai'i like any other state, the former government and crown lands of Hawai'i would have become part of the enormous federal land reserve. Instead these lands were assigned to the administration of the State of Hawai'i's Department of Land and Natural Resources. They were managed by a Land Board, which was appointed by the governor. The Land Board was chaired by the director of the department, who was also appointed by the governor. Viewed as history, the perpetuation of the land trust through the State of Hawai'i was one of the acknowledgments at statehood that Hawai'i was different from any other state. It reflected an inherent squeamishness on the part of the United States regarding the circumstances of annexation, and it also reflected a desire on the part of government in Hawai'i to manage its own lands.

The effect of the archipelago's decentralized geography long since had been offset by the persistent trend of centralization. While the reasons for centralization varied over time, invariably they had to do with organizing the Hawaiian Islands to deal with the larger world, which was successively defined as marauding man o' war, great naval nations, the American sugar market, American expansionism, and eventually the federal government of the United States.

In his 1959 analysis of statehood, Jack Burns had equated "centralization" with oppression. Centralization was the work of the *hegemony*, a relatively unused word that is still widely recognized by scholars in connection with colonialism and the rule by an elite to the benefit of the few. Burns predicted that statehood would be the cure for centralization. "Traces of it still remain," Burns said with his trademark confidence, "but statehood will enable us to dispose of them." The next step was for the Democratic Party to take over the extraordinarily centralized powers of the new state government. For Burns personally the question was whether he should try to become the first elected governor or stay in Washington.

TO THE VISITOR from Hawai'i, a fourth of the globe away, Washington is especially compelling. From the periphery, Washington appears as the all-powerful center, as a dense aggregation of symbols and design, history and culture. The domed and spired capitol, with its classical columns and arches, obviously borrows from the grandeur of Rome. The impression is heightened by the scale of the Mall, the Declaration of Independence at the National Archives, and the monuments to Washington, Jefferson, and Lincoln.

After the U.S. government made Hawai'i a state, there was an outpouring of affection for Burns from both Democratic and Republican members of congress. The enthusiasm suggested that his base in Washington was ready-made. Perhaps it also reflected a certain level of agreement with Burns' assertion that statehood opened "a whole new area of possibility, for Hawai'i and for the Nation."[2]

A Senator Burns would have been well suited for the political program of a pivotal figure such as Lyndon Johnson. Being respectful of the South, Burns knew how to court Southerners and move them along politically. In his ease of relationship with nonwhite people in Hawai'i, he simultaneously made a statement that the world was changing.

At the time Burns' campaigns were coordinated jointly by Aoki of the 442nd Club and Tokunaga of the Club 100. Aoki had gone with Burns to Washington while Tokunaga stayed home. When the statehood vote was imminent, Aoki telephoned Tokunaga and told him to prepare for a special statehood election. Tokunaga wanted to know what Burns had decided. He also wanted to know what the overall Democratic Party slate of candidates would be, and above all that Burns would return to Hawai'i as quickly as possible and take all the credit he could for statehood.

Burns was on an extension of the telephone line. He interjected that he was working with Lyndon Johnson on a bill to create a center of East-West education at the University of Hawai'i. Johnson was warming to the idea, and if Johnson would put his name on the bill it would pass. Hawai'i would have a $10 million a year addition to its economy through an international educational institution that expressed Hawai'i's new possibilities. The crusher for Tokunaga was the next line. Burns was not coming back to Hawai'i, but was staying on in Washington and tending to the work.

Tokunaga believed that Burns should run for the U.S. Senate, as did Aoki. They were aware that the move to Washington had not been easy for Beatrice Burns, and they believed Burns had earned the life of a senator. Aoki would tell of Burns receiving a telegram from a Big Five executive promising his support for a senate candidacy and his opposition to a gubernatorial candidacy. Finally Burns said that he would run for the Senate only if he wanted to inflate his own ego: "I'm going to run for the governorship because if you want to build the Democratic Party up, we've got to take the governorship."

Burns' decision said implicitly that the development of the state government, the Democratic Party, and the people of Hawai'i were synonymous. His decision also said something about Hawai'i as a unique society with a unique destiny. Where most governors try to parlay their positions into a Senate seat, he traded a sure Senate seat for a difficult governorship contest.

THE 1959 ELECTION

As a window to the first statehood election, the perspective of Walter Heen is revealing, because he looked at it in context of a long reach of time and with a deep sense of the Democratic Party's island nature. His grandparents' generation brimmed with Hawaiian royalists. His Chinese grandfather, Chung Muk Hin, was a citizen of the kingdom. Chung Muk Hin became known as Harry Heen, fathering ten children with a Hawaiian woman from Lahaina, Maui, the best-known of whom were William Heen and Ernest Heen, Walter's father.

Walter Heen would serve as a legislator, city councilman, judge, and finally as chairman of the Democratic Party. He thought of his family as opponents of the oligarchy and progressives on social and economic issues, but they also talked with business people and became suspicious of the Communist taint of the ILWU.

Walter Heen attended his first Oʻahu county Democratic Convention in 1956 on his return from law school. There he supported Thomas P. Gill, a brilliant young attorney who was attached to the interests of the emerging urban trade unions. A Burns supporter argued that since Burns and Tom Gill did not get along, Gill should not be elected county chairman. Walter Heen rose to argue that since Burns was serving as delegate to Washington and was no longer territorial chairman, the issue was moot.

After being elected to the legislature, Heen again sided with Gill in a 1959 battle within the Democratic Party over control of the House of Representatives.[3] This was a famous incident in which Gill's group produced the largest number of Democratic votes but fell short of the required majority of the entire House. Rather than accede to Gill's plans for how he would run the House, the Democratic minority formed a coalition with the Republicans. Such bipartisan coalitions would recur through the statehood period. Burns, although enjoying a reputation as the founder of the modern Democratic Party, wrote a letter congratulating the winners and urging them to get on with their work—effectively giving his blessing to the alliance with Republicans. Burns' critics could not help but note that his most immediate allies—made up of Neighbor Island Democrats and the ILWU—had been the key players in the coalition.

It was not that Heen disliked Burns, but he saw Burns as surrounded by AJAs. As a Hawaiian he asked himself, "Where are we in this picture?"[4] With the approach of the state of Hawaiʻi's first gubernatorial election, Heen's personal relationship with Burns warmed somewhat. One of Burns' inner circle floated a plan for Heen to run for lieutenant governor with Burns, but the idea languished because Heen was not of a constitutional age to run for executive office.

Meanwhile, Heen's companions in the House continued to brood over the Republican-Democratic legislative coalition far into the campaign season. As it became apparent that the ticket of Burns and Mitsuyuki Kido was in trouble, a meeting was held downtown at the Alexander Young Hotel. Gill and several others unloaded on Burns. Heen would remember Burns repeatedly tying one of his shoes. Thereafter, "we decided what-the-hell, he's our candidate for governor," but to no avail. Disunity, combined with Burns' strategic errors, led to his defeat. The beneficiary was the incumbent Republican appointee, William F. Quinn, whose impact on history would be nil, despite his being Hawaiʻi's first elected governor.

The Democratic Party also lost control of the Hawaiʻi Senate in 1959. It won only one of the two U.S. Senate seats and the single U.S. House seat.

In Washington, this first statehood election confirmed the impression that Hawai'i really did have a two-party system, and that the pendulum well might be swinging back to the Republican side.

Attorney Katsugo Miho would say he came within an hour of becoming a Democrat, but was instead elected in 1959 to a long career in the State House as a Republican.[5] Miho's success was yet another reminder that the new political establishment was based on a bipartisan center that was balanced by the political involvement of the nisei. Miho was the younger brother of Katsuro Miho, a pioneering prewar attorney and a founder of the Emergency Service Committee. Katsugo Miho—the younger "Kats"—had come of age with an acute awareness of the military intelligence investigations and his brother's web of relationships (for example, with Hung Wai Ching, Hemenway, and Shivers). Thereafter, Miho had served in the 442nd and was one of the several founders of the 442nd Club. At George Washington University law school in Washington D.C. Miho roomed with the future Democratic Senate president, John Ushijima of the 442nd, and they socialized with Dan Inouye, their law school classmate, also of the 442nd. By 1958, Democrats Tadao Beppu and Donald Ching were on the telephone to Miho, announcing they were on their way to Miho's house with his Democratic Party membership card.

Before they arrived, Miho was called to a meeting with Republicans Neal S. Blaisdell and Hiram L. Fong, who insisted he join the Republican Party. Fong prevailed. Never one for subtleties, Fong argued that it was in the best interest of Japanese Americans to be represented by both political parties.

THE 1962 ELECTION

After 1954, 1962 was probably the closest the Democratic Party came to developing a clear, widely held plan of action. Brought up short by Burns' 1959 loss, the party and its allies in the ILWU put a high priority on Burns' successful campaign for governor. Large Democratic majorities were elected in both houses of the state legislature, and Tom Gill was elected to the U.S. House in Washington. Finally consolidating all the possibilities of 1946, 1954, and the passage of statehood, the Democratic Party of Hawai'i in 1962 achieved a monopoly control on state government. Thereafter, where many had argued that Hawai'i had developed two parties of roughly comparable strength, the two-party idea would prove to be an illusion.

The Democratic Party of Hawai'i would become unique in America for its unbroken control in the last half of the twentieth century of the governorship, both legislative houses, the State judiciary, and a majority of the congressional delegation (usually the delegation in its entirety). It would also be unique for its exercise of power by a majority nonwhite electorate within America. Its record, if better known, would probably overshadow— in terms of durability and real effectiveness—the best-known political machines in American history, such as Tammany Hall in New York, the Cook County machine in Illinois, the Boston machine, and the organization first mobilized by Huey Long in Louisiana. It was to differ from these political machines in many respects, but most of all in governing a geographically self-contained place that had been a separate country and continued to function more like a nation than did any of the other forty-nine American states.

The immense role of political power in Hawai'i, and the way political power anchored social, economic, and racial relationships, created the inner reality of a state that was otherwise befogged by imposed images. Most prominently from this early period came the images of James Michener's *Hawaii*, along with its motion picture adaptation; *Blue Hawaii*, starring Elvis Presley; and the network television series *Hawaiian Eye*, which was followed closely by *Hawaii Five-O*, which in turn was followed by *Magnum P. I.* This imagery was enhanced by the rapid evolution of mass travel to Hawai'i and the almost perfect coincidence of the jet age. In its outward manifestations, Hawai'i became a travel poster. To a considerable extent, the pre-statehood understanding of Hawai'i's strategic significance was buried under a mountain of travel industry propaganda, but it was on this mountain that the post-statehood economy of Hawai'i was reconfigured.

A BOOM ECONOMY

While people remember John Burns and the early-day Democratic Party as agents of change, little thought is given to the changing economic context from which they benefited politically. The growth of Hawai'i's economy in the 1960s coincided with the rapid growth of the American economy. Within Hawai'i, the economic boom was attributed substantially to statehood. However, an understanding of Hawai'i's economic history in a longer time period leads to a more subtle conclusion. While occasionally the economic trends of Hawai'i and America have converged, as they did in the early statehood period, they often have diverged. Hawai'i has been consistently different. Much as Hawai'i is geographically separate, its economy after statehood evolved as significantly separate from the American economy.

A dimension of this story was told by an erudite bank economist, Thomas Hitch. Originally a staff economist in Washington D.C. for the President's Council of Economic Advisers, he was recruited in 1950 to be the research director of the Hawai'i Employers Council, then became a bank economist. As a student of economic history for four decades, Hitch

developed an eye for seeing beneath the surface of political events to underlying issues of policy. He carefully documented the differences in growth
rates between the Hawai'i economy and the American economy, beginning
in 1876 with passage of the Treaty of Reciprocity. While the U.S. population and labor force grew threefold between 1876 and the beginning of
World War II, the population and labor force of Hawai'i grew eightfold.[6]
During the 1930s, Hawai'i was significantly less affected by the Great
Depression than mainland America.

During World War II, the differences between Hawai'i and mainland
America became much greater. Despite the attempts of martial law to freeze
wages and keep the work force in place, total real personal income in Hawai'i
between 1940 and 1944 rose 36 percent a year, at nearly three times the rate
in the continental United States.[7] To pursue the Pacific war, the population
of Hawai'i almost instantly doubled. War construction became a huge factor.

In the immediate postwar years, the unionization of Hawai'i's work force
occurred in a faltering economy. For the years 1946 to 1949, Hitch com-
puted a 15 percent yearly decline of total real personal incomes. In addition to the mass exodus of American military, a quarter of the civilian
population left Hawai'i. These years coincided with the dock strike, the Red
Scare, and the rise of the Burns faction to a central role in modernizing the
Democratic Party.

As the Democratic Party approached 1954, Hawai'i's economy began to
work better. In contrast to a comparatively sluggish mainland economy,
Hawai'i grew at a rate of nearly 4 percent a year from 1949 to 1958. Then
a combination of events occurred that was even more fortuitous for Burns
and the Democratic Party. While previously the plantation economy had generated much of its own capital, economic growth in the 1950s created a
demand for outside capital. Prior to statehood, Hawai'i's remoteness worked
decidedly against investors putting money into Hawai'i. Indeed, many people continued to be unaware that Hawai'i was an integral part of the United
States. Hitch told a story about asking his insurance company in New York
to change his insurance policy. His insurers wrote back saying he would have
to get a physical from a doctor recommended by the American consul. Hitch's
correspondence with an economist in the White House came to him with
postage for a foreign destination.[8]

Just after statehood, the Kennedy administration whole-heartedly
embraced the Keynesian theory of promoting the flow of capital into markets through fiscal and monetary policies, setting off a period of prolonged
economic growth. American investors had more to invest and suddenly
Hawai'i was there as a model investment for the development of what was
to be a vast global boom in travel.

Hawai'i was a tropical, exotic destination, but it was also a state of the United States. It was friendly, safe, sanitary, English-speaking, and unimaginably appealing in both the manners of its people and the quality of its scenery. The word *Hawai'i* was on everyone's lips. The development of commercial jet flights coincided perfectly with statehood. When Sanford Dole's missionary parents had sailed from New England to Hawai'i in 1839, they were at sea for five months. When young Sanford returned to visit his New England relatives, he rode the first steamship out of Honolulu in a trip that took five weeks. Eventually ocean liners to the West Coast took five days. Propeller aircraft reduced the journey to a noisy, exhausting nine to ten hours. In 1959 a jet from the West Coast to Hawai'i took five hours.

Tourist travel grew throughout the 1950s at an average annual rate of 20 percent a year. Typically such high growth rates are sustained by an emerging industry only for short periods, since the numbers are compounded. For rapid rates of growth to be maintained, the real numbers must get bigger by the proverbial leap and bound. Nonetheless the 20 percent growth rate was sustained throughout the sixties and well into the seventies.

As incomes rose in America, the cost of air travel declined. Where the first tickets on prop planes had cost more than the annual income of the average American, that cost would eventually decline to 2 to 3 percent of average income. And it was in this context that Americans began to chat with one another about their island-by-island travel trophies. Yes, one may have been to O'ahu, but what about Maui? Kaua'i? Moloka'i?

Hitch would summarize his historical analysis by writing, "Hawai'i seemed to go its own way economically,"[9] and nothing would separate Hawai'i from the patterns of the American economy like the impact of Japan. In the mid-1960s, when the Japanese began to make money, and Japan began loosening its restrictions on foreign travel, they began making tourism-related investments in Hawai'i that would run into billions of dollars.

MORE THAN ANY other single factor, the rise of mass tourism paid the bills of Hawai'i's political liberalism. Tom Gill, the quintessential liberal, said: "Having been both rich and poor, rich is better." At least in the case of Hawai'i, rapid economic growth was a powerful companion to the Democratic Party's goal of developing a politically progressive, multiracial society. Not only could the political actors take credit for economic growth at election time but the flow of money also increased their belief that they were doing right. Economic growth and the unleashing of human potential through democracy seemed as logical a combination as they had to those delegates to the U.S. Constitutional Convention of 1776 who read a new writer, Adam Smith, in spare moments. Money created jobs and financed development. Business profited, labor got a bigger slice, and government raised ever more tax revenues.

Much to the point of maintaining a political coalition between Burns' veteran-based group and the ILWU, rapid economic expansion held hard political choices at bay. Potentially, that choice was between the essential conservatism of the veterans group and the historic radicalism of the ILWU. Because the economic pie kept getting bigger, the problem was consistently muted.

Strong protections were enacted for working people, along with a regulatory regime that allowed government to check the power of business. Although various proposals were debated to allow homeowners on leased land to buy their house lots, few ventured into the deeper question of land redistribution. The feudal landownership system—the system that had merged, then ossified, the worst features of the Hawaiian and oligarchic systems—remained essentially intact. This land was in America, where ownership was inviolable. Neither was wealth heavily taxed, not even inherited wealth. Neither was there reform or repeal of the most regressive feature of the tax system—a 4 percent excise tax on the movement of most goods and services through the economy, with the tax pyramiding at every step.

What was the answer to the question of how each person was to develop to his or her highest potential? The most essential answer was through the traditional system of private enterprise, somewhat fettered but essentially unchanged in its form and function. The second and related answer was more government. The Hawai'i of the 1960s could afford more government. With higher education previously confined to the University of Hawai'i at Mānoa, Democrats transformed the existing vocational schools into an island-by-island network of community colleges. School budgets, while always the subject of criticism, increased significantly. Huge sums went to creating infrastructure—water systems, sewage systems, highways, harbors, and airports. The expanded budget also financed more generous welfare payments for the needy—and reputedly became the most generous payments in the United States. When funds were needed to match federal innovations, ranging from Medicaid to the "war on poverty," as it was called, the money was readily forthcoming.

The possibilities of the new Hawai'i seemed boundless. Although Burns was sometimes portrayed as a pragmatist among the reformers, he was simultaneously thought of as the ultimate dreamer. On his first day in office, and every day thereafter, he got up early to go to Our Lady of Peace Cathedral to attend Mass. He talked about inspiring "a Pacific Community of Nations, a spiritual unity of people of diverse ethnic origins." Echoing the old internationalism, he said,

> We see this as our special role and duty and destiny by reason of the
> precious gift of American freedom given to us, by reason of our unique
> geographical location, by reason of our total blending of the cultures
> of East and West in our interracial unity and harmony, by reason of
> our extraordinary prosperity and attractive physical and social envi-
> ronment, and by reason of our proven history of dedication to man's high-
> est ideals.[10]

"Hawai'i," said Burns, "is at the hub of the Great Wheel of the Pacific." Beyond
its devotion to "man's highest ideals," the Democratic Party story of early
statehood was one of common-sense reform. It was a set of social, political, and economic adjustments that were widely agreed upon. Taken together,
they created a new status quo. The potentially conflicting political power
of various ethnic groups was brought into a new balance and harmony—
thanks probably above all to the moderation and restraint of the Japanese
Americans.

The idea of private enterprise was not only preserved but strengthened
by diminishing the mercantile proclivities of the Big Five and diversifying
the mix of entrepreneurs. The hated Big Five became merely the Big Five.
The potentially revolutionary aims of the ILWU were moderated. A new stability was effected between business and labor. The public sector was given
more nourishment, mostly by way of investment in human resources and
infrastructure.

Where the statehood issue in Congress had sharpened partisanship in
Hawai'i, the actual experience of statehood muted partisanship. Washington was far away. The imperative of island life was to find agreement, and
the vision of a multiracial society with both business and labor at the table
was bipartisan.

Long afterward, the 442nd veteran Kats Miho, who served eleven years
in the State House as a Republican, recalled, "Everyday life is no different
whether you're Republican or Democrat. . . . We would introduce bills under
our names, which would not become law but a comparable, similar bill would
be introduced by a majority member, and that bill would pass."[11]

Miho's deeper attachment was to a social rather than partisan interpretation of history. He thought that nowhere else was there a group of war
veterans who had such an opportunity "to control their lives and that of
their families in the way we have been able to do in Hawai'i."[12]

Within the bounds of this far-reaching bipartisanship, the Democratic and
Republican parties might have achieved a dynamic in Hawai'i not unlike the
American system. That is, the Democrats might have settled in as the gov-
ernment tinkerers, while the Republicans might have positioned themselves

as the brake on government excess. The Democrats might have maintained a closer relationship with labor, and the Republicans with business. While these themes were not totally absent, they were of relatively little consequence. The main trend was Hawai'i's development as a one-party state in which change was negotiated by factionalism. Increasingly the office of governor—not the legislature, which first had lifted the Democratic Party—was the center of power. It was in this context that politics in Hawai'i became more and more obsessed with who would be governor.

THE QUESTION OF SUCCESSION

As Jack Burns approached the end of his first four-year term of office, he was lean and straight. His movements were quick. His energy level usually seemed high. He loved to talk with people—to the consternation of his devoted secretary. Nonetheless he seemed older than his fifty-six years. He had given a great deal of himself, and he had punished himself. He had not drunk alcohol for many years but he had smoked. His skin was deeply lined.

In conversation people called him The Old Man, Stone Face, and The Great White Father. While these words may seem strange today, they were both respectful and affectionate in context of the mixed plate of Asian-influenced political culture. In Confucian terms, an old man is to be accorded special respect, while a person with a stone face is admirably stoic. Were the words *white father* tongue in cheek? No. I heard them used many times matter-of-factly, or even in awe. The imagery was of a potent father figure, benign and disarmingly friendly provided one bent to his will, which was presented as the will of the democratic electorate. One did not forget he prayed daily, often before dawn. One wondered if for Burns the issue of will was wrapped up not only in the people's will, but also God's will.

It was with a sense of discovery, years later, that I read about Father Alphonsus, the Belgian priest of Kalihi who served as a role model for Burns in the absence of his father. And it was in the context of Burns as The Old Man that a skein of stories developed over who would be the best person to succeed Burns as governor.

In 1959 Burns had run for governor on a ticket with Mitsuyuki Kido. They had lost to the Republican ticket of William F. Quinn, who was haole, and to the part-Hawaiian James Kealoha. Thereafter Burns was criticized for being too close to the AJAs and not reaching out to other ethnic groups. In 1962, he won with the part-Hawaiian William S. Richardson as his running mate.

The overt *pilikia* (trouble) over succession began in 1965 when Burns delivered on his promise to Richardson that after Burns' first term Richardson would be appointed to the Supreme Court. As it turned out, Richardson became chief justice and had a huge impact on court decisions from a native Hawaiian point of view. It was at this time that I, as a young reporter, got to know some of the people around Burns and then Burns himself. I was intensely interested not only in Burns but in the period. This led in a few years to *Catch A Wave*. True to the temper of the times, this book was pre-occupied with the here and now and with unfolding events—particularly with new techniques of campaigning, survey research, and the impact of television on elections.

KENNETH F. BROWN

The scene for *Catch A Wave* was set by Burns' choice of Kenneth F. Brown to run with him for lieutenant governor. The oft-told story is about Brown's lack of political experience, but what Burns saw was what many other people in Hawai'i would gradually come to see—that Kenneth Brown was an extraordinarily capable and caring person. Brown's ancestry was one-quarter Hawaiian and three-quarters haole. On his Hawaiian side he was a direct descendant of John I'i, a famous figure in the Kamehameha dynasty. Although Brown grew up as part of the landed gentry of Hawai'i, he also grew up with a painful awareness that the races were arrayed in an imposed hierarchy, with haoles on top and Hawaiians at least halfway down the ladder. His father was half-Hawaiian but looked Caucasian. Brown noticed that at parties in Kāhala his father would stand next to the Hawaiians who had been brought in to play music. Brown sensed that beneath the drinking and the laughter lay a profound sadness. In the faces of the Hawaiians, he read a despairing question, "What have we come to?" Reflecting on this prewar period, Brown would say, "It was like a conspiracy. We didn't understand, but each person played their part."

One day he and his father and mother were in a Hawaiian outrigger canoe in Kealakekua Bay, on the island of Hawai'i. A Hawaiian man paddled the canoe. The idea was to paddle across the bay to see where the British explorer James Cook had been felled by the Hawaiians, but the canoe began to pitch with the incoming ocean swell. His mother became anxious. In the excitement, his father spoke with the Hawaiian man in the Hawaiian language. Kenneth was astonished to learn that his father actually spoke the native language of Hawai'i.

Brown's family home near Diamond Head harbored a staff of Japanese servants, including maids who created atmosphere by wearing kimonos. As a boy Kenneth played with their children, but with age he and the Japanese children grew apart. The Japanese went to public school while he was driven to Punahou in a black sedan by a Japanese chauffeur who wore leather leggings. He then went off to Princeton to study architecture.

Returning to wartime Hawai'i with an architectural degree, he again went to Punahou every day, except now it was to work in a temporary office of the U.S. Army Corps of Engineers. There he made drawings alongside people of Chinese and Japanese ancestry, and he began to sense a tremendous vibrancy in Asian Americans that previously had been obscured to him. He eventually set up his own architectural firm with an AJA partner, Ernest Hara, and got into business. He golfed avidly, following in the footsteps of his uncle, Francis I'i Brown, a famous sportsman, and on the golf course he met the newly inaugurated governor, John Burns, who captivated him with his understanding of the people of Hawai'i.

"Burns," he would say, "had a knowledge of the world that I was starving for."[13] Soon thereafter Burns asked him to coordinate an international golf tournament that was designed to show off Hawai'i in the big league of golf. One day Burns said, "I want you to be my successor." One might imagine that lengthy discussion would precede such a decision, but the opposite was true. Brown thought that Burns' proposal was not the result of calculation but intuition. ("When he was convinced something was right, he just did it.") Thereafter it would be said over and over that Brown was politically naive. This was by definition true, in that he had no experience running for political office.

Family members besieged him. How could he run as a Democrat? How could he abandon them? At the Cypress Point Country Club in Pebble Beach, an elderly white lady turned to him. Without announcing the subject of her sentence she asked, "Kenny, how *could* you?" He replied, "Don't worry, my dear, it will be all right."

Burns' most immediate political circle, along with the ILWU, did what it could for Brown's candidacy, but many Democrats turned away from what seemed to be an eccentricity on Burns' part. When Brown lost by a wide margin to Thomas Gill, Burns was in Africa representing President Johnson at the independence ceremony of Botswana. On Burns' return to America, he was met by Brown at LaGuardia Airport. "My God," Burns said, "I never thought you would talk with me again."[14]

Brown saw Burns as a strong individual "whose world had been crushed," because voters had rejected his choice. Brown and his wife drove Burns to Washington D.C. to meet with Inouye. The meeting was controlled and purposeful. Inouye empathized with Burns but guided the conversation around to the work yet to be done in Hawai'i.

Brown then took Burns to his country club on the West Coast to play golf. The press in Hawai'i was clamoring. Where was the governor? What was his reaction to the election? Would he campaign with Gill? The governorship was in danger of being lost. Those closest to Burns were in a state of intense anxiety. Burns' younger brother Edward, who knew a great deal about Jack's capacity for being high-strung, feared his brother was coming apart.[15] With Burns still on the mainland, Burns' wife, Beatrice, called the party chairman, Bob Oshiro,[16] and a few others. She asked what could be done. Matsuo Takabuki was designated to see Burns in California. In his memoir, Takabuki would only say, "Burns seemed to have lost the desire to campaign."[17] Ariyoshi, then a state senator, would recall Takabuki's mission as telling Burns, "We're ready to help you get reelected, but you've got to decide whether you want it." At one point in California, Burns announced to Brown, "I'm not going back." But Brown thought that playing golf helped Burns: "Every day, he got better."

The scene at the airport in Honolulu became etched in the political memory of Hawai'i. It occurred in the last days of stair-steps from airplanes onto the tarmac. Tom Gill waited while Burns walked down the steps. Gill offered his hand, but Burns walked past him.

The indelible impression was of a man in a rage. Guided by those closest to him, Burns talked repeatedly with a Catholic priest. "It was more or less catharsis . . .," Oshiro would say, "to get it all out of his system." More than half of the campaign period for the general election elapsed without Burns campaigning. Only in the closing days did he revive sufficiently for the Democratic Party to patch together a coordinated effort, at which point he and Gill barely warded off a weak Republican ticket.

That Burns could survive such mistakes said something about the underlying strength of his political base. That his extraordinary behavior could be interpreted by Oshiro and Brown as Burns being Burns—as Burns doing whatever he thought was right—was a reflection of the way Burns so deeply gripped the feelings and imaginations of people who knew him well, and the way he would—within a few years—come to be regarded as all but godlike. In conversation, the historian Gavan Daws[18] would ask rhetorically if Jack Burns was a great man of history. Although Daws thought of Burns as flawed, he had an answer: Yes.

While Burns' behavior in 1966 might be dismissed as an aberration, it reveals the extent to which society in Hawai'i lived in a realm beyond conventional politics. This was not to be understood by stirring the American stew known as the Democratic Party, but a story about the time the ruling chief fell ill. His plan for succession was thwarted by an ambitious younger chief who was not in his favor. For many days thereafter, the ruling chief did not go abroad in the land.

IN THE 1968 ELECTION, a second major disturbance occurred when the Republican mayor of the city and county of Honolulu (O'ahu), Neal S.

Blaisdell, retired after sixteen years as mayor. Blaisdell was a charming part-Hawaiian man who was originally a noted athlete and coach. In 1941, as the roof was trembling over the Japanese community, a youthful Blaisdell took over as coach of one of the best Japanese baseball teams, the Asahi. The new general manager was the police captain John Burns. For the duration of the war, their team was known as the Athletics. Despite belonging to different political parties, Burns and Blaisdell got along well.

Blaisdell was succeeded by a nominal Democrat, Frank F. Fasi, who had been running for mayor throughout Blaisdell's long tenure. Fasi was the proud offspring of Carmelo Fasi of Hartford, Connecticut. He had come to Hawai'i as a marine during the war, stayed on, and made money in the salvage business. With less than kindly intent, some people liked to refer to Fasi as a junk dealer. He was sensitive to being treated as an outsider. Campaigning, he would tell people that if they could open up his chest, they would read an inscription on his heart: "Made in Hawai'i."

When Frank Fasi won the 1968 Democratic primary, Carmelo Fasi and his wife came to visit him. At a milling-about political gathering at the Japanese Chamber of Commerce, Frank Fasi was called away to talk with a group of politicians in the low light on the far side of the hall. Carmelo Fasi could not resist an indulgence in sentiment toward those whom he imagined had kept his son out in the political cold all this time. He raised his arms in a universal gesture, right arm up, left arm intersecting. To no one in particular, about no one in particular, he said, "To hell with the sons of bitches."[19]

In the same election, Walter Heen moved from the state senate to a seat on the city council, where he and Fasi almost instantly clashed. Although Heen had been closer to Gill than to Burns, Heen was repeatedly invited to breakfast with Burns at Washington Place, and there in the kitchen they engaged in increasingly candid conversations. Reference points were all-important: In their character typing, there were those who understood and cared about the unique experience of Hawai'i's people, those who cared but did not wholly understand, and those who neither cared nor understood.

With statehood and a booming economy, the population of newcomers from the mainland was rising rapidly. The political center of gravity was increasingly being influenced by those with little or no information on the historical background of political events in Hawai'i. Stylistically, Burns set the tone for the island politician who talked in great depth with people at close range but minimally with the mass media. Such a style was being challenged by politicians who were less personally connected but were more adept at communicating through the media. Gill was snapping at Burns, and Fasi was a great practitioner of media-based theater, and then there was a third person who at that time was merely a multimillionaire broadcaster who oozed ambition and bristled with opinion, Cec Heftel.

Burns and Heen more or less agreed on the varying qualities of these three persons, all of whom aspired to be governor. Gill knew a great deal about Hawai'i. He was undeniably caring and brainy but had a deadly defect: He was arrogant in a way that suggested superiority; he liked people mainly in the abstract. Fasi was frightening because (here Heen lent his firsthand testimony from City Hall), "It was impossible to deal with him. You could never tell his direction from one moment to the next." And Heftel? Heen remarked, "He's worse than Frank." Burns slapped the breakfast table. "You're right," he exclaimed.[20]

Burns had recovered from his precipitous decline of 1966. It was the Burns of slates, the Burns who was determined above all to empower the AJAs, the Hawaiians, and more generally anyone who shared his intense devotion to racial and ethnic equality. What else could matter so much? Certainly not the fact that Gill, Fasi, and even Heftel were all Democrats in good standing. Who understood Hawai'i's story? Who really cared how much the people of Hawai'i had suffered?

Gill was obviously planning to run for governor against Burns in 1970. Burns asked Heen to consider running for lieutenant governor as his supporter. On the desirability of Heen as a running mate, both Gill and Burns agreed, as Gill would later ask Heen the same thing. If Heen were to become lieutenant governor, he might then become the first elected native Hawaiian governor and the first nonwhite governor of an American state. Although opposition to Burns was practically part of Heen's political birthright, he experienced Burns as "constantly reaching out." Nonetheless he had been a friend of Gill's a long time. He was tired of being caught in the middle between two people he once referred to irreverently as God and Jesus Christ. After he declined Burns' request, Burns turned to another candidate for lieutenant governor, with results that reached far into the future.

For deeply rooted reasons, Japanese Americans supported statehood more actively than any other group.

Initially, the unique identity of native Hawaiians seemed to be further obscured by statehood.

This photo gives a rare glimpse into the interest level of 1954. Courtesy of Hawai'i Archives

After repeated and bitter infighting, John Burns became the leader of the dominant faction of the Democratic Party.

The young congressman Daniel K. Inouye greets President Kennedy and Vice President Johnson. Courtesy of Hawai'i Archives

President John F. Kennedy and Governor John A. Burns in Honolulu.
Courtesy of Hawai'i Archives

The Burns consensus included the ILWU in the person of Jack Hall (left) and Republican stalwarts such as U.S. Senator Hiram L. Fong (right). Courtesy of The Honolulu Advertiser

State Senator Nadao Yoshinaga translated ILWU power into far-reaching social legislation.

Clashes between Burns and Thomas P. Gill (left) recurred from 1952 to 1970. Courtesy of The Honolulu Advertiser

Gill's programmatic and intellectual liberalism made a mark on the politics of Hawai'i for several decades. Courtesy of The Honolulu Advertiser

Frank F. Fasi in one of his early campaigns for mayor of Honolulu. Courtesy of The Honolulu Star-Bulletin

Chapter 9

In the Middle

While George Ariyoshi's story is distinctly a nisei story, it is a reminder of the many variations on its themes.[1] Neither Ariyoshi nor his family experienced plantation life. He came of age as World War II was ending. Although he was influenced by the war, its effect on him was less direct than on people a few years older. After living in various places around Oʻahu, the Ariyoshi family moved into Chinatown when young George was entering the second grade. There he was enrolled at Robello School in Pālama and also at a nearby Japanese language school, the Pālama Nihongo Gakuen. On his first day at Robello School, he was confronted by the class bully, who grabbed him by the shirt. George struck back. Thereafter, on his way home from language school, he was periodically in fights. To change the pattern of his day, his parents transferred him to the Japanese language school of the original Hongwanji Buddhist Mission on upper Fort Street. Ariyoshi's father also enrolled young George in judo. He trained for three years but to his puzzlement, his father never allowed him to enter competition. He went to class only to learn the discipline and psychology of judo. He learned how to use the force and weight of his opponent and how to fall lightly by relaxing and rolling. Papa Ariyoshi told George he was not in judo class to compete, but to learn the inner peace that came with knowing he could defend himself if necessary.

By almost any description except his own, the Ariyoshi's place in Chinatown was a tenement house. People walked through a shared outside hallway to a shared kitchen and a shared bath. In two rooms, overlooking the corner of Smith and Pauahi Streets, George Ariyoshi and his mother, father, brother, and four sisters lived, ate, and slept. They brought their futons out at night and put them away in the morning. Nonetheless, what Ariyoshi would remember was not the cramped quarters or the communal kitchen, but the enveloping security of his family, the immediacy of his father, and the unceasingly pleasant company of his mother.

Ariyoshi's father, Ryozo, had completed the third grade in a village in Fukuoka Prefecture on the island of Kyushu in southwestern Japan. As a boy he had gone to sea, and when he was nineteen his ship docked in Honolulu Harbor. Once ashore, he decided to disappear into the Japanese community and in so doing became an illegal alien resident of an American territory. He lived with the possibility of being picked up and deported, but he did not allow his status as an illegal alien to dampen his zest for living. He participated prominently in sumo, which was a popular sport before the wartime suppression of Japanese culture. He was a skilled stevedore, a stone mason, and a dynamite blaster in the stone quarries.

Ryozo Ariyoshi worked on the waterfront at a time when the longshoremen's union was just trying to organize. Men sometimes fought over who would be selected to work. Passersby were hijacked for loose change. Young George would go down to Pier 16 to check whether his father's crew had been called for work. Formally the work crew was designated as Gang Number Three and informally as Sylvester's Gang. Around the pier George heard it said that a person looking for trouble should avoid Sylvester's Gang, and in particular avoid his father. Ryozo had thrown stevedores much bigger than himself off the docks into the water.

George was the number one child and the number one son. He would remember his mother, Mitsue, as often praising and never criticizing. At four-thirty each morning, she rose to cook in the communal kitchen. When she fixed the children's favorite foods, she would pretend to not be hungry, leaving them more to eat. When he went out to play, he told her where he was going. If he decided to play somewhere else, he reported back to her with his new location.

Mitsue recited prayers each day of her life thanking God for her family and friends, who she would list at length by name. She made people feel good. A family friend called her "the thank-you lady" because she always made the rounds to acknowledge those who helped her son.

TEACHERS WATCHED ARIYOSHI with anticipation. At Central Intermediate School, which was three blocks from Smith and Pauahi, one of the teachers assessed George along with a boy who had the same initials and who would be his lifelong friend, George Akita. The teacher predicted that the outgoing Akita would become a politician (he instead became a historian), while the introspective young Ariyoshi would grow up to be a professor. Young Ariyoshi first thought of himself as a potential journalist. Prompted by his eighth grade teacher to visit the attorney Arthur Trask of the famous Trask clan, he was told that attorneys helped people in trouble. Thereafter he was an attorney in the making. He announced his plan to his father, who replied in Japanese: *Hadaka ni nattemo*. It meant that Ryozo would give the shirt from his back to see that his son had the education he wanted.

Although nisei stories of growing up in the Territory of Hawai'i are typically about second-rate opportunities, they are often about first-rate teachers. Ariyoshi's stories suggest a period in which teachers devoted their time and effort unreservedly, and the transforming power of education was of utmost importance.

The most revered of all his teachers was Margaret Hamada, who hovered over Ariyoshi for parts of all three of his years at Central Intermediate School. She guided him while he worked on the school newspaper, and she sent him to see Arthur Trask. She observed that when he spoke, he lisped. Sometimes he became so intent on forming words that he would lose his train of thought. If he did not overcome his speech problem, he could never be a lawyer. Mrs. Hamada directed him to come to her class on weekends. She would begin these sessions by engaging him in a few classroom chores. Now, she would say, let us read. Aloud. He made great improvement. At Central Intermediate he participated in a mock court. When he moved on to McKinley High School he won a place on the debate team. Mrs. Hamada was sometimes in the audience, remarking on how well he was doing.

On the morning of December 7, Ariyoshi returned home from Buddhist temple to find his mother had packed a bag for each family member, in case they were abruptly uprooted. Soon thereafter his family was designated as among the Japanese living too close to a strategically important facility, in this instance Honolulu Harbor. They were forced to move.

The Japanese word for adversity—for an accumulation of difficulties— is *kurō*. In traditional Japanese culture, the proper response is to push on. Ariyoshi liked their two-room tenement in Chinatown, but he also enjoyed a new life with his cousin, in the freer, greener environment of upland Mānoa Valley.

Although sheltered by his family, Ariyoshi was not sheltered from hard work. At fifteen, he joined work gangs to clear a defensive field of fire along O'ahu's coastlines in the event of a Japanese invasion. Thereafter he was among the student laborers who were virtually conscripted under martial law to work in the sugar and pineapple fields. The summer he was seventeen he stacked cans in a pineapple cannery, and the following summer he was a cannery timekeeper, a hint of the ability people saw in him even at a young age.

As he grew up, his cultural influences became more diverse. He participated in both the Young Buddhist Association and the Young Men's

Christian Association. McKinley High was derided as Tokyo High, but it offered both intellectual stimulation and a challenging tradition. Its reputation had been enlarged by the class of 1924, which produced the brilliant Masaji Marumoto, the entrepreneur Chinn Ho, Hiram L. Fong, who would become a United States Senator, and also many of the members of the 100th Battalion and the 442nd Regimental Combat Team, including Daniel Inouye.

At McKinley, Ariyoshi caught a glimpse of the school's famous principal, Miles Carey, an impassioned progressive who was caught up in John Dewey's vision of human potential. Carey made Ariyoshi feel good simply by asking, "How are you *today?*" Not unlike Ariyoshi's parents, Carey created a sense that each day was a great day. America might be at war, but life was good. In Ariyoshi's sophomore year, Carey left his school to live at Poston Detention Center in the Arizona desert, where he organized classes for Japanese children who were interned.

In addition to working on the school newspaper and participating in debate, Ariyoshi was president of the senior class, following in Marumoto's footsteps. As a young teenager Ariyoshi was rail thin, with thick black hair that he combed back in a modest pompadour. He had strong, even teeth and smiled readily. After graduation, he enrolled at the University of Hawai'i and waited to be drafted.

Perhaps because he had been senior class president at the mostly AJA high school, he was the youngest person to be invited to the Emergency Service Committee conference in January 1945 to discuss the future of Japanese Americans. While Ariyoshi would remember only the drift of the day's dialogue, he remembered the people vividly. Stanley Miyamoto—who discussed liquidation of the Japanese language schools—was married to the Central Intermediate teacher who had predicted he would become a professor. Robert Murakami—who cautioned against Japanese Americans taking a public position on starting a multiracial organization—was one of Ariyoshi's career role models, being one of the few AJA attorneys in Honolulu. Mits Kido had coached his friend George Akita in speech at Farrington High. Best known to Ariyoshi was the charismatic Shigeo Yoshida, who had talked about "eliminating all vestiges of alien influences" inconsistent with American ideas. Young George Ariyoshi regarded Yoshida as the best speaker in the Japanese community and, in addition, Yoshida's brother was a good friend of Ryozo Ariyoshi.

Reviewing the notes of the conference many years later, Ariyoshi was careful to acknowledge that the speakers were under immense pressure, but nonetheless he was not in agreement with the drift of their thinking. Yes, he wanted to be a good American. Yes, the Japanese community had to avoid criticism. Undeniably it had to go to extraordinary lengths to get through the war. But no, the Japanese community should not give up its cultural identity in the process. Japanese Americans should not try to change completely, but should be themselves and contribute to the building of a community by being themselves. It was one of the essential themes of Ariyoshi's life.

DRAFTED IN THE CLOSING DAYS of the war, Ariyoshi was assigned to the Military Intelligence Service Language School at Fort Snelling, Minnesota. In the early days of the American occupation of Japan he was shipped to Tokyo. There, in the ruins of the great city, hungry children hung around U.S. Army headquarters hoping to shine a pair of shoes. In what for him must have been a struggle of conscience, Ariyoshi smuggled a peanut butter and jelly sandwich out of the cafeteria in violation of army regulations, giving it to a destitute seven-year-old boy. All his life he remembered that the boy took the sandwich home to his three-year-old sister.

Where most of the prominent nisei political figures had participated in battle, Ariyoshi had not. Where most had seen Europe, he had seen the homeland of his parents and reflected on its devastation. By the time Ariyoshi returned to Hawai'i, the University of Hawai'i campus was alive with war veterans. People hovered around Dan Inouye. The camaraderie was intense, and so was the sense of celebration. Ariyoshi recoiled from the atmosphere of drinking and partying. Although handsome and athletic, he was not one of the boys. Partying might divert him from the goals that he had been carefully defining since grade school.

He left Hawai'i precipitously, thinking he would attend the University of Michigan at Ann Arbor. He arrived to find that enrollment had closed. From there he went to East Lansing, Michigan, where he was accepted at Michigan State. On graduation, he returned to the University of Michigan and earned a law degree. As always, he came straight home.

For the first time in seven years, he spent considerable time with his father in 1952 and 1953. The sumo wrestlers of his father's youth had formed an association called Sumo Kyokai, but his father thought they spent too much time reminiscing. He wanted them to develop young sumo wrestlers. He also argued for opening up sumo to other racial groups. Since sumo was then an exclusively Japanese sport dating to the eighth century A.D., the senior Ariyoshi was taking an unconventional position.

Like few other institutions, sumo was at the heart of traditional Japanese culture. Ryozo Ariyoshi decided that Hawai'i needed a new sumo association, which he called the Rikishi Club. The center of the club would be a sumo ring, a *dohyo*, which consists of a clay mound encircled by a giant rope, four poles decorated by spiraling red ribbons, and a pagoda-shaped roof. A Japanese temple in Nu'uanu Valley agreed to provide space. Young George Ariyoshi not only drew up the papers for the club but worked alongside his father in the construction of the *dohyo*. With a new place to train, Ryozo Ariyoshi brought together some of the old crowd of wrestlers and tutored a new, multiracial generation in sumo.

The year 1952 was the year the immigration and naturalization law was amended by the McCarran-Walter Act. Part of the stimulus for this historic change was the heroism of the AJAs in battle. While the 1952 law was still weighted in favor of white European immigration, it allowed the original Asian immigrants—who for so long had been denied U.S. citizenship—to become naturalized citizens. A less well-known provision allowed people who had been residents continuously since 1924 (the year of the Japanese Exclusion Act) to become permanent residents—regardless of how they had gotten into the country. In one of Ariyoshi's first acts as an attorney, he filed residency papers on his father's behalf. For the first time since Ryozo had jumped ship in 1919, he was a legal resident.

Financial opportunities for young Japanese American lawyers in Hawai'i were so limited that Ariyoshi proposed to a particular Caucasian that he initially work for free. He started on a small salary. Slowly he sensed a ceiling above him, based on kinship and privilege, beyond which he was not likely to rise. This perception—which would be stated and restated as his connecting link to John Burns, to the Democratic Party, and to his original campaign for public office—was mainly remarkable for how temperately he stated the issue. In telling this story, Ariyoshi was always careful to say that this system of prejudice applied to whites who were not connected to the elite as well as to nonwhites.

In contrast to Burns' talk about ending the rule of the hegemony, Ariyoshi's description of an invisible ceiling lacked color, but its careful wording reflected Ariyoshi's earnest belief that it was a definable problem for which a solution was possible. In broad terms, the intense belief of the nisei of Hawai'i in the democratic ideal was pervasive and overwhelming. So far as Ariyoshi can be relocated as the young man just returned from law school, what stands out is his mixture of determination and optimism. Although society gave him little reason to feel secure, he enjoyed an inner security that would show itself again and again. As if he had escaped the scars of the war, he hewed to the prewar conception that had been developed by such figures as Tasuku Harada, when he taught that nisei could embody the best of both worlds. Ariyoshi was comfortable being both American *and* Japanese. He did not merely pay respect to his immigrant parents but stayed close to them and supported their cultural activities. He spoke the Japanese language. He discussed values in Japanese as well as American terms.

He also balked at the idea of dismantling the Japanese culture and its institutions. As the racial climate improved, a move was made to close down the ethnic chambers of commerce, including the Japanese Chamber of Commerce, and merge them into a single chamber of business. Ariyoshi disagreed.

After the war, Ariyoshi was away from Hawai'i during the events that divided people: the sugar strike of 1946, the dock strike of 1949, and the worst of the anticommunist crusade. He was fresh, energetic, well dressed, tall, photogenic, and in the terms of the time only modestly frustrated by the continued influence of the wealthy haole.

THE BURNS-ARIYOSHI CONNECTION

Less than five weeks before the 1954 primary election, Ariyoshi was invited by a friend named Tom Ebesu to a Democratic Party meeting at the Nu'uanu YMCA, which nine years earlier had housed the Emergency Service Committee. Ebesu said they would be meeting his friend Burns, chairman of the Democratic Party. Burns wanted people to talk. How did they feel about life in Hawai'i? Was everyone being treated fairly?

Ariyoshi responded by saying that after returning from law school he realized Hawai'i was being run by a closed circle of privileged people. Ariyoshi said if you were not part of that circle your chances for advancement were limited. Burns replied that if he felt that way he should do something about it and run for the legislature. Ariyoshi thought Burns surely could not be talking about him. He had been out of school only two years. He turned around to see if Burns was speaking to someone sitting behind him, but there was no one there.

Ebesu grabbed onto Burns' proposition. He was one of the manager and organizer types who in the early days of the party were nearly as important as the candidates themselves. He had played a role in the 1952 City Council election of Matsuo Takabuki, the first member of the 442nd Regimental Combat Team to win a public election. Ebesu and Ariyoshi were nearly the same age, and Ebesu knew Ariyoshi well enough to talk freely with him.

Ebesu lived in Kalihi near Burns' mother's house. He often would pick Burns up and drive him around, and in the process they engaged in long talks. Years later he would tell his daughter, Sandy Ebesu, that he particularly respected Burns because he had risked his reputation in the early war years on behalf of the Japanese community. Given Ebesu's close acquaintance with Burns, it is conceivable that he had told Burns about Ariyoshi before the meeting, and that in a modest way they were conspiring to bring in a new recruit.

The next day Ebesu picked up nomination papers and engaged Ariyoshi in a long conversation over a plate lunch in Ala Moana Park, next to the ocean. It was only two days until the deadline for filing the papers that would put Ariyoshi's name on the ballot. The primary election itself was only a month away, resulting in an extremely short campaign period. The two talked for hours about the Hawai'i of their youth and the kind of place they wanted for their families. Ariyoshi then consulted his mother and father, who gave their blessing and pledged their support. Ariyoshi was running for public office, with little notion of how to win.

A GOOD FIRST-TIME POLITICAL CAMPAIGN is a friends and family affair, which Ariyoshi's was. His parents went door to door daily. Ryozo spoke in English about "my boy, my boy." Mitsue thanked everyone. Friends coalesced, reflecting the untapped political potential of the previously inactive. James Takushi, who was to figure repeatedly in Ariyoshi's career, was attending the University of Hawai'i that year. Takushi was from a large family in the neighborhood. His father was Kamada Takushi, who had emigrated from Okinawa and had first worked at Kohala Plantation on the Big Island. On the plantation Kamada Takushi had distilled home-made *okolehao* whiskey, then moved to Honolulu and made tofu. When the Aloha Soda Water Company went up for sale, he saw a way to make money by brewing and bottling legal stuff. His orange drink was a big seller.

Kamada Takushi pried bottle caps off with his teeth, taught his five sons to box, and maintained a friendship with Ryozo Ariyoshi. James Takushi grew up knowing Ryozo Ariyoshi as a former sumo. By then Ryozo had a dry-cleaning business and came around the Aloha Soda Water Company in his truck. Everyone lived in the neighborhood just above Chinatown. The Takushis—along with their bottling operation—lived at the corner of Kukui Street and College Walk, where the Izumo Taisha (Shinto) temple stands today. By this time Jack Kawano, destroyed as a union organizer by the anti-communist crusade, was running a liquor store on the same street. The most visible Democratic Party worker was "Dynamite" Takushi (no relation to James), who would effusively inquire of an acquaintance, "And how are you, my handsome gentleman?" James Takushi's brother Tetsuo, who became a doctor, had been in George's class at Central Intermediate. Already James Takushi had signed a Democratic Party card, inspired at the university by the civil libertarian Alan Saunders, and soon James was out walking door to door with Ryozo Ariyoshi handing out campaign literature. After a day of canvassing, Ryozo would announce, "Okay, Jimmy, my son no drink, so let's have a beer."

A picture of George Ariyoshi with his friends survives as an artifact of 1954. All are of Asian descent, a blending of graduates from the two inner-city public high schools, McKinley and Farrington. Ariyoshi sits in the foreground, next to Tom Ebesu. Ariyoshi believed his campaign group was one of the largest to spring up that year. Its size and vibrancy would eventually explain in part why he could be independent of the labor unions and, on notable occasion, independent of the Democratic Party as well.

AN INDEPENDENT DEMOCRAT

Just as Hawai'i society was divided into two tiers, O'ahu was divided into two House districts. Although these districts have since been repeatedly subdivided, the shadow of their political and demographic traits remains. The old Fourth District was East O'ahu, a bastion of the Republican Party. The old Fifth District was West O'ahu—Ariyoshi's district. It was heavily Japanese, as well as Chinese, Korean, Hawaiian, and Filipino. It was the district in which Mitsuyuki Kido had won in 1946 as proof of the viability of a new Democratic Party.

The old Fifth District was a multimember district with six candidates to be nominated. To win, a candidate had to reach the inner city above Honolulu Harbor, as well as the immigrant-packed Kalihi and Pālama neighborhoods and, not far beyond, the sugar and pineapple plantation camps of West O'ahu, which reached up between O'ahu's two mountainous spines to the North Shore. From there the sugar fields reached down the coastline past the northern tip of the island, Kahuku Point. The district continued through Waiāhole and Waikāne, where Hawaiians still grew taro, past the piggeries and pineapple farms of Kahalu'u (an Okinawan enclave), to Kāne'ohe, which was a small country town. Cows and horses grazed on their tethers. The candidate had to reach out to dock workers, cannery workers, plantation workers, small farmers, and native Hawaiians who clung to a semblance of their land-based lifestyle by retreating into the countryside. The population of Ariyoshi's Fifth District was comparable in size to the privileged Fourth, but it spread across several times as much space.

One of the ironies of Ariyoshi's political success was that he was immensely shy. To understand how he could still succeed requires setting aside stereotypes of the American politician. James Takushi watched as Ariyoshi greeted people, then searched for something to say. He became convinced that people actually liked Ariyoshi not in spite of his shyness but because of it. He spoke better, dressed better, and was better educated than the mass of his constituents. But in a culture where the great majority of people had struggled for a web of reasons having to do with ethnicity, a limited grasp of English, or the nature of their work, Ariyoshi had a special appeal. He was reticent to put himself forward, but he put himself forward. Where other candidates adapted to the political scene with extravagant eloquence, Ariyoshi was subdued and perpetually courteous. In the primary election, Ariyoshi ran fourth. Given the short period of the campaign, he made a strong showing.

WHAT ARIYOSHI WOULD REMEMBER most vividly about the general election campaign was his brush with the ILWU, when the ILWU insisted that all the Democratic candidates pool their resources into a single piece of campaign literature. Ariyoshi objected. The union pressed. He dug in. Ryozo counseled him to resist the pressure and redouble his individual efforts.

Far from being about inconsequential bickering, Ariyoshi's vignette touched a fundamental nerve center in Hawai'i's political development. By organizing and politicizing workers, the ILWU had paved the way for the Democratic Party, but it possessed a streak that was nearly dictatorial. Guided by a radical understanding of Hawai'i's stratified society, the union sometimes behaved as if elections were not a celebration of democracy but a conceit of the upwardly mobile bourgeoisie. Lawrence Fuchs' description still rings true: The ILWU picked candidates based on "their willingness to recognize ILWU power at the polls, to make deals based on that power, and to live up to them."[2] They often preferred conservatives who were willing to make deals on specific legislation and stick to them:

> The only group of politicians despised at union headquarters were the so-called independents in each major party, who, because of a liberal, pro-labor record, believed they were entitled to union support without being obliged to take 'advice' from the ILWU. . . . The Democratic independents, especially, came in for abuse. Who were they to masquerade as liberals when it was union power that had so diluted the power of the oligarchy in Hawai'i?[3]

Despite his snubbing of the union, Ariyoshi ran away with a House seat, finishing third in the race for six seats. Those who failed to be re-elected included the Republican entrepreneur Hiram L. Fong, as well as the usually popular Republican Yasutaka Fukushima. The fact that Ariyoshi started out as an independent Democrat in politics, and that he remained an independent force in politics, flies in the face of the often-repeated assertion that he was a creation of Hawai'i's Democratic machine.

RECONNECTING WITH BURNS

By the time George Ariyoshi was approached to run with John Burns for lieutenant governor in 1970, he was forty-six years old. He had a successful law practice. He and his family lived in a nice house in Nuʻuanu valley above Honolulu. He had invested in condominium apartments and dabbled in development. His three children were in private school and approaching college, which meant that the greatest demands on his earning power were also approaching. He was thinking of running for one more term of office, then retiring from politics.

After Masaji Marumoto was asked in 1961 to be a director of Bank of Hawaiʻi, Ariyoshi was asked in 1963 to be a director of First Hawaiian Bank. These were Hawaiʻi's two largest banks, both institutions of the oligarchy. Ariyoshi had agonized over being both a bank director and a Democrat, but decided that to accept would further the opening up of society. Thereafter he also became a director of the Honolulu Gas Company.

In this sense Ariyoshi's résumé set him squarely in the conservative wing of the Democratic Party, but—as he was to demonstrate—he was not easily categorized. During Bill Quinn's tenure as governor in 1961, Quinn had nominated a prominent Republican, Samuel P. King Jr., for judge. Several Republican senators wavered on King's confirmation, which meant that the Democrats had enough votes to block it. This had created an opportunity to embarrass the opposition.

Behind the closed doors of the Democratic caucus, Ariyoshi asked whether King would make a good judge. The answer was yes. If that was so, he said, then the Democratic Party was opposing King merely because he was a Republican. Ariyoshi recalled his original reason for running: Beyond a certain level, opportunity was reserved to people with friends in high places. "Now," Ariyoshi argued, "we're going to say that Sam King shouldn't be a judge simply because he is not our friend, and we're going to hold up his nomination."[4] To this he added a line that he would eventually recite to his protégés many times:

> *It is so easy to stand up for principle when the principle works in our favor, but we've got to stand for principle when it's not working in our favor.*

With Ariyoshi's vote, King became a judge. Thereafter, the 1963 session of the legislature further established Ariyoshi as a person who went his own way. This was the first legislative session with Burns as governor and both houses solidly Democratic. Ariyoshi was thirty-six and in his ninth year in office. He was elected to chair the Senate Ways and Means Committee, one of the several most influential positions in the legislature, since it addresses the state budget.

With Democratic office-holders having promised so much to their constituents, Ariyoshi made a careful analysis of the state's finances. In response to a variety of spending proposals that exceeded the budget proposed by Burns, Ariyoshi said no. One of the most compelling people he turned down was then-senator Patsy Takemoto Mink, who wanted to exceed Burns' already increased education budget. Mink, soon to be Congresswoman Mink, responded by walking out of Ariyoshi's committee. She was followed by Nadao Yoshinaga, a brilliant but temperamental legislator who was the ILWU's key actor in the Senate. One of Yoshinaga's friends, John Ushijima, also walked out, leaving Ariyoshi in danger of being a finance chairman without a quorum to move the budget bill out of committee.

For those who mistakenly saw the Democratic Party as a matter of AJAs supporting one another, the incident was interesting. While three AJAs had walked out of the committee, Ariyoshi's work as chairman was salvaged by the support of a part-Hawaiian Democrat, Harry Fields; Democrat Benjamin Menor, of Filipino ancestry; and an archetypal haole Republican, Randolph Crossley. It underscored the essentially centrist nature of what was romantically thought of as the Democratic revolution. Further, it was the beginning of Ariyoshi's identity as a prudent fiscal manager. It put him in harmony with Burns in the face of pressures from ILWU-aligned Democrats to spend money more freely.

His image as a conservative Democrat was further solidified during the 1963 session by his position on land reform, an issue that had taken on a life of its own with Burns' election. Aroused by the Democratic hold on both the legislature and the governor's office, supporters of land reform revived their campaign to transform the leasehold land under home sites to fee simple ownership. Patterned in some ways after Maryland's attempts to change its long-time, plantation-inspired land tenure patterns, the proposal became known as the Maryland bill.

With votes in the Senate split evenly, Ariyoshi voted no, and the bill died. He received a telephone call from Burns, who said that Ariyoshi's vote in opposition had saved him the politically onerous task of vetoing the bill. Otherwise Ariyoshi was heaped with abuse and outrage. In my own perception as a political reporter, nothing so contributed to isolating Ariyoshi prior to 1970 as did his vote on the Maryland Land Bill. He was perpetually blamed for its failure and never credited for his subsequent work in developing an alternative.

His isolation became nearly complete as the result of the bitter and widely reported factional feud that ensued from Tom Gill's rift with Burns in 1966.

One side of the Senate Democratic caucus was led by Nelson Doi, the other by Nadao Yoshinaga. If Ariyoshi had gone along with one side or the other, he could have been president of the Senate. Instead he had clung to a lofty position of insisting that the two factions negotiate a compromise based on a genuine sharing of power. When the two sides finally struck a deal without him, he was shunned. His influence in the 1968 session was nil. While the combatants raged, he sat near the back of the chamber next to the clock, infinitely patient and courteous, a study in serenity.

He did not seem to be a real politician. He did not run on adrenaline, stay out late at night, or speak loudly. He was not self-important. He was not pushing for anything. He was pleasant, polite, well groomed, and relatively Asian in manners and mannerisms. The warriors of the Capitol held him in a certain contempt. The harshest criticisms reconstructed his history to prove that he was not really a Democrat: He wasn't friendly to the unions. He had screwed up the Democratic caucus by voting to confirm Sam King's judgeship. He had held hands with the Republicans on the first budget bill, then sunk the Maryland bill. He was the director of two corporations. In the litany, he was what was going wrong with the Democratic Party.

In a regrouping of the Senate for the 1969 and 1970 sessions, Ariyoshi re-emerged as majority floor leader, a kind of legislative management job of coordinating the passage or rejection of legislation after it leaves committee. Since it has to do with floor action, it lends itself to generating a certain amount of publicity, but Ariyoshi played his role in such a low-keyed way that the impact on his modest political stock was negligible.

His role in the 1970 gubernatorial election therefore came as a surprise, even to himself. James Takushi, who was by then in Burns' cabinet, was as close to Ariyoshi as anyone. He went to a meeting at Ariyoshi's house in which he proposed that Ariyoshi run for lieutenant governor. Ariyoshi said no, that even then, in the late sixties, the public was probably not ready for a lieutenant governor of Japanese ancestry.[5]

Thereafter Takushi went along with Ariyoshi to a meeting initiated by the ILWU's chief lobbyist, Eddie DeMello, who was known in political circles for being tight-lipped, shrewd, and tough. In Ariyoshi's account, two others were involved. One was Nelson Prather, a public relations person for the sugar industry. The fact that he and DeMello worked together would have been no surprise, because in dealing with government the sugar industry and the union had become frequent bedfellows. The third person was the highly respected Bert Kobayashi Sr., who had been Ariyoshi's law partner and was now attorney general of Hawai'i. Had he wished, Kobayashi could have run with Burns for lieutenant governor, but he had passed up the opportunity. DeMello, Prather, and Kobayashi proposed that Ariyoshi run for lieutenant governor. Ariyoshi asked for Burns' position. They said Burns wanted him and to expect a telephone call. Within hours, Burns was on the telephone asking for a meeting. He told Ariyoshi that he had in mind not only 1970, but who would become governor in 1974. Ariyoshi struggled with the idea, then agreed.

WHY BURNS NEEDED ARIYOSHI

It is now a largely forgotten fact in Hawai'i that by the time Tom Gill ran for governor against Burns in 1970, Burns seemed to be a waning force. Tom Gill operated from a well-developed political base within the Democratic Party (much more so than did Frank Fasi, who was largely a media phenomenon). Gill was the centerpiece of a coalition of urban trade unionists, university-based liberals, a variety of old-line Democrats including the Heen family, and a new generation of political activists for whom the catalyzing experiences of World War II were merely history.

Although Gill came wrapped in the armor of public issues, he approached power with a certainty of purpose, in much the way that Burns and his people approached power. Why did the ILWU oppose him? Tom Gill said it was because he would make Eddie DeMello come through the front door of the governor's office rather than up the back stairs. Gill always wanted to sit where Burns sat, first in the Democratic Party, and then in the governorship. Had he played it safe, he could have represented Hawai'i in the congressional delegation indefinitely, but like Burns he believed that what mattered was the governorship. He understood the governorship was the center of gravity in the political culture of Hawai'i, and he was determined to get hold of and move the center. What Burns described as a new consensus, Gill described as a sell-out of the Democratic agenda of social change. The Burns crowd, he contended, had merely wanted in the door, and once they got in they had wallowed in their new connections and new comforts.

Setting aside the judgments, there was an essential description of the terrain to which all accounts referred. After seizing the governorship in 1962, Burns defined a new, moderate center that held the door open to traditional rivals. It was an island solution and also one that resonated with the lessons of Lyndon Johnson in Congress, and even with what Johnson was trying to do as president.

One of Burns' first priorities as governor had been to end the interlocking corporate directorships of the Big Five, which were the contemporary expression of the old oligarchy. Burns' attorney general, Kobayashi, gave the corporations a choice. Would they like to resign their multiple, interlocking directorships, or would they like to engage in a long, costly court battle in which they would almost certainly lose? The historic showdown on the interlocking corporate directorates was settled quickly and quietly.

Burns found common ground with big business. Just as his relations with middle-of-the-road Democrats were good, so too were his relations with Republicans who wanted to find their way into the broad center. In Hitch's description, these were old-time Republicans who "were more politician than they were Republican."[6] A pillar of the Big Five corporations, Malcolm MacNaughton, chief executive officer of Castle and Cooke, told of meeting Burns after Burns was first elected to the governorship. MacNaughton asked Burns if he could dispense with describing the Big Five as "the hegemony." Burns laughed and said he could.[7]

GILL AND THE LIBERAL LEFT

The serious challenges to Burns were no longer from the right but from the left, and most of all from Tom Gill. In his memoir, Matsuo Takabuki would explain the Burns faction as moderate and relatively conservative on fiscal policies:

> *While they were sympathetic to labor, they were also concerned about business, especially small business. Labor would always be given an audience, but the Burns faction was not going to be controlled by them. Tom Gill, however, was more labor-oriented.*[8]

Tom Gill was in many ways a traditional American liberal who was nonetheless a unique derivative of Hawai'i. His mother was a writer and his father an architect. He grew up in a house on the mountainside above Honolulu. Instead of attending Punahou, as his race and class might have indicated, he attended Roosevelt High School. He fought in the Philippines in World War II, where he was wounded, then studied on the Berkeley campus of the University of California. As a young labor lawyer, he shared the goals of the mainstream AFL-CIO unions. His clients prominently included Art Rutledge, who represented the hotel workers and teamsters; Akito "Blackie" Fujikawa, who represented electrical workers; and eventually, with their unionization, the public school teachers.

He founded a law firm, Gill, Doi, Shim, McClung, and Naito, which became a history piece on the reach of labor into the halls of Hawai'i's government. Herman S. Doi helped write the laws of transition from territory to state status, then served as director of the Legislative Reference Bureau and as the first ombudsman of Hawai'i (and the United States as well). Alvin Shim served at strategic moments as House attorney but also stayed on in the law firm and eventually had sixty union clients, large and small, who depended not only on his legal work but on his guidance. David McClung became a member of the House of Representatives, then president of the State Senate. Yukio Naito, while the least known, came to be regarded as the leading thinker of the Office of Legislative Auditor and then of the Public Utilities Commission.

Gill was a late arrival on the Democratic scene in comparison to Burns, or even to Frank Fasi. He nonetheless snatched the chairmanship of the Oʻahu County Committee from Burns' group in 1952, a position Burns himself had held four years earlier. Although he worked as a legislative attorney, he did not run for the House of Representatives until 1959. In 1962 he was elected to the U.S. House. In 1964 he lost a U.S. Senate race to Republican Hiram L. Fong, and thereafter he was appointed by Burns to run the state's Office of Economic Opportunity. There he expanded his base among social workers, low-income people, and native Hawaiians.

In 1966 Gill telephoned Dr. Thomas Ige, an economist at the University of Hawaiʻi, and asked him to serve as manager of his campaign for lieutenant governor. Ige was an even-tempered, congenial man who had served on Inouye's staff in Washington. Put off by Burns' choice of Kenneth F. Brown, Ige agreed to help Gill. When Burns heard what had happened, he telephoned Ige and complained bitterly. Ige replied that they were not opposing him but the unknown newcomer, Brown. Burns refused to soften, insisting that he personally was being challenged. After that exchange, Ige wrote, "I was completely cut off and never had any contact with Burns or his establishment after that time. He never spoke a civil word to me again."[9]

As the winner, Tom Gill enjoyed an image of the upstart against the new establishment, a David against Goliath. Thereafter he crafted a complex set of strategies and positions aimed at ousting Burns from the governorship if Burns insisted on running for a third term. Already Burns had seized on grand themes to create a special role for the state of Hawaiʻi as his imagined "hub of the Great Wheel of the Pacific." Gill created a different set of themes, but they too revolved around what set Hawaiʻi apart as an island state from the continental states.

Gill had grown up in proximity to the watershed preserves above Honolulu and had acquired a lifelong interest in the workings of an island ecosystem. He was aware, for example, that Westerners had set loose goats, pigs, and cattle that had destroyed the upland native forests. With the destruction of the forest, the water supply of Honolulu was threatened, because the function of the forest was to catch rain and cause it to seep into the underground water supply. To its credit, the Republican governments of the Territory had overseen a massive campaign of replanting fast-growing alien species and creating an enormous forest reserve. The forest was an object lesson in how quickly human society could destroy its own resource base on islands, but also how islands could be managed. Foreseeing that Hawai'i would experience great changes in terms of population, growth, and demands made on limited resources, Tom Gill wrote and pushed through the legislature, with singleminded determination, a statewide land zoning law, designating all of the Hawaiian islands to be either conservation, rural, agricultural, or urban. The land use law was designed to protect watersheds, prevent prime agricultural lands from development, and protect environmental, cultural, and historical features and sites. It attracted a variety of supporters, including the sugar and pineapple industries, the ILWU (as protectors of agricultural employment), urban planners, managers of water systems, and the beginnings of an environmental movement.

Remarkably, it became law in 1961, in the first full-blown legislative session after statehood. Almost unnoticed, it added a new increment to the already enormous powers of the governorship. Zoning was assigned to a Land Use Commission, which was appointed by the governor and confirmed by the Senate. Administration of the conservation district was assigned to the State Land Board, which was appointed by the governor and confirmed by the Senate. The zoning powers commonly identified with incorporated municipalities—in this instance, the four city/county governments of O'ahu, Maui, Kaua'i, and Hawai'i—were confined to urban-zoned lands.

Perhaps it was the sort of law that the conqueror King Kamehameha would have liked, but those he defeated, such as Kaumuali'i of Kaua'i and Kahekili of Maui, would not have liked. It was a further centralization of power at a time when the one-time dispersed kingdoms—Hawai'i, Maui, O'ahu, and Kaua'i—now functioning as the Neighbor Island counties—had just been granted zoning powers.

Gill pushed the bill through the legislature as a member of the House, with the support of the Democratic Party. It was a mark of Gill's intellectual conceit that he would boast of not fully explaining it to his fellow Democrats, believing they might then not vote for it. He would ridicule his House colleagues by saying that when he described it as a Green Belt law, some thought it had to do with judo.

Probably because Gill was thought of as the Democrat most eager to expand and use the power of government, the contribution of the Republican Party to the land use law has been obscured. The Land Use Commission came into being with the approval of a Republican majority in the Senate and a Republican governor, William F. Quinn. What Gill had in mind was a more rational approach to land use, with an emphasis on arresting piecemeal urban sprawl and on stopping the environmentally damaging and costly effects of rural subdividing, which was driven not by development but by speculation. In the process the bill created greater security for the tax sheltering of land dedicated to forest watershed preserves and also for agriculture. To the extent that it protected the sugar and pineapple domains of the corporations from higher taxes, it was attractive to Republicans. Seven of the twelve supporting Republican senators were directors of or employed by such interests as Bishop Estate, Damon Estate, C. Brewer, Parker Ranch, First National Bank (later First Hawaiian Bank), and the Hawaiian Telephone Co.[10] The resulting Land Use Commission was appointed by Quinn and approved by the temporarily Republican Senate, and it proceeded to behave in a stereotypically Republican way. It set the temporary district boundaries in a private meeting at the Pacific Club, then formalized its work in a brief public meeting.[11]

Despite these beginnings, the Land Use Commission was widely regarded in Hawai'i as the wave of the future for a more land-conscious America—the answer to urban sprawl and the destruction of rural resources. Arguably it was the most successful effort by the Hawai'i state government to gain effective control over and to manage its resources. It provided a template for additional ideas that, taken together, came to be the new central theme of Hawai'i's body politic: The control of Hawai'i's destiny through the state government.

All the resources Gill could muster—the old law firm, the researchers, the social workers, the occasional liberal economist or socially conscious businessman, the government planners—went into developing and giving credibility to a detailed redesign of island development: A mass transit system for Honolulu, a new energy base (Gill seriously explored nuclear power), a large new revenue source (a hotel room tax), a restructuring of tourism (with an emphasis on upscale travelers), and the creation of a government-sponsored housing market for lower-income island residents.

Gill seethed over lax enforcement of, and exceptions to, the land use law. Since the beginning of statehood, rezonings had accommodated a fifteen-fold increase in tourism, with shocking effects on the landscape. Everything was running out of control. Gill was convinced that Burns in his capacity as governor was adrift in an ill-defined center. Gill talked publicly about erstwhile reformers turning into Babbits, referring to Sinclair Lewis' vapid denizens of *Main Street.* He insisted on referring to Burns as Jack, rather than as Governor. Yet even in his most scathing critiques he could not bring himself to attack Burns directly. Jack, Gill said, in his most famous phrase, was ill-served by "alarming friends."[12]

LEGISLATING THE FUTURE

The incessant tension between these two remarkable people ironically contributed to an outpouring of legislation in 1970 that was to define the future of Hawai'i as a distinct island society. In context of the reaction to a rapidly growing population, abortion of an unborn fetus was made legal—for the first time in America. The legislature supported a variety of planned parenthood and birth-control initiatives. It created a commission on population control.

Environmental controls were enacted that were possibly the most elaborate in the country. These included creation of an office of environmental quality control, strict air pollution standards, an open space plan, a shoreline setback on construction, new controls on water and sewage discharge into the ocean, and a natural area preserve system to protect endangered flora and fauna. The legislature capped off what some saw as an island mania for long-range planning by forming a Commission on the Year 2000. It also took steps to facilitate and fund a sizable, government-directed housing market. The fact that all of this happened in 1970 in Hawai'i, far ahead of the American curve, was the result of Hawai'i being an island state in which population pressures and the limits of resources were conscious concerns.

This body of legislation, which guided Hawai'i into the twenty-first century, resulted from an oddly cooperative effort between supporters of Burns and Gill. It created talking points for Burns' drive for re-election, and it gave Gill the tools he wanted in the event that he should win. If it were possible to untangle the personalities from this record, it might be more objectively seen that Democrats in Hawai'i, across the spectrum, were willing to go to great lengths to use the powers of government to shape island life. In this regard, Hawai'i Democrats were still adding to the power of government even as the public's ardor for government was cooling across the country, a fact punctuated by the 1968 presidential victory of Republican Richard Nixon over the liberal hero of the Democrats, Hubert H. Humphrey.

THE STATE, THE STATE

Around this time a survey researcher, Jim Dannemiller, began several decades of exploring what was on the minds of Hawai'i's voters. The most recurring element of political surveys is to find out what people see as problems and where they look for solutions. Dannemiller came to believe that for almost every problem people in Hawai'i turned for a solution to, in his words, "the state, the state, the state, and the state."[13]

"Hawai'i," he thought, "is going to give up liberalism at the point of a gun."

WHAT ARIYOSHI DID FOR BURNS

The 1970 campaign for Burns' re-election was the first of many million-dollar campaigns. Polling became more sophisticated. Television rose to a new level of importance. It was the beginning of the half-hour campaign film, catching an American trend that would endure in Hawai'i long after it had fizzled elsewhere. All of these trends further aggregated political power in the governor's office. It underscored that what really moved people and interests was who sat in the governor's chair.

The changes of 1970 were ushered in by a network of people who would direct and stage-manage the politics of the governorship for the rest of the century—the advertising executive Jack Seigle, the Washington consultant Joseph Napolitan, and the strategist and manager Robert Oshiro.

The manipulation of information, money, and television were aimed most basically at voters' sense of the past. Although Tom Gill dominated the discussion of policy-making, he was no match for Burns in the evocation of history. Although Gill began the campaign with a wide lead, as the campaign went on a majority of AJA voters migrated back to Burns. This shifting of votes was far from uniform, but it resulted in a substantial majority for Burns. While not an appeal to ethnicity per se, it was an appeal to something more central to nisei culture than to anyone else's—the idea of obligation.

More explicitly than anyone, Ariyoshi struck the themes that revived Burns' base of support. At the dinner launching his campaign for lieutenant governor, Ariyoshi greeted the crowd with a phrase in Japanese: *Okage sama de*. It was widely understood among nisei and would come to be understood by others, but it was remarkable that Ariyoshi would say it aloud. In an environment that had suppressed Japanese culture, the Japanese cultural value of mutual obligation was being stated in the Japanese language: "I am what I am because of you."

Ariyoshi sketched his postwar story: The humble dwelling on Pauahi Street, his parent's willingness to sacrifice for his education, the barriers that divided the elite from the mass. Addressing his children by name, Lynn, Todd, and Donn, he reminded them of how fortunate they were to live in a society where equality of opportunity was a reality, a society "where you can dream." Hawai'i was not always like this.

If any man in Hawai'i is to be given credit for this change, it is your present governor, our dear friend, John A. Burns.[14]

The Ariyoshi who had been contemplating retirement was suddenly engaged. He was saying what he wanted to say. He was being himself by acknowledging his cultural roots and refocusing the Japanese experience in Hawai'i. On the face of it, this was a seemingly uphill battle. He proceeded to do what he had done in 1966: talk in small groups, night after night, fueling the base of people who believed what he was saying or who at the least accepted his sincerity.

As the weeks went on, the competition was less and less about Tom Gill's program and more and more about Burns' person. As if to punctuate this triumph of person over program, Burns narrowed his eyes in his campaign film and said with a sudden ferocity: "Any damn fool can take a stand."

FOLLOWING TRADITION, the Democratic primary campaign closed the night before the election at a public rally in the park by the bay in Hilo. After the rally, Ariyoshi returned to O'ahu with Burns early on election day. As they parted, Burns said he was certain Ariyoshi would win, but that he himself might not. Ariyoshi hurt for him.

Inconclusive polls were being run, but a disproportionate number of AJAs were saying they had not decided. It was a polite way of telling survey researchers to not pry. While many AJAs had given Tom Gill their votes for high office in past elections, it was not for the deeply rooted, emotionally charged reasons that they now continued to support Burns, who won by the substantial margin of 82,000 votes to 69,000.

A history that had been obscured was being retrieved. If someone had helped you in a difficult time, you helped them in a difficult time. It was a history that nisei typically understood but which the haole newcomer usually did not. No longer was there the one big story about Hawai'i's golden people moving confidently toward a shared future, but a more complicated and perplexing story. It was the beginning of an enduring phenomenon of the post-1970 period: Multiple narratives and diverging understanding of what mattered. Different stories were being told to different audiences and being received differently.

In the general election, Burns and Ariyoshi easily defeated a credible Republican ticket of Sam King and a former superintendent of schools, Ralph Kiyosaki. The governorship, which the Republicans had won in 1959, and nearly regained in 1966, now was securely in Democratic hands.

As many have observed about American politics, the Republican Party functions more or less as the party of the status quo, and the Democratic Party as that of change. The Republican Party had failed to capitalize on the deepest of Democratic Party schisms—that resulting from the issue of how far left the party would go through the person of Gill. Thereafter the

Democratic Party of Hawaiʻi was to become an all-encompassing island party, and Hawaiʻi was to become a one-party state. Inexorably, the Democratic Party of Hawaiʻi was to double as both the party of change *and* the party of the status quo. As more and more Republicans ran as Democrats, the Democratic Party became the party of conservatives as well.

THE EMBLEM OF the one-party state became the hyphenated Burns-Ariyoshi relationship. In keeping with his concern for succession, Burns devoted a large amount of time to giving Ariyoshi first-hand exposure to the problems of being governor. Burns often would invite Ariyoshi to his office in late morning. Ariyoshi participated in Burns' office meetings and chaired cabinet meetings. From their late-morning starting time, they would work through the day and often eat dinner together at Washington Place. Sometimes they would talk into the night.[15] They engaged in a level of collaboration that was unprecedented and is unlikely ever to be approached again.

In the spring of 1973 Burns confided that something was wrong with his health. More and more, Ariyoshi crossed the fifth floor of the capitol not to learn about the governorship but to assume its responsibilities. One day, Burns reversed the pattern, walking into Ariyoshi's office. His erect posture was one of his trademarks, but he was uncharacteristically stooped. He faltered. He braced his right arm against the wall for support. He nonetheless stalled going to the doctor. He finally underwent surgery in mid-October 1973 and was diagnosed with cancer. Ariyoshi assumed his duties immediately after the surgery (the first of five) and moved into the governor's office in the summer of 1974.

Chapter 10

The First Japanese American Governor

By the time George Ariyoshi became acting governor, the post-statehood economic boom had ended. In one of John Burns' last acts in office, he appointed a commission to analyze how much revenue the state government was taking in versus how much it was spending. The panel was called the Commission on Operations, Revenues, and Expenditures (CORE).

CORE settled on the ratio of increased revenues to increased population as a key indicator of government's ability to embark on new programs and expand old ones. It found the state government had been living in the luxury of rapid economic expansion. Between 1961 and 1971, both the population of Hawai'i and the state government had grown rapidly, but state expenditures had increased at a phenomenal eight times the rate of population growth.[1] This was made possible by increased personal income, increased federal aid (resulting from Johnson's Great Society programs), and a general tax increase passed by the 1965 Hawai'i legislature. In dollar amounts, spending by state government had increased at roughly 10 percent a year in the first half of the 1960s, and 20 percent a year in the second half.

The chill descended in 1971 and 1972, when spending suddenly exceeded revenues. CORE was concerned that while tax revenues were flattening, demand for government services was still rising—what Dannemiller called "the state, the state, the state, and the state." CORE argued that Hawai'i's rapid rate of in-migration, which had been affordable in the sixties, had become a liability in the seventies, straining Hawai'i's ability to provide housing, health care, education, and welfare. Accordingly population growth rates became a concern, and the idea of trying to discourage rapid growth developed analytical and intellectual underpinnings. CORE said that while "there may not be consensus on what the population limit for the State should be,"[2] everyone agreed that in-migration was a problem.

If the CORE report had been more explicit, it would have said that being a state of the United States was proving to have its own problems. The in-migration triggered by statehood had set off a population growth rate nearly double that of the United States as a whole. With a rapidly growing population and a constantly rising number of tourists, the landscape was changing with a disconcerting rapidity. Many people seemed to be in shock over the physical changes of building mass and skylines. The sense of Waikīkī and other destination resort areas as local or Hawaiian places waned drastically.

Simultaneously, the changing ethnic composition of the population led to a sense of the social fabric unraveling. In the process the certainties of early statehood were giving way to questions about what Hawaiʻi was and where it was going. Japan was investing heavily in Hawaiʻi, provoking a negative reaction. A wide, deep trend of political activism was beginning to energize many native Hawaiians. Community-based protests were erupting across the islands. These arose from attempts to preserve lifestyles, landscapes, or agricultural activities that were jeopardized by development. Increasingly these protests were supported by, then coordinated by, a New Left movement that turned to the texts of the traditional left for guidance. From place to place there were bitter fights for control within these movements, pitting studied radicals against single-issue activists.[3] Variations of protest flowed from the environmental movement, which eagerly generated lawsuits opposing government policies.

The second deep, pervasive division in society was over the Vietnam War. While the divisiveness of the Vietnam War became a standard description of the United States, the war afflicted Hawaiʻi in ways that went to the heart of Hawaiʻi's identity. The Japanese American community had avoided internment because it had been cleared by, then policed by, the military intelligence agencies. The nisei had been lionized for their military exploits. Statehood had been a celebration of Asian American entry into the mainstream of American society—in context of a Cold War waged heavily in Asia.

Hawaiʻi had become what was intended in the 1898 annexation—the base for projection of American military force in the Pacific. This was the meaning of Pearl Harbor, the Battle of Midway, the staging of the Korean War, and now the Vietnam War. The fact that Hawaiʻi was an armed fortress was often strangely obscured in the civic dialogue. The presence of the military tended to be treated (and is treated today) as a "military sector" of the Hawaiian economy. The military relationship was even reduced to a dimension of the tourism story, as Hawaiʻi became a major destination for the rest and recreation leave—R & R—of servicemen from Vietnam.

However, the agony of a controversial war revived contention over the enormous U.S. military presence in Hawai'i. It also served as a reminder of the alliance of Burns with Lyndon Johnson that had done so much to secure statehood. As Johnson's war policy was coming undone, he travelled to Hawai'i repeatedly in a seven-month period between December 19, 1967, and July 20, 1968, to confer on military strategy and to meet with the various military despots who held down America's satellite government in South Vietnam. It was in the spring of 1968 that he had written to Burns, "Each time that I return from your lovely island, I wonder how I can ever repay your hospitality."[4] In a strange moment, Burns devoted his entire State of the State address in 1968 to supporting Johnson's war policy. The press began to joke uncertainly about Hawai'i being the only state with a foreign policy. The legislature defied Burns by passing a resolution condemning the war.

The campus of the University of Hawai'i was shut down by antiwar demonstrations, and the administration of a popular university president, Thomas H. Hamilton, was ended by the conflicting pressures placed on him.[5] Young people condemned the war, burned draft cards, and made highly publicized flights to Canada. Again, for AJAs, the sense of intergenerational conflict was particularly intense.

In the midst of this turmoil, Ariyoshi had to seek election to the governorship in his own right. He approached the task in a weaker political position than can now be readily imagined. He did not have a large, solid statewide following. In some insidious way, he actually seemed diminished by his close association with Burns, most pointedly when, in a flippant moment, Burns had referred to him as "Boy-san." Ariyoshi appeared to many to be an understudy with no flair or will of his own. One of his most cutting critics was *The Hawai'i Observer,* an alternative weekly news magazine that was widely read in the 1970s before its financial demise. *The Observer* described Ariyoshi as a practiced follower in a spent movement.

> *The Democrats are, in 1974, split into a half-dozen squabbling factions. The goals they espoused in 1954 have been accomplished, forgotten or discredited.*[6]

Key people next to Burns were no less lacking in enthusiasm. Mike Tokunaga, looking back on the period, would describe Ariyoshi as an unemotional candidate and a "cold fish." Burns appointees in the cabinet resisted Ariyoshi's leadership. The daily press was unfriendly, giving the "Boy-san" story major play. Reflecting on this period, a writer named Paul Phillips described Ariyoshi as having "led a career of quiet obscurity," adding: "A seemingly less prepossessing choice could hardly have been found."[7]

David McClung, who as Senate president had aligned himself with Burns, competed for the same potential supporters. Burns did not actively support Ariyoshi. In fact Ariyoshi had moments of wondering why Burns, if he had wanted him to be governor, didn't push for him to be governor. The competition was intense. Frank Fasi had established a reputation as a capable, if needlessly contentious, mayor, and Tom Gill's traditional following was very much with him.

OPENING UP THE DEMOCRATIC PARTY

Two years into Ariyoshi's term as lieutenant governor, the 1972 Democratic convention in Hawai'i had provided an early indication that Ariyoshi was not what he had been made to appear, and that he would incrementally set his own course, if necessary to the dismay of Burns' followers. The convention itself was a window into the conflicts of the day. Gill's faction again was trying to take over the Democratic Party, this time with an assist from Fasi. The tradition of factionalism was intensified by bitterness over the war. The cry for overturning the Democratic machine bosses across America was integral to a process of more direct representation in the selection of the Democratic candidate for president—an impulse wrapped in moral certainties that eventually led to the politically disastrous nomination in 1972 of the South Dakota populist, George McGovern, for the presidency.

The idea of overturning the party establishment particularly resonated in Hawai'i, because Burns ran the party autocratically in concert with a handful of others. The selection of delegates to the national nominating convention was a case in point: They were typically chosen by Burns, Dan Aoki, and Inouye over breakfast, with input from no more than a few other people, then handed to the convention for rubber-stamping.

Ariyoshi told Burns that he was going to advocate opening the party to newcomers and dissenters. Burns merely looked at him. At the convention podium, Ariyoshi argued that a political party must constantly renew itself: "If it is to continue to be a dynamic vehicle for action," he said, "it must be open to new ideas and be willing to accommodate diversity." He pleaded for renewing "the vigor of '55" and for an end "to old differences and personality splits." While openness might lead to family fights, "the purpose of a family fight is not to drive opponents from the arena." He argued that the Democratic Party had to choose between opening up or cutting off real debate and sending a slate of familiar faces to the national convention. To open a slot for dissidents within the party, Ariyoshi announced he would not run for delegate to the national convention. When he had taken a similar position in the faction-ridden Senate fight in 1966, he had been held in contempt by the political warriors of the capitol. Now he was taking essentially the same ideas to a wider arena.

His speech was a clue to the Democratic Party's ability to periodically redefine itself as "the party of the people." It also was a clue to Ariyoshi's ability to see that change was needed, and to act on that perception. In the same convention, a conciliatory party man, Minoru Hirabara, was elected chairman. He went to considerable lengths to comply with the letter and spirit of the national party guidelines on open participation, and back-room slate-making was substantially curtailed.

Although probably in closer touch with Burns than anyone, Ariyoshi was already resented as insufficiently loyal to the old group and the old definition of the party. Two years later, by the time of the 1974 convention, when Burns was gravely ill, his loyalists wore shirts cut from a cloth that had been printed for his 1970 campaign. Participants talked privately about the *bushidō,* which prescribes the practice of loyalty, faith, and valor, with loyalty foremost.

UNLIKELY AS IT MAY HAVE SEEMED at the time, the fact that the Democratic Party vigorously debated the Vietnam War became a part of its continued success. Thousands of people joined the Democratic Party of Hawai'i as a means of voicing opposition to the war. A man named Chuck Huxil attended his first Democratic precinct meeting in Mānoa Valley in 1968 because he loathed the war. In response, a Burns supporter in the precinct rammed through a motion to not discuss the war. Two years later, Huxil returned with enough new members to take over the precinct and elect delegates to the state convention. Wanting to not unduly offend the Burns people, he offered them several convention seats, but some of his own supporters became upset. One of the Burns people took Huxil aside and advised him to take all the convention seats, since otherwise his group would fragment. Huxil became a devoted Democrat who worked with all factions at the grassroots level. He felt that within the Democratic Party his vote was equal to that of a governor, a bank president, or a union boss.

Starting out in the Burns faction, Sandra Ebesu, daughter of Tom Ebesu, went to her first convention at age twenty-one in 1972. She sat next to her sister, who was also a delegate. Her father's friend sat behind her and was constantly telling her how to vote. When the chair asked for voice votes, he would lean over and say, "Yell louder." Distressed, she went home and asked her father why he had not attended. He said the party needed new people. Sandra Ebesu became a key supporter of Ariyoshi and of building a new, conciliatory center among younger members of the Democratic Party.

Turmoil created possibilities. Although under attack for its conservatism, the Democratic Party was in the vanguard of issues that mattered most to the burgeoning women's movement. With legislative passage in 1970 of the right to a legal abortion, Hawai'i became the first state in the country to allow women a choice over reproduction. That same year Hawai'i was the first state to support the Equal Rights Amendment to the United States Constitution.

These were significant beginnings of a long-term alliance between the feminist movement and the Democratic Party in Hawai'i. When a young third-generation AJA, Carol Fukunaga, enrolled in the University of Hawai'i, she knew implicitly that her parents expected her to study hard and make good grades. She also knew that she was departing from their expectations when she joined the antiwar sit-in at the administration building in 1968. Her father had fought in the 100th Battalion. Now, for the first time, she heard people criticizing the U.S. military. She came to believe that the Vietnam War was a colonial war, and that people from Hawai'i were dying for no democratic purpose. In 1972 she joined a legislative campaign for a first-time candidate, Anson Chong. For her, it was a children's crusade, run out of a garage. Periodically the boys drifted off "planning a mysterious thing called strategy," while the females typed, stuffed envelopes, and answered the telephone.

That fall, the university opened its law school (substantially because of Burns), propelled by the theme of widening the opportunities of Hawai'i's young people. Those who might not be able to afford a law school on the mainland had a school of their own. Fukunaga was admitted to the first class, most of whom were young political activists. A third were women, reputedly the largest percentage in a law school in America. Thereafter, Fukunaga became a successful candidate in her own right and an influential figure in first the State House, then the Senate.

Along with Mazie Hirono (who became lieutenant governor in 1994) Fukunaga was the most enduring of the female politicians of the 1970s, but she was one of many—including Patsy Mink, Jean S. King, Marilyn Bornhorst, Joan Yim, and Amy Agbayani—who gave meaning to the Democratic Party's rhetoric of equality. As the decades passed, this trend became not less but more pronounced, as women voted more and more disproportionately for Democratic candidates on a national level. It was yet another instance in which a change in Hawai'i foreshadowed changes in the entire country, which then reinforced the dominant position of the Democratic Party in Hawai'i.

THE IDEOLOGY OF THE FUTURE

In 1969, a young professor arrived at the University of Hawai'i named James Dator, whose core concern was the relationship of turmoil in the present to possibilities of the future. Dator would write about "surfing the tsunamis of change" by studying alternative scenarios and acting on them in an informed way. "There are no future facts," he was fond of saying, "but there are no past possibilities."[8] He had developed his first courses on the future while teaching for six years at Rikkyo University in Tokyo, and he thought of himself as a Japanophile.

Despite his unconventional image—a flying page boy haircut, tee shirts, and a motorcycle—Dator made an almost instant connection with some of the most influential people in Hawai'i. "Because the future is the arena of the possible and of the preferred," he would write, "rather than of the foregone and predetermined, it is also the arena of dreams and values." In a moment symptomatic of the early seventies, Dator captured the rapt attention of a joint session of the Hawai'i State Legislature. He became the key academic figure of the Commission on the Year 2000, which was chaired by the editor of *The Honolulu Advertiser*, George Chaplin. After the year 2000 had actually arrived, Dator observed that society becomes interested in the future for one of two reasons. One is that society is doing so well it begins to ask the utopian question, "What more can be achieved?" The other is that when the status quo is suddenly jeopardized, society casts about for ways to ward off decline. From Dator's experience, he believed that during his brief but meteoric celebrity, both had happened in quick succession. The sixties had seemed to pose infinite possibilities, which were abruptly diminished in the early seventies.

Following the report of the Commission on the Year 2000, the legislature appointed Dator to a citizen's committee tasked with anticipating the future. Then came the energy crisis of 1973, precipitated by the Organization of Petroleum Exporting Countries suddenly shrinking the world oil supply in cartel-like fashion. Because Hawai'i depended almost exclusively on imported oil, people in Hawai'i felt especially vulnerable to manipulation of a scarce resource. Drivers formed long lines, sleeping overnight in their cars to maintain their positions. A few times people actually fought with one another over cutting into line. Suddenly Dator understood the legislature's question to be, "How do we get out of this problem?" The committee's answer was that they had not been formed to deal with crises, and that they had no ready remedy.

THE VULNERABILITY OF ISLANDS

In the developing competition for the governorship, the energy crisis of 1973 turned out to be another defining moment for Ariyoshi. Against Frank Fasi's claim that only he was man enough to deal with such a big problem, and against Tom Gill's call for government rationing, Ariyoshi in his capacity as acting governor devised a simple, workable response called GasPlan. People with even-numbered license plates were allowed to buy gas on even-numbered dates, and those with odd-numbered plates were allowed to buy gas on odd-numbered dates. Topping off tanks was prohibited. It was an approach that relied on communication and community concurrence. Calm was restored, and the sense of panic passed. It was a significant moment in Ariyoshi taking on stature as acting governor.

Ariyoshi similarly though less publicly coped with the state's economic and fiscal problems. With the downturn of government revenue, Burns had frozen government hiring and then approved each exception to the spending freeze. When Ariyoshi became acting governor, he set expenditure guidelines for the department heads and expected them to balance their own budgets—adopting an essentially less personal but more policy-oriented approach. With influential Democrats starting to talk about a tax increase to cover the deficit, Ariyoshi took the position that if the fiscal pain was widely shared on the spending side, a tax increase could and should be avoided.

The common denominator of these successes had to do with managing change. While he was constantly critiqued as a plodder, Ariyoshi's devotion to calm and rationality was beginning to give him increased credibility. The turmoil of the times also was intersecting with his intergenerational understanding of how life worked. From his devotion to his parents and his 1970 speech addressing his children, it was a short step to his organizing political theme: The preferred future.

In Ariyoshi's formulation, interested publics were to come together, identify scenarios, and make choices. A scenario commanding wide support was a preferred future. As part of his competition for leadership, Ariyoshi's code-phrase about Hawai'i—"a special place"—was the "preferred future."

Initially this formulation seemed like a comfortable descendant of Burns' preoccupation with the development of Hawai'i's people, and with their "first real opportunity for full, genuine emergence" in the context of statehood. The preferred future was democratic and participatory. Situationally, it was a response to the turmoil of the times. Ariyoshi's party speech in 1972, two years in advance of the campaign, talked repeatedly about "preferred futures." For example, "if we do not innovate our preferred futures, we are doomed to cope—and to cope inadequately—with crisis after crisis." Stylistically, a sort of futurism was part of Burns' semi-Confucian tradition, in which the function of leadership was to set broad parameters, after which solutions were to flow up through the democratic process.

However, in the realm of government policy-making, Ariyoshi's seemingly safe formulation led to an extraordinary turnabout, because it was his passageway into substantially slowing down the pace of Hawai'i's physical development. It was a passage into political territory that Gill had previously had all to himself. If Burns, the practitioner of rapid development, was disturbed by this turn of events, it went unrecorded.

By the time of the election campaign, Ariyoshi, Fasi, Gill, and McClung were all putting forward ideas about shaping growth, managing growth, and controlling growth. While no one wanted to embrace the idea of zero growth as articulated by elements of the environmental movement, the agreement on slowing down the growth of the sixties was unmistakable. Ariyoshi broadened his political appeal in the context of this dialog. For example, a young man named Dan Ishii was looking for someone to support. He went to coffee-hour discussions by both Gill and Ariyoshi and went away believing they were talking about essentially the same thing. The difference in his mind lay in the fact that Gill proposed one way to accomplish controlled growth—his way—while Ariyoshi opened doors to involving others. For that reason, Ishii decided to back Ariyoshi.

The poll standings at the beginning of the campaign reflected the large, established followings of Fasi and Gill. Each had about a third of the Democratic electorate. Ariyoshi had a fifth, but was nonetheless far ahead of McClung, which allowed Ariyoshi to rally people who wanted neither the unpredictability of Fasi nor the inflexible certitudes presented by Gill.

ROBERT OSHIRO AND TEAM

The way that key elements then organized around Ariyoshi became fundamental to popular definitions of the Democratic machine. The most important unions to endorse Ariyoshi were the Hawaiian Government Employees Association and the ILWU. Walter Dods, then the rising young man of First Hawaiian Bank, played a role in strategy and communication. He had gotten to the table as an early supporter of Ariyoshi's 1970 campaign and subsequently had married Dianne Nosse, Ariyoshi's press secretary. The national consultant for strategy was Joseph Napolitan of Washington D.C. Napolitan's work was coordinated by Jack Seigle, who was becoming a storied figure in advertising and public relations in Honolulu. Seigle was in charge of media production and, to some extent, press strategy. In tandem, Seigle and Napolitan had been the media dimension of the *Catch A Wave* campaign that had re-elected Burns in 1970.

The ultimate strategist was Robert C. Oshiro, who served as a recruiter, organizer, philosopher, and manager. Although small in size, Oshiro had a great, resonating voice. He could deliver even casual conversation with a combination of penetrating sincerity and ferocious intensity. He evoked intense emotion.

Oshiro's father had been a plantation laborer, a cowboy, and a truck farmer. Oshiro had grown up pulling weeds on a three-acre farm outside Wahiawā, a country town in the rural plain of Oʻahu where Schofield Barracks and Jim Dole's pineapple company converged. Oshiro always kept something of Wahiawā about him, and for most of his life he maintained a simple law office there, despite his achievements and influence.

For the many people who came to stereotype him as the ultimate machine Democrat, his inside story may seem flabbergasting, in that his mentor was not Burns but Gill. His first political involvement was with the Oʻahu County committee under Gill's chairmanship. As an organizer of old-time rallies in Wahiawā, he said, "I always looked upon myself as . . . working for Tom [Gill]. And that's how I got started in the political process."[9]

Like Gill, Oshiro was a New Deal liberal influenced by the work of the National Labor Relations Board.[10] But where Gill's main tendency was polarity, Oshiro's was the pursuit of commonality. As a law student he was interested in labor-management relations. As an early-day party worker, he became interested in creating a united front within the Democratic Party. The initial focus of his work was recovering from the surprising losses of the 1959 statehood campaign.

Oshiro believed the idea for a fact-finding committee for 1962 started at the precinct level with Gill, but it became an idea for which Oshiro himself was widely credited. The goal was to determine who the strongest candidates were in a way that the main forces of the party could agree upon. The committee idea was embraced by the Democratic chairman, who asked Oshiro to chair it because, in Oshiro's words, "being from the country, I was removed from all personality problems." The key finding for the purposes of 1962 was that Burns continued to have wide support for the governorship despite his loss to Quinn. The fact-finding committee agreed on supporting Burns for governor and Gill for Congress. Thereafter, Oshiro became chairman of the Democratic Party. As chairman, Oshiro helped Burns and Gill pull together the last-minute campaign in 1966 that preserved the Democratic Party's hold on the governorship.

Along the way Oshiro came to see Burns as a heroic figure, while becoming progressively more distant from Gill. After completing his tenure as chairman in 1968, Oshiro was approached by members of Burns' circle to create a re-election campaign for a third Burns term. Contributions by cabinet members created a fund for Burns' support that paid Oshiro a $3,000 monthly salary. Although he would organize the first media-heavy million-dollar campaign in Hawai'i, he thought of himself as primarily a practitioner of grassroots politics. He believed he had been repeatedly elected a state legislator—and survived a challenge by the ILWU—because of his willingness to go door to door and sit with people and talk about their lives.

When Oshiro started rebuilding Burns' base in early 1969, he often went to meetings in nearly empty rooms; one time there were only two people. The challenge was "to get them to believe again in the dream that we had." Eventually he counted thirty thousand active grassroots supporters for Burns—"thirty thousand people who are locked in, and no media can dislodge them."[11]

By the night of Burns and Ariyoshi's victory in 1970, Oshiro was exhausted. As Ariyoshi attempted to organize in 1974, Oshiro stayed in Wahiawā and watched. Then he received a telephone call from Burns. Long after the fact, Oshiro quoted Burns as saying, "Bobby, unless you get involved, this man isn't going to make it. I want you to look at it from a standpoint of what it means to all of us at the party."[12] Oshiro's story contradicts Ariyoshi's perception that Burns did not actively support him, although it is understandable in context of the reverence and awe in which Oshiro came to idealize Burns. For example, Oshiro would say, elliptically, that he had been guided by Burns' farewell address to the legislature, quoting Walter Lippmann on the death of Roosevelt: "The final test of a leader is that he leaves behind him in other men the conviction and the will to carry on." Oshiro kept this saying in his top desk drawer and said "it was as though he was talking to me personally."[13]

With Seigle and Napolitan again handling media, Oshiro turned to building support for Ariyoshi from the bottom up. A worker was a "sparrow." A good sparrow set aside ego and practiced teamwork. Through teamwork came success. It was a perfect, simple formulation with overtones that resonated in local culture. Oshiro regarded his Okinawan heritage as particularly significant. He was aware that as immigrants from the southernmost and most recently annexed prefecture of Japan, Okinawans had struggled to be treated equally by the Japanese themselves. On a wider scale, he would talk about Okinawan, Japanese, and native Hawaiian cultures all placing a higher value on cooperation than did the intensely independent and competitive cultures of the West.

In 1970, he had said that the deeper cause of the Burns re-election campaign was developing respect for the ethnic cultures of Hawai'i. On his blackboard he had written the word WASP in foot-high letters, representing the cultural force of the mainland, and from there had drawn an arrow to multicultural Hawai'i, which he represented with a circle. Coming at this time, and in such large numbers, Oshiro said, the WASP wave might engulf Hawaiʻi, so that his children and others would lose the sense of diversity that was unique to Hawaiʻi. At a minimum, time was needed to reaffirm what was good and workable in the ethnic cultures of Hawaiʻi, so the young would not be overwhelmed by the new migration.[14]

In 1974, he located his comparable theme in a speech that he wrote for delivery by Dan Aoki to the Club 100, the social club of the 100th Battalion. It recounted the veterans' sacrifices and celebrated the resulting social and economic progress of Hawaiʻi. But, Oshiro asked, how often had they heard that Hawaiʻi was not ready for a Japanese governor? "Must we wait for another war," he asked, "to open to our children the doors to the highest offices of the state?" And,

> *Isn't this also saying that no Chinese can be governor, or no Hawaiian can be governor, or no Filipino can be governor? . . . are we being tested again as to whether or not we are Americans? Must you and I think, act, and live like the Mainland Americans to be identified as an American?*[15]

If Ariyoshi could be elected, it would mean that "your sons and daughters" likewise could aspire to society's highest roles. A young campaign worker for Tom Gill, Paul Murakami, confronted Ariyoshi at a rally at the University of Hawaiʻi and asked if Ariyoshi was telling people to vote their race. Ariyoshi responded, to applause, that in his view, most of the racism in the campaign had been directed at him.[16] From a liberal viewpoint, Ariyoshi's answer was inadequate, because of the liberal presumption that a just society regarding race and ethnicity had been achieved. Elections were no longer supposed to be about race or ethnicity but about issues.

From this viewpoint, what Oshiro had defined as the cause of the 1974 campaign amounted to playing a race card to maintain a regime that had run out of ideas. Indisputably, it was an appeal on behalf of a candidate who was playing catch-up. The words that Oshiro said aloud for Ariyoshi would obviously have gone unsaid for someone with the popularity of Dan Inouye, if Inouye had decided to return to Hawaiʻi to run for governor.

But unless a person believed that it was meaningless to have a Japanese American governor, then the liberal view was an idealized view stripped of historical context—a history that had begun with the labor recruiters and their contracts of peonage and with the assertion of white supremacy.

When the organizing belief in white superiority had waned, whites nonetheless had continued to hold the highest positions of leadership, even when—as with Burns and Hall—the primary constituents were not Caucasian.

Thereafter AJAs had succeeded as legislators but were thwarted from holding executive office. Mitsuyuki Kido had been passed over for secretary of the territory. Kido was also defeated in 1959 in his candidacy for lieutenant governor on the ticket with Burns, and Burns had won the governorship only after turning to a part-Hawaiian running mate. As late as 1970, Ariyoshi had told Jim Takushi that Hawaiʻi was not ready for a Japanese American *lieutenant* governor.

Although Ariyoshi was immensely self-controlled, during the 1974 campaign Takushi saw him lose his temper in response to a racial insult. Takushi and Ariyoshi were out driving. At a stoplight a young man in an adjacent car said to his car full of friends, "No Jap's going to be governor." Ariyoshi bit his lip. The slur was repeated. Ariyoshi yelled, "Come on, you punks. I'll take you on."[17] For Ariyoshi such a breach in self-control was unmentionable, but years later in his autobiography he disclosed that throughout his tenure as governor he was consistently the target of hate mail. He not only concealed this information but ignored it, in the belief that to acknowledge its existence was to give it power.

Ultimately, Oshiro's appeal for the election of a Japanese American governor was like a Rorschach test, evoking different responses from different people, but in historic terms it was barely a whisper on the wind. In an interview a dozen years later, Oshiro said that in the absence of other factors

> *a voter is going to vote based upon the one common thread that he has with the principal. . . . We can't look at voters as what we think they should be . . . you have to work with people as they are.*[18]

In 1974, he said, ethnicity "was a factor. A big one."

DRIFT FROM LIBERALISM

Ethnicity was an identifiable (if not quantifiable) factor in what was otherwise a confusing campaign. The quieting of the statehood celebration, the widespread protests, the search for a new slowed-growth paradigm, all had an effect, in which the illuminating events of 1970 gave way to a sense of confusion in 1974. Ariyoshi, positioned as a candidate of the business-labor consensus, talked about preferred futures. Gill, the candidate of governmental controls, talked about helping the faltering economy. Fasi was perhaps the most clearly in character: He talked about himself and what a great job he had done as mayor. Near the end of the campaign, David McClung acknowledged he was out of the running by answering the question of who he would support other than himself. Having long since turned against his old law partner, Gill, and having joined the Burns wing, he nonetheless said he would vote for Gill. He said he doubted Ariyoshi's ability to lead.

Underlying all of this was continued widespread support for a strong state government, even though the exuberant liberalism that had molded Gill was slipping. After Humphrey's 1968 loss to Nixon, McGovern lost to Nixon in 1972 by an enormous margin. The very word "liberal" that came to people's mind with Gill would soon be called "the 'l' word." In Hawai'i, the urgency of the liberal cause had been dimmed by its success. The battles of labor, as defined by the moderate goals of the American labor movement, had been substantially won. The package of Earth Day bills had been adopted. The issue of land reform had been blunted. The feminist movement was making gains. The consumer movement had racked up victories on many fronts.

In such a climate, personalities and character mattered more than ever. Just as Gill was more comfortable with ideas than with people, others were more comfortable with his ideas than with him. Walter Heen said Gill liked people in the abstract. There was the deadly cult of Gill's intellect. Even Burns, who was reputed to have an IQ in the genius range, described Gill as the most intelligent person on the scene. Gill's admirers were entertained by listening to him say cutting things about others. Once playfully caustic, Gill had become embittered by his defeat in 1970. People left his presence wondering what he might say about them in their absence.

Once again, the question became how people of Japanese ancestry would vote. While Gill had many AJA supporters, he was something of a cultural mismatch. If anything, he attracted AJAs who were trying to shed the influence of traditional culture. In 1955 Gill had published a booklet on issues through the Oahu Democratic Committee. It included some quaint advertising—one by Dot's Restaurant in Wahiawā, for example. Gill boasted that none of the advertisers "tell us what to write." Encased in his self-righteousness, he rejected even the most innocuous forms of mutuality. He nonetheless realized that he should be concerned with the special history and influence of AJAs. When he saw in 1970 that the AJA vote was migrating to Burns, he belatedly recruited a popular state senator, Vincent Yano, to run with him. In 1974 he recruited former senator Nelson K. Doi as a running mate, in what became an example of the strangeness of the times.

THE NELSON DOI FACTOR

Nelson Doi was an eloquent speaker with a gravelly voice and a firey personality. He had served as Senate president in the early sixties. After losing the factional battle of 1966, he took an appointment to the court bench from Burns. Because he had been critical of Burns, his tenure as judge was an interesting example of the power of a governor eating away at his opposition over time. By the spring of 1974 Doi was ready to return to politics, his reputation apparently enhanced by the dignity of the court. Meanwhile, he had taken a self-realization seminar by Werner Erhard—Erhard Seminar Training (EST).

Like Taoism or evangelical Christianity, EST led participants down a short, quick path to the ineffable. A person who succeeded at EST "got it." In the 1970s the acronym EST became a part of Hawai'i's vocabulary. Thousands of people took EST. Gill was surrounded by EST. His old friend Vincent Esposito took EST, as did Royce Higa, who had resigned his appointment with Burns in 1970 to support Gill, as did Alvin Shim, the remaining practitioner in Gill's old law firm. Shim thought that if Gill took EST he might become more approachable and show greater respect for others. One day Shim asked Royce Higa how the Gill campaign was going. Higa again was supporting Gill but also happened to be the person closest to Nelson Doi. He replied, "Great, except for one thing—Tom Gill."[19]

At the time Ariyoshi was at around 20 percent in polls and Fasi was at 30 percent. Gill had a new poll that showed high voter approval of a Gill-Doi team. He had started ahead of Ariyoshi, and with Doi's announcement the poll showed him moving into the lead—this in spite of his being out of office for four years.

Meanwhile, Doi was pressing Gill for commitments on the distribution of political appointments, which meant they were already wrangling over the spoils of an imagined victory. The Gill of 1954, who was not influenced by a neighborhood restaurant in Wahiawā buying an ad in his party newsletter, was not to be similarly compromised by Doi. Neither was he to be compromised by seeking the favor of large groups of voters who determined the outcome of elections. In addition to AJAs, the ILWU was such a block. By 1974 the ILWU was losing membership but was nonetheless still a major political force. Without Burns, it could choose between the long pro-labor record of Gill or the spotty labor record of Ariyoshi, who had once voted against a Democratic Party minimum wage bill. In pursuit of a meeting with the ILWU, Gill went to see Shim, who was potentially the key to the door to the most important elements of the Democratic coalition—meaning the unions and the AJA. Shim could talk to not just some but all of the unions, including the ILWU; he was also in tune with Royce Higa and Nelson Doi, whose support was fundamental to getting the requisite number of AJA votes. What happened next had vaguely to do with the unrest of the times.

Shim had originally thought of himself as a person who questioned why things were as they were. When he was a small boy, his uncle had given him a book called *One Thousand Questions*. As a thirteen-year-old at Kamehameha Schools, a friend wrote in his annual, "Here's to Kamehameha's skeptic." His early involvement in politics was motivated by a perception that Hawai'i was in the grip of socialism for the rich. After earning a law degree at Georgetown University (as a classmate of Inouye), Shim returned to Hawai'i and became involved with organized labor. He was not only a labor attorney but an original thinker who was dedicated to replacing "socialism for the rich" with "capitalism to the 'max,'" a kind of participatory version of capital formation, distribution, and consumption.

In the early '70s he found more and more people wandering a landscape of philosophy, religion, culture, and cults, asking questions that had not previously been asked. He had resisted taking EST but then acceded. Through Erhard's training, he felt more in touch with himself and his feelings. As a person who "got it," he saw himself as "smaller than the smallest, bigger than the biggest." In the words of Erhard, life was an experience, not a concept.

One day in the early 1970s, Shim saw a small, brown-skinned man in robes arriving at the Honolulu International Airport, surrounded by an entourage. The skeptic in Shim caused him to think of the man as a fake. For no apparent reason, the man smiled and winked at Shim. As Shim wondered to himself, "Who is this guy?" the man said to him, "You will get the answer by reading my books." It was the Indian mystic Muktananda, who had been invited to Honolulu by Erhard.

A friend asked Shim to a meditation session with the swami. When Shim closed his eyes, Muktananda walked by and touched the top of his head. Shim felt weightless, floating up into a sky of brilliant blue stars. For a person whose life was organized by rationality, it was both exhilarating and frightening. While Shim worked with Muktananda, he continued to be the most influential labor lawyer in Hawai'i, which gave him a kind of dual mystique: He waded through the primordial swamp of politics and soared through the blue lights of heaven.

When Gill went to see Shim, he found an EST trainer named Ted Long at the meeting. Shim remembered Gill immediately adopting a cold, impersonal demeanor. Discussing the ILWU meeting Shim had arranged, Gill said, "Don't expect me to kiss their asses." Shim, who was part-Hawaiian, also remembered Gill saying to him, "I want you to get the Hawaiians in line," or words to that effect. Shim was particularly offended by that, because he had become involved with the beginnings of a Hawaiian renaissance, in which Hawaiians were not to be merely lined up but involved and consulted. All the while Gill avoided talking to the EST man, Long. As Gill turned to leave,

Long blurted out, "If you want to be governor you have to treat people like people."

Shim canceled the meeting with the ILWU. Gill said Shim was angry because Gill refused to take EST, to which he added, "I told those guys I didn't need a lobotomy."[20]

Thereafter Nelson Doi arrived in Shim's office with Royce Higa and announced he was pulling out of the campaign partnership. When word went around that Gill and Doi had no sooner joined forces than parted ways, it effectively destroyed Gill's opportunity to personify a reinvigorated Democratic Party. It reinforced the sense that Gill was not a haole who reached out, but one who talked down. Gill responded by becoming increasingly insistent on the power of his thinking.

ARIYOSHI AS GUBERNATORIAL CANDIDATE

George Ariyoshi not only was of Japanese ancestry but was guided by a politically unlikely, traditionally Japanese cultural style. Where Dan Inouye and Vincent Yano were masters of a sunny, outgoing type of campaigning, Ariyoshi was comparatively subdued. Beyond being properly Japanese in his manner and bearing, he was shy. James Takushi, who had been with him since the old downtown days, understood Ariyoshi in ways that others did not. After Ariyoshi had voted no on the Maryland land bill, Takushi would wait for him on the lanai of 'Iolani Palace so Ariyoshi would have someone to talk to during recesses. Thereafter a legislator had introduced a resolution to the Democratic convention to expel Ariyoshi from the party, and Takushi made the rounds pleading for the resolution to be withdrawn. As the 1966 election approached, Ariyoshi's campaign manager, a man named George Tashima, was stricken with a fatal illness. Tashima implored Takushi, "Help George. He is so naive in many ways. He needs protecting."[21]

Because Ariyoshi worried that he would offend people by not remembering their names, the outgoing Takushi would drive him to events and scan the crowd, putting names to faces. One night he arrived with Ariyoshi at a boxing match at about the same time as David McClung, who began working the crowd and calling people by name. Takushi turned to find Ariyoshi in his seat, in conversation with a boy who happened to sit next to him.

Nonetheless Ariyoshi was an energetic campaigner who was effective in his own way. He stayed in excellent physical condition. When he made a commitment, he was unequivocal and systematic. He kept up a strong, steady pace. In 1966, shunned by the Democratic Party for his vote on the Maryland bill, Ariyoshi had talked with several small groups each night, carefully explaining the intricacies of his position. In 1974 he demonstrated a capacity to open himself to the changing scene and to articulate the themes of the time. What he lacked in obvious political skills, he made up for in more subtle ways. In his lack of rhetorical flourish, he came across as thoroughly sincere. By being so transparent in his thinking aloud, he acquired a certain gravity. He had an inner clarity that affected audiences, even when he was repeating himself, as successful candidates must do.

The ILWU joined the Hawai'i Government Employers Association (HGEA) in backing Ariyoshi. Dan Aoki and Mike Tokunaga backed Ariyoshi. With the approach of election day, Robert Oshiro organized a rally of ten thousand people for Ariyoshi at McKinley High School. Everyone ate a plate lunch together.

Late in the campaign a then little-known Hawaiian candidate, Daniel Akaka, filed to run for lieutenant governor. Akaka was a handsome and personable educator and the brother of Abraham Akaka, who was well known as pastor of the missionary Kawaiahao Church. Ariyoshi's campaign quietly backed the younger Akaka, but Doi had built up a large lead.

On election day, Ariyoshi won the three-way gubernatorial race with 36 percent of the vote, and Doi beat Akaka by a wide margin, which meant that accidents of personality and timing had led to two AJAs on the ticket. What would previously have been unthinkable did not seem to matter, as if seven decades of anti-Japanese sentiment had finally evaporated.

Ariyoshi and Doi were opposed in the general election by Randolph Crossley, who had nearly beaten Burns in 1966, and Benjamin Dillingham, the inarticulate son of Walter Dillingham. On general election night, Burns watched for results from his hospital bed with Robert Oshiro. When it became clear that Ariyoshi would succeed him as governor, Burns clasped Oshiro's hand. Ariyoshi went to the hospital to thank Burns. "I should thank you." Burns replied, "You have made all my dreams come true."

HOW ARE THE BOYS?

By the following spring, Burns' disease had worsened to the point where treatment was discontinued. He returned to his home in Kailua. He told an old friend, Pundy Yokouchi of Maui, that Ariyoshi's victory was a victory for equality.

"You know what this means," Burns said.

"What is that, governor?" Yokouchi asked.

"After this," Burns said, "a Hawaiian can become governor. And then—who knows?—maybe a Filipino can become governor."[22]

Burns' daughter, the psychologist Sheenagh Burns, daringly described Burns' hard edges, but also the soft places. As a child she shared a love of baseball with the man she called "Pops." Analyzing major league players one day, she came to an early-day black player. Sheenagh said he was not really that good. Pops argued with her. Give the man a break, he urged. She resisted. He said she should bear in mind the hard times that black people had been through.[23]

She had grown up with the words of Burns' 1969 State of the State address—about a "subtle inferiority of spirit that is totally unwarranted." She heard his litany not from the gallery of the capitol but at close range as a child while he talked to people on the telephone: Hawai'i had to change. People who felt put down got hurt—not only the Japanese, but everyone who had been confined by the old system.[24]

He dreamed of adopting children of every race as a symbol of humanity's oneness. He taught Sheenagh to be proud that she was "local," that she was not a foreigner to Hawai'i, but part of Hawai'i. She came to believe that her father, after a lifetime of struggling with issues of self-worth, came to accept that he was loved. "This set him free," she said.

Alvin Shim took Muktananda to see Burns, who was by then terribly weak. Muktananda asked Burns if he would like to make peace with his pain. Burns smiled. The healer had brought an apple, and he held it over Burns while he prayed. Muktananda then left Shim at Burns' bedside. Suddenly energized, Burns thumped Shim on the chest. "Get me that apple," he said, and proceeded to eat it. He asked Shim, "How are the boys?" Shim said the boys would be all right. Burns said, "Remind them we have plenty of poor haole kids out there. Tell the guys to help them, too."[25]

FROM HIS OBSCURE ORIGINS, Burns had led the Democrats to their victory in 1954, served two terms as delegate to Congress, negotiated statehood, and served three terms in what was probably the most powerful governorship in America. To record his personal story, his son, James Seishiro Burns, organized an extraordinary effort known as the Burns Oral History Project. A team of historians conducted ten audiotaped interviews with Burns before his death on April 5, 1975. The project interviewed nearly a hundred contemporaries. Most idealized him, but a few, such as Gill, were critical.

In death his reputation grew. Where Ariyoshi's relationship with him was real and substantive, successor candidates for governor—not only Democrats but Republicans—would hold up their scraps of brief moments with the great man. John Waihe'e, after serving two terms as governor, would lament, "If I could only have had fifteen minutes with Jack Burns."[26] Ben

Cayetano, in his campaigns for governor, routinely described with great solemnity his only brief conversation with Burns. Republican Patricia Saiki suffered politically for attempting to embrace the Burns tradition across party lines, while old political horses such as Gill and Fasi gained a certain authenticity merely for having opposed Burns. In a 1994 survey, nearly two decades after his death, 69 percent of the public identified Burns as the governor who had done "the most for Hawai'i."

His public acclaim rose even though much of what was written about him was usually less than complimentary and often scathingly critical. Such books as *Land and Power* and *Hawaii: Islands Under the Influence* persisted as staples of published analysis without apparent affect on Burns' personal reputation. Although *Catch A Wave* was in many ways a book about how high finance and media were manipulated to ensure Burns' victory over Gill, increasingly it came to be described by readers as a book "about Governor Burns," as voters absorbed what they wanted to absorb.

Sheenagh Burns' psychological portrait of her father, published in 1990 in *The Hawaiian Journal of History*, received only one notice in the mass media and was otherwise ignored. It was a marginalized view until publication of Burns' biography in the year 2000, on the twenty-fifth anniversary of his death. The biography was followed by an hour-long documentary, produced by John Burns' daughter-in-law, Emme Tomimbang. Both film and book reiterated Sheenagh Burns' description of an angry young man whose bouts of drinking mirrored the example set by his father. In this narrative Burns was rescued from self-destruction by becoming the exact opposite of his father, engaging in a "heroic struggle with 'the devil within.'"

> *Gradually, by sublimating the powerful energy of that anger into more useful channels, he became more like his mother and his priest. . . . He could then choose all the people of Hawai'i as his children. Like a mother, he would care for and nurture them. Like a priest, he would surrender and dedicate his life to them.*[27]

Freed of his followers' contention that he was a perfect being, Burns became an even more interesting figure. He not only had adapted his life to society's needs but was adapted in memory to symbolize all that was heroic in the mid-Pacific movement for equality and justice in American society.

Chapter 11

Special Place

When George Ariyoshi took the oath to serve as the third elected governor of Hawai'i, he stood at the far end of a long sequence. The journey had begun with the forced opening of Japan in 1853 and the ensuing question posed by the Social Darwinism of the times: Were white Europeans and Americans—sailing in superior ships, bearing superior arms—inherently superior beings? Other questions followed: If some nations were obviously superior in power, would they always be? Why had Japan's emigrants been barred from voting in the Republic of Hawai'i, then barred from citizenship in the Territory of Hawai'i? Was equality achievable? Despite hard work and sacrifice, why had Americans of Japanese ancestry continued to play roles at least one level removed from the top level of power?

By arriving in the office of governor, Ariyoshi touched the core of what defined Hawai'i. After its long period of colonization, Hawai'i had asserted its multiethnic identity by electing a nonwhite chief executive. As America became more racially diverse, might not Hawai'i lead the country to a new level of diversity?

Like others who had broken racial and ethnic barriers, Ariyoshi was under intense pressure and scrutiny. In traditional Japanese culture, which had been perpetuated in Japanese American values, Ariyoshi was at all costs not to bring shame, *haji*. While avoidance of embarrassment is a behavioral goal of people around the world, in Japanese culture it is a paramount value, like loyalty. Ariyoshi had so internalized the idea of *haji* that it resulted in a style of caution and personal conservatism that obscured the more experimental and intellectually vigorous person beneath. Other pressures surrounded him. Among Burns' followers, he was supposed to carry on for The Old Man, while many of Burns' opponents wanted him to change government in some way. The U.S. State Department had a special interest in

Ariyoshi as an Asian American, and the government of Japan was intently looking over his shoulder as an overseas son.

For all these reasons and more, many images were held up as conventional wisdom about Ariyoshi, to the detriment of his being seen clearly and understood rationally. Above all, the image of Ariyoshi as a status quo figure was reinforced by his identification with Burns. The roots of this identification between the two were in their complex relationship, but it extended among Ariyoshi's critics, such as Frank Fasi, who vociferously argued that Ariyoshi was the inheritor of the Burns political machine. Noel J. Kent's *Hawaii: Islands Under the Influence* said, dismissively, "the changes that did transpire were largely in the realm of rhetoric."[1] Cooper and Daws' *Land and Power,* the most widely circulated book during Ariyoshi's tenure in office, contended that Ariyoshi was an extension of Burns in land policy, conjuring a "Burns-Ariyoshi consensus on development."[2]

The fact was that even as Ariyoshi invoked the legacy of Burns, he departed from him on many of the crucial issues facing Hawai'i. How he did this was essential to the Democratic Party holding on to power, idealizing Burns as a founding figure while adapting to new ideas and priorities.

Compounding the confusion of image and reality was the fact that the new directions set by Ariyoshi were usually not brought home forcefully and repetitively to the public. Much like Burns himself, Ariyoshi had a sort of neo-Confucian belief that good works would be recognized as such. He also tended to interpret political and governmental change as having been sanctioned by Burns himself, if only in a general way. Ariyoshi would say that during the long hours he spent as Burns' lieutenant governor, Burns stressed that he must be himself. A paraphrase would be, "I did what Governor Burns wanted me to do, which was to be my own man."

Contrary to the drift of the book *Land and Power,* the changes brought about by Ariyoshi become clearest when examined in those terms—land and power. Like other stories of the period, the story of Ariyoshi as an innovator in land policy necessarily begins with the extreme difference of Hawai'i from other states.

IN POLYNESIAN TIMES land tenure was governed by a system of use rights, as opposed to ownership rights. As the Polynesian settlement evolved, distribution of lands fell progressively into the hands of ever more powerful ruling chiefs. The last step in this evolution was Kamehameha's success in the wars of conquest. From his base on the island of Hawai'i, Kamehameha conquered and then redistributed lands across the islands. To reward several key chiefs, he proclaimed that their new lands could be held in perpetuity, meaning the lands could be passed on to heirs.

As Western influence spread through the development of plantation agriculture, pressure mounted for the mid-nineteenth-century redistribution of land in fee simple, which became known as the great division of the land (*māhele*). The result of the division was that most land was owned outright by a small elite—first by Hawaiian chiefs, but more and more by haole planters.

The essentially feudal nature of the chiefly system, which had been tempered in pre-Western time by mutuality, ossified into a system reminiscent of the Middle Ages in Europe. An agricultural system organized along streams and inside valleys, with many participating farmers, became a system of highly industrialized plantations owned by investment corporations. Missionaries who believed they had come to save Hawaiians from depravity lived to see their children and grandchildren become lords of the feudal manor, with palatial homes, maids, drivers, overseers, and translators who issued orders to a largely Asian work force.

LAND REDISTRIBUTION

Over time, as plantation society shifted into the hands of professional executives, the control of land became progressively anonymous. Private lands belonged to a few large corporations or to hereditary estates that typically leased land to the corporations. In the postwar period, as the resident population grew, house site development occurred more and more on land that was leased by individual homeowners from the large owners.

One of the stated goals of the postwar Democratic Party was to change the feudal pattern in one respect: To allow lessees to buy the underlying fee simple ownership of their house sites. With land reform, people would at least own the land on which their homes sat. Although this was a modest definition of land reform as it often has been undertaken in feudal societies, it was widely portrayed as an assault on the sanctity of property rights in the American context. America, after all, was a progressive society with a large middle class and wide distribution of land ownership. The paradox of feudal land distribution in a democratic society resulted from the fact that America had unilaterally annexed Hawaiʻi as an island nation, then supported the continuation of its feudal distribution of ownership.

In that regard, Democrats in Hawaiʻi who were interested in land reform within the American constitutional context were left to improvise. What reform was acceptable? After promising land reform in the 1954 election, the Democrats gained enough power in the 1962 election to actually make land reform possible. When Ariyoshi as a state senator had expressed his misgivings about the Maryland bill, the Senate leadership had pressured him to hold off on taking a public position. As the tension mounted, the leadership threatened to strip him of the chairmanship of the Ways and Means Committee. He invited them to go ahead. Two of the leaders of the AFL-CIO unions came to his office, demanding that he vote yes on land reform and threatening to see him defeated in the next election if he did not. Ariyoshi pointed toward the door. Dozens of people called his house at night. Some calls were so abusive that friends came over to support Ariyoshi's wife Jean in answering the telephone.

After Ariyoshi cast the deciding vote in the Senate against the Maryland bill, a Democratic House member submitted a resolution to the next State Democratic convention to expel Ariyoshi from the party. When the campaign season got underway, one of Ariyoshi's Democratic colleagues in the Senate told him that his vote was an embarrassment. When Ariyoshi spoke at a rally in the plantation town of Waipahu, the ILWU business agents glared at him and the crowd stared without applauding. When he approached people to shake their hands, they avoided him. He recalled telling the audience,

If you want someone who is a rubber stamp, you shouldn't vote for me. But if you want someone who will study an issue and then vote according to conviction, I hope you will consider me.[3]

In a speech to the Japanese Chamber of Commerce he said if a legislator was merely supposed to follow the party platform, the Constitution should give the Senate three days to pass Democratic bills, followed by three days for the House, after which the legislature could turn over its work to the governor. To the faithful Jim Takushi he announced, "All we have to do is tell people the truth."

The problem was that Ariyoshi's idea of truth regarding land reform was obscure, complex, and never really understood. It began with his observation that leases are a form of contract protected by the U.S. Constitution. If existing leases were included in the Maryland bill, the bill would be an unconstitutional attack on contracts. If only new leases were covered by the law, the result would be an extreme inequality between neighbors. He believed the government would be "creating two categories of people living side by side, one with an existing lease but no option to buy, as contrasted to one with a new lease that carried with it an option to buy."[4] He argued that leased homes would become progressively unattractive and their value destroyed.

When the ILWU had pressured Ariyoshi in 1954, his father had counseled him to go his own way and redouble his efforts. This was what he now did in response to the storm of criticism that descended. Retreating from party rallies, he asked friends to organize coffee hours and invite voters to in-depth discussions. Sometimes he would do two or three coffee hours a night. He calculated that in thirty days he reached several thousand people directly. He sensed that some audiences agreed with his reasoning, while others at least appreciated the care he had given it. He asked people who responded favorably to spread the word. On election night, he became convinced that circles of knowledgeable voters had created a ripple effect. With four candidates to be nominated, he ran a strong second in a closed, Democrats-only primary. In the general election he led the ticket.

Thereafter, Ariyoshi's position on the Maryland bill became the key to the eventual conversion of leasehold to fee simple. On populous O'ahu, the estate of Princess Bernice Pauahi Bishop was by far the largest owner of leased residential land. Bishop Estate would often be demonized for its size, influence, and generous pay to its court-appointed trustees, but it had its own historical legitimacy and its own beneficiary constituents. Its holdings—about one-tenth of the total land mass of Hawai'i—were a remnant of the lands once held by descendants of Kamehameha I, and its revenues supported the Kamehameha Schools.

From a native Hawaiian point of view, land reform at the expense of Bishop Estate was yet another of many devices to separate Hawaiian beneficiaries from their supporting land base. Land reform was potentially land theft. To simultaneously see the opposing ideas of injustice through the eyes of a lease-holding tenant and the Kamehameha Schools (as beneficiary of Bishop Estate) was to realize that the issues of feudalism had never been resolved in modern Hawai'i.

In 1967, a state senator named John C. Lanham asked Ariyoshi what lay behind his opposition to the Maryland bill. Ariyoshi restated his belief in the sanctity of contracts and the inequity that could result from enhancing one person's property while undermining the value of a neighbor's.

In the meantime Ariyoshi had been approached for advice by a trustee of Bishop Estate.[5] Ariyoshi said the estate should voluntarily sell off as much residential property as possible to lessees. Although the estate was opposed to forced conversion, it was so cash-poor that its trustees were hard-pressed to balance the Kamehameha schools budget. They chose a neighborhood in Ariyoshi's senate district, Hālawa Heights, just west of Honolulu, as a model for conversion. They also asked Ariyoshi to perform the legal work. He declined, saying that it would render him suspect and ineffective. He nonetheless followed the process closely. The community negotiated an acceptable price, and Bishop Estate sold off the house lots. From this experience Ariyoshi came to believe that neighbors could cooperate effectively in converting their leases to ownership.

With Lanham, Ariyoshi worked out the essential ideas of a new lease-hold conversion bill. It encouraged lease-holders to organize and land own-ers to negotiate with them. The bill required that at least half of a given community participate if the landowner was to be engaged in a negotiation. If the negotiations failed, the bill provided for a process whereby fair mar-ket value would be determined and the state government would use its power of eminent domain to condemn the land on behalf of homeowners who were willing to pay "fair market value" for the land.[6] The bill passed in the 1967 session of the state legislature.

Burns demonstrated his deep reservations by not signing the bill, but he allowed it to become law without his signature. It was an instance of Burns creating the appearance of deferring to the legislature while not really bend-ing to their will. For his seven remaining years as governor, Burns did noth-ing to implement the law. While land reform faded as a political issue, the problem of construction on leased land actually became much more acute. Where in 1950 every twentieth owner-occupied house was on leased land, by 1970 every fourth house was on leased land.

When Ariyoshi was elected governor, leasehold conversion was a test of what he had learned from Burns. Would he return to the issue of lease-hold or would he ignore it, as Burns had done? Ariyoshi moved in careful steps, but all in the same direction. He hired an executive from private indus-try to spearhead leasehold conversion. In his first year in office, the 1975 legislature put a ceiling on how much landowners could charge in the rene-gotiation of leases. Thereafter the process of neighborhood organization and negotiation began. When Bishop Estate challenged the constitutionality of the law, the state defended the law in a five-year court battle in which the State of Hawai'i ultimately prevailed in the United States Supreme Court. By the end of Ariyoshi's tenure, nearly seven thousand leases had been con-verted to fee simple ownership under the terms of the law.[7] Thousands more likely were sold privately by large landowners who read the political mes-sage of the legislation and the willingness of Ariyoshi's administration to do battle in court.

Subsequently some of the same people who faulted Ariyoshi for vot-ing against the original Maryland bill criticized leasehold conversion. *Land and Power* pointed out that by the 1980s three-fourths of the remaining lessees were on Bishop Estate land. Many lessees were affluent and lived in Republican-leaning political districts. Therefore, leasehold conversion was a matter of a prosperous group securing "a useful economic benefit . . . over the objections of the representatives of a socially deprived and oppressed group."[8]

Other than in the Hawaiian perspective, land reform faded as a political issue. A conflict that had caused such intense feelings left the scene with little remark, a seeming metaphor of the Democratic era. Nothing evoked the wonder of the original cry for justice, but conversion worked. Most people were satisfied, as were most interests. The edge of discontent was no longer about land tenure per se, but about rapid growth, rapid development, and the question of who benefited and who did not.

LAND AND POWER

The central thesis of the book *Land and Power in Hawai'i* was that young Democrats had come into office advocating "radical reform" only to become middle-aged and absorbed with "getting re-elected, getting established financially, getting ahead." Published in 1985, the book became a phenomenon in the niche book market of Hawai'i. It resulted from a meeting one night between a young researcher, George Cooper, and the widely acclaimed historian, Gavan Daws. After a few drinks, they shared their sense of mutual outrage over the state administration's determination to build a multilane freeway through a pristine valley and over the fluted Ko'olau Mountains of O'ahu.

In lighter moments Daws described himself as a historian of the Victorian period who had discovered the environmental crisis. In the 1970s he played a significant role in the island-based environmental group Life of the Land. He shared Cooper's sense of mission, but was away from Hawai'i much of the time, filling a special chair in history in his native Australia. As a result, most of the research and writing of *Land and Power* was the work of Cooper, a painfully sensitive person who pursued his task with utter sincerity.

In the course of their work, Daws would return from Australia to review hundreds of new pages of manuscript, which he would substantially reduce, only to return on his next visit to new hundreds of pages. While Daws himself was an elegant writer, *Land and Power* was nearly encyclopedic, running to more than five hundred printed pages. If the text was not widely read, the index was. With its simple, oft-repeated theme, it became an influential code for defining Hawai'i as the glow of statehood faded.

Near the end of the book was a chapter profiling Ariyoshi, recounting his involvement in a variety of modest-size real estate developments. For example, in 1960 Ariyoshi was a member of an investment group that bought and later sold sixty acres of land in Maui. The group included Vincent Yano, who would run against Ariyoshi for lieutenant governor in 1970, and Bert T. Kobayashi, soon to be Burns' attorney general. A second transaction occurred in 1962, when Ariyoshi drafted partnership papers for a rural sub-division on the Big Island, for which he was paid in shares. In 1965, along with a law partner, he bought four house lots on Oʻahu, then built and sold four houses over a period of years.

Cooper and Daws proceeded from the premise that Hawaiʻi Democrats were at the center of one of the most heated real estate markets in the world. As a result, involvement in real estate was ubiquitous. Ariyoshi, they concluded, was "a representative figure" but "development was not the major part of his life, nor was he anything more than a small player in the field."[9]

Attempting to define Ariyoshi politically, Cooper and Daws quoted Ariyoshi as believing in "small and safe steps."[10] Recounting Ariyoshi's positions on boards of directors, they wrote that by the early 1960s Ariyoshi "was well on his way to a personal, professional, and business accommodation with Hawaiʻi's old landed interests." As a candidate Ariyoshi stressed "unexceptional issues, often with a conservative cast to them: a balanced budget, governmental efficiency, an improved school system, promotion of local industry." Unlike many Democrats, Ariyoshi's votes had sometimes parted with labor.

The Cooper-Daws analysis erred fundamentally in its belief that Ariyoshi and his colleagues had come into office advocating "radical" reform, which they then conveniently abandoned. Their analysis was oblivious to the centrist, small-business orientation of many urban participants in the Democratic Party, prominently including Japanese Americans. In fact, Ariyoshi was nothing if not consistent. Cooper and Daws conceded, "Unlike some of his contemporaries he had not started out on the left wing of the party, where the idea of land reform as social justice was important, and then drifted in a more conservative direction." Rather, Ariyoshi had never been "a left-liberal, much less a radical."[11]

What the elusive labels of *Land and Power* failed to capture were the original and sometimes paradoxical ways that Ariyoshi—from 1974 forward—pursued island solutions to island problems. This led him to a concept of "managed growth" that not only ran counter to Burns' promotion of rapid development but was without precedent in American politics.

SLOWING DEVELOPMENT

In the early statehood period, Hawaiʻi's population was growing at approximately three times the national average. In context of such unsettling change, the writer Alvin Toffler's *Future Shock* seemed apt: Future shock was "the disorientation and stress brought on by trying to cope with too many changes in too short a time."[12] The effects of "future shock" caused people to re-examine critically the idea that development was inherently good. It was also in this context that the environmental movement began to ignite an understanding of the fragile nature of Hawai'i's living space, and a New Left movement seized on rapid development as the crux of public disenchantment. In the background, the war in Vietnam dragged on, creating its growing legacy of public acrimony.

Arguably the turbulence of the times gave Ariyoshi room to experiment; at heart he was ever the earnest student, obligated to address problems as they were presented to him. In his inaugural address he talked about stewardship. For people who saw him as a caretaker of the Burns legacy, the idea of stewardship was perhaps a further reason to dismiss Ariyoshi. But stewardship is also a word that suggests caring for relationships and resources over long periods of time. Just as Ariyoshi often operated outside the realm of politics as usual, his recitation about stewardship could not really be located on the political continuum of left, center, and right. The good steward cared for the vineyard. The good steward was mindful of preceding generations. The good steward was ultimately an island blend of Biblical, Polynesian, and Confucian teachings.

With land issues churning, Ariyoshi made two appointments that changed the chemistry of the State Land Use Commission. One was a native Hawaiian activist, Collette Y. Machado, and the second was a leader of the League of Women Voters, Carol B. Whitesell. Controversies over land use raged on all islands, but the most intense were on the windward side of O'ahu, where the towns of Kailua and Kāne'ohe had grown rapidly. From there developers had turned up the windward coastline to places where cows still grazed, streams flowed in their original stream beds, people still fished, and a passing driver could stop to buy bananas and papayas. With continued development, the plains of O'ahu were in danger of becoming a single, vast city, devoid of countryside.

THE BATTLE FOR WINDWARD VALLEYS

The most revealing and historically important confrontation was over the future of Waiāhole and Waikāne valleys, which lay directly beyond the developed residential regions of Kāne'ohe and Kahalu'u. These are wet valleys rimmed by steep cliffs and fed by waterfalls and beautiful streams. They were originally perfect places for Hawaiians to settle and grow taro. In the twentieth century they had been acquired by the famous water developer, Lincoln McCandless, and then passed on to his daughter, Elizabeth McCandless Marks. The arable lands were on short leases to household tenants and small, often part-time, farmers. As a combination of large land holdings and powerless tenants, Waiāhole-Waikāne reflected the perpetuation of an elitist, feudal system into post-statehood Hawai'i.

Productivity was low, rents were low, and Marks' return on her land was
also low. Seeking a higher return, she entered into a development agreement
with a near caricature of the politically connected developer in postwar
Hawai'i. His name was Joseph R. Pao. He was born on Kaua'i of Portuguese
ancestry. A graduate of the Catholic St. Louis school in Honolulu, Pao was
a frequent partner of Mitsuyuki Kido, Burns' comrade in the reformation
of the party. Pao's cousin was James P. Ferry, who was Burns' director of the
State Land Board, and Ferry's deputy was Mitsuyuki Kido's brother, Sunao
Kido. Pao had vacationed in Las Vegas with his friend Neal S. Blaisdell, the
mayor of Honolulu, who was on such comfortable terms with the Burns faction despite his membership in the Republican Party. Pao's accountant, Herman Lemke, chaired the City Council, and Pao's favorite planning
consultant was the city's former director of planning, George Houghtailing.

Pao frequently partnered with big landowners, including Bishop Estate
and American Factors, and his agreement with Marks was in that tradition.
Marks had the land and he had the power. He created Windward Partners
for investors, broadening the base of support to include prominent leaders
of the AFL-CIO.

If Ariyoshi had followed the script of *Land and Power*, he would have
postured, then stepped aside in the name of progress. Joe Pao would have
brokered his deal; the crops would have died; the agricultural tenants would
have been removed; and the land would have been subdivided.

In examining what actually happened, a great deal of importance must
go to the influence of community organization in opposition to development. The most pivotal grassroots person was Robert Nakata, who was as
far from being a stereotypical radical as Ariyoshi was from being a stereotypical politician. Nakata spoke softly, smiled shyly, and dressed plainly. He
belonged to one of the Okinawan farm families in Windward O'ahu. By the
early 1970s Nakata was an ordained minister who was paid by the Methodist
church to engage in community work on the windward coast. He began to
hear stories of people driving in limousines down the dirt roads of Waiāhole
and Waikāne. A review of the city's planning map showed the region was
intended to be a huge urban development. Nakata asked to meet with a dozen
or so people in Waiāhole and got twice that many. After Pao's plan emerged
through Land Use Commission records, several hundred alarmed people
turned out for a subsequent meeting.

Nakata, thinking this small community needed all the help it could
get, reached out in several directions, simultaneously setting up liaisons with
the governor's office; windward legislators (including Republican Senator

D. G. "Andy" Anderson); Life of the Land; a regional Hawaiian group (which only recently had begun organizing); and activists in ethnic studies at the University of Hawai'i. From ethnic studies, Nakata found one of the most charismatic organizers of the time, Pete Thompson, a handsome young Hawaiian with a flashing smile and penetrating voice. Thompson was, all in one, a researcher, writer, and high-powered orator who could move a crowd with the spoken word. Thompson was involved with protests across the Hawaiian Islands, as community after community lined up to fight rezonings in a mandatory five-year review of the Land Use Commission boundaries.

Within the Waiāhole community group, the Okinawans were mostly farmers, and the Hawaiians and Filipinos were mostly residential tenants. Initially the farmers circulated letters and wrote petitions while the tenants held back from openly opposing development, fearful that they might be evicted on short notice. In response, Thompson paid special attention to the Waiāhole tenants, spending endless hours building up their confidence to resist the development plan openly. Valley residents particularly were schooled to speak up before the Land Use Commission. Thompson stressed that most of the people on the commission were local people, and if community members testified they would be made comfortable and would be understood, even if they spoke pidgin. If people who did not speak English wanted to testify, their testimony was translated.

Not long after Ariyoshi's narrow victory in the 1974 election, the valley's residents won their own victory with the Land Use Commission, which turned down the rezoning petition of Joe Pao. The following year Pao came at his development plan from another angle, aiming not at Waiāhole but Waikāne. Community tension heightened. Rents, originally low, were raised. Community members agreed among themselves to not pay the increased rents, but instead to pay their existing rents into an escrow fund. By 1975 it also had become apparent that what Nakata called "the ethnic studies folks," and what often was called The Movement, were being led by a Hawai'i affiliate of the Revolutionary Communist Party of America. For a relatively brief moment, an ongoing feudal practice again became joined to a studied, communist opposition.

For the most part the residents of the valleys reacted the way dock and sugar workers had reacted a quarter century before—by accepting the help of people who stepped forward. Departing from a widespread pattern of disrupting Land Use Commission proceedings, the Waiāhole-Waikāne residents maintained a tenuous relationship with the commission. At one hearing, two members of the audience took out bullhorns with the idea of stopping the proceeding—a tactic that had shut down LUC meetings elsewhere. Nakata remembered one of the grassroots leaders of Waiāhole tapping the person with the bullhorn. "This is our show," he said. "We don't want it shut down." The commission again ruled against Pao's development plan.

Thereafter the ax fell. The valley residents were notified that they would be evicted. They went to court to block the eviction. Losing, they appealed. Losing again, they appealed to the Hawai'i Supreme Court, which said that if the community wanted to stop the evictions even temporarily they had to post a bond. Three years had gone by. After their heady victories, the residents were drifting to ever more desperate tactics. They debated whether to raise the money to post the bond or meet the eviction with nonviolent resistance. The community was split.

Throughout, the Kahalu'u Methodist Church kept a collection box dedicated to supporting the people of Waiāhole and Waikāne. Nakata got fifteen Methodist ministers to sign a pledge that, if all else failed, they would go to jail in support of the community. Nonetheless the Okinawan farmers were uncomfortable with the idea that only civil disobedience lay between them and eviction. Many argued for posting the bond. Nakata calculated that Thanksgiving was coming, then Christmas, and then the legislature would meet again. He told himself that something good would happen. By the narrowest of margins a community decision was made to engage in nonviolent resistance to eviction, should it come to that.

The question then became what the residents would do if the police arrived. A siren was to sound the warning. Residents and supporters were drilled in locking arms and forming human circles around houses, but it became apparent that the community was too spread out. As an alternative they decided to block access to the valleys on both ends of the island-encircling Kamehameha Highway.

A rumor reached the community that the police would evict the residents right after the new year. The community invited supporters to camp out in the valley. More than five hundred people came out, but nothing happened. The number of campers dwindled. Nakata told his liaison in the governor's office, Sus Ono, they were thinking about moving everyone to the capitol for a camp-out. In truth their mighty effort was running out of ideas. Nakata thought to himself that after all the work, they were staring failure in the face.

On the fifth day of the new year, the community steering committee was holding its nightly meeting. They received a call from a CB radio operator who had volunteered to watch for movements of police. He reported with great excitement that the police were moving out of the regional police station. The Waiāhole siren sounded. The valley dwellers rushed out to block the highway. Traffic began to pile up. It took the police several hours to convince the protesters that the fervent call had been a false alarm. The alert had been sounded a few minutes before the eleven o'clock change of police shifts. When the valley people opened the highway, they held hands along the side of the road and sang "Hawai'i Aloha." Drivers who had sat for hours honked and waved their support as they passed by. No one was arrested.

All the while, Nakata maintained communication with the governor's office through Sus Ono. Could the governor intervene? There was no answer. From the community's point of view, Ariyoshi—entering his third year in office—was an essentially uncommunicative, do-nothing governor. He made friendly noises and met with them occasionally, but nothing happened.

Unknown to them, Ariyoshi was meeting privately with Elizabeth Marks and her attorney at the governor's mansion, Washington Place, appealing to her to sell her land at a modest price to the State of Hawai'i. Marks was a remote figure from an earlier day. Nakata was the only protester who had talked to her, at a single meeting in which she referred to valley residents as "my people." She complained that the residents of the valley had gone to her baby luau in 1906, and now they were speaking ill of her.

Ariyoshi told her that selling the land would relieve her of an otherwise insoluble problem and allow her to do something good for posterity. It had become apparent that her land would not be rezoned for development. Selling was a way out of the mess. Their meetings continued.

In mid-February 1977 the state's Windward Regional Plan was reaching final form. Beneath the surveys, guidelines, and alternative scenarios for the future lay a commitment to keep Waiāhole and Waikāne in agriculture, and to block development. On one occasion Ariyoshi met with representatives of the protest to find himself confronted with angry words. He was carrying documents that reflected his concern for their issue. Provoked by verbal attacks on his integrity, he raised his voice. "If you read these," he said, "you will know I am trying to help you people." He threw his papers on the table and walked out. It was the only loss of temper as governor to which he would confess. As late as February 25, tenant leaders met with Ariyoshi and left frustrated. What was Ariyoshi doing?

After repeated meetings, Marks agreed to sell six hundred acres in the heart of Waiāhole at ten thousand dollars an acre. If the land had been rezoned, it would have sold for several times and perhaps many times that amount. Ariyoshi believed it was the best six million dollars the state ever spent. On February 27, 1977, he announced the state government was buying the prime agricultural areas of Waiāhole Valley. Details remained, but most of the problem had been resolved.

Ariyoshi's move set off a furor of criticism from legislators. He had acted without their concurrence. He also had used funds intended for the construction of housing. His preemptive stroke was uncharacteristically rash, but it resolved the situation. It was also further proof of his willingness to use the powers of the governorship.

As history, the Waiāhole decision and the leasehold conversion program run together. Both addressed the legacy of a feudal pattern of ownership. In both instances, the State of Hawai'i had used its power to redistribute land. Perhaps it was a faint echo of the function of ruling chiefs in pre-Western times. Indisputably the importance of use rights over fee simple rights figured heavily. While Waiāhole was the most important conflict over development in the middle and late 1970s, it was one of many that reflected Hawai'i's island nature. In what other state in America would such a thing have happened?

THE PIECES OF A PLAN

In his autobiography, Ariyoshi described asking himself a fundamental question:

> *What can we do to preserve a part of old Hawai'i—the Hawai'i we knew as youngsters? Does it still exist in some places? . . . Can we enable our grandchildren to experience the environment of old Hawai'i that we experienced?*

His answer was to draw the line on urbanization not only in Waiāhole but up and down the windward and north shores. In response to one land use conflict after another, Ariyoshi became a land-banker, one who puts land away. He intervened repeatedly on behalf of preservation by acquiring strategically located sites that had been targeted for development: Not only Waiāhole and Waikāne but places with such magical names as Mālaekahana, Kaiaka Point, and Sacred Falls. Previously Burns had bought another large windward valley, Kahana, and the city developed Kualoa, the northern tip of Kāne'ohe Bay, as a regional park. As a result of all these efforts, the windward side of O'ahu remained a lightly populated area interspersed with agricultural preserves and parks.

While some of Ariyoshi's steps were obviously influenced by events of the moment, the Windward Regional Plan provided a systematic rationale. This plan was an early step into a more rational, consistent approach to planning and development. Through survey research, it asked members of the general public what they thought and wanted. This was to become a basic feature of Ariyoshi's planning efforts. Naturally the public favored preservation of rural, open spaces.

The plan led the reader through a careful analysis of pressures for urbanization and suburbanization on the one hand versus agricultural use and open space on the other. The resulting tilt toward agriculture and preservation provided the rationale for both land-banking acquisitions and opposition to widely varied development schemes. The confrontational climate of Waiāhole-Waikāne made headlines, but the overall movement to protect the countryside of Oʻahu went all but unnoticed.

Nonetheless the effort to preserve Oʻahu was of historic importance. Poorly planned development was slowed down. In Windward Oʻahu it virtually stopped. A standard was set for development to be more reasoned and less dependent on the connections of the developer. Not least, the Windward Oʻahu Plan provided an impetus within the Ariyoshi administration for more ambitious plans to moderate and manage Hawaiʻi's growth.

SLOWING POPULATION GROWTH

In the evolution of managed growth, land use considerations merged with the closely related question of population growth. As a state of the United States, with no control over in-migration, how could the government of Hawaiʻi deal with all the people who wanted to reside within its boundaries? How fast could Hawaiʻi grow?

Because of limited land space and tight control of land ownership and land use, rapid population growth was probably more stressful to Hawaiʻi than to any other place in the continental United States. Several factors drove Hawaiʻi's extraordinary growth rate, the most obvious being the accelerated movement of people from other states to Hawaiʻi. A second was the liberalized 1965 immigration law, which increased migration from Asia. A third was the resettlement of refugees from the Vietnam War, which was generating refugees throughout Southeast Asia. Finally, Hawaiʻi had a young population and an increasingly good health care system. As a result, Hawaiʻi had a high birth rate and a low death rate.

The Burns-appointed Commission on Operations, Revenues, and Expenditures described "an air of helplessness" about Hawaiʻi's rate of population growth. Burns himself thought of rapid in-migration as an inevitable consequence of the open, accessible society he had strived for. James Takushi could remember small-group conversations in which Burns said that local people would have to compete with haole from the mainland and also accept that their grandchildren well might be of mixed ancestry.

While there was a widespread concern for maintaining "local culture," newcomers were among those who most actively supported population controls—a phenomenon that Gill had described as the drawbridge phenomenon. Newcomers crossed the Pacific and shouted, "Raise the drawbridge!"

A temporary Commission on Population Stabilization was created by the 1970 legislature, then replaced by a Commission on Population and the Hawaiian Future. The enabling legislation talked about achieving a "desired equilibrium" of population size and density and government services. The commission sought to determine optimal populations in the four counties and to control the number of incoming residents.

The 1970 session also created a Commission on the Year 2000. Like the Population Commission, it generated themes of taking charge of Hawai'i's future, rather than allowing the lifestyle of Hawai'i to be washed away by waves of change.

Such commissions often reflect an active concern but a lack of resolve or clarity. By the time Ariyoshi became governor in 1974, both commissions had generated research, ideas, public discussions, and publicity for the issue of growth. In a general way, both helped expand support for controlling growth, while the specific managed-growth policies were being generated by Ariyoshi's administration.

The thinking on managed growth converged along several paths. One was a constitutional battle over residency requirements for welfare and employment by the State of Hawai'i. The second was a task force appointed by Ariyoshi to find ways to manage growth. The third was formulation of a Hawai'i State Plan.

Of these, the controversy over residency requirements was the most emotionally charged. It began in the early seventies as orderly communities reacted to the highly visible arrival of unemployed young people from the mainland. As a group, these new migrants reflected the turmoil of drugs, free sex, rebellion against authority, and opposition to the war that were sweeping the country. Young people came to Hawai'i not only because of its reputation as a physical paradise, but also its reputation for being a welfare paradise.

In 1971, during Ariyoshi's first year as lieutenant governor, the community reaction catalyzed. The *Honolulu Star-Bulletin* editorially attacked a "Welfare Jet Set." *The Honolulu Advertiser* not only located "mainland longhairs" at the welfare office but also found one who confided, "Just between you and me, I don't need this money, but I want to see what I can get."[13]

Nationally, residency requirements had come to be thought of as crude devices to discriminate against new arrivals and immigrants. The liberal justices of the U.S. Supreme Court of the sixties had consistently struck down state residency requirements for a variety of benefits and services. So when the Democratic regime in Hawai'i looked at residency requirements, it did so at a potential sacrifice of its liberal image. The residency bill was pushed by a prominent senator, George Toyofuku of Kaua'i, whose district was a favorite haven for the young migrants. Whole beaches had been taken over by nude young people, and at least one of their camps was demonstrably a public health risk.

Toyofuku's residency proposal attempted to establish a compelling state interest that would allow it to withstand the scrutiny of the courts. Toyofuku said that most of the youthful transients "are without sufficient funds to support themselves, are unwilling to seek employment and frequently congregate in and around small communities which wholly lack public facilities and services to cope with such vast increases in population." He went on to say that local people "keenly resent this influx" and that a breakdown of law and order might possibly result from ill will and hostility.[14]

A bill passed that maintained federally supported programs for the blind, disabled, medically needy, and families with dependent children but imposed a one-year residency requirement on a purely state-funded program of general assistance. As the bill awaited Governor Burns' signature, Ariyoshi endorsed it as a "desperate move" that was necessary under the circumstances.[15] He cited a study by the Department of Social Services and Housing showing that more than half of all applicants for general assistance in early 1971 were new arrivals from the mainland.

Previously, in the name of an open society, Burns had opposed everything from out-of-state tuition to a hotel room tax on visitors. Signing the welfare bill therefore reflected a shift both for Burns and the political climate of Hawai'i. What might have been a conflict over low-income people in another state was, for Hawai'i, a conflict over its relationship with the rest of the United States. Ariyoshi regretted aloud that the State government had come to "discriminating between resident and transient," saying,

> *While I believe that a person in legitimate need of assistance should be helped regardless of his state of origin . . . the reality of the situation demanded that the rolls be cut and soaring costs halted.*[16]

In practice, the State continued to give short-term emergency payments to people who searched for work. It was the sort of contradiction that caused a State welfare administrator to say, on his retirement, that he started his job "as a flaming liberal" but was leaving as a "burned out bureaucrat."[17] The welfare issue underscored the fact that Ariyoshi was neither an ideological liberal nor an ideological conservative but an islander fixated on the related issues of resources and population. He campaigned for governor in 1974 by saying that Hawai'i should become the first state in America to adopt a policy of slowed growth, saying, "It is irresponsible for public officials to discuss Hawai'i's future in terms of unlimited growth."[18] A slowing of growth was not only economically feasible but imperative "if we are to enjoy the kind of life we want for ourselves and those who will follow us."

By 1977, the issue of rapid growth had become more intense. Excessive population, he told the legislature, "seems to be central to nearly every problem in our state." He listed competition for jobs, agricultural land, parks, and scenic vistas. Too many people translated to increased crime, "too much pressure" on public institutions, and the erosion of "the aloha spirit." In short, "too many people can spell disaster for this State."[19]

The Ariyoshi of 1963 who had argued that the Maryland bill was unconstitutional was now ready to challenge the existing interpretation of the United States Constitution. At his urging, the 1977 legislature passed a one-year residency requirement for local government employment. It was quickly struck down in the federal circuit court. In 1978 the legislature passed a variation, giving preference to newcomers who filed local tax returns. Similarly, a new general-assistance welfare law skirted the constitutional issue by denying aid to future applicants who were able-bodied, childless, and under fifty-five.

In pursuit of the population issue, Ariyoshi also moved from the subject of residency to immigration. Reflecting Hawai'i's mid-Pacific location and Asian relationships, the state had experienced a proportionately larger influx of foreign immigrants than any other state. Because recent immigrants tended to bring more immigrants, the largest group was from the Philippines. In 1976, a record year for in-migration, seven thousand people immigrated to Hawai'i under terms of the new U.S. law. Added to this were two thousand refugees displaced by the Vietnam War.

Ariyoshi argued to the federal government that as a small land space with a comparatively small economy, Hawai'i was not in a position to absorb a disproportionate number of refugees. At a symposium in California he argued that it was hypocritical of the federal government to regulate immigration but not allow the states to have a voice in determining how many immigrants they could absorb. Turning to the broader theme of the symposium, which was federal reorganization, he proposed a "return to a system of governance and decision-making that once again recognizes the sovereign and very necessary role of the state government."[20] It was an extraordinary statement that would become even more significant in years ahead as native Hawaiian nationalists began to agitate for control of Hawai'i's borders.

The relationship of Hawai'i to the rest of America was again the issue, and Ariyoshi again reflected how quickly the political climate had shifted in Hawai'i in the post-statehood period. Was Hawai'i to be like other states? Or was it to be a semiseparate society that periodically struggled with its role as a state? Did Hawai'i follow the liberal political tradition of America? Or did it strangely have something in common with Southern states that were chronically at odds with the federal government?

The Hawai'i of the seventies had experienced a sharp economic downturn. It had few resources and no apparent, quick way to bring good times back. In the tradition of his tight-fisted chairmanship of the Senate Committee on Ways and Means in 1963, Ariyoshi insisted to many unhappy pleaders that the government budget was like a family budget. If you spent beyond your means, you were in trouble.

As the idea of managed growth evolved, it was therefore not only a land use or planning issue but also a fiscal issue. Proof of this emerged in the task force organized by Ariyoshi in 1977. It was overseen not by professional planners but by the director of his Budget and Finance Department, Eileen R. Anderson. Thirty-eight people served on the task force, many of them representing government agencies. They produced a book-length document titled "Growth Management Issues in Hawai'i,"[21] which cautioned that managing population growth would require a fundamental shift "in some of the basic political, economic, and philosophical values of our modern society":

> *We may see a new kind of attitude—an attitude that calls for enhancing the conservation ethic, questions the growth ethic that "more is better" and recognizes our residents' unity with our natural environment.*[22]

The result, it said, might be "the evolution of a 'growth management ethic.'" "Growth Management" weighed various strategies against the likelihood that they would be found unconstitutional. The authors distinguished between different direct and indirect controls. Direct controls were likely to conflict with the United States Constitution, but indirect controls over natural resources were not. The movement to slow growth needed a larger framework of indirect controls. This was to become one of the motivating factors of the Hawai'i State Plan.

THE HAWAI'I STATE PLAN

To the curious visitor, Hawai'i may have seemed intoxicated with the making of plans. The young state conceived of itself as a place of dreams and visions. Planning was the rational way to make visions manifest and the State of Hawai'i, from the beginning, was devoted to planning. Hawai'i was just small enough, centralized enough, separate enough, and otherwise self-contained enough to tempt intelligent people to believe they could see Hawai'i as a whole. Hawai'i could be planned. The most strategy-conscious agency of its government, the Department of Planning and Economic Development, fused at least nominally its two often-conflicting pursuits into one effort. Implicitly, planning was on a par with economic development.

In the early years of statehood, organizations ranging across the political spectrum embraced the cause of planning. The Chamber of Commerce created the O'ahu Development Conference under the leadership of an erudite planner named Aaron Levine. The League of Women Voters embraced planning as synonymous with good government. The ILWU, while its positions on rezoning sometimes reflected pursuit of its members' self-interest,[23] became a major force in planning. Early on, these organizations backed the effort to preserve the profile of Diamond Head from development. This watershed controversy occurred in 1966, combining an outcry of protest with the meticulous efforts of a planner, Robert Van Dorpe, through which the view planes of the famous landmark were preserved.

The Burns administration had attempted to devise early-day computer models of the economy. To develop more rational government, it had invested in a Planning, Programming, and Budgeting System, PPBS, which for a while was treated with reverence. It also wrote an early version of a State general plan. Yet under Burns these plans operated more as pleasant background noise, because the political consensus that guided the early statehood period revolved around rapid economic development.

When the consensus supporting rapid growth came unstuck around 1970, many forces and interests had to be involved in creating a new plan. The tortuous path that wound through everything from welfare issues to Waiāhole Valley led eventually to a resolution that was passed by the 1975 legislature. It directed the administration of the new governor to revise the State of Hawai'i's general plans. In context, George Ariyoshi obviously was not the instigator of planning, but he was to become its champion. What had begun as a discussion of rational stewardship became a proposal for the most encompassing plan imaginable.

Although fed by budgetary concerns, the draft of the plan was generated in the Department of Planning and Economic Development (DPED) under the direction of Hideto Kono. Kono's career had been what Ariyoshi's might have been if Ariyoshi had not gone to law school and not run for public office. Like Ariyoshi, Kono was articulate but reflective. He was trim, erect, and always well dressed, with a big smile, square jaw, and wavy grey hair. Like Ariyoshi, he had served in the Military Intelligence Language Service. At the University of Hawai'i, he had studied social psychology, then earned a master's degree in political science. He was first a civilian executive of the army, then an increasingly senior business executive. He had repeatedly taken leave from executive jobs to help staff the institutions of change in Hawai'i, including the constitutional convention of 1950, the first Democratic legislatures, the statehood reorganization commission, and finally the formation of the East West Center.

Kono had gotten started in the private sector as an assistant to the assistant to the president of Dole Pineapple Company. Eventually he was given the job of developing the Dole brand in East Asia, where he spent eight years, returning to Hawai'i just in time for Ariyoshi's ascent to the governorship.

Like a good student of political science, Kono saw a world composed of ever-changing centers of influence.[24] He once reminded the president of Amfac, Henry Walker, "Your group [the Big Five] used to run the whole show, more or less from the Pacific Club." The 1954 election had created a new power center in the Democratic Party, and the new and the old necessarily had to interact—hence his corporate beginnings as assistant to the assistant to the president of Dole. In his view the drive for statehood had temporarily unified people, but unity had given way to the formation of multiple power centers. If people did not get their way they would "make their point with loud squeaks rather than the greatest good for the greatest number."

In such things as state government public works, Kono believed the budget was in danger of becoming an aggregation of projects backed by special pleaders. Initially Kono had thought the central task of planning would be to develop rational guidelines for public works, "because if you do it based on friends, there's no end to it." Rational decisions were especially important because Hawai'i's territorial infrastructure was aging while its population was growing rapidly. He saw the Planning, Programming and Budgeting System started by Burns as generating massive amounts of data without any meaningful benefit.[25] At some point his and Ariyoshi's thinking took a leap based on their evolving experience with preserving the rural character of Windward O'ahu—what Kono described interestingly as "an urban panic." It was in this climate that long-range planners within DPED began to formulate a more encompassing plan for the State of Hawai'i.

Informed communication was central to this new thinking. Kono believed that a diverse democratic society, like Hawai'i in the seventies, lacking the controls of a monarchy or an oligarchy, must make a special effort to engage in dialogue. Where disagreements existed, one element of society at least could understand the assumptions, beliefs, and needs of another element. Through discussion, an aggregation of narrow interests could be subtly transformed to a broader public interest. When Kono's department took the first draft of the State Plan out for public review, the county governments wanted in on the decision-making structure. The counties were added to a policy council, which Kono was to chair, with the lofty admonition that members behave "as trustees of our children's children."

ARIYOSHI PRESENTED THE MAIN FEATURES of the draft State Plan in the beginning of his fourth year as governor. He told the legislature the real question was "whether we have the spiritual determination to be masters of our destiny,"[26] a query that would echo through the political world of Hawai'i for at least a dozen years. With the extinction of the sovereign Hawaiian nation in 1898, Hawai'i had explicitly lost any semblance of being self-directed. With statehood, Hawai'i had regained some measure of autonomy, but how much? Ariyoshi represented a deep impulse in Hawai'i to push the boundaries of self-direction. The plan, Ariyoshi said,

> *is the beginning of us finally taking control of our destiny. It will serve notice that we know what is good for this State, what is proper and what is achievable.*[27]

The plan was built on a descending hierarchy of theme, goals, objectives, and policies. The theme had to do with Hawai'i's people valuing self-sufficiency at the individual and family level, as well as social and economic mobility and a healthy community. The first of three goals was a strong, viable economy "characterized by stability, diversity, and growth." The second goal was a beautiful, stable, clean, quiet environment. The third goal was about individuals and families in context of healthy, caring communities. Among the thirty-five objectives, population was covered first. There were no fewer than 167 objectives. The senator who chaired a special committee on the State Plan, Francis Wong, said the plan was a step toward creating an orderly government process "rather than reacting to brush fires which often time become roaring forest fires."[28] The year of its introduction, the plan passed the Senate unanimously and passed the House by forty-nine to two.

Ariyoshi spoke about the plan over and over with great intensity. He described the new law as second in importance only to the state constitution. He portrayed it as another instance of Hawai'i leading the nation in innovation and good government. This idea of Hawai'i selectively leading America was then still current. Land use reformers from around the country had studied Hawai'i's land use law, and there was a widespread expectation that the island-based ideas generated in Hawai'i would become germane to a continent.

Time proved otherwise. By adopting growth management, Hawai'i was distinctly not leading America, but underscoring its differences with America. In fact Hawai'i had institutionalized a system of comprehensive planning that in the continental states was virtually unthinkable.

Otherwise, the State Plan was an example of the journey being more interesting than the destination. The plan was refined for six years through hearings, public surveys, workshops, conferences, committee meetings, and finally legislative amendments. One key provision called for the adoption of functional plans in twelve areas—agriculture, conservation, education, energy, higher education, health, historic preservation, housing, recreation, tourism, transportation, and water resources. These plans were laboriously developed by teams of public servants and citizen advisers. The legal issues usually had to do with the extent to which the State Plan, as an act of the legislature, had the force of law. Was it a sort of supra-law that might override other laws? Was it a mandate? Was it a set of regulations?

Step by step, the idea of the State Plan as law-giving yielded to the idea of guidance. Finally the 1984 legislature amended the law to explicitly state that the functional plans were "guidelines" for the four counties and "statements of policy to guide" state agencies.

One of the most cogent descriptions of the State Plan was made in a paper by Kent Keith, a resident intellectual of Ariyoshi's cabinet. Keith argued that while the law amounted only to guidelines it nonetheless created a process for making complicated decisions. In this sense, Keith argued, the Hawai'i State Plan was akin to laws covering administrative procedures and environmental impact statements.[29] A member of the Land Use Commission of the day said, "It was like the Bible. Different people quoted different passages in opposition to each other. We still had to make the hard decisions."

Repeated surveys of public opinion, conducted for the plan, supplied a broad public perspective on growth-related issues. In a 1981 survey, members of the public were asked whether Hawai'i's population should grow faster, at about the same rate, slower, or not at all. Half said slower, and 21 percent said not at all. Did the respondent agree or disagree with the idea that "every effort should be made to keep agricultural and conservation lands from changing to urban use." Four-fifths agreed. Similarly, survey research overwhelmingly validated the state government's strong hand in planning. When asked whether government should have a "major role" in planning, or whether planning should be left to the private sector, 93 percent favored government planning. When asked if state government should in general do more, less, or about what it was doing, half the sample said more, and more than a third said about the same. Only 10 percent suggested less

—this only a year after the conservative Ronald Reagan had been elected president on a platform of downsizing government. The mere existence of such widely publicized survey research surely had an effect on both the executive and legislative branches of government.

In a similar vein, the plan succeeded in generating a large amount of direct public participation. The workshops had a sprawling, village-meeting quality. People knitted their brows and thought deeply. Inevitably they thought about their own spheres of interest, but they also struggled to think about the whole. On the downside, it seemed that people could not hold so much stuff in their brains at once.[30] While undoubtedly everything does relate to everything, as the ecologist Barry Commoner proclaimed, the individual mind is unaccustomed to such an exercise.

Nonetheless, in significant measure through the plan, Ariyoshi achieved a sense of wide inclusion. His passion was genuine. He helped move the center of gravity from rampant growth to managed growth. Beyond the obvious island impetus for the plan, there was something that had to do with an evolving Hawai'i culture, in which Euro American, Asian, and Hawaiian concerns fused. All things were governed by webs of relationship. Through good relationships, order was achieved. Ariyoshi had embarked on his journey with a call for the people of Hawai'i to become masters of their own destiny. In 1984, with hindsight, Ariyoshi told the legislature the plan was a gift to the next generation. It had tended to right things: "We were losing our balance," he said. "We were losing our way."

THE INTERSTATE HIGHWAY

Like the controversy over Waiāhole-Waikāne, the issue of whether to build an additional freeway to Windward O'ahu deeply divided people along pro- and antidevelopment lines during the 1970s and well into the 1980s. The freeway battle—in some ways unique in the country—was a prime example of how the power and largesse of the federal government together undermined the idea of Hawai'i working out its own future.

As subsequent lobbying was to prove, the most enduring attraction of the freeway was that the federal government supplied 90 percent of the money for interstate defense highway construction. As an economic stimulus, the federal highway fund was the next best thing to free money. The idea of building three federal interstate defense highways on O'ahu had developed in the pro-growth environment of the Burns era. As one writer would observe, to expect Burns to let "thousands of construction jobs to slip by, when he needed a crutch to prop up Hawai'i's failing economy, would be expecting too much."[31] In fact, the three highways had been considered a political coup, since by definition no highway on an island could be interstate. The rationale of national defense was only slightly less feeble. H-3 was designed to link Pearl Harbor on the leeward side to Kāne'ohe Marine Corps Air Station on the windward side. But given the fact that the only threat of war was nuclear, the idea of linking the two military bases by a multilaned freeway was an anachronism.

By the time Burns left office in 1974, H-1 along the leeward side of O'ahu and H-2 up the central plain of O'ahu both had been built without significant opposition. H-3 had been in planning for a decade, and strong opposition had set in during preliminary construction. The idea survived the election season, because Ariyoshi was the only Democratic gubernatorial candidate to support continued development of the freeway. A year after Ariyoshi's election, the activists Pete Thompson and Bob Nakata joined forces to fight not only for preservation of Waiāhole-Waikāne but to stop the freeway, which they suspected would put pressure on land values and act as a stimulus to development. Three thousand people filled the capitol in 1975 demanding an end to the freeway's development, but their views were offset by the lobbying of the construction industry and the general support of windward commuters, who increasingly found the existing Pali and Likelike intermountain highways to be congested.

ENVIRONMENTAL ACTIVISTS AND THE NATIONAL ENVIRONMENTAL POLICY ACT

Had it not been for the federal highway fund, H-3 would never have been started. Had it not been for federal environmental legislation, H-3 would never have been stopped.

Originally the highway was routed through the botanically and archaeologically rich Moanalua Valley, just outside urban Honolulu. Moanalua was owned by the estate of Samuel M. Damon, whose descendant Frances "Patches" Damon[32] sought to understand where the highway was actually to be built, and how the highway would affect the valley's archaeological and botanical features. "Patches" Damon would remark that she could easily be mistaken for a little old lady in tennis shoes, but in fact she possessed a law degree and had studied at Oxford. While hiking, she asked botanist Paul Weissich what would happen if the highway didn't go through the valley. He replied that the highway was "almost" there. She said "almost" was the key word: "It isn't here yet, and it is not going to be either." Thereafter she would say the idea was not hers, but "came from somewhere else," possibly from her deceased mother, Gertrude Damon, who had taken notes on the oral traditions of Moanalua from a Hawaiian woman, Namakahelu.

Namakahelu was blind, she chanted, and she was attached to the valley in the symbiotic way that traditional Hawaiians were attached to their *ahupuaʻa* (land section from mountain to sea).[33]

When Damon discovered her mother's notebooks on Moanalua, she stayed up twenty-four hours reading about the creation of the ancient Hawaiian migrations and settlement. Grandfather Damon had created Moanalua Gardens, a park in the mouth of the valley that was open to the public and maintained by the Damon estate, and "Patches" now led her family into transforming the upper reaches of the valley into a 3,000-acre park. By walking up an old carriage road, the visitor could experience an unspoiled environment in which native flora abounded. A beautiful stream flowed, and next to the stream sat a huge flat-faced boulder that was filled with Hawaiian petroglyphs. Realizing that no one could appreciate the valley without seeing it, "Patches" assembled a staff who converted visiting hikers into supporters of maintaining the land as it was.

The botanist Weissich was sent to show the park plan to the Department of Transportation (DOT). In a conference room filled with government engineers, he unrolled a nine-foot long map. "Gentlemen," he said, "you are not going to build a highway through Moanalua Valley." A long silence followed. In the next meeting, Dr. Fujio Matsuda, Burns' transportation director, announced that the highway was indeed going to be built through Moanalua, and that the highway would become a scenic parkway, opening up new vistas to the motoring public. Further, he argued, the institutions of democracy supported it, most importantly the legislature. "The voice of assent rarely is heard," he would say, "but the voice of dissent is loud and prominent."

The environmental group Life of the Land (LOL) had just begun to explore the Environmental Impact Statement (EIS) requirements of the National Environmental Policy Act, which had been passed in 1970. A young activist named Jo Ann Yukimura, who later became the antigrowth mayor of Kauaʻi, wrote a brief on the EIS. The pioneering environmental activist (and LOL founder) Tony Hodges was simultaneously pushing for Damon to file a law suit. Believing prophetically that native Hawaiians had the greatest long-term potential as protectors of the land, Hodges also began encouraging Hawaiians in the windward area to defend their traditional *kuleana* lands from incursion.

In the meantime, a young attorney named Boyce Brown had begun building a legal case against the highway even though he had no client. Working initially for nothing and always for below-market fees, he devoted much of his life to this one issue. Brown's first move was to argue that an EIS was required for completion. In response the State highways division produced a twenty-three page document, which Brown successfully attacked as inadequate. Work stopped for two years while a new EIS was developed that eventually filled eighteen volumes.

Brown next turned to a provision in the highway law that reflected society's growing sensitivity to the negative effects of freeways. This provision, 4(f), prohibited the use of federal funds if a highway required land from parks, historic sites, wildlife preserves, and so on. The U.S. Department of the Interior had in the meantime placed Moanalua Valley on the national register of historic places, and Brown successfully blocked construction through Moanalua. The petroglyphs had prevailed. While the engineers studied alternative routes to Pearl Harbor, another four years passed. When H-3 was revived, the route had been moved one valley over to a path of lesser but still considerable resistance.

In the meantime, a federal flood control project had created a small lake and park, known as Hoomaluhia, beneath the windward path of the highway. To prevent urbanization of the buffer area between the park and the freeway, the county government had expanded the park up the mountain to the planned highway. As a result, one federally initiated project was touching a second. This sent Boyce Brown back to court with another 4(f) suit, arguing that H-3 would illegally impinge on the expanded park. In other words, an innocuous park project, planned in tandem with H-3, became the new basis for stopping H-3—a position eventually upheld by the Ninth Circuit Court of Appeals in San Francisco.

Ariyoshi by this time had invested heavily in windward planning, as well as the preservation of windward open spaces and agriculture. He believed that the level of windward development was an ongoing management issue, and that if people worked at preserving Windward Oʻahu as he had, then it would not be overdeveloped as a result of the highway. He ran out of patience with the law suits, as had a consulting engineer named Stanley Kawaguchi, who spent even more of his life than Brown working on H-3.[34] Kawaguchi wrote a paper arguing that environmental law was out of balance with community needs and desires. Further, he contended, the federal court had gone from being an interpreter of law to administrator and decision-maker, concluding,

> *We should not permit our courts to usurp this role. As for the H-3 project itself, the record clearly shows that it is indeed time to say enough for the environment.*[35]

At a joint meeting of the state and federal highway divisions, Kawaguchi summarized several options, the most desperate being to seek a congressional exemption from federal law. To his surprise, Ariyoshi's director of transportation, Wayne Yamasaki, got Ariyoshi's support for pursuing the unprecedented exemption.[36]

By this time, Dan Inouye had been a United States senator for twenty-four years and was a major national figure. Spark M. Matsunaga, a veteran House member, was the junior senator, having replaced the Republican Hiram Fong. Dan Akaka represented the neighbor islands and Windward Oʻahu in the House, and the broadcaster Cec Heftel represented Honolulu. While the tactic of an exemption was not without risk, proponents of the exemption were secure in H-3 gradually having won the battle of public opinion.[37] Inouye, Matsunaga, and Akaka personally attended joint meetings[38] and signed on to a two-year strategy, which was developed with the help of a state-hired lobbyist. The lobbying scenario assumed that the highway bill, as a key part of the entire budget, would be hung up in a congress divided between a Democratic majority in the House and a Republican majority in the Senate. In a perilous last step, the exemption was to be moved into the House and Senate Appropriations committees, on which Akaka and Inouye, respectively, sat.

A nationwide reaction to environmental regulation played a significant part in the strategy. Accordingly, the proposed exemption was a test of how well Hawaiʻi's congressional delegation, reputedly one of the nation's most liberal, could work in a conservative environment. Yamasaki and Kawaguchi met eventually with all 100 senators. These conversations invariably turned on the way that the planned expansion of Hoomaluhia Park had hung up H-3 in Federal Circuit Court. Kawaguchi argued that doubling the park size up to the highway boundary was good planning, which by almost any standard it was. Therefore, he argued, the court decision, carried to its logical extreme, could force highway agencies to oppose all parks that approached highways, as well as the designation of historic sites, wetlands, and other protected areas.[39]

In a concerted effort to protect 4(f), many of the environmental organizations in the country enlisted in opposition to the H-3 exemption, including the Sierra Club, Friends of the Earth, the Audubon Society, and the National Wildlife Federation. Mayor Fasi—who originally had supported the highway—retained a lobbyist who led a furious effort to rededicate the money to mass transit or some other combination of traffic programs. An influential Republican senator from Vermont, Robert Stafford, chairman of the Environment and Public Works Committee, emerged as the key opponent in the Senate. In the spring of 1986 Stafford wrote a public letter urging Ariyoshi and Fasi to work with him on transportation alternatives for Oʻahu. Ariyoshi denounced Stafford for interfering in Hawaiʻi's affairs.

As a result of Stafford's opposition, the prospects for the exemption seemed stronger in the Democratic House. At the last moment of the last committee-level amendments to the national highway bill, Akaka said he had an amendment on the clerk's desk. It passed without debate, roll call, or stated opposition. A congressman from California, who had promised the environmentalists that he would watch out for the exemption, asked Akaka, "Was that your highway bill?"

Thereafter partisan conflict between the two houses hung up the budget, as predicted. The next step was to insert the exemption inside a Continuing Resolution, the goal of which was to keep the federal government functioning on the old budget until a new budget could be adopted. Attention initially focused on what was widely interpreted as a showdown inside the public works and environmental committee between Inouye and the committee chair, the Republican Stafford. Amendment after amendment arose to the public works bill, but not the exemption. The opponents of H-3 interpreted the lack of action as a defeat for the vaunted Inouye.

Fasi's lobbyist in Washington was insisting that the environmental groups take an uncompromising stand against the exemption so Fasi could appear to be the voice of reason by promoting the transfer of H-3 funds to alternative projects. Instead Fasi called a press conference in Honolulu to gloat over Inouye's apparent inability to sway Stafford's committee. He appeared at City Hall in a cleric's collar and conducted a mock funeral over a cardboard headstone that said "H-3 RIP." Rick Ziegler of the Stop H-3 Association thought Ariyoshi and Inouye were "both justifiably insulted and that any hope for a compromise had ended."[40] Ziegler was painfully aware that the Stop H-3 Association was losing the battle for public opinion; it had become a coordinating group that relied on Boyce Brown's legal maneuvering. He thought what Stop H-3 needed was a solid alliance with the Hawaiian community, and he remembered crawling through the brush along the new route in Hālawa Valley looking for Hawaiian cultural artifacts. "Lord, just one good petroglyph," he said to himself.

On September 23, Inouye moved the exemption onto the Senate floor in the form of an amendment to the Continuing Resolution. The floor debate had curious moments in which the question of Hawai'i's relationship to the rest of the United States flickered strangely. "It all began in the summer of 1959," Inouye said, when Hawai'i entered the union. Shortly thereafter the Hawai'i delegation succeeded in including the new state in the Interstate Highway Act, and the federal and State highway divisions mapped out the three highways, the last running "from Pearl Harbor, our nation's most important naval facility in the Pacific."

"We have been waiting since Statehood," Inouye said. "I'm not suggesting that since this highway happens to be in Hawai'i, we can do whatever we want with it—no." But he wanted his colleagues to know that the State had dealt with every issue except the peculiarities of 4(f). Stafford responded, "This is not a vote on Hawai'i. H-3 happens to be in Hawai'i, which many of us regard as a national treasure." The only senator who spoke for Stafford's position was the Republican John Chafee of Rhode Island, who said, "Hawai'i, abide by the rules." Otherwise, Stafford was deserted on all sides. Even his vice chairman voted for Hawai'i's exemption, as did the Republican majority leader, Robert Dole of Kansas, whose bond with Inouye dated to an army hospital where both were treated for war wounds. The resulting Senate vote was seventy-eight to sixteen.

Given the intensity of partisan conflict between the two houses, passage of a unified version of the Continuing Resolution was still not a foregone conclusion. The September 30 deadline for transfer of funds to alternative transportation projects, such as mass transit, was fast approaching. Ariyoshi drafted a letter to the United States secretary of transportation asking that $716 million be released to the City and County of Honolulu to develop alternative projects. The letter went into a bottom drawer and was never mailed.[41] Ariyoshi talked to the congressional delegation, who confirmed Kawaguchi's view that the exemption would not be debated in the House, virtually ensuring its passage.

The Continuing Resolution came out of conference in mid-October. The conference committee found that alternatives were neither prudent nor feasible, and also that archaeological sites—specifically the Luluku agricultural complex that had been discovered belatedly at the base of the Ko'olau Mountains—were not to be subjected to review under 4(f). The joint resolution passed the House by a one-vote margin that included the vote of the freshman congressman from Hawai'i, Neil Abercrombie, who had temporarily replaced Heftel while Heftel waged a campaign to succeed Ariyoshi as governor. Although Abercrombie was a political dissident and longtime opponent of H-3, he said H-3 was a "done deal."

H-3 WAS IMPORTANT in itself. It also showed that even though Hawai'i was a small state, it had accumulated an extraordinary amount of influence through its two votes in the Senate. While Hawai'i's delegation was routinely flailed by political conservatives for supporting liberal legislation, H-3 revealed Hawai'i's effectiveness—particularly Inouye's effectiveness—in organizing bipartisan support for what he wanted. It also underscored Inouye's instinct for working the bipartisan center. Subsequently, House Speaker Tip O'Neill tried to get an exemption for the redesign of a freeway that runs through

Boston, but failed,[42] and no exemption comparable to H-3 has since passed Congress. Neither was Section 4(f) of the Highway Act amended, even though seventy-eight senators had agreed that it lent itself to being misconstrued.

H-3 was completed by Ariyoshi's successor in 1997. Originally estimated to cost a quarter billion dollars, it eventually cost $1.3 billion.[43] The resulting traffic relief considerably exceeded the most optimistic engineering projections. Contrary to the beliefs of its opponents, it has not at least initially set off a cycle of growth in Windward Oʻahu. The activist Ziegler thought that while the antihighway forces had lost on the highway battle they had awakened many against excessive development, a view echoed by Nakata.

Above all, H-3 illustrated the extent to which Hawaiʻi was shaped by outside forces, or what the writer Noel Kent called "Hawaiʻi under the influence." The courtroom manipulations of federal environmental law, the vehement protests that were unsupported by public opinion, the State fixation on "free" federal money, the fact that the phenomenal costs were virtually immaterial—all had one thing in common: They contradicted the idea of Hawaiʻi mastering its own destiny. H-3 was about federal dollars, federal facilities, federal regulations, federal lawsuits, and finally an extraordinary federal resolution of a deeply rooted conflict within Hawaiʻi over the nature of what was desirable development.

George Ariyoshi was the youngest of the 1954 Democrats, filling a void among Burns' followers.

Ariyoshi's courteous demeanor obscured his underlying determination and focus.

Governor and Mrs. George Ariyoshi.

Protests against development of Waiāhole and Waikāne valleys. Courtesy of The Honolulu Advertiser

*Republicans D. G. Andy Anderson
(top),* Patricia Saiki (left), *and Fred
Rohlfing (bottom)* underscored the
Republican Party's failure to win in
Hawai'i even when it had skilled,
attractive candidates.

Anderson engineered a hollow partisan victory with Fasi's comeback as a Republican. *Courtesy of* The Honolulu Advertiser

Alvin Shim was a ubiquitous mentor who constantly prodded the Democratic establishment. Courtesy of The Honolulu Advertiser

The much sought-after Walter M. Heen was a reminder of the Hawaiian past who foreshadowed the Hawaiian political revival. Courtesy of the Heen family

Robert C. Oshiro eventually managed five winning gubernatorial campaigns. Courtesy of The Honolulu Advertiser

Governor Ariyoshi with a new lieutenant governor, John Waihe'e, circa 1982. Courtesy of The Honolulu Advertiser

With Burns in failing health, Ariyoshi served as acting governor.

Carol Fukunaga was one of the most enduring politicians to come out of the political renewal movement of the 1970s. Photo by Tom Coffman

Protests in the 1980s increasingly focused on native Hawaiian issues.

Chapter 12

The Pacific and Asia

One day in 1967, a packet arrived in the governor's office from Osaka, Japan, announcing Osaka's coming international exposition, Expo '70. The packet was routed to a young development officer, Tom Sakata, in the Department of Planning and Economic Development. Sakata had traveled to Japan as a child and spoke a modest amount of Japanese. He had served as president of the Japanese Junior Chamber of Commerce during the early statehood controversy over integrating the ethnic chambers of commerce, a move he had opposed.

Sakata recommended that Hawai'i participate in the Osaka fair. He cautioned that presenting Hawai'i in Japan would be expensive, but said it could be worth it. As Governor Burns considered the idea, he received a letter from the Expo president evoking Hawai'i's century-long relationship with Japan and "the main role of Hawai'i as a link between East and West."[1] Burns signed on, and to Sakata's surprise the legislature appropriated nearly a million dollars with no strings attached. Overnight, Sakata's life changed, as he became a trans-Pacific commuter. Less apparently, the future of Hawai'i had changed as well.

The opening of a special relationship with Japan reflected not only culture and geography but Hawai'i's need for outside investment capital. In the nineteenth century, the plantation economy had been capitalized by New England money and made profitable by the subsidies, quotas, and price supports of the United States government. By the time Burns responded to Sakata's recommendation with such enthusiasm, the sugar industry was incrementally retreating in Hawai'i. It continued with an ever-changing combination of quotas and price supports, but these were not keeping the more marginal plantations open. At one point, Hawai'i sugar was selling into the protected domestic market for eighteen cents a pound, while sugar from other nationally protected markets—together forming a world "dumping" market—was selling for as low as four cents a pound. In other areas of Hawai'i's economy, the Vietnam War had swollen the military sector, but war by definition was a boom and bust proposition, and by 1971 a majority of Americans were clearly sick of the war.

While economic planners pored over ideas to diversify the economy, nothing worked faintly as well as tourism. It required investment in public infrastructure, but private capital responded by building resorts. From the 1950s onward, Hawai'i's local corporations were no longer able to generate enough capital to propel resort development, so a key feature of the statehood period was an ongoing search for low-interest money from bond markets and private investment.

Burns was acutely sensitive to the opinions of Wall Street investors (as all subsequent governors would be), because Wall Street rated bonded debt, set interest rates, and bought bond issues. As an investor of public capital, Burns cut a famous deal with Laurance S. Rockefeller on construction of one of the world's most tasteful resorts, the Mauna Kea Hotel in the north Kona district of the Big Island. The State built the highway that ran past the resort and Rockefeller built the resort itself. Other than resort investment, a significant amount of American capital came to Hawai'i as a result of new condominium property development strategies, which were devised by the famous financier Chinn Ho and the attorney Matsuo Takabuki, who was Burns' all-purpose adviser.

Otherwise, for a capital source, there was Japan, a nation of savers recently recovered from war. Japan had successfully played host to the 1968 Olympics in Tokyo and was now reaching out to other countries through the Osaka exposition. In the Cold War and the prosecution of the Korean and Vietnam wars, Japan had become America's indispensable ally and, partly because of favorable trade agreements with the United States, an often-remarked economic miracle.

As Japan's people were again getting out in the world, they rediscovered Hawai'i. Japanese sumo executives visited Hawai'i in 1964 looking for opponents for their young wrestlers. On Maui they found a young Hawaiian athlete named Jesse Kuhaulua, who wrestled with the Maui Sumo Club. They subsequently put him into training in Japan, where he was given the name Takamiyama. Excitement over Takamiyama peaked in 1972 when he won the emperor's cup at the Nagoya *basho,* one of the four main tournaments of the year. When Takamiyama returned for a three-day tour of Hawai'i, George Ariyoshi was so moved by Takamiyama's successes that he stayed with Takamiyama day and night.[2]

Extensive Japanese travel to Hawai'i also began in the 1960s as Japan loosened its restrictions on overseas spending. For Japan's growing number of overseas travelers, Hawai'i provided something familiar as well as something different. Japanese could find their language, food, drink, television shows, architecture, religions, and cultural practices in both an island and an American setting. They could experience a taste of Hawaiian culture, which as music and dance they embraced with Japanese enthusiasm. The number of Japanese visitors to Hawai'i doubled between 1960 and 1965, then nearly quadrupled between 1965 and 1970.[3] While the total was still small compared to what it would become, the trend was set. Thereafter the travel industry had its eye on the Japanese visitor count to the point of obsession.

In the big picture, the Japan connection fit with Burns' view of Hawai'i as the hub of what he imagined to be the Great Wheel of the Pacific. The original theme of the Hawai'i exhibit at Osaka was, "Hawai'i, the Center of the Pacific Community." The attention Burns paid to the Osaka exposition was reminiscent of his level of concentration on statehood. He engaged in dozens of meetings and wrote hundreds of letters. Would Hawai'i be inside an American pavilion or shoulder the added expense of a free-standing pavilion with its own identity? "Since Hawai'i is unique and different from the other American states," Burns wrote to the Expo, "we prefer not to be situated within the American Park complex." When the location of a free-standing pavilion became an issue, his secretary slipped him a note from Sakata in Japan that said, "We're not going to get anything worthwhile without some kind of pull." Burns then communicated directly with the Minister of International Trade and Industry, Masayoshi Ōhira (who was later to become a prime minister of Japan), an early clue of Hawai'i's access to Japan's elite.

Originally the exhibit was heavily conceptual, portraying Hawai'i as the point of convergence for ideas and cultures. When it opened, it was criticized for being cold and abstract. Burns was critiqued in the daily press ("the haole press") for micro-management, but was lavished with praise by the surviving Japanese community newspaper, *The Hawai'i Herald*. The pavilion closed briefly for an emergency makeover. In came more landscaping and a troupe of Hawaiian singers and dancers. From Osaka, Sakata wrote, "The main problem now is to continue with as much live entertainment as we can afford. Japanese public doesn't seem interested in a sophisticated approach."[4] As one of the few pavilions with regular performances, it was a popular success, but like the travel industry itself, it was successful at a price. However much Hawai'i sought to be a high-concept society, visitors wanted it to be an exotic but secure escape, the land of swaying palms where people sang and danced.

Burns, accompanied by Mrs. Burns, led a Hawai'i delegation to Osaka. Sakata thought the Japanese liked Burns' stoic, quiet bearing. Hawai'i's pavilion contractor in Japan booked the historic Tsuruya Teahouse in the cultural center of Kyoto in Burns' honor.[5] Traditionally visitors sat at low tables on tatami mats, but to avoid calling attention to Beatrice Burns' wheelchair, the hosts stripped the room, carpeted it and equipped it with Western-style furniture.

Burns made a presentation to the Keidanren, a sort of supra-chamber of business that is described in English as the Economic Federation of Japan. For the enthusiast of Japan, the Keidanren symbolizes a purposeful society guided by a spirit of cooperation. For Japan's critics, it is a perpetuation of the *zaibatsu* combine from the prewar period. While the Keidanren has often been criticized in North America, it has been regarded more dispassionately in Hawai'i as a facilitator of business and investment. The goal of the Keidanren meeting was to stimulate Japanese investment in Hawai'i, against a backdrop of rapidly expanding Japanese travel to Hawai'i. Burns said it was a special honor to "be fed and hosted by such distinguished gentlemen and then turn right around and try to take their money away." In describing his Pacific Community, he predicted that in the twenty-first century Japan would assume and share Pacific leadership not only in economic development but "social, cultural, technological, and ecological harmony":

> *One cannot help but marvel at the New Japan, bursting at the seams with such unparalleled energy and productive force that the twenty-first century is now being described as the Century of Japan.*[6]

Burns invited the Japanese executives to come to Hawai'i to explore investment opportunities. The most dramatic presentation was on Kaua'i, where a fleet of helicopters flew them along the southern coastline, up through the wilderness of the Waimea Canyon, down along the Nāpali Cliffs of the northern coast, to a new destination resort, Princeville. One of the Japanese said to Sakata, "I feel like an emperor."

When a second Hawai'i delegation returned to Japan, Burns turned the leadership over to Ariyoshi, by then lieutenant governor. Ariyoshi had seen the devastation of Japan as a young soldier, and now he was seeing Japan's economic recovery at close range. Like Sakata, he suddenly found a reason to retrieve the Japanese he had spoken with his parents and at language school. On occasion Ariyoshi spoke Japanese in the Hawai'i-Japan meetings, instead of waiting for his English to be translated—to the consternation of some of the Hawai'i representatives.

These exchanges culminated in formation of the Japan-Hawai'i Economic Council in Honolulu, under sponsorships that included the Japan Chamber of Commerce and Industry, the Japan Federation of Economic Organizations, and the Keidanren. Only three other trade and investment councils involving Japan then existed in the United States (the Japan-California Council, the Japan-Texas Council, and the Japan-Midwest Council). According to a statement of the secretariat of the Japan-Hawai'i Council, none were sponsored at such a high level in Japan. The Japanese delegation in Honolulu included the president of Nissan; several top executives of Mitsubishi; the chair of Nomura Securities, which was absorbing and investing the savings of the Japanese citizenry; the president of Asahi Urban Development Corp.; the executive managing director of New Otani Hotels; an investment advisor of the Industrial Bank of Japan; and top executives of Sumitomo Bank, the Japan Travel Bureau, and Tokyu, one of Japan's largest developers. In sum, the delegation represented a large slice of what would soon become the world's second largest national economy.

That such a delegation would sit across from a Hawai'i delegation may seem outlandish, but it indicated that Japan was prepared to treat Hawai'i as not only a major investment but as a special point of entry into America. The intangible factor at work was the political, cultural, and social organization of Hawai'i. Sakata believed, "They always considered us to be like a country."

Historically, the foreign policy goal of Meiji Japan was equality with western powers. Just as in 1894, when Japan had requested that its emigrants be granted the right to vote, the Hawai'i of 1972 was a sort of litmus test on how Japan would be treated in the world. Both Japan and Hawai'i were island societies that excited people who thought in paradigms. For example, Akio Morita's Sony Corporation would create a separate corporate entity, Sony Hawai'i, to field test not only market penetration of products but Sony's ability to service those products outside Japan. Morita became so enamored that he bought a home in Hawai'i and gave large sums of money to Punahou School.

The comfort of Japan's people in Hawai'i was not only cultural but political. The Liberal Democratic Party (LDP) of Japan had come to power in 1955, just as the first Democratic-controlled legislature of Hawai'i was being seated. The LDP operated on the mystique of consensus. The idea of consensus as a guiding political concept had gained a brief currency in America through Lyndon Johnson's simultaneous pursuit of social goals and his courtship of big business, but probably nowhere in America was consensus taken as seriously as in Hawai'i. Rule by the oligarchy had reflected a type of consensus, however much it had been vilified. Burns had fashioned the first post-statehood consensus, and Ariyoshi was to become heavily involved in creating yet another consensus.

This habit of struggling for consensus was reflected in who sat at the table for Hawai'i, across from the leaders of Japanese business. The Hawai'i delegation included the presidents of the Big Five (Amfac, Castle and Cooke, Alexander and Baldwin, C. Brewer, and Theo. H. Davies) and the Dillingham Corporation (including scion Lowell Dillingham in his capacity as board chairman and Herbert Cornuelle as president). It also included the electric and telephone companies, the two largest banks (Bank of Hawai'i and First Hawaiian), Sears, and the industrialist Henry J. Kaiser. Chinn Ho was the only well-known name among the five representatives of businesses owned by Asian Americans. Although the part-Hawaiian president of First Hawaiian Bank, John Bellinger, was elected chairman, the delegation's composition was a reminder that although political power had passed to nonwhites, the ownership of the largest corporations and their lands had not.[7]

Formation of the Japan-Hawai'i Economic Council was followed by a gusher of Japanese yen. Although it is impossible to assign a precise value to the council, or to Ariyoshi's participation, or to his election to the governorship two years later, the subsequent record of Japan's spending and investment in Hawai'i was staggering. At one point, somewhere between one-third and one-half of all Japanese investment in the United States was in the State of Hawai'i.

SPECIAL RELATIONSHIPS WITH JAPAN

The personal story of George Ariyoshi returns often to his father, Ryozo. Ariyoshi was not merely proud of his father but also reassured by his strength. In Ariyoshi's first political campaign, to his surprise, he heard people greeting his father as Yahata. He asked what the name meant. Ryozo Ariyoshi said it was his sumo name, Yahata Yama.

After Ryozo Ariyoshi had become a legal resident of the United States, he was free to travel in and out of the country without fear of detection and deportation, and he often traveled to Japan. The year after Ariyoshi's election to lieutenant governor and just after his forty-fifth birthday, Ryozo engaged his son in a conversation on the eve of another trip to Japan. In Japanese, he said that George was now a mature adult in the fullest sense, and that he would continue to grow as a person. George also took this statement as a prediction that he would become governor. Thereafter Ryozo and Mitsue Ariyoshi attended the celebration of Ryozo's brother's birthday in Fukuoka. Ryozo's health failed, and he was hospitalized. It happened that George Ariyoshi was in Tokyo, waiting to receive the second trade delegation to Japan. By the time Ariyoshi got to his father's bedside in Fukuoka, the doctors warned that his father would likely not recognize him.

"Papa," Ariyoshi said, "can you hear me?"
"Hai," Papa said.

With effort, he put his once powerful arms around Ariyoshi. When Ryozo Ariyoshi died, his body was returned to Hawai'i.

AFTER ARIYOSHI'S ELECTION to the governorship, he, his wife, and their daughter Lynn toured Japan as guests of the Foreign Ministry and the National Governor's Association. They visited Kumamoto in central Kyushu, Ariyoshi's mother's home prefecture, and Fukuoka, his father's prefecture, in northern Kyushu. Their Japanese hosts not only located Ryozo Ariyoshi's home village but also his report card, which showed excellent marks up through the third grade, his last year in school.

By protocol, governors of American states met with governors of Japanese prefectures, but the excitement in Japan about an American governor of Japanese descent caused protocol to be drastically altered. In Tokyo, Ariyoshi met with the prime minister of Japan, Takeo Miki, and also with the minister of agriculture and forestry, the foreign minister, and the head of the Ministry of International Trade and Industry—the fabled MITI.

Governor and Mrs. Ariyoshi then met with Emperor Hirohito and Empress Nagako in the imperial palace. Hirohito, thought to be a person of few words, had recently praised Japanese immigrants to America for helping create an "eternal friendship" between the two nations. The protocol officer of the imperial household hovered near the audience, as did the U.S. ambassador. The ritual fifteen-minute meeting with the Emperor stretched to forty minutes. This was the beginning of an ongoing relationship between Ariyoshi and the imperial family of Japan.

The possibility that the governor of Hawai'i could be so important to another country was, for most people, beyond imagining. As a result, Ariyoshi's relationship with Japan was never adequately understood in Hawai'i, let alone around the United States. He went about it quietly. There was possibly a reluctance on the part of the press to write about it at length, for fear of resurrecting the anti-Japanese themes that had haunted Hawai'i's none too distant past.

Extraordinary moments went unreported. Late in Ariyoshi's term of office, he was chosen to be one of four speakers at a Japanese government-sponsored gathering of Japanese descendants who had emigrated abroad.[8] Prior to delivering his scheduled speech, Ariyoshi met a person from Brazil who said, "I am Brazilian." Ariyoshi asked, "But aren't you also Japanese?" The man replied, "No, I am Brazilian." Ariyoshi was supposed to speak in English from a text that had been translated into Japanese. Disturbed by his conversation with the man from Brazil, he made a spontaneous decision to discard his translated remarks and to speak in his less than perfect Japanese, despite the presence of Crown Prince Akihito. As he spoke he imagined himself directly addressing the man from Brazil:

> *None of us need be ashamed of saying who we are, what we are, or where we've come from. We can take off the shackles of the past, and we can reach out and dream.*[9]

Ariyoshi turned and saw the man was in tears. Akihito was peering at Ariyoshi trying, Jean Ariyoshi imagined, to assess whether the governor of Hawai'i was indeed speaking impromptu. Subsequently Ariyoshi was invited to, and attended, Hirohito's funeral, as well as the enthronement of Akihito.

REACTION

Japanese travel and Japan's investments flowed together like currents in a stream. In Hawai'i the reaction was far from uniformly favorable. As early as 1970 Tom Gill complained that visitors from Japan came on Japanese package tours, arrived on Japanese airlines, moved on Japanese buses, stayed in Japanese hotels, and shopped in Japanese shops. Frank Fasi voiced less focused yet equally negative complaints. The Economic Research Center of the University of Hawai'i conducted a poll in 1973 showing that a majority of Hawai'i residents opposed further Japanese investment in Hawai'i, an irony in light of the fact that the tide of yen was then only starting. In February 1973, the Association of Hawaiian Civic Clubs supported a resolution advocating a ban on the sale of land to foreign nationals.

Late in 1973, Senator Inouye brought a subcommittee on commerce and tourism to Hawai'i to inquire about Japanese investment. Keidanren staff watched Inouye with concern and Ariyoshi with a sense of reassurance.[10] Ariyoshi's testimony revolved around maximizing the benefit of investment. He suggested that joint ventures be encouraged, and that speculative or quick-profit investments be discouraged. He urged that the traditional culture of Hawai'i be respected by new ventures and that a majority of the resulting employees, not only junior but high-ranking, be from Hawai'i. Further, he urged that Japan invest not only in real estate but other industries (something they were always essentially unwilling to do). In effect he was speaking from Hawai'i's self-interest while supporting the idea of continued Japanese investment and advising Japan in a polite way.

In mid-1974 Shelley Mark, long-time director of the Department of Planning and Economic Development, summarized the long-term picture on foreign investment. "We've always had it," Mark said, "we've needed it, we've welcomed it, we've benefited from it, and as long as America believes in freedom, in free enterprise, in business competition, in expanded trade and social and cultural relationships, we will always have it."[11]

HAWAI'I BETWEEN TWO GIANT ECONOMIES

Japan's investment eventually became so large and prolonged that Hawai'i's economy began to follow the broad cycles of Japan's economy more closely than those of the United States. As the island state on the edge of America, Hawai'i gradually came to float ambiguously in economic terms between the two great powers.[12] During the late 1980s and early 1990s, Japanese investment in Hawai'i consistently exceeded two billion dollars a year. As late as 1990, Japanese investment in Hawai'i—at $2.86 billion—represented more than one-fifth of Japan's total investment in the United States.[13] Reading numbers in Los Angeles, an accountant described the cumulative effect of Japan's special attachment to Hawai'i: "It was really the first market they became involved in, and they are more heavily involved there than anywhere."[14] In the span of several years, investors from Japan bought up much of the available inventory of real estate, including both resorts and private homes. Japanese investors became so bold (and American investors so timid by comparison), that very little new development occurred without an infusion of Japanese yen.

Japanese travelers came in ever-greater numbers and spent staggering amounts of money. Studies were conducted by the Hawai'i Visitors Bureau that showed the Japanese traveler spending an average of $586 a day compared to an average $119 daily expenditure by travelers from the U.S. mainland.[15] While the extent of this disparity would be disputed, everyone agreed there was a huge difference in the spending patterns of Japanese and Americans. This particular study concluded that Japanese represented 22 percent of the Hawai'i travel market but 43 percent of market receipts, or about four billion dollars annually.

In retail stores, restaurants, and nightclubs, the Japanese were the new super-rich. Just as the issei generation was dying (along with many of the shops, restaurants, and theaters that served them), new and visibly Japanese establishments sprang up to serve the traveler from Japan. Retailing tilted heavily toward expensive, internationally recognized branding that validated the Japanese traveler's trip abroad. By learning to speak Japanese, young people in Hawai'i could be certain of getting a job in the visitor industry. Entertainers translated their songs into Japanese and developed audience patter in Japanese. Signage in areas of heavy visitor traffic typically became bilingual, as did airport and airplane announcements.

Nonetheless the impact of the visitor on the culture of Hawai'i was marginal compared to the earlier impact of the immigrant. The sushi bar was not the saimin shop. Only occasionally, it seemed, did Japanese Americans from Hawai'i bridge the distance between America and Japan. Among these exceptions, Pundy Yokouchi attracted investment capital from Japan, as did the influential developer Herbert Horita. Wally Yonamine, renowned for his contribution to Japanese baseball, stayed on in Tokyo and ran a high-quality jewelry business. The sumo of Hawai'i became big stars in Japan. People sometimes found their relatives in Japan, and a surprising amount of travel occurred from Hawai'i to Japan.

A study conducted in 1978 found that 56 percent of the Japanese Americans in Hawai'i had visited Japan. One-fourth had visited more than once, and 5 percent had visited many times. Likewise remarkable was the large number of non-Japanese Americans who had visited Japan—35 percent, including the same core of 5 percent who had gone many times.[16] Where else in America had there been even faintly this much human interaction with Japan?

A STUDY OF JAPANESE CHARACTER

The travel data was part of a long-term research project entitled *The Study of the Japanese National Character,* begun in 1953 by the Institute of Statistical Mathematics in Tokyo. In 1971 this study was extended to Hawai'i through a member of the political science faculty of the University of Hawai'i, Yasumasa Kuroda. The objective was to broaden research on Japan's national character to the Japanese Americans of Hawai'i and eventually other Americans. Large surveys were conducted in 1971, 1978, and 1983.

Perhaps the most recurring longitudinal theme was the similarity of AJA to other ethnic groups in Hawai'i. Japanese Americans were asked, "What (socioeconomic) class do you belong to?" Sixty-five percent of AJA said the middle class, as did 62 percent of all other respondents. Did the respondent agree or disagree with the view that children should be taught that money is the most important thing in life? All groups disagreed by margins of nine to one. Even where Japanese Americans were significantly involved in an activity related to Japan, people of other ethnic groups were involved to a considerable degree as well. For example, 87 percent of AJAs sometimes watched Japanese television channels, but so did half of all others. Half the AJA population went to Japanese movies, but so did nearly a third of the entire population.

Even regarding culturally loaded or "value" questions, the differences seemed modest. The respondent was asked to choose between visiting a father on his deathbed or attending a meeting to "decide whether his firm is to go bankrupt or to survive." Sixty-seven percent of AJAs returned to the imagined bedside, but so did 58 percent of non-AJAs. When nudged semantically, these differences became only slightly more pronounced. For example, the survey asked, "Would you say you are on the whole more inclined than the average to honor your ancestors or less?" Sixty-one percent of AJAs said yes, compared to 48 percent of non-AJAs.

Was it true that individual Japanese Americans deferred to group processes more than others (a stereotype of the Japanese often advanced behind closed doors by politicians in Hawai'i)? Not really. When people were asked whether they adhered to rational principles at the expense of interpersonal harmony or vice versa, harmony was more valued by a margin of 73 percent among AJAs and 64 percent of non-AJAs.

Responses seemed to diverge more significantly when history weighed more heavily, but even then with interesting results. People were asked how satisfied they were with life in the United States. More AJAs were "completely satisfied" than non-AJAs, by 38 percent to 25 percent. Was equal justice in America not merely an ideal but a reality? Despite the wartime experience, AJAs were more inclined to believe in equal justice (52 percent versus 41 percent). Would "people's freedom" likely increase or decrease in the future? AJAs were more optimistic about the future of freedom (52 percent compared to 38 percent).

Finally, did the respondent support the Democratic or Republican Party? Suddenly the scales tipped. Where non-AJAs supported the Democratic Party by a ratio of about two to one, Japanese Americans supported the Democratic Party by a margin of *nine* to one.

However, in terms of ideological orientation this seemed to mean little. When asked if they were "favorably or unfavorably disposed" to conservatism, the answers were AJA 30 percent, others 29 percent. Liberalism? AJAs responded favorably at a rate of 35 percent, compared to 38 percent for others. Democracy? AJAs weighed in at 88 percent, compared to 84 percent for all others. In other words, AJAs described themselves as no more "liberal" than the general population. This data seemed to reinforce the impression that over time the Japanese American in the isolation of Hawai'i had migrated into the Democratic Party, and had simply been given no compelling reason to leave.

Other dead-center views emerged as well. For example, the idea that the interests of employers and employees are mutual and that labor and management should cooperate, was strongly endorsed. Gradual social reform was supported, while "radical change" and "revolutionary action" were not.

Try though they did, the researchers found relatively modest differences within the local population of Hawai'i. They came to believe that

> *those who grow up in the Aloha spirit appear to develop a common culture of their own, irrespective of their ethnic backgrounds (which is) unique, when compared with mainland American culture.*[17]

As they worked the data, the research team began to explore other possibilities, contrasting the Hawai'i-born (regardless of ethnicity) and the haole who had recently arrived from the mainland. The research found that islanders were more likely than haoles to believe in "the System," more likely to be satisfied, more likely to honor their ancestors, and more likely to emphasize the value of obedience to their children.

Of particular interest to the researchers, recently arrived haoles were more likely to nurture an interest in their children "in how and why things happen." Accordingly "mainlanders are interested in new values and creative activities more than islanders. . . ." Therefore, they concluded, without a continuous flow of mainlanders, island culture "may not be able to develop itself as effectively,"[18] which was surely one of the nicer things that had been written about mainland haoles in a while. Further, the authors were impressed by the power of mainstream American culture as it interacted with island culture:

> *Despite the ethnic awareness sweeping the United States in recent years and the call for the "local boys," the wave of acculturation and assimilation seems to be of such a magnitude that nothing can prevent ethnics from assimilating to American culture at large.*[19]

While this view arguably was being proven wrong, it was nonetheless provocative and formulated with care.

As to the nisei, the authors believed that by empirical means they had located the Pacific "golden man" of James Michener's description, but the nisei was a fleeting figure—a child of Japanese immigrants, at home in both the East and West, most likely in his or her fifties, and soon to be retiring from active life.

KANYAKU IMIN, A CELEBRATION OF IMMIGRATION

In 1982, George Ariyoshi's third term as governor coincided with the pending centennial of the arrival in 1885 of the Japanese immigrants. The celebration was named *Kanyaku Imin,* or "contract immigrant." Although the fiftieth and seventy-fifth anniversary observances had been led by the United Japanese Society, Ariyoshi formed a coordinating committee sponsored by the state government to oversee the year-long events of 1985.[20] Ariyoshi was chairman but turned much of the work over to Hideto Kono, who by then had resigned from the cabinet after two terms. The executive secretary was the same Tom Sakata who had coordinated numerous relationships in Japan and elsewhere in Asia after making the original Expo '70 connection. The staff also included Dr. Albert Miyasato, an educator on leave from the governor's office.

So far as the centennial had to do with healing, Miyasato's personal story was particularly poignant.[21] Before World War II, he had been taken by his parents to study in Japan. He learned about the attack on Pearl Harbor as a young teenager on the grounds of a Buddhist school in Fukuoka, where his fellow students shouted a hearty *banzai.* He was constantly barraged by military propaganda and was carried along by the fervor of his fellow students, many of whom eventually volunteered for the suicidal missions of the Kamikaze Youth Corps.

His boyish identification with his parents' homeland was dashed when he was moved to Tokyo, where he and other Americans of Japanese ancestry were placed in a special school and expected to work for either a newspaper or radio station. Because Miyasato had a deep, resonant voice, he was assigned to radio broadcasting. He lived under surveillance on a near-starvation diet. As Japan's fortunes declined, he thought constantly about food. He was pushed through rehearsals to the brink of making broadcasts but was rescued by the emperor announcing Japan's surrender.

Desperate to reunite with his family in Hawai'i, Miyasato was told by Occupation officials that he had been in a spy school and might lose his American citizenship. He struggled in Tokyo for eighteen months to gain passage to Hawai'i. During that time he worked as a translator. On his return home, he was stricken by guilt whenever he was asked, "Where were you during the war?" Most remarkably he found

> . . . it was not easy to participate in free discussion. All my training in Japan was geared to subservience in thinking. It was a difficult burden to think for myself again after years of being controlled in thought and in action.[22]

In his struggle to regain a sense of wholeness, Miyasato became an educator. At age forty-one he completed his doctorate and rose quickly within the Department of Education, then joined Ariyoshi's staff. He avoided the anxiety of returning to Japan until 1974, when he was obliged to go as part of his work. There he was amazed that he could experience positive feelings for both Japan and the United States simultaneously.

Miyasato's was one of many stories reconstructed during *Kanyaku Imin* that admitted not only to immigrant sacrifice but to a painfully conflicted past. Framing a hundred years, *Kanyaku Imin* helped create a multigenerational narrative that previously had relied inordinately on the single-generation legend of the nisei soldier. Geographic origins in Japan were relocated. Community-building in Hawai'i was acknowledged. Picture brides were honored. In the process, nisei could recall being criticized by their elders for marrying outside their villages or prefectures, or across the boundaries of national origin and race. By the time of *Kanyaku Imin*, nearly half of all marriages involving Japanese Americans in Hawai'i were of mixed ethnicity.[23] Accordingly, participants in the celebration spanned the distance from the remote villages of Meiji Japan to arguably the most racially mixed society in the world.

Jane Komeiji and Dorothy Hazama's book, *Okage Sama De,* helped popularize the phrase that not only Ariyoshi but many nisei were fond of: "Because of you, I am what I am." It became a metaphor of gratitude to the founding generation, much as did Dennis Ogawa's *Kodomo no Tame ni, For the Sake of the Children.*

Jean Ariyoshi led a drive to plant a million trees. Fundraising concentrated on developing an Imin Center for conferencing at the East West Center, echoing the internationalist themes of the twenties and thirties. Senator Mike Mansfield, who prided himself on his friendship with both Inouye and Ariyoshi, joined in the celebration. He would soon be named ambassador of the United States to Japan. Emperor Hirohito came, a reminder that where Japan was concerned, Hawai'i was indeed a special place. The concluding event honored individuals who had helped the Japanese community from their first moment through their moment of greatest danger. Led by the attorney Ted T. Tsukiyama, an avid community historian, the celebration revived the memory of such figures as Charles Hemenway, Robert Shivers, and Hung Wai Ching.

BE YOURSELF

In his 1959 article on statehood, John Burns wrote that Hawai'i's people had achieved a measure of identity but now could "achieve that identity as best they can."[24] In his 1969 address to the legislature, he echoed the student Shunzo Sakamaki's phrase of forty-one years prior about "a sickening sense of inferiority." Burns talked about a "subtle inferiority of spirit" that plagued certain unspecified people in Hawaiʻi, even though, he was quick to add, it was totally unwarranted. I covered this speech as a young reporter, putting this jarring phrase in the top of the story, a choice that brought a rare, terse word of approval from Burns. Thereafter the idea of a subtle sense of inferiority was repeated over and over in Hawaiʻi, sometimes by other members of the press, at other times by Burns' admirers, usually as evidence of Burns' deep understanding of Hawaiʻi. Despite its wide currency, the meaning of this phrase was not systematically discussed or debated. It suggested something, but what it really meant to different people, and what might be done in response, were never dealt with publicly. Despite its vagueness, the phrase had something to do with appreciating Asian and local culture and healing the hurts of the past.

In this regard, Ariyoshi echoed Sakamaki's contention that people who abandoned their cultural heritage were in danger of being "cut adrift from the ancient moorings." Ariyoshi told a story about two Filipino American girls who confided to him after a speech that they sometimes felt inferior and wished they were something other than Filipino. He told them if they bought into the idea of inferiority, they would automatically be setting limits on who they were and what they could become. "Be yourself," he told them. "Be proud of who you are."[25]

Much in the way that Sakamaki had rallied nisei to live in the "best of both worlds," Ariyoshi invested political capital in affirming the inherent worth of all ethnic groups. By definition all cultures have values, but the nisei presented a special preoccupation with cultural values that dated to Confucius and the bushidō code. (For example, a woman named Tomoe Yamaguchi described the president of a Japanese social club leading a discussion of Japanese values in the plantation town of Waipahu in the 1920s.)[26] Although public discourse on Japanese values had disappeared with the onset of World War II, the embrace of Japanese values had quietly continued. In conversations Ariyoshi now shared with others, his father had talked about *otagai* (mutual obligation), *okage sama de,* and *shikata ga nai* (accept what cannot be changed).

Haji—the imperative of not bringing shame on one's family—was cited over and over by parents as their sons went to war. When young Dan Inouye approached the coast of Italy, he asked his comrades their thoughts as they approached their first battle. He recalled, "It wasn't, 'I hope I don't get injured. I hope I don't die.' Everyone said, 'I don't want to bring shame to my family.'"[27] The writer and teacher Shigeo Yoshida, who had exhorted the 1944 Oʻahu conference on the future of the Japanese to eliminate "all vestiges of alien influences," was to write in old age that Japanese values had "much to do in determining the behavior of our people."[28]

As an alternative to the traditional image of America as a melting pot, Ariyoshi proposed that America be a "mixing pot." If America was a cultural stew, each element should retain its form and taste and add something special. The goal was not a new uniformity of either experience or outcome, but an equal opportunity to achieve one's potential. In Ariyoshi's formulation, "To be proud of what you are is to be a self-confident contributor to the whole."[29] Other individuals during this period developed their own image of diversity. A Honolulu attorney, Kenji Kanazawa, described differing ethnicities making a "tossed salad." Kay Uno Kaneko, who had been interned as a child, suggested an American tapestry, in which different threads retained their color and shape.

When the Japanese Cultural Center of Hawai'i was organized in the 1990s, its founders discussed core Japanese values at great length. The process involved dozens of people who shared an active interest in Japanese American cultural history. The theme of the standing exhibit became *Okage Sama De*. Eleven values were inscribed on stone obelisks in kanji for exhibit purposes. *Giri* referred to duty, *chūgi* to loyalty, *gisei* to sacrifice, and so forth.[30] *Ganbare* was restated in a film inside the exhibit as "don't give up" or—in the motto of the 442nd RCT—"go for broke." *Kansha* referred to the gratitude owed by Japanese Americans to such figures as Robert Shivers and Jack Burns. Finally, one learned that the word for filial piety was *kōkō*, the value Ariyoshi observed by citing his father's instructions.

CONSTRUCTION OF THE ASIAN-PACIFIC

Although Japan was of special importance in Hawai'i in perpetuating ethnic identity, it was only part of an intricate community-building process that was simultaneously transnational, American, and local. Following the pattern of Japanese studies, the University of Hawai'i developed study centers focused on Korea, China, the Philippines, the Pacific Islands, and, finally, native Hawaiians. The university built up one of the best research libraries in the Asian-Pacific region and one of the better Asian collections in the world. Year after year, as part of the legacy of Lyndon Johnson and Burns, the East West Center educated new Asian and Pacific Island leadership.

In the sciences, Hawai'i served as a base of inquiry into tropical and subtropical agriculture, aquaculture, forestry, marine resources, soil formation, vulcanology, alternative energy, oceanography, meteorology, ocean thermal transfer and, through the astronomical observatories on Hawai'i Island, the universe.

While these activities occurred openly, their strategic importance in reinforcing America's preeminent world role was often overlooked (in much the same way that an understanding of Hawai'i as the base for projecting American military power was usually lost on both residents and visitors).

ARIYOSHI AS INTERNATIONALIST

During Ariyoshi's third term, he and a small group of staff and cabinet members confidentially shared "think" pieces around the theme "Creating Our Own Destiny."[31] In what was almost certainly Ariyoshi's own composition, one far-ranging four-page paper said Hawai'i had come a long way since statehood but success had changed things: "The old rallying points of providing greater opportunity, dignity, and support for all the people of our community have lost their effectiveness as touchstones for the development of solutions to our modern problems."[32] Hawai'i needed a new rallying point ("a vision, reaching the hearts and minds of our people"), organized around a delicate balance between Hawai'i controlling its own future and playing a unique role in the Pacific region. Hawai'i was a relatively small place in which seemingly small events could have a great impact; therefore, in expanding its Pacific role, Hawai'i should not "turn our future over to the events of other parts of the world." To this Ariyoshi added, "We must become a more knowledgeable society in order to understand ourselves, and to understand others."

Starkly, one contributor asked, "Where does an American island state, with strong Oriental and Polynesian influences, make its new mark? Can it utilize its multicultural environment to its advantage, or will it just be an anomaly in the Pacific—a society of ethnic *poi* dogs?" (meaning merely people of mixed ancestry).

Another cited the 1973 world oil crisis as the "symbolic end" to the early statehood period. The intrusion of world events, in this view, had triggered two interrelated movements—first the Hawaiian renaissance and second "controlled growth." This writer correctly predicted that economically there would be nothing in the future faintly comparable to the economic boost of tourism in the 1960s. Another participant wrote that since Hawai'i's people seemed to be most concerned about not being engulfed in the culture of the mainland United States, Hawai'i must concentrate on strengthening its "cultural grammar." By doing so, Hawai'i could become a model "of possible unions between the various parts of the Pacific Basin . . . the basis for greater involvement in affairs of the region, which can lead in turn to greater economic opportunity for Hawai'i's people."

Ariyoshi said that if Hawai'i's people could "retain the initiative in the events that affect us, we can achieve greater things than we now imagine."[33] Philosophically, this discussion echoed the pre–World War II pan-Pacific internationalism in which local community-building efforts such as Hands Around the World, the Hawaiian Japanese Civic Association, and Lions International had developed in parallel with the Institute for Pacific Relations. In Ariyoshi's terms, by an individual finding himself or herself, he or she could make the greatest contribution to others. By answering the question, "Who am I?" or "Who are we?," Hawai'i's people might not only expand their horizons but their livelihoods. The possibilities for success would be enhanced by the Pacific region becoming ever more important, along with the importance of relationships between communities and nations. Further, this vision would be influenced by a multipolar world: "No one country will be in complete control."

Propelled by his internationalist analysis, Ariyoshi increasingly devoted himself to Hawai'i's relationships among Pacific islands and with Asia. In the process he attracted a level of interest that was not accorded to him in the forty-nine continental states of the United States. Reminiscent of his special relationship with Japan, Ariyoshi was given special treatment in many of the countries of Asia. In Peking, Ariyoshi and his entourage stayed in the compound where Nixon and Kissinger had stayed. In Manila, they stayed in Malacanang Palace. In Malaysia they dined with the king and queen and in Thailand with the prime minister.[34] Ariyoshi's wife Jean often went on these trips, by all accounts adding a dimension of charm and sparkle. Sakata usually went, as did the head of the Hawai'i Visitors Bureau (HVB), for most of the period Stanley Hong. Ariyoshi hewed to a schedule of five or six events a day and refused to play golf or relax during the week.[35] The doors of Asia were open but, in the view of Hong, only the travel industry was really organized to systematically capitalize on these initiatives. Try as he did to promote a diversity of economic interests, Ariyoshi's successes mainly had to do with opening new HVB offices throughout Asia in combination with the Department of Planning and Economic Development.

There were a few breakthroughs, as when Ariyoshi brought President Reagan and Japanese Prime Minister Yasuhiro Nakasone together in support of a Pacific International Center for High Technology Research, which was devoted to finding new technologies for the Pacific and particularly Pacific islanders.[36]

More complex issues of Pacific island societies came to be routinely addressed. These efforts were concentrated in Ariyoshi's second and third terms and involved both U.S. territories in the Pacific and newly formed Pacific island nations. People who observed Ariyoshi thought that he relaxed and enjoyed himself with Pacific islanders.[37] He saw Asian and island cultures sharing "a certain indirectness and subtlety of communication that is a matter of politeness and courtesy."[38] With this perspective as his guide,

Ariyoshi became a conduit for communication between Pacific islanders and the U.S. government (as indeed was the entire Hawai'i congressional delegation, in varying ways).

Ariyoshi's role was most apparent in his relationships with the governors of the U.S. territories of Guam, American Samoa, and the Northern Marianas Islands.[39] They began conferring with Ariyoshi in response to the differences between island and continental concerns at venues such as the Western Governors conference, which could be consumed almost entirely by interstate highways, forests, dams, and the distribution of river water.

In the late seventies, the territorial governors began meeting with Ariyoshi in Honolulu, identifying their own agenda before traveling on to regional and national meetings. In response to a recommendation by the Western Governor's Conference,[40] the Carter administration organized a federal interagency task force on territorial policy. This led to a 1980 federal conference at the Kuilima Hotel on the northern tip of O'ahu, in which people from Hawai'i played prominent roles. Conferees focused on the shared interests that resulted from the fragile ecological systems of islands, their limited land areas, and their distances from supply sources and markets.[41] The conference identified priority concerns of fisheries, coastal management, telecommunications, ports, transportation, trade, tourism, energy, and the provision of municipal services.

Seemingly as a matter of course, Hawai'i was not merely a host but a participant in the discussion of territorial issues. Thereafter a Pacific Basin Development Council (PBDC) was formed that was made up of the American flag islands and the State of Hawai'i. The secretariat was based in Honolulu, and meetings of the chief executives rotated from Hawai'i to Pago Pago in American Samoa, Agana in Guam, and Saipan in the Northern Marianas Islands.

The same year, Hawai'i took on a special role among recently decolonized Pacific nations. Twenty-three entities, mostly microstates, formed the Pacific Island Development Council (PIDC), which was based at the East West Center. Most had been colonized by European powers in the wave of imperialism that occurred between 1875 and 1900. The start of decolonization nearly coincided with statehood for Hawai'i, beginning in 1962 with New Zealand's grant of sovereignty to Western Samoa. During this period Britain and Australia likewise pulled out of colonial relationships. By 1980, the decolonization movement was punctuated by the combined British-French grant of independence to Vanuatu (previously the New Hebrides) in the Western Pacific.[42] Resisting the tide, France hung on to the Society Islands, which included Tahiti, as well as related islands that continued to be known as French Polynesia. Alone among the Pacific powers of the West, America not only resisted the tide of decolonization but convinced itself that it had never been a colonial power.[43]

With the continuation of the Cold War, small tremors in the Pacific caused major reactions in America. In the words of Robert Kiste, head of the university's Pacific islands studies program, the U.S. government saw "a communist behind every coconut tree." The importance of these far-flung islands was highly subjective. Most had small land masses with small populations, disjoined from neighbors by great distances of water. However, their strategic military importance can be decoded by retracing place names of World War II battlegrounds. For example, Guadalcanal was part of the new Republic of the Solomon Islands, Tarawa Beach was in Kiribati, and Saipan was part of the United Nations Trust Territory (before it became the capital of the U.S.-affiliated Commonwealth of the Northern Marianas). In the age of nuclear weapons testing and intercontinental missiles, the strategic importance of Pacific islands increased.

Particular attention was focused on the new microstate of Kiribati, where a young student named Ieramia Tabai had campaigned for office throughout the widely dispersed islands of his new country by exalting "the people" and criticizing the government.[44] By 1985, Tabai, as head of state, executed a fishing rights agreement with the Soviet Union, causing shock waves that reverberated from U.S. Pacific naval headquarters in Honolulu to the Departments of State and Defense in Washington. Ariyoshi was one of the few American civilians who had ever been to Kiribati, representing the U.S. government at the national celebration of Kiribati independence at Tarawa in 1979. During proceedings of the PIDC, Ariyoshi asked Tabai if anything lay behind the Soviet agreement. Tabai said no, that it was a matter of generating revenue for his tiny nation.[45]

Through PIDC, Ariyoshi formed a friendship with the Fijian leader, Sir Ratu Mara Kamisese, who was then gaining wide recognition in the reconfigured Pacific. While widely separated by distance and history, Hawai'i and Fiji were in some ways analogous. Each was a distant reach of Polynesia. Each had about a million people, as well as the largest islands between the Americas and New Zealand. If Britain had exercised its opportunity to make Hawai'i a British protectorate, as it had Fiji, and thereafter decolonized, Hawai'i and Fiji in 1980 might have more obviously been comparable centers in the Pacific.

THE ISSUES OF ISLANDS

To what extent Hawai'i suffered from island-related problems is impossible to say, since the question was never raised in public discourse, even though

Hawai'i obviously had much in common with other Pacific islands. The fact that the State of Hawai'i, in a single year, 1980, took formal steps to align itself with overseas territories (through PBDC) and with Pacific microstates (through PIDC), while unofficially acknowledging the submerged Hawaiian nation through an Office of Hawaiian Affairs, has never been examined.

To what extent was Hawai'i like other islands, even though it was America's fiftieth state? The scholar Robert Kiste sketched a picture of Micronesia under U.S. Trust Territory administration as beset by rapid urbanization, inadequate urban infrastructure, inadequate housing, and an ever-increasing reliance on imported food, which resulted in dietary disorders and malnutrition. Urban centers attracted students and working-age people, while a "correspondingly large number of older people and young children are left at home in communities severely depleted of their productive work forces." Traditional skills were being systematically lost, along with the ability to sustain a subsistence economy. The authority of family, kin, and traditional leaders was declining, and teenage delinquency and alcohol abuse were rising. Education was outpacing employment opportunities, yet aspirations were higher than at any time in the past.[46] Kiste's description of Micronesia was in many ways a description of indigenous Hawai'i.

The nationally renowned ecologist Peter Vitousek suggests that the Hawaiian Islands enable conservation biologists to more readily see what is less readily apparent on continents. "They are," he says, "like a miner's canary."[47] For a place that functioned simultaneously as a regional outpost, a state, a microstate, and a submerged indigenous nation, Vitousek's definition of Island Hawai'i cuts through all others: Hawai'i is a miner's canary, chirping in the depths of the mine.

Chapter 13

Native Hawaiians in the New Hawai'i

Within the modern Democratic Party in Hawai'i, a long-term effort was made to include native Hawaiians and to incorporate their concerns into broad Democratic themes. As John Burns argued, Hawaiians and AJAs together formed an unbeatable majority. This coalition worked increasingly well in the sixties and seventies, as more Hawaiians became politically active and also tended to migrate from the Republican to the Democratic Party. Nonetheless, a day of reckoning awaited, in which native Hawaiian history would be rediscovered and the interests of Hawaiians might then diverge.

As the 1970s unfolded, it would be one thing for people of Japanese, Chinese, Korean, or Filipino ancestry to "take off the shackles of the past" (in Ariyoshi's phrase) and another for native Hawaiians to do so. Asian Americans were descended from people who had come to Hawai'i of their own will, even if they had encountered a semi-closed society on arrival. In response to Burns' question of 1959, "Who am I?" all could say, "By choice, I am American." They enhanced Ariyoshi's American stew. In contrast, native Hawaiians who asked "Who am I?" found themselves on a distant, dark hillside, conversing with ancestral ghosts. They were the remains of a vibrant, indigenous nation that had been taken away.

Although Lawrence Fuchs in *Hawai'i Pono* (1961) had located little Hawaiian opposition to statehood, he wrote about a reluctance on the part of many to close the door on the once independent kingdom into which the elderly Hawaiians of that time had been born. Fuchs portrayed Hawaiians as looking to an illusive past, but he would remember only one person he thought of as a proponent of a truly separate Hawaiian identity,[1] Dr. Richard Kekuni Blaisdell, who would eventually advocate Hawai'i's complete independence from the United States. An essential part of Blaisdell's position would be that Hawaiians had been asked in the 1959 plebiscite only whether they favored statehood or opposed it, not whether they wanted their country back.

Among a half dozen people who in the 1950s had consistently orchestrated opposition to statehood, only Alice Kamokila Campbell was of Hawaiian ancestry. At various times she had participated in an Anti-Statehood Committee and in a second group advocating a commonwealth status for Hawai'i. With such allies as former Democratic governor Ingram Stainback and a well-known Republican senator, William H. "Doc" Hill, she had rummaged through antistatehood tactics that were variously anticommunist or anti-Japanese. Kamokila was the daughter of Kuaehelani Campbell, who arguably had been the most effective opponent of America's annexation of Hawai'i and who, after the death of James Campbell, had married Prince David Kawānanakoa, brother of Kūhiō.[2] Alice Kamokila Campbell was therefore an extension of the royal family, which—given the temper of the times— probably made it easier for most people to dismiss her views. By the time of the statehood referendum, neither Kamokila nor any of her haole friends bothered to campaign for a "no" vote.

The outcome was a reminder that such a referendum is the culmination of a purposeful campaign that invites the entire electorate to climb on a bandwagon. In 1984, the historian Roger Bell sought to put the statehood referendum in perspective by summarizing the sketchy survey research conducted during the approach to statehood.[3] During these several years, the research suggests that significant numbers of Hawaiians were ambivalent about statehood. About a fourth of Hawaiians on O'ahu described themselves as opposed to statehood, while roughly one-third favored it. Interestingly, Caucasians voiced a similar range of opinions. Only Japanese Americans, at 62 percent, clearly supported statehood in this survey.

Bell believed that subsequent events revealed less real opposition than the surveys suggested. However, opposition to statehood among native Hawaiians was possibly understated, since many lived in remote settings and outlying islands and were not represented in this oft-quoted research. What comes through most clearly is that the Japanese community was highly favorable to statehood while Hawaiians and Caucasians were significantly less so. Nonetheless, with congressional approval, the electorate uniformly caught the fever for statehood. The turnout among registered voters—encompassing more than four-fifths of the eligible population—was a record 99 percent. The vote was 132,938 in favor, 7,854 against, a margin of more than seventeen to one, surpassing not only Burns' expectations but everyone's.

Like other big American events—World War I, World War II, the Korean War—statehood seemed to diminish the unique identity and political consciousness of native Hawaiians, at least initially. If an arc of the vitality of indigenous life could be reconstructed, the low point would probably be 1959. America was the shining city on the hill, and everyone looked to its light. During this period it seemed that the vast body of knowledge that defines a culture was being relegated to Bishop Museum.[4] A handful of people clustered around Mary Kawena Pukui, a woman of profound cultural knowledge and amazing memory. Throughout the islands a relatively small but indeterminate number of people perpetuated different areas of the Hawaiian culture, often centering on fishing and farming, oral tradition and hula. Such people as Iolani Luahine and Maike Aiu in hula, Ka'upena Wong in chant, Harriet Ne in oral tradition, and Papa Auwae in the healing arts were walking repositories of what was widely described as a doomed culture.

In the few years after statehood, Hawaiian life began to stir. Not completely unlike the network of people who formed in 1941 to resist a mass internment, there was no plan of action, no script, and no key lines of rhetoric that adherents might cling to. What drove this reawakening is a matter of conjecture. Herb Kawainui Kane, who designed the replicated Hawaiian voyaging canoe Hōkūle'a, believed the Hawaiian movement was catalyzed by a relatively few disjoined people who saw that their ancestral heritage was rapidly slipping away. Some debt was owed to the example of the Japanese American, and some to the self-assertion of Afro-Americans in the civil rights movement. Around the world indigenous people—about one-tenth of the earth's population—became more assertive in the course of the 1970s. A shift was occurring in the relationship between the colonizing societies and those who had been colonized.

JOHN DOMINIS HOLT

No voice cried out so eloquently to awaken Hawaiians as that of John Dominis Holt. Holt was born in 1920 into a once well-to-do family that was sinking, financially and otherwise. In response to the family's decline, Holt's mother turned to Jesus and his father to drink. John was a promising but erratic student who fled to the mainland as soon as he could, seeking to discover himself. He vividly remembered the exhilaration of lurching down the streets of America's great cities, inebriated, anonymous, and free of restraint.

He enrolled at Columbia University in New York City, hoping to study under the legendary anthropologist Franz Boas.[5] More than any other academic figure, Boas had effectively challenged the belief in the superiority of the white race,[6] otherwise defined as "scientific racism" or Social Darwinism. This was of immediate importance to Hawaiian history, because Social Darwinism had galvanized the views of such men as Sanford Dole and Lorrin

A. Thurston and their American cohorts—such as Theodore Roosevelt and Captain Alfred Mahan—in their annexation scheme.[7] As an alternative to Social Darwinism, Boas developed the theory of cultural relativism, based on the belief that all cultures have their own integrity, and that no one culture is inherently more valuable than another. The great scholar W. E. B. DuBois, who would go on to organize the National Association for the Advancement of Colored People, described Boas' lecture on the ancient kingdoms of black Africa as a life-changing experience. "I was too astonished to speak," wrote DuBois. "I came then and afterwards to realize how the silence and neglect of science can let truth utterly disappear or even be unconsciously distorted."[8]

By the time Holt arrived at Columbia, Boas had died, but his work lived on through several famous protégés. Holt worked with Ruth Benedict, who eventually would write *Race and Racism* and *Patterns of Culture*. When World War II began, Benedict relocated to the Office of War Information in Washington D.C. Holt stayed on in New York but worked under her direction, generating material for booklets on cultures that American soldiers were likely to encounter in their global war. One project evolved into Benedict's enduring work on Japan, *The Chrysanthemum and the Sword*. Benedict was arguing in print for America to "clean its own house and get ready for a better twenty-first century."

> *Then it could stand unashamed before the Nazis and condemn, without confusion, their doctrines of a Master Race. Then it could put its hand to the building of the United Nations . . . sure that victory in this war will be in the name, not of one race or of another, but of the universal Human Race.*[9]

In contrast to the German fixation on the myth of pure Aryan blood, Benedict looked to Hawai'i as a place "where the code of racial separatism is conspicuously lacking."

> *Intermixture in Hawai'i does not have to be illicit; marriages between the most diverse races take place in the churches. There is no discrimination against the offspring of such crosses; they can hold eminent positions if they have ability.*[10]

During Holt's six-year sojourn in New York City, he attended the lectures of leading writers and thinkers, socialized with artists and musicians, and drank with figures of the political left, such as Mike Gold of the *Daily Worker*. He returned to Hawai'i in the early postwar period with cultural tastes and intellectual interests for which there was no apparent use. In frustration, he became obsessed with the beauty of plants. He worked as a gardener for Tripler Army Hospital, but was laid off in the Red Scare as payment for hob-nobbing with socialists in New York. He started his own landscaping busi-ness. Times got better, and he began to make money.

In contrast to many well-off Hawaiians, he admired what the Democ-ratic Party was doing in the 1950s to, in his words, "get out of this stran-glehold." He was interested in Japanese Americans in Hawai'i and what black people were beginning to do on the mainland. Periodically he engaged in horrendous drinking bouts with impoverished Hawaiians, dancing the hula in Chinatown and sleeping off the binge in public housing projects in Kalihi. Finally he began to fulfill the promise of his youth. He haunted the collec-tions of Bishop Museum and the archives of the State of Hawai'i, which once had been the archives of the kingdom and territory. Controlling his distaste for the missionary tradition, he tackled the Mission House library as well, not imagining that one day he would be on its board of directors.

From a collector he bought a copy of the voluminous Blount report on America's involvement in the overthrow of Queen Lili'uokalani. He now pos-sessed one of the few remaining copies of what the historian Tennant McWilliams would describe as the most far-reaching indictment of Ameri-can behavior overseas.[11] He began to lecture, write, and publish. He was amazed at the gap between what he was learning and what others did not know or care to know. Conservative Hawaiians particularly appalled him. When he would talk about Hawaiian imprisonment or ill health, he said, "They wouldn't believe it. They wouldn't pay any attention to it."

He was accused of being negative and of dwelling on the past. "Nobody wanted to review history. . . . They wanted to sort of cover it all up and say it's all great and fine and let's go on. 'I'm doing well. Why can't Joe Blow down at Nānākuli do well too? What's his problem?'"[12] Among his histo-ries, poems, novels, and plays, his twelve-thousand-word essay titled *On Being Hawaiian* was probably his most influential.

On Being Hawaiian was published in early 1964, as the civil rights debate in America was beginning to peak. Twelve years before Herb Kane's repli-cated voyaging canoe, Holt resurrected the image of the "fantastic naviga-tional feats of our ancestors." He talked about "the pain of being alienated from our own roots and our land." This he associated with the legacy of Social Darwinism, the "glib, pseudoscientific statements which have been made to describe the ancient social order." Hawaiians had been "pummeled into accepting the stranger's view of ourselves as being cute, all-abiding, friendly nincompoops, charming and lovable, but certainly inferior as humans—and in need of being looked after by superior beings."[13]

Holt was heartened by young people who sought their roots and engaged in political protest. Prophetically, he wrote, "we want to run our own show—at long last—as an ethnic and political conglomerate on our own terms."[14]

As a person of distinction who maintained a fierce pride in being Hawaiian, Holt was far from alone. Such traditional organizations as the Queen Ka'ahumanu Society, the Order of Kamehameha, the Sons and Daughters of Hawaiian Warriors, and the Hawaiian Civic Club maintained ties among Hawaiians. Under the guidance of the pioneering Hawaiian social worker, Clorinda Lowe Lucas, and her son-in-law, Myron Thompson, the Queen Lili'uokalani Children's Center (QLCC) engaged in a conscious re-evaluation of what it meant to be Hawaiian.

The venerable Mrs. Pukui of Bishop Museum worked at QLCC as a cultural consultant, and one day a young social worker, Richard Paglinawan, brought the case of a deeply troubled child to her attention.[15] Conventional intervention had failed. Mrs. Pukui said the child was troubled by conflicts rooted in Hawaiian culture. She prescribed a religiously based process of conflict resolution that had been almost entirely suppressed: *ho'oponopono*. From such exchanges, a cross-cultural working team emerged, examining the lives of troubled Hawaiians from a dual Western and Hawaiian point of view. The team published *Nana I Ke Kumu*, which means "look to the source." It described a world of torment in which the native culture had been devalued and then suppressed, but had not obligingly died.[16] *Nana I Ke Kumu* became a foundation stone of an ever-widening definition of Hawaiians as a distinct people with a distinct culture.

THE HAWAIIANS

Among the many initiatives that eventually became known as the Hawaiian movement, one of the earliest was simply called The Hawaiians. Its most visible leader, Pae Galdeira, started as a youth worker in the heavily Hawaiian community of Waimānalo, on the eastern tip of O'ahu facing Moloka'i. He was employed by the Community Action Program, a federal antipoverty agency that had been developed as part of Johnson's Great Society, through which Galdeira was exposed to theories of community organization. One night, he drove a youngster home in the middle of a storm. He found a family of nine clinging to a tent on the beach, trying to prevent it from blowing away. One was a baby. He soon found twelve families living similarly on the beach. He began to ask why they were homeless nearly half a century after Prince Kūhiō had secured the Hawaiian Homes Act in Congress. He was both shocked and angered, a response that would be multiplied by many thousands of Hawaiians in the years to come as they reflected on their relationship with the governmental institutions of America. Reaching out to others around Oʻahu, Galdeira formed The Hawaiians. After trying repeatedly to air their grievances with Governor Burns, they put up a picket line at the capitol.

Their demonstration became entangled with Aloha Week, an invention of the travel industry designed to tone up a soft spot in the autumn tourism market. As a focal point of Aloha Week, a king, queen, and court are selected each year from the Hawaiian community to ritually harken the image of ancient royalty. As the Aloha Week court approached a ceremony at the capitol, they stopped at the sight of protesting Hawaiians. Burns spoke at the Aloha Week ceremony, then approached Galdeira and inquired in pidgin, "What the fock you doing?"[17] Galdeira swore angrily, accusing Burns of giving him a runaround. "Bullshit," Burns muttered. After more angry words, Burns invited not only Galdeira but the hundred or so protesters to meet in his conference room later in the day.

Arriving on the fifth floor, walking beneath the enormously high ceiling that Jackie Kennedy had suggested, the protesters were greeted at the door by the governor. Many of the older people melted, regretting their demonstration. Burns asked what was on their minds. Since no one spoke, Galdeira began to describe their grievances with the Hawaiian Homes Commission. Others joined in. With Burns was Myron Thompson, who had been recruited by the governor from the Queen Liliʻuokalani center to be his chief of staff during his second term. As complaint piled on complaint, Burns periodically turned to Thompson. "Is that right?" he would ask, and Thompson would say that it was. "We've got a bad program," Galdeira was to quote Burns as saying. "How are we going to make changes?"

Through the Community Action Program the federal government subsidized the development of many elements of Hawaiian activism, including the work of such notable figures as Rose Victorino and Lena Riverio in welfare rights, Arnold Kidder in legal aid, and Randy Kalahiki in mobilizing against development. Similarly, a new generation of Western-educated Hawaiians gained experience through the somewhat more conventional Model Cities Program, including a future governor (John Waiheʻe) and a future speaker of the State House of Representatives (Henry Peters).

A two-part pattern of reaction and action evolved. On the rawest level was the pervasive sense of reaction against the rapid development that threatened the remaining links of Hawaiians with their traditions and with their living spaces. Across the islands, Hawaiians engaged in protests against development schemes that damaged the land, streams, beaches, bays, and fisheries. The second track had to do with more systematically assessing what it meant to be Hawaiian, and to map out what needed to be done to repair the damage and survive as an identifiable people and culture. On the most elemental level, this occurred in the form of quests, or fact-finding and culture-affirming expeditions.[18] People who were to become widely influential, including Walter Ritte Jr., George Helm, and John Waiheʻe, all systematically sought out elders with a root question: What does it mean to be a Hawaiian? Such efforts created examples for more systematic efforts involving thousands of people, such as an organization developed in the mid-1970s named Alu Like.

ALU LIKE

Although Alu Like became, as intended, a provider of services, it was initially important for bringing Hawaiians together. One of the key founders of Alu Like was Myron Thompson,[19] one of those rare individuals who lived in perpetual excitement over the possibility of improving society. He was lean and intense, with Hawaiian-brown skin and prematurely grey hair. His activism and social conscience made him a ready convert from the Republican to the Democratic party.

Thompson was driving to the airport after a work session in Washington D.C. when he heard on the radio about congressional action on the Native American Act. He asked himself why native Hawaiians were not included, turned around and went back to the city. There he worked closely with Senator Inouye and various Native American Indians, and as a result Congress eventually amended the definition of native Americans to include native Hawaiians, opening the way to federal funding of numerous social and economic programs.

By this time, a core group of politically conscious Hawaiians was working to capitalize on the federal initiative, many of them brought together by an ad hoc organization called the Home Rule Movement, which had borrowed its name from the party that last had elected Robert Wilcox as delegate in 1900. The Home Rule Movement served to develop political ties among a widening circle of college-educated Hawaiians, including such renowned figures as John Holt, John Waiheʻe, and Alvin Shim.

Daniel Akaka, soon to be a United States representative and then a senator, was working in the newly elected Governor Ariyoshi's office. At Ariyoshi's direction, he pulled together a network of Hawaiian leaders in the governor's conference room to develop a program under the Native American Act. This was done on a crash basis in two steps, first to form the organization and second to delineate the needs of the Hawaiian community.

The name Alu Like—*working together*—was given by Mrs. Pukui, who more than anyone had come to symbolize the preservation of the Hawaiian culture. Where the Community Action Program had called for the "maximum participation" of its economically disadvantaged beneficiaries, Alu Like was based on the maximum cultural participation of its Hawaiian beneficiaries. The head of the guidance counseling program at Kamehameha Schools, Winona Rubin, was recruited to head the new organization. Rubin would remember being immensely excited, meeting many Hawaiian activists and the earliest of the modern-day Hawaiian nationalists for the first time.[20] Her first office was in Mayor Wright Housing, which then was one of the roughest, most crime-ridden of the public housing projects. The immediate challenge was to communicate widely with Hawaiians throughout all islands and to conduct an assessment of community needs. In Rubin's view, the baseline work of the book *Nana I Ke Kumu* made a significant difference, as volunteers numbering in the hundreds were given training that drew on its findings. Native speakers were sought out and hired as key field workers. They were deployed as part of a dual-language approach in situations where older Hawaiians were deemed most comfortable speaking the Hawaiian language. Aunt Edith Kanakaole, a giant figure in traditional culture, played an important role in sensitizing people to making a bicultural contact with Hawaiians.

Alu Like was, in a certain way, a shift from working on an illness model to working on a wellness model, focusing not so much on what plagued Hawaiians as what Hawaiians could do, with a helping hand, to help themselves. Repeatedly the answers had to do with Hawaiians gaining political awareness, and with linking the cultural remembrances of an older generation to the potentials of a new, educated generation. What Ariyoshi had to say about the importance of culture was much like what Hawaiians were saying in a different context. "We believed that unless you knew the roots from whence you came, you could not contribute as well in the present," Rubin was to recall. "When you know your roots, you can give others respect."[21]

A young girl named Norma Wong had just graduated from high school when she went into the field for the new Alu Like. She was eventually to become a state legislator and then key staff for a Hawaiian governor, but in 1975 she was in her late teens, opening doors, stimulating conversation, and taking notes. In meeting after meeting, up and down the Hawaiian Islands, she heard refrains that linked a seemingly distant past to hope for the future.[22] At the time, fewer than a thousand people were reported by the U.S. census to speak Hawaiian which was widely regarded as on the verge of extinction. Nonetheless, at even the smallest gatherings an older person would typically be asked to speak in Hawaiian or pray in Hawaiian. Others listened, deeply moved by the sounds of their ancestral language.

Education was a frequent concern. In Wong's perception as a field worker, people were satisfied with public schools up to the third or fourth grade, at which point they felt Hawaiians were being subtly put down and left behind. The desire for access to land also pervaded conversation, as did frustrations with the Hawaiian Homes program. People also wanted to know how to protect traditional water rights. Across a broad spectrum of issues Hawaiians wanted to become more assertive. People talked not only about supporting sympathetic candidates but about more Hawaiians themselves running for office. Job development, training, and placement became an immediate and enduring program, substantially as a result of Inouye's support, and subsequent programs dealt with health, education, housing, business assistance, literacy, and native rights. In most instances, the federal dollars flowed into Hawai'i because of the congressional delegation's successfully including Native Hawaiians in provisions for Native Americans. This de facto change in status occurred even though Hawaiians were not recognized as a sovereign native people by the United States government, a factor that came back to haunt Hawaiians at the end of the century.

The debate over native Hawaiian sovereignty lay in the future, but the process of bringing people together for discussion had an immediate impact. A series of extended meetings were held—in Wai'anae, at Kamemeha Schools, and at McKinley High School—each involving one hundred to two hundred leaders as identified by a grassroots selection process. These meetings culminated in one hundred elected delegates coming together in a three-day gathering in Wai'anae, called *Puwalu,* which means uniting cooperatively. *Puwalu* was dedicated to developing a clearer understanding of a Hawaiian agenda, with land, water, language, cultural preservation, and political action as its core.[23] Norma Wong thought of the *Puwalu* as the last time Hawaiians assembled out of sight of the mass media. Serendipitously, the *Puwalu* intersected with preparations for another constitutional convention of the State of Hawai'i. When Hawaiians said they must do something, they increasingly had in mind the Constitutional Convention of 1978.

While significant to the political evolution of Hawaiians, Alu Like also reflected the continuing evolution of the Democratic Party in Hawai'i. Burns' gospel was to unite the Hawaiians politically with AJAs. Tom Gill had reached out to Hawaiians through the Community Action Program, as had Frank Fasi through the Model Cities program. Myron Thompson connected strongly not only with Burns but also with Ariyoshi and Inouye. Moments in the governor's conference room on the fifth floor of the capitol—Burns with Galdeira, Dan Akaka with the organizers of Alu Like—were slices of time that further introduced the Hawaiian revival to the Democratic Party.

In the years ahead, expressions of Hawaiian nationalism—sometimes simply expressions of rage—strained the local coalition of Hawaiians and AJAs, but for the time being at least a special relationship held sway. As all the voting and survey data argued, AJAs were the most fervent practitioners of the democratic process, and the Hawaiian movement was about awakening and working together. When Alvin Shim organized a workshop on political action for Hawaiians, all of the resource people—the political scientist Richard Kosaki, the attorney Yukio Naito, for example—were of Japanese ancestry. Dan Inouye traced his extensive relationships with Hawaiians to his mother, who was orphaned at a young age. Homeless on the streets of Lahaina, Maui, she was taken in and nurtured by Hawaiians. As a result, she could speak a pidgin Hawaiian and in old age took Hawaiian language classes at the university. "She made it very clear to me from the time I was very young,"[24] Inouye would recall, "'I owe a lot to the Hawaiian, and I expect you to repay that debt.'" Inouye would remember his first act as a legislator in 1955 was to propose that the territorial legislature vacate 'Iolani Palace "even if it means going out in a tent," arguing that it was "a sacrilege" to meet in the throne room of the last Hawaiian queen. He thought of Alu Like, with its mostly Hawaiian board of directors and staff, as an early beginning, reversing negative stereotypes and generating evidence that Hawaiians could manage their own affairs.

KAHO'OLAWE

A dramatic explosion of Hawaiian political consciousness can be dated precisely to January 3, 1976, when nine Hawaiians boated in to a small, reddish-brown island named Kaho'olawe, eighth in size among the Hawaiian Islands, eleven miles from east to west and less than seven miles from north to south. It was a place where no one in recent time had dared to travel, and no one lived. When imaginations soared, one could see with a nudge that Kaho'olawe had the shape of a fetus.

Archaeologists subsequently developed evidence that Hawaiians had created a small but sustained settlement on Kaho'olawe about 1000 A.D. Subsequent Western attempts at settling the island had failed. Kaho'olawe was dry to begin with, and the Western introduction of goats and cattle—split-hooved grazers—stripped the land of plant life and reduced its capacity to attract passing rainfall. In 1953, President Eisenhower issued a decree allowing the United States Navy to use Kaho'olawe as a practice range for aerial bombing. In the tradition of trivializing the identity of the Hawaiian Islands, Kaho'olawe became known as the Target Island. The top of the island was reduced to a red hardpan, the landscape was cratered, and even the stones were broken and strewn about. On seeing the disaster done to the natural systems of Kahoʻolawe, one of the young men from the boat, Walter Ritte Jr., wept uncontrollably for hours. It was a reaction that in the coming years would be shared by many.

Ritte and his companions had been called out by an older activist from Maui, Charley Maxwell, who previously had been involved in a movement known as ALOHA, which had sought reparation from Washington for America's taking of native land. For Maxwell, a person such as Ritte was a logical recruit. Ritte's parents—a nurturing Hawaiian mother, an eccentric haole father—had settled on the small, rural island of Molokaʻi when he was seven, and Ritte had returned to Molokaʻi after college hoping to make a living and raise his family. In addition to hunting, he acquainted himself with older Hawaiians and with their stories.

The nature of Molokaʻi life—and the deep involvement of Molokaʻi people—illustrated the extent to which Kahoʻolawe was a symbol for deeply held hurts and grievances. The east half of Molokaʻi was held by a small handful of owners. The central plain was a pineapple plantation, which even then was a declining industry. Most of the west half of the island was owned by Molokaʻi Ranch, which had devastated both the landscape and the surrounding reefs by the heavy grazing of cattle. Wild goats and pigs were eating their way up the mountains, continuing their long-time destruction of the native forest and degradation of the watershed.

Human settlement was scattered along the leeward coast and in small farms in the upland plain, which was under lease to long-term Hawaiian tenants by the Hawaiian Homes Department of the State government. The island was part of Maui County which, by virtue of population, not only dominated state and local elections but housed the agencies of local government. Maui ruled.

Molokaʻi's unemployment rate often ran to 20 percent, and subsistence hunting, fishing, and gathering were an essential feature of community life. Pig, deer, and fish in the deep freezers of Molokaʻi were a consistent substitute for money. For those who might not grasp the idea of feudalism continuing into modern Hawaiʻi, a visit to Molokaʻi was a clarifying experience. Hawaiian hunters were to Molokaʻi what Robin Hood had been to Sherwood Forest. A few interests owned the countryside, and the struggling populace was marginalized for trespassing and poaching. Despite all this, Molokaʻi became a cradle of hope. It remained the most Hawaiian of the islands, not only in demography but in its powerful sense of the Hawaiian past.

As Hawaiians became politically active, the Molokaʻi community generated a shared vision of a golden age of the none too distant past, when the land was widely populated and cultivated. The largest traditional settlements logically had been in the cool, water-rich valleys of the windward side, which were now virtually inaccessible by any reasonable or legal means. The areas of lightest settlement were in the hot leeward plains, to which most of Molokai's people were now confined. On the southeast-facing coast, cooler breezes blew, and more rain fell. There, in the center of the island, was a partially overgrown stone temple of great mass that testified to the work and religiosity of many thousands of people. On the shore, a lei of human-made fish ponds—sixty in all—stretched from the midpoint of the island to the east end, where the traveler could find Hālawa Valley, a natural Eden that once had supported hundreds of families. A waterfall in the back of the valley fed a stream system that had supported more than five hundred taro fields, in which the water ditches and rock walls were still much in evidence, despite the invasion of alien trees and weeds.

Such a vision begged the question, where were the people of old, *ka po'e kahiko*? What had caused this disaster? When Hawaiians wept for the land in public meetings, was it for this that they wept?

The year before the Kaho'olawe expedition, a community group known as Hui Alaloa ("the group of the long trails") had engaged in long, overland marches across Moloka'i. The protesters hiked to the bays and reefs of the west end of Moloka'i, and also to the valleys of the windward side of the island. For a small community, Moloka'i generated a startling depth and breadth of leadership that touched all the islands. Along with Ritte, the most visible was George Helm, a Hawaiian singer, poet, and native son of Moloka'i. Others in the young, activist, and educated generation included Emmett Aluli, a medical doctor who had traded the certain successes of Honolulu for serving a remote community in a culturally sensitive and accessible way. Yet another was Collette Machado, an effective activist who had found the cause of her life by relocating from Honolulu to Moloka'i.

In their attempts to rediscover what it meant to be Hawaiian, Ritte and Helm traveled widely, looking for elders to connect them to the Hawaiian past. In the process they found an underground of fishermen and taro farmers, healers and religious practitioners, as well as people who still spoke fluent Hawaiian. Some of the most valuable sources were on Moloka'i and were to become symbols of the revived role of *kūpuna*, the respected elder. These included Aunt Harriet Ne, who provided a window into the powers of memory that Hawaiians had developed in their pre-Western oral culture. Mrs. Ne seemingly could recite everything she had experienced, heard, or seen from the age of two.[25] She was a bridge to the nineteenth century and a repository of legends and chants that originated from centuries before the arrival of Cook. Aunt Clara Ku was a homesteader who had resettled on the land in the 1920s. With a voice that could be heard at a great distance, and features so powerful they could have been sculpted from lava rock, Clara Ku became an emblem of the *kūpuna* across the islands. When the demands of organizing or protesting arose, Aunt Clara would pack and travel with her friends, Aunt Lani Kapuni and Aunt Mary Lee, in the spirit she originally had resettled the Moloka'i plain.

The first landing on Kaho'olawe was planned in secrecy, but while the boats of the Hawaiians lay offshore, to Ritte's surprise a reporter appeared in a fishing boat. U.S. Marine helicopters appeared overhead, shouting warnings to not set foot on the island. Most of the people in the boat complied, but Ritte decided he had gone too far to turn back. He went ashore with the group of nine. He and Aluli explored the island for two and a half days, hiding from the searching helicopters. They immediately came to two conclusions: First, they must do whatever needed to be done to stop the bombing, and second, Kaho'olawe must be restored as a sanctuary for the Hawaiian people. When their demands were initially ignored, they returned with Ritte's wife, Loretta, and his sister Scarlett. After another expedition around the island, Ritte began a diary, in which he wrote: ". . . Kaho'olawe represents the binding agent, the strength and steadfast courage, for our Hawai'i people." Despite the damage, they had found shrines and petroglyphs as evidence of habitation, as well as meadows of grass and reef life to support human occupation. "We love her," wrote Ritte, "and we will guide her future, for now it lies in our hands."[26]

With the navy, the FBI, and the courts stirring, sixty-five Hawaiians gathered for the third access in mid-February 1976. At the dock on Maui, FBI agents warned Ritte that federal authorities would take great offense if he went again. One of the few living kahuna of the ancient religion, Sam Lono of Windward O'ahu, called Ritte out and demanded that he nonetheless go, arguing that he had a right of access to Kaho'olawe for native religious purposes. Not only Ritte but the entire group went, including all of the aunties from Moloka'i, despite their advanced ages. One of the most important participants was Aunt Emma DeFries, also a religious practitioner, who became a teacher to many of the younger people. She was a visually stunning woman with olive skin and straight, steel-grey hair who always wore a red wrap and a hair band. Two young musicians, Jerry Santos and Robert Beaumant, followed her around and wrote about "the light in the lady's eyes." Music became politically important in Hawai'i again, as it once had been around the time of overthrow and annexation.

Thereafter there was a long lull in the Kaho'olawe story, marked by haggling but no agreement. Nearly thirteen months after the first access, the fourth access took place in January 1977. The group consisted of young, athletic Hawaiians who knew one another well—Ritte, George Helm, Richard

Sawyer, Francis Kauhane, and Charles Warrington Jr. All assumed they would be arrested for criminal trespass. On the first night they carried large quantities of water ashore and buried them in scattered places, then Ritte and Sawyer settled in for a long-term test of will with the navy. To their shock, the navy conducted bombing and strafing practices despite their presence on the island. Part of their time was spent running and hiding. Dizzy and weak from lack of adequate food and water, they read, wrote, slept, and dreamed. The idea of redirecting the course of history by retrieving the past had become a constant theme. "We have so little of our history now," Ritte wrote, "and we must save whatever we can now for us and our future generations, or forever shall our proud Hawai'i past be gone."[27]

As days and then weeks passed, the public drama heightened. George Helm addressed the Hawai'i legislature and then went to Washington to appeal to the congressional delegation. Returning to Hawai'i, he had a dream that Ritte and Sawyer were in trouble and needed help. Slipping past Coast Guard patrols, he and a young man from Maui named Kimo Mitchell landed in the dark on surfboards. Ritte and Sawyer had lit a bonfire, but high winds blew the sparks across a wide area, creating confusion. Not finding Ritte and Sawyer, Helm and Mitchell set off on their boards for the south shore of Maui. George Helm was a writer, poet, and speaker. He played Hawaiian slack-key guitar and sang in the classic Hawaiian falsetto style. He had a warm, engaging smile, dark eyes, a full beard, and unruly long hair. Through his participation in the Hawaiian movement, he was transformed from a stylish young perfomer into a person whose research and personal honesty compelled people to stop and listen. Breaking with the greatest taboo of Hawaiian experience in Western time, he more than any of the young activists turned to the ancient gods, and to such figures as Emma DeFries for religious guidance. "Though many of our spiritual attempts were very awkward," Ritte wrote, "they were done with great conviction. . . . George played the key role . . . as we all looked to him for decisions and knowledge. . . ."[28] Helm and Mitchell were lost at sea, Mitchell at age twenty-five and Helm just short of his twenty-seventh birthday. In preparation for the occupation, Helm had written, "The breath in man is the breath of Papa (the earth). Man is merely the caretaker of the land that maintains his life and nourishes his soul. Therefore, *'aina* (the land) is sacred."[29]

AFTER THIRTY-FIVE DAYS on Kaho'olawe, Ritte and Sawyer surrendered. The same Samuel P. King who had run against Burns, now a federal judge, gave them the maximum sentence for federal trespass, which was six months in jail. Throughout, Ritte maintained a stance of informed defiance, tempered by professions of nonviolence. "This is Hawai'i," he wrote, "a unique and different culture. No matter how hard one tries to make us all Americans, our differences must be respected."[30]

The political fallout of Kaho'olawe remains incalculable, but some attempt at description must be made. Hawaiians were once again culture heroes in their homeland, not only to fellow Hawaiians but to a generally admiring and sympathetic public. Second, Kaho'olawe altered the nature of the Hawaiian movement. What had begun as a series of initiatives to secure help from the government—with modest experiments in autonomy, such as Alu Like—had been transformed into a spiritual and nationalistic movement. Around this time, the word *"lāhui,"* (nation) was revived. Reflecting on Kaho'olawe, Aluli wrote in 1978, "We must pay heed to the strange callings of our inner voices, and trust they are coming from the well-hidden past."[31] After dedicating a quarter century of volunteer effort to the occupation of, negotiations over, and cleanup of Kaho'olawe, Aluli wrote: ". . . Each time we pick up a stone that has fallen from a cultural site, we pick ourselves up as a people. We lay the foundation for a nation."[32]

THE DEMOCRATIC PARTY AND THE MYSTIQUE OF CHANGE

When the social order is deeply disturbed, as it was in the 1970s, one of the standard political scenarios is that the party in power loses its hold on the institutions of power. This was essentially what had happened to the national Democratic Party in the aftermath of the 1960s, but in Hawai'i, just the opposite occurred. The Democratic Party repositioned itself as the party of change, molded change, and co-opted change. As with other disturbances of the status quo, such as the antidevelopment movement, the women's movement, and the antiwar movement, the Democratic Party became the political beneficiary of the Hawaiian movement.

This was so even though many Democratic Party figures were initially conflicted. Inouye particularly was caught in the middle, not only because he was an American military hero but because his mission in Congress revolved heavily around bringing defense appropriations home to Hawai'i (as indeed was true to a lesser extent for the entire delegation). Despite the considerable animosity directed at him by Hawaiian activists, Inouye pleaded with President Jimmy Carter to pardon Ritte and Sawyer. He said the occupation had made Kaho'olawe a "symbol of the resurgence of the Hawaiian people, a movement formulating for many Hawaiians a renewed respect for their culture and their history."[33] The cultivation of Hawaiian votes by the old Burns faction was instrumental in minimizing the distance between Hawaiians and non-Hawaiians. As a byproduct of the Japanese Hawaiian coalition, Dan Akaka had by this time been elected to the U.S. House. At the

moment when Inouye seemed immobilized, Akaka led the congressional delegation in easing the navy out of Kaho'olawe, ending the navy's tenure, clean-
ing up the island, and turning it over to the Hawaiian people. All of this
was eventually accomplished in collaboration with a stable, enduring Hawaiian nongovernmental organization, the Protect Kaho'olawe 'Ohana, led by
Emmett Aluli.

JOHN WAIHE'E AND THE 1978 CONSTITUTIONAL CONVENTION

During the year of the first Kaho'olawe access, John Waihe'e was graduating from law school and passing the bar. He had worked for Alvin Shim's
firm as a student and then associated as an attorney. His first case was a
defense of Walter Ritte, a distant cousin, against charges resulting from hunting deer on other people's property. His second client was Charles Warrington,
who was hauled into federal court for trespass on Kaho'olawe along with
Francis Kauhane, Ritte, and Sawyer. While these cases provide a glimpse of
Waihe'e's roots in the Hawaiian movement, his background in rural Hawai'i
provides more telling information about his ability to reach out to all ethnic groups, and particularly the Japanese. He grew up in a modest but orderly
house in a neighborhood of forest, small farms, and ranches called Āhualoa
on the island of Hawai'i. While Āhualoa is situated in the cool upland flank
of Mauna Kea, it overlooks what then were sugar fields of the water-rich
Hāmākua district. Waihe'e's father, John David Waihe'e II, was both a Democrat and a sympathizer with organized labor. He had his own issues as a
Hawaiian and would die on the waiting list of the Hawaiian Homes Commission, but he nonetheless actively supported the people who labored and
periodically went on strike in the plantations.

One of John Waihe'e's earliest memories was going with his father to
the soup kitchens of strikers in the picturesque sugar mill town of Hon-
oka'a, next to the sea. He also remembered the ILWU business agent and
state representative for the region, Yoshito Takamine, dropping by the
house to talk, bringing a sense of the faraway state capitol in Honolulu
to the family doorstep. Although wrapped in his family's Hawaiianness,
Waihe'e was constantly exposed as a child to the virtues of the Japanese.
He played around in the back row at elementary school while maintaining the friendship of a studious Japanese girl in the front row, who shared
her class notes with him at test time. In a brief flurry of activity, he became
an Eagle Scout, then got into enough hometown mischief to be sent to
boarding school in Honolulu. There he met his future wife, Lynn
Kobashigawa, and together they attended Andrews College, a sectarian
religious college in Wisconsin.

Energized and focused by the activism of the civil rights and antiwar movements, he won the office of student body president. He broadened his social experience and his political vocabulary. He worked in a steel mill and learned about labor organization. He was swept up in the excitement of Martin Luther King Jr. and the 1968 presidential campaign of Robert F. Kennedy. As someone who was always thought of as having great potential, he was a constant work in progress—the rascal child who became an Eagle Scout, the C student who was a classroom brain, a Hawaiian who was intimately connected with the Japanese, a country jack who knew about the city, and eventually an islander who knew about the wide world.

At the Model Cities program Waiheʻe was called a planner. In law school many of his classmates thought of him as the smartest member of the first class. John Dominis Holt, in his quest to revitalize Hawaiian culture, hired Waiheʻe to interview Hawaiians about what it meant to be Hawaiian, in essence creating a subsidized quest for identity. Waiheʻe was one of a hundred Hawaiians who sequestered themselves in Alu Likeʻs three-day *Puwalu*. Varied people looked at him and saw something of themselves, and perhaps also what they would like to be: a real Hawaiian.

Shim was a good fit as a mentor, because he was both a proud Hawaiian and passionately committed to broad liberal causes and to the labor movement in particular. At the time Shim was tired of losing law partners to politics, so he imposed a general prohibition against members of his firm running for office. In this spirit, Waiheʻe thought seriously about modeling himself after Shim—that is, being influential without ever standing for office.[34] At Shimʻs firm, Waiheʻe periodically took over the conference room on Saturday and brought in his friends to pick the brains of well-known guests. He was well on his way to being a behind-the-scenes operator like Shim: He was active in the *Puwalu* process, active in a small group that sought to elect a Hawaiian governor, and also active in a downtown group called Goals for Hawaiʻi, where he worked on a committee dealing with land use issues. With the approach of the Constitutional Convention, he was working on the campaigns of no fewer than six other candidates. The day of the filing deadline, Shim called him in and announced a reversal of office policy: He wanted Waiheʻe to run for a seat in the convention.

Waiheʻe raced from house to house in a rainstorm, securing signatures from his neighbors in Kalihi for his filing papers. Through Shimʻs firm he had become friends with Norma Wong, who by then had graduated from doing field work for Alu Like, and it was a short step to a meeting in her garage with a group of other candidates for the convention. Participants included a law school classmate, Franklin Hayashida, who had sat next to Waiheʻe at the Model Cities agency and gotten his signature on his first Democratic Party card. Five others were to become future members of the legislature: Carol Fukunaga, Anthony Chang, Tom Okamura and Gerald Hagino of O'ahu, and Anthony Takitani of Maui. All except Waihe'e were Asian American, and all shared an interest in making a maximum impact on the convention.

ONE OF THE EXCITING ASPECTS of a representative gathering is that those elected must organize themselves. It is like going to a party and finding out who likes to talk, who likes to drink, and who likes to dance. People who go home early serve on committees, and those who stay up late preside. At the 1978 convention, nearly half of the delegates were loosely aligned with State capitol politics as it had been played up to that point. Another group of approximately equal size, nearly half, identified with some new cause or suggested reform. The balance were derived from the meeting in Norma Wong's garage, with its origins in the University of Hawai'i Law School, under the leadership of Waihe'e.

In the public buildup to the convention, the proposals for change centered on the words *initiative, referendum,* and *recall,* a formula for direct citizen participation in government and a bypassing of the legislature. In this package, citizens were to be given the right to initiate legislation (initiative), bring it to a public vote (referendum), and to dismiss legislators (recall) with whom they were unhappy prior to the end of their terms in office.[35] These ideas were imported principally from California, but as a way of legitimizing them in Hawai'i, proponents gathered twenty thousand signatures on a petition that was submitted to the convention.

The romance of such ideas reflected the widening suspicion of the legislative process, a distinctly stronger trend among haole newcomers than among local or long-time residents. Cries for reform played in tantalizing and confusing ways against a sense that public calm might be returning. The Vietnam War was over. Development had slowed. Ariyoshi had bought Waiāhole Valley for the state. H-3 was tied up in court. A new State Plan was about to sail through the legislature. The New Left of Hawai'i was going the way of the Old—which was into the death grip of Marxist-Leninist orthodoxy. What should the convention do? "Next to nothing," said the liberal of old, Tom Gill,[36] expressing a view shared by downtown business, as well as by unions.[37]

Ariyoshi notably took exception to the drumbeat for the convention doing as little as possible. In his remarks to the delegates, he said that some people looked at constitutions as akin to the Biblical ark of the covenant, but constitutions must move "hand-in-hand with the progress of the human mind," and each generation must make its own way. He reiterated his view of Hawai'i as unique in geography and people, problems, and solutions. He warned against assuming that something that was good for another place was good for Hawai'i—seemingly a veiled reference reflecting his opposition to initiative. "We must adopt Hawaiian solutions for Hawaiian problems," he said.

LEADERSHIP FROM BELOW

The maneuvering for leadership of the Constitutional Convention was complicated by the fact that none of the three groups had a clear majority—neither the practitioners of state capitol politics nor the independents, and certainly not Waihe'e's small group. As a standoff was being defined, a leader of the independents, Jeremy Harris (then of Kaua'i, later a major political figure on O'ahu) suggested to Waihe'e that he take the presidency. Waihe'e declined, deferring to a delegate in the status quo group, William Paty. Paty was a plantation manager with a craggy face and burnt, deeply lined skin, a Republican who was widely liked in his home community—Waialua, on O'ahu's North Shore—as well as around downtown and the capitol. Paty as president suggested a status quo convention, reminiscent of the Republican Hebden Porteus presiding over the do-nothing convention of 1968. There the analogy ended. Paty arose each morning at four and swam in the ocean, and he approached events with an uncommon level of excitement, which was perhaps at the root of his affinity for Waihe'e.

As the person who tipped the scales toward the keepers of the status quo, Waihe'e was asked what he wanted for himself. He replied that he wanted nothing for himself but to be at the table when committee chairmanships were handed out. Thereafter he helped nail down chairmanships for friends, including Anthony Chang and Carol Fukunaga, but most importantly for a person who was a step removed from his immediate group, A. Frenchy DeSoto.

FRENCHY DESOTO AND THE HAWAIIAN AFFAIRS COMMITTEE

DeSoto was the matriarch of a large family and had originally worked as a janitor, then as a patronage employee in the state senate as a sergeant at arms. She represented the substantially Hawaiian, low-income district of Wai'anae, O'ahu. She had a husky, cigarette voice, which she used to great advantage, gliding seamlessly from perfect English to pidgin to a partial but expressive grasp of Hawaiian. As a child she had been orphaned and abused, and within her powerful frame there was a reservoir of dismay and rage that was counterbalanced with hopefulness and a warm sense of aloha.

She first had became involved in Wai'anae community issues, then in both the *Puwalu* of Alu Like and the Protect Kaho'olawe 'Ohana. She was among the sixty-five participants in the third access of Kaho'olawe, of which she would say: "It became apparent that this was not just about fighting another power, but a cultural thing respecting the land. That was when I got into *aloha 'āina*,"[38] meaning a philosophy based on reverence for the land.

She also was one of dozens of Hawaiians Shim had gotten into EST without charge, owing to the generosity of Werner Erhard, who had wanted to know why so few Hawaiians took his course. They were too poor, Shim replied. During the EST seminar DeSoto had, in Shim's view, journeyed through anger to an extraordinary statement in which she reduced the audience to tears, an indication of her power as a speaker. Thereafter she called Shim and asked if she had what it took to run for the Constitutional Convention. Shim said that if she thought she did then she did, and if she thought she did not then she did not.

DeSoto chaired the Hawaiian Affairs Committee. At the time, the affairs of Hawaiians were the presumed backwater of the legislature, in which members nagged the executive branch about the failures of the Hawaiian Homes program. The Hawaiian Affairs Committee in the 1968 convention was likewise regarded as a backwater, and on the surface nothing in 1978 seemed to have changed. Jim Shon, then a young haole researcher, prepared a briefing paper for the convention on behalf of the Legislative Reference Bureau about Hawaiian issues. Hearing no new ideas, he focused on the long-standing wisdom that since Hawaiian Homes had been established by federal statute, little could be done. Thereafter Shon was elected to represent Waikīkī in the convention and actually briefed DeSoto's committee on his findings or, more accurately, his lack thereof.

As a result of the distance between the Hawaiian community and the political status quo, the emergence of a Hawaiian agenda seemed amazingly spontaneous. The actual situation was that the Hawaiian ideas and relationships predated the convention, but the strategy for their passage was developed as the convention progressed. Winona Rubin gave the committee the ideas developed in *Puwalu*. She and Ariyoshi's director of Hawaiian Homes, Georgianna Padeken (previously of QLCC on Moloka'i), would appear weekly with stew and rice to feed DeSoto's committee staff and "talk story." DeSoto called Ritte and said, "Boy, get down here." Ritte flew to O'ahu and, after two days, called his wife and asked her to send more clothes. He particularly set his sights on native rights, access and gathering rights, which he had worked on for several years, but he also lobbied for the entire Hawaiian package. With Ritte's recent celebrity at Kaho'olawe, he could get into delegate offices easily, and there he made much the same presentation—do something for Hawaiians—over and over. The staff included Francis Kauhane and Steve Kuna, a recent graduate of Howard University Law School. Interestingly, an outspoken young activist named Mililani Trask, a descendant of the Trask political clan, likewise worked a while but parted ways with the committee over fundamental Hawaiian strategy, only to emerge in the public spotlight as an outspoken Hawaiian nationalist.

Outreach was important. DeSoto was deeply aware that Hawaiians tended to live in outlying or Neighbor Island neighborhoods. Since her constituents were not in Honolulu, she took her committee to them, with Paty's support for travel. The testimony she most remembered was that of a poor, elderly Hawaiian man who had always supplemented his diet by fishing. One day he found that his path to the sea was blocked by a fence, which had been erected by a developer. To get over the fence, he built boxes on both sides, then climbed over. When the property owner caught him, he was arrested for trespass and put in jail. Having no money, he could not defend himself, let alone engage in a lengthy battle to protect his traditional right of access to the sea.

Waihe'e met often with DeSoto to review what was coming out of her committee and what might and might not actually get the convention's support. In the meantime, a simple motion on how to set a calendar and proceed had been voted down on the convention floor, raising a question of discipline and how the convention was to function.[39] As the majority coalition tried to regroup, a senior Democratic legislator, Donald D. H. Ching, began to refer to John Waihe'e as "majority leader," after which Waihe'e began to chair the meetings and line up votes. To track the positions of delegates, he set up a system of party captains, or whips. This was a conventional enough step, but he proceeded to set up a second set of captains among the independents, with whom he also maintained close contact. This more inclusive system would become the key to continuously forming new alliances and mustering a majority vote on a wide range of controversial issues.

"WE RESERVE THE RIGHT TO CONTROL OUR OWN DESTINY"

As proposals moved from committee to the floor, initiative posed a particular problem. The most thoughtful attack on initiative was mounted by delegate Gerald Hagino, who contended that it would destroy the traditional lawmaking process and put it in the hands of mass media or those who spoke loudest. Hagino echoed a tract called Palaka Power, written by his brother David Hagino, who at the time was out campaigning for a legislative seat. A diluted version of initiative actually made it onto the floor of the convention. In a confused maneuver, it passed on a roll call vote, but a delegate then called for a division of the house, in which the Waihe'e group joined hands with the status quo group. Initiative died.

A second package had to do with environmental protection, including explicit protection of land, water, agricultural activity, marine resources, and a safe environment. This package also included a prohibition against the use of nuclear energy. Independents who had lost on initiative found much to their liking in the environmental package, and the whips of the independent delegates began to coalesce with Waihe'e, who began to call the independent Jeremy Harris "my floor leader." A new coalition was invented to make up for conservatives who thought the environmental amendments were going too far down the road of legislation.

A seemingly innocuous discussion of the preamble of the constitution provided a revealing glimpse into the redefinition of Island Hawai'i that was inherent in the Hawaiian movement. Gerald Hagino moved to amend the preamble by deleting the words "State of" from the first sentence in favor of "We, the people of Hawai'i." The proposed preamble described Hawai'i's people as mindful of the Hawaiian heritage "and uniqueness as an island state." It went on to say, "We reserve the right to control our destiny." Frenchy DeSoto seconded Hagino's motion.

Delegate Paul E. DiBianco, an attorney from the mainland who was influential among the independents, objected to deleting "the State of" in the first line. "We are a state," he said. Delegate Paul L. Lacy interpreted the phrase about "control our destiny" to mean "we're declaring the right to control our destiny as if we were a sovereign nation." By a wide margin, the delegates passed the new Preamble, which now referred to Hawai'i as a place or society, not a state.

There were five Hawaiian amendments. One mandated the study of Hawaiian history, culture, and language in the public schools. One made the Hawaiian language the official language of the State, along with English. One protected traditional and customary Hawaiian rights (such as the right of access to the mountains, the ocean, and religious sites). One limited the taking of ownership of land by adverse possession, a process by which many small Hawaiian landowners had lost their lands. One mandated the state to form a semi-autonomous political entity to be known as the Office of Hawaiian Affairs (OHA).

DeSoto's committee's report credited the rise in ethnic consciousness to the American civil rights movement, in which the struggle for acceptance had become a celebration of ethnicity. The committee report also cited new thinking in biology, in which the value of preserving the diversity of species had displaced the preoccupation with Darwin's survival of the fittest: ". . . variety rather than sameness enhances the possibilities for survival," the report said, and "a culturally diversified society is a source of strength for a nation." It went on in this vein by saying, "we may evaluate existing models of society and perhaps thus discover alternative models of structuring society." It described in positive terms the Hawaiian emphasis on the *ohana* system of the extended family, and devotion to group success rather than individual success. It differentiated Hawaiian culture from other nonwhite cultures of Hawai'i by noting that the cultures of Japan and Korea, as examples, were being preserved in those countries, but for Hawaiian studies "the State of Hawai'i is the 'home country.'"

In support of the education plank, the report said that the subject of Hawaiians had been reduced to a small subset of social studies in the schools and "lost in the wave of western standards and the emphasis on assimilation or (the) 'melting pot' model in America."[40]

The Hawaiian man who had encountered the fence on the way to the beach lived on in DeSoto's floor speech: Such events, coupled with government neglect, "have resulted in making Hawaiians strangers in their own homeland," she said. Echoing the Boas school of anthropology, delegate Patricia Nozaki supported the education package by saying, "It is time to recognize the fact that Hawaiian values are as important as other values in our multicultural State, and that these values should be given equal consideration and recognition." Delegate Kekoa Kaapu recalled the decision of his father, David of Punalu'u, to live in a grass house and tend his taro patch wearing only a *malo*. People—including FDR—had come from all over to see how he lived, yet some of the Hawaiians in the neighborhood were ashamed of his wearing only a loincloth, because they had been taught to think that way in school.

The several-day debate provoked a cascade of thoughts and stories. The wording of the committee report on OHA is of particular historical importance. ". . . People to whom assets belong should have control over them," it said. Further, the committee said it intended OHA to be "independent from the executive branch and all other branches of government," although it would be administered as a state agency. The committee hammered redundantly on its hope for an autonomous new organization: "The status of [OHA] is to be unique and special . . . a separate entity independent of the executive branch of the government." By this time the organizations of American Indians had drawn serious attention in Hawai'i, particularly the settlement of the massive Alaskan native claims against the United States government. The report said that one of OHA's potential purposes was to receive reparations from the U.S. government, but nothing resembling the Indian tribal model or the native Alaskan model of beneficiary corporations was even faintly suggested. In fact, so far as OHA was inspired by the experience of others, the idea was influenced by the Office of Maori Affairs in New Zealand, a place many Hawaiians had visited for inspiration and which was increasingly known by its Polynesian name, Aotearoa.

It was not at all obvious at the time that problems with the United States Constitution might result from structuring OHA inside Hawai'i state government. Delegate H. William Burgess, who was to participate many years later in the court attack on an all-Hawaiian election, nibbled at the edges by asking what new rights were being created and at whose expense. None, he was told. Tradition was merely being protected. Delegate Akira Sakima asked specifically if there was a constitutional problem with holding a State election involving people of only one racial group (which was to be the basis for a famous ensuing U.S. Supreme Court case). John Waihe'e, who often dealt with floor opposition, said OHA would be constitutional because it was in essence a board of directors for a trust. While this was something less than a convincing answer, it illustrated Waihe'e's role as the extraordinary delegate of the entire convention.

In the calls to action, a longer version of Hawai'i's past came alive. Delegate Mary Ann Barnard quoted from Queen Lili'uokalani's autobiography, in which the Queen recounted being warmly greeted by thousands of people in Washington during the period she pleaded against annexation. In contrast to the missionary descendants in Hawai'i, these people were, in her words, "the real American people." Delegate Barnard said that to vote for the amendments would be in the tradition of the real American people. Delegate Shon, having previously thought that the Hawaiian Affairs Committee could do little, now said, "in all fairness, the entire State should belong to native Hawaiians."

In broad terms, the convention reflected the course of the decade, in which first the environment and then Hawaiian culture were the overriding concerns, propelled by the idea of Hawai'i taking greater control over its future. In all, the convention adopted 116 amendments, five times the number of 1968. The only clear-cut concession to the independents was establishing an eight-year, two-term limit on the governorship.[41] The limit did not apply to Ariyoshi's first term, but it was to mean that no one in the future would serve the long, almost dynastic terms of Burns and Ariyoshi.

Ariyoshi had maintained his usual distance from the work of others, but when the convention adjourned he embraced a yes vote for all 116 proposals as a package. In many ways the package validated the direction he had set during the preceding four years, generally by strengthening state controls over resources and specifically by giving the State government new powers over water rights. Traditionally control over the pumping of water had been divided among the counties, the plantations, and the military, and

Ariyoshi had become convinced that water was an endangered resource. The resulting State Water Commission, with its power to regulate usage and allocate water between wet and dry parts of the islands, was a significant addition to the already enormous powers of the governorship.

For good reason, the design of the ballot for the ratification vote was criticized as being weighted in favor of adoption. The public was given two options. The first was voting yes or no on all amendments. The second was an assumed yes vote unless a specific negative vote was cast against a given amendment. All amendments were ratified, but the Office of Hawaiian Affairs passed narrowly, with less than 52 percent of the vote. The Hawaiian amendment regarding "traditional and customary rights"—the access and gathering rights amendment—got more than 55 percent support, while "population growth management," which sounded like an Ariyoshi theme, got more than 66 percent support.

A TURNING POINT

In the ensuing election of a nine-member board of trustees for OHA, Frenchy DeSoto became chairperson. She was backed by Walter Ritte, who chaired a committee on culture dedicated to perpetuating Hawaiian life. At the oath-taking ceremony, John Dominis Holt gave the keynote address. Only fifteen years had passed since Holt had written in *On Being Hawaiian*, "we want to run our own show."

Almost from its first moments, OHA was embroiled in conflict with the State of Hawai'i, of which it was a part. The enabling legislation gave OHA 20 percent of the revenues that the State received on lands that once had belonged to the Hawaiian crown and kingdom. Interpretation of this law was a matter of dispute between OHA and a succession of State administrations. As a result, the scope of OHA's operations was chronically in flux.

Beneath the question of funding lay the question of autonomy. Contrary to the wishful thinking about autonomy that pervaded Hawaiian Affairs Committee reports, the limits to OHA's semiseparate status quickly became apparent. As a creature of budgeting, appropriations, legal opinions, civil service, and other administrative procedures, OHA was a relatively small agency that was subordinate to the State of Hawai'i. Clues to the tensions in which OHA would be caught had actually surfaced within the convention, although they went virtually unnoticed at the time. On one side, a young Mililani Trask had parted ways with Frenchy DeSoto and quit her staff. She said that in good conscience she could not support an entity that was part of the State of Hawai'i, but favored instead developing a sovereign relationship with the federal government through an independent nongovernmental organization, which she would proceed to form to great effect—called <u>Ka Lahui</u>. On the opposite side was the questioning voice of delegate H. William Burgess, who urged people to explore the possibility that because OHA would be a racially based creation of the State government, elections to OHA would be unconstitutional unless open to all voters—precisely the contention that would stagger OHA and carry the day in a U.S. Supreme Court ruling in a famous case, *Rice v. Cayetano,* in 2000.

While virtually no one was happy with OHA, it was nonetheless a step on a difficult path. Its very existence posed the issue of Hawaiian self-determination. It reminded people that Hawai'i's history had begun not with statehood, or 1954, or 1941, or with the overthrow, but with the arrival of the first settlers nearly two millennia prior. As dissatisfaction with OHA increased among Hawaiians, support grew for the *Ka Lahui* formula of a "sovereign" indigenous nation operating within the American nation-state. Beyond this essentially American formula for dealing with native peoples lay the vision of a truly restored and independent Hawaiian nation, led by *kanaka maoli,* "true Hawaiians"—a retrieved definition that gained increasing currency in the 1990s.

From almost any imaginable perspective, the Hawaiian amendments made the convention a turning point. Hawaiians had led, and the haole and AJAs who were in agreement had listened and followed. That in itself was a break with the past. The first significant payment for Hawaiian participation in the original Democratic coalition of 1954 had come due. It had been made, but the future was fraught with social, political, and ethnic ambiguities. The status of Hawai'i—as a nation, submerged nation, colony, state, or bifurcated state—again was an issue. While this came as a surprise to almost everyone (and seems to amaze even otherwise well informed visitors to this day), it was a development that was deeply rooted in history. The status of Hawai'i had been an active point of contention from the late 1840s until statehood. In the framework of a history that was constantly being retrieved and refocused, the certainties of statehood—let us say, occurring between 1959 and the 1978 convention—were a brief respite from tensions over the status of Hawai'i, tensions that continue today and seem an inevitable part of Hawai'i's long-term future.

Otherwise, the convention was about continuity. The power of the State government and the office of governor were further enhanced. OHA itself was a State-level solution. In the face of disconnected independent demands to diminish the State's aggregation of powers, delegates who were young, local, activist, or otherwise critical of the political establishment, all coalesced to preserve the system, as if they could sense the next step was taking the system into their own hands. John Waiheʻe would say, "We set the agenda for the next twenty years." Jim Shon would say, "John's group saw themselves as a generation of new leaders who wanted to take over from the establishment and pursue a superior agenda."

Images of the once-thriving Hawaiian world were revived as part of the Hawaiian renaissance. Drawing by Choris, 1816

The writer John Dominis Holt spoke up about Hawaiians when all was silence. Photograph by Tom Coffman

Walter Ritte. Courtesy of The Honolulu Advertiser

Walter Ritte (right) *asked a Hawaiian* kupuna, *Walter Keawe, about ancient trails.*

Ritte (foreground) *searched barren Kahoʻolawe in vain for George Helm. Courtesy of Walter Ritte*

Aunt Clara Ku became a symbol of renewed respect for elders. Photograph by Tom Coffman

A. Frenchy DeSoto, mother of the Office of Hawaiian Affairs. Photograph by Tom Coffman

Myron Thompson. Courtesy of the Thompson family

To a much greater extent than was generally known, the political skills of John D. Waiheʻe III were developed in the Hawaiian movement. Photograph by Tom Coffman

Chapter 14

Democratic Reinventions: Status Quo and Change

Having won the three-way Democratic primary of 1974 with only 36 percent of the vote, George Ariyoshi was in a politically insecure position during his first four years in office. The nature of his insecurity was punctuated on the night of his election victory, when Tom Gill gave up his eight-year quest for the governorship, leaving to Fasi the potential for getting a majority vote in the next Democratic primary.

The scale of Frank Fasi's ambitions was illustrated to me as a political reporter in 1968, when it was becoming apparent that he finally would be mayor of Honolulu. In his campaign office, facing his desk, a five-step projection of his imagined future was written on a board: Step one was mayor of Honolulu. Step two was governor of Hawai'i; step three, United States senator; step four, vice president; and step five, president of the United States.

As he evolved in his role of Mister Mayor, he developed a somewhat more lighthearted presentation of himself. He might be a feisty fellow, but he was looking out for the little guy. He might be a rambunctious player, but it was all in a good cause. When he held his voice in check, he was a good impromptu speaker. When he succeeded in suppressing his seething temper, he was good in the give and take of a press conference.

Long after the fact, many of his opponents would concede that he created a record of accomplishment as mayor.[1] He was a demanding, businesslike administrator who lived by the idea that to get results for the public was to get their vote. He accumulated lists of what he had done: fountains, free summer fun, paving and planting the City Hall parking lot, and above all the city's increasingly efficient bus system, logo typed TheBus. If people forgot about TheBus, they remembered it when they saw Fasi in his van, which was TheMayor'sBus. In contrast to the politics of ethnic healing, metaphysics, and negotiating Hawai'i's relationship with the world that were so much a part of the mainstream Democratic Party, Fasi focused simply on delivering the goods and reminding people at election time.

Lots of energy went into feuds—with the City Council, the daily newspapers, the governor, and the legislature—in a way that completely contradicted the spirit of consensus. A feud orchestrated by Fasi was political theater that played effectively to the needs or grievances of sizable audiences. For example, the City Council had a history of zoning variances and ethical violations; the daily newspapers, through a joint operating agreement, had become a virtual monopoly; and it was indeed true that the governor had too much power.

Some people who knew him liked him and clung to him over a lifetime, such as the nisei war veteran Iwao Yokooji. More typically, to know him was to distrust something in him—the intoxication with power, the breezy manipulation of information, the intensity of his hatreds, or his self-fulfilling prophesy that the world was against him. The political scientist Dan Tuttle had managed Fasi's first campaigns, sacrificing himself to Fasi's advancement, only to be alienated by Fasi's indiscriminate anger. Walter Heen had been driven into Jack Burns' arms by Fasi. Tom Gill had supported Fasi in 1968, only to learn he had played with fire. Editors and reporters loathed Fasi. Although Ariyoshi's compulsion was to get along with everyone, he privately fumed when he talked about Fasi.

After becoming mayor, Fasi was never literally alone, because he had patronage, but he was always alone in more elemental ways. Relatively few who actually knew him spoke up for him vigorously, even those who owed their jobs to him. He was the antithesis of the prevailing political culture of Hawai'i, in which people got to know each other and made judgments based on firsthand impressions—a culture that made Honolulu the world's largest small town, or in the words of author Richard Pratt, "an international city with small-town characteristics."[2]

Fasi often said he represented "the little man." The little man was out there, disconnected, unreachable by ordinary means, but nonetheless the little man was what Fasi knew about. The little man was a political force of widely dispersed people who shared Fasi as their political common denominator. For nearly half a century, a seemingly irreducible minimum of one-third of the electorate routinely rallied to Fasi. Another large group in the middle would consider him from situation to situation. After winning three mayoral elections, in 1968, 1972, and 1976, Fasi felt winning the governorship was only logical. As Fasi embarked on the campaign, there were many believers and few skeptics among the people around him. "There was no doubt that Frank would be governor—that we were with a winner," in the words of Bob Dye, "and we would go beyond."[3]

AT ANY GIVEN MOMENT, the job of being governor is not about State Plans or H-3 or land reform, but about any one of thousands of pieces of a mosaic. It is about managing the government shop and balancing the community's demands against the reality of revenues. Ariyoshi's stamina as a manager was like Fasi's stamina as a campaigner. He went at it year after year with the same diligence and energy. He had a passion for the art of management.

Ariyoshi got an early start on the day, often attended a community function with his wife in the evening, returned to his office, then worked at a desk in the upstairs apartment of Washington Place. He did calisthenics morning and night, aiming for a total of fifty pushups and one hundred to two hundred sit-ups. He apportioned time for details, time for problems, and time to talk about ideas. He prided himself on his retention of numbers and rapid mental calculations. As his budget director, Eileen Anderson, gave presentations, he routinely cross-checked her figures while she spoke. His friend James Takushi would occasionally build an intentional mathematical error into his own presentations on employee costs and collective bargaining, believing that after ferreting out the error Ariyoshi would be more relaxed.

Public expectations of the state continued to accelerate while the growth of revenues slowed. The one far-reaching change instituted by the 1968 constitutional convention was collective bargaining for public employees. It created widespread expectations of improved pay and benefits even though it was enacted almost simultaneously with the economic downturn. In the course of holding the line on spending, Ariyoshi faced a series of strikes by teachers, blue-collar workers, and white-collar workers. These were strikes in which government unions established their turf, but in most other respects were dissimilar to the early dock and sugar strikes. Rather than moralistically pitting the working class against the Big Five, the government strikes were mundane: How much money did the state have to modestly raise the pay of its employees?

The government was also under pressure to compete with the private sector for high-level talent. Ariyoshi agreed to an advisory panel's recommendation that cabinet officers and judges be paid more, but unknown to the public he refused to take the pay raise himself. He reasoned that he had made a pact to serve at the salary in effect at the time of his election. He diverted his salary increases to charity. If he had used this information to deflect public criticism, it might have been interpreted as political astuteness. Privately, he believed that not taking pay raises helped his mental outlook. "To do a job, you can't have a serious conflict within yourself . . ." he would write. "You have to feel good about what you do."[4] Feeling that he had done right, he could, in his words, hold his head up and "with an inner clarity and clear conscience" ask people for their support at election time.

He was happiest talking about government principles and methods of management. He engaged young staff in long discussions about political history and public service. People in government needed to be given responsibility, then held answerable for their sphere. He reminded people that if they worked hard and well, the state could avoid hiring more people and thus pay its existing personnel better. He tried to walk through every government agency during each term in office and thank each person in the state work force for his or her effort.

If things were going along smoothly, the tendency of government was to continue on its way. If something went wrong it was not necessarily bad, but an opportunity for improvement. He believed that government should beware subsidizing volunteer groups, because government funding and regulation tended to cripple the zeal of volunteers. He preached fiscal responsibility, observing that when revenues are tight, government tends to tighten up. It responds to good times by immediately spending more money. As an alternative he advocated setting money aside and building a cash cushion against downturns. This fortified him in denying requests for new spending even when tax revenues became more available. It was the basis of his favorite maxim: A governor was condemned to reacting when times were bad; his opportunity for managing wisely was when times were good.

During his first several years in office, the government was in a dire fiscal condition. He worked closely with the government work force to balance the budget, while publicly projecting a sense of optimism about the state's economic future. He developed a strict philosophy relative to business that again set him outside the liberal-conservative spectrum. It revolved around his belief that a healthy business climate primarily required a level field of competition—a view that can readily be interpreted as a reaction to the days of the Big Five. This led him to oppose both tax increases and targeted tax cuts—in his view, tax giveaways—with equal vigor. While he was aware of the impact of national economies on Hawai'i, he also saw an important role for state government in the fact that the performance of regional economies differed widely. "In this regard," he wrote, "Hawai'i is a region unto itself."[5] From this perception, the job of state government was to maintain a stable flow of public construction, stable public employment, and—as a result—a relatively stable level of confidence among consumers. A rapid rise in spending and the layoff of employees were to be equally avoided.

The writer Richard Pratt said of Ariyoshi, "The fiscal conservatism evident throughout his public career . . . would have permitted, or forced, him to be a Republican in another setting, but never was, at least visibly, an issue within the Hawai'i Democratic Party."[6] A liberal legislator of the time said simply, "We didn't pay that much attention to George. He didn't have any money to spend." In response to the limited resources of the 1970s and to Hawai'i's island constraints in general, Ariyoshi foreshadowed various attempts around the country to alter the free-spending traditions of the national Democratic Party. Most prominently, Jimmy Carter's presidency (1976–1980) attempted to make a virtue of conserving resources. In California, Jerry Brown, then a young governor, was preaching the necessity of streamlining government and doing more with less. At the National Governor's Conference, Ariyoshi was to make the acquaintance of the young governor of Arkansas, Bill Clinton, who convened a new Democratic policy council dedicated to a more fiscally conservative party.

While Ariyoshi took an active interest in national trends, his fiscal approach was always deeply rooted in his perception of Hawai'i as a semi-separate society that could influence its future. With a certain AJA twist of thinking, Ariyoshi talked repeatedly about obligation to the future. He believed that if government fixed its thoughts on an intergenerational span of time, it would make wiser decisions and perform better. When his aides advised him to stop buying scenic lands that could not be turned quickly to political advantage in the form of parks, he corrected their thinking as short-term.

While none of this could be communicated to the general public on a given day, the political effect was cumulative. Ariyoshi was centrist and moderate. He not only talked about political tolerance but practiced it. He usually ignored criticism. He often referred to Burns' advice that a person who opposes you in one moment may support you in another. He drew both staff and cabinet members from among the planners and social workers whose original loyalty was to Tom Gill. He dismissed political affiliations as irrelevant to doing a good job. When the social worker Masaru Oshiro opposed Ariyoshi on an issue of conscience, he submitted his resignation. Ariyoshi asked him to continue; failing that, he gave Oshiro other jobs. Through such acts, Ariyoshi helped create a climate of greater tolerance for diverse thinking and views.

He projected the idea of an orderly community that evolved incrementally. People who dealt with him tended to support him, even if they only partially agreed with him. He was even tempered. People around him thought that only Fasi could upset him, but then not for long.

WHILE THE TESTIMONIAL SUPPORT of cabinet members is to be expected, the nature of their testimony is significant, returning over and over to Ariyoshi's managerial framework of authority, responsibility, and accountability. "I never felt I was being second-guessed" and "I had a job to do, and he helped me do it," were comments that reflected the relationships of cabinet members to the governor. Ariyoshi gave his appointees broad guidelines within which to exercise authority, for which they were then held responsible. "I felt it was my job to encourage people, not to control them," he was to write. "To treat people with dignity, you have to recognize they are capable of doing things on their own, and you can't control them successfully by treating them like robots."[7]

Cabinet members often thought of him as someone they got to know slowly, but who would reveal a little more of himself over time. The sense of order and the sharing of responsibility through tumultuous times also helped keep Ariyoshi on track, something that cannot be taken for granted in politics. He had taken over the governorship in 1973. If he were to be re-elected in 1978, he would begin the new term with more than five years behind him, a point at which many political executives begin to burn out.

THE ORIGINAL PERCEPTION of a post-statehood island machine had come from the bipartisan hand holding between Jack Burns' capitol and Neal Blaisdell's city hall. This image had been reinforced by Burns' grooming of Ariyoshi, by the large sums of money spent on the 1970 and 1974 elections, and by the capacity of the State administration to raise campaign funds. From this collection of images, Fasi postulated the existence of "The Machine" and invited voters to think of him as the independent-minded alternative.

If indeed the Burns and Ariyoshi years met the American definition of a political machine, it was a profoundly island definition that described an idealistic, quixotic, and at times even eccentric political operation. Burns had nearly abandoned the aggregated powers of the governorship in 1966. While Ariyoshi advanced the idea of a Burns legacy, he changed many of Burns' policies. Ariyoshi continued to believe that people would appreciate his plans and his land-banking, even as the climate became increasingly impersonal and media-dominated. He took seriously the quote from the Chinese philosopher Lao Tsu, who taught that a leader is best when the people hardly know he exists. "And of that leader the people will say when his work is done, 'We did this ourselves.'"

It was the sort of thing that moved Pratt, in his *Hawai'i Politics and Government,* to contend that island political culture was built on "moralistic and traditionalistic orientations."

It is moralistic in the commitment to use public authority to serve a broader community of underrepresented interests. It is traditionalistic in its protection of historic, shared values and in a deep reluctance to open up the political process to those who may not understand or share those values.[8]

As America became progressively more conservative in the 1970s and entered the era of explicit conservatism with the election of Ronald Reagan in 1980, Hawai'i became one of the last predictably Democratic bastions. Paradoxically, as post-statehood Hawai'i was becoming less the inspirational dream of Fuchs' multiracial democracy and more a semiseparate political culture organized around the governor's office, public enthusiasm for electoral politics was slowly but surely declining. The role of money, mass media, physical and demographic growth, and the accompanying depersonalization of relationships, all took a toll. In these ways, Hawai'i was becoming more like other states, even as it self-conciously sought to define itself as different.

THE 1978 ELECTION

Around the end of March 1976, on a day when Mayor Fasi was traveling out of state, a chubby, talkative developer named Hal Hansen dropped into the City Hall office of Bob Dye and proceeded to tell a story.[9] He said that in his zeal to secure the city-controlled development rights for an urban renewal block known as Kukui Plaza above downtown, he had approached Fasi's campaign finance chairman, Harry C. Chung. He asked Chung what it would take to get the project, to which Chung allegedly replied with a large sum. Hansen said he then attempted to siphon this money from his development company.

Dye stopped Hansen long enough to say that whatever he said was going straight to the city prosecuting attorney, which Hansen understood. Thereafter Dye telephoned Fasi, who was traveling abroad. Dye thought Fasi was genuinely surprised. Fasi told Dye he had done the right thing and asked only that he try to keep it from the press until he returned to Hawai'i. After the story broke, Kukui Plaza took on a life of its own. First there was an investigation by the City Council, which established that Hansen was an eager influence-peddler who had succeeded in giving business or preferential sales treatment to Fasi's associates. (For example, the city prosecutor had lived in a Kukui Plaza apartment rent-free for two months, and a Fasi staff member received a loan.) Hansen was also readily shown to have illegally skimmed money from his own company, which meant that he was desperately in need of a plea bargain.

After six months of this, the state's attorney general, Ronald Amemiya, got involved in the case. Amemiya called the nationally renowned prosecutor Leon Jaworski, who had been the special prosecutor of President Nixon in the Watergate case. Jaworski declined but recommended several possibilities, including Grant Cooper of Los Angeles, who was best known for his insanity defense of Sirhan Sirhan, who murdered Robert Kennedy. Cooper was contracted as the special prosecutor of Fasi and Chung. Dozens of witnesses were assembled for a case that ultimately succeeded or failed where it started, which was on the credibility of Hansen's story. Cooper secured a grand jury indictment, but when Hansen was called to testify, he refused to do so, citing his constitutional right against self-incrimination. After a brief period of the court holding Hansen in contempt, the charges were dismissed. Eighteen months after Hansen first contacted Dye, the trial was over.

Why Hansen refused to testify would remain a matter of conjecture. While awaiting prison Hansen laid out his version to an able reporter for the *Honolulu Star-Bulletin,* William H. Donham, with the idea that it would become a book. He said he had agreed to testify against Fasi believing that Fasi lay behind the conversation with Chung, but he had no direct evidence to offer—that is, he never discussed a payoff with Fasi. After agonizing over whether to testify, he suffered, in Donham's words, "a sudden attack of ethics." As he was leaving to serve his sentence, Donham advised him against publishing the manuscript on the belief that he had enough problems and would need friends when he got out. Thereafter Hansen served 17 months in jail and prison. He died shortly thereafter.

Although Ariyoshi's administration had conducted the prosecution, Ariyoshi portrayed himself as above the fray. He said nothing publicly about Kukui and never met with Cooper, who left a voluminous report of his findings that Ariyoshi neither read nor released.[10]

IN THE AFTERMATH, Fasi appeared to have survived politically as a person who was regarded as innocent until proven guilty. He began the campaign year of 1978 looking more than ever like a winner of the coming gubernatorial election. *The Honolulu Advertiser's* Jerry Burris wrote that "Fasi was confidently making plans for the inauguration ceremony," while Ariyoshi's popularity was at rock bottom.[11] Both Dennis O'Connor, an influential state senator, and Maui mayor Elmer Cravalho, considered running as third-force, white-knight candidates. Gill gave a long, nasty interview from retirement saying, "Our choice for change at the moment isn't very encouraging—so we replace a dummy with a dingbat?"[12] When asked what he thought of Ariyoshi's efforts to control growth, Gill said he didn't think Ariyoshi was "entirely off base," but added that Ariyoshi didn't really know what he was doing and was engaged in "random wobbling."

By this time Ariyoshi had a record of protecting Windward O'ahu and of formulating the Hawai'i State Plan. He had developed initiatives in diversified agriculture and aquaculture. Following through on his experience with GasPlan, he was pressing forward with making Hawai'i a major center of research and development on alternate energy. However, nothing was felt in the political climate comparable to the stagnation of revenues. The post-statehood boom—the eight-fold increase of revenue growth over population that Burns had enjoyed—was now history. Ariyoshi had spent six years reining people in and saying no.

At one point he was quoted as saying, "Being the 'no' man is a lonely and unpopular position to be in much of the time," but he vowed to not leave a legacy of financial ruin.[13] At the midway point in his first elected term, he attempted to make a political virtue out of fiscal necessity. The veteran *Star-Bulletin* writer, Doug Boswell, wrote that Ariyoshi had developed a "new assurance and an aura of self-confidence,"[14] quoting a speech to Hawai'i's mayors, including Fasi, in which Ariyoshi said, "Everyone is in favor of fiscal responsibility until such time as it may get in the way of one's own self-interest. . . . So I ask you in all candor: Are you really for fiscal responsibility even if it adversely affects something you think is important?" He would claim that in his first three years he had spent a third of a billion dollars less than the legislature had allocated. He was starting to build a small cash reserve. He had turned back calls to increase taxes, and the antitax Tax Foundation of Hawai'i said Ariyoshi had saved the state from a deficit.

Inevitably the issue of tax revenues and economic growth became intertwined in the campaign. Fasi accused Ariyoshi of a "sudden change of heart" on economic growth and development. He promised to reverse the "current negative thinking about making these Islands into Fortress Hawai'i." Hawai'i was supposed to be the crossroads of the northern Pacific, Fasi said, but a "no-growth policy" was stifling new investment and the development of new jobs.[15]

In response, Ariyoshi cited reports quoting Fasi as saying that Hawai'i had more land space than his native Connecticut and neighboring Rhode Island combined,[16] so Hawai'i could triple its population. Ariyoshi raised the specter of an O'ahu with three times the number of hotel rooms, high rises, businesses, and dwellings. Hawai'i was "a different kind of state, and we ought to find our Hawaiian solutions to our Hawaiian problems rather than look to other places and play copycat."

THE OSHIRO FACTOR

Fasi's advantage at the opening of 1978 was one of several times when the hold of the supposed Democratic juggernaut hung by a proverbial thread, and the name of the thread was Robert Oshiro. In 1968 Oshiro had stepped down as chairman of the Democratic Party and decided not to run for re-election to the legislature. He thought wistfully of returning to his alma mater, Duke University, to work on a doctorate of law, only to become the manager of Burns' 1970 re-election campaign. In 1974, he was called in by Burns to help Ariyoshi. Thereafter Ariyoshi asked him to be part of a small advisory committee to his new administration. Oshiro would remember thinking, "I've done my job, you're on your own,"[17] and once again he was nominally out of politics.

Two years later Oshiro had become involved in an interesting Democratic schism over a congressional race. It began with Ariyoshi asking Oshiro to organize the congressional campaign of Dr. John Craven, an oceanographic engineer and marine designer. Craven had played an important role in the country's *Polaris* nuclear submarine program, then relocated to the University of Hawai'i in the late 1960s as an innovator of marine technologies. He was a force behind the development of more stable marine platforms and semi-submerged dual-hulled ships. But it was Craven's revival of the theory of ocean thermal energy conversion (OTEC) that most attracted Ariyoshi's attention. The idea of OTEC was to use the ocean surface as a solar collector, then convert that energy to a usable form through an underwater heat exchange process—a concept that the State of Hawai'i would actually put into practice on a demonstration basis within a few years, thanks to Ariyoshi's dogged pursuit of support from the federal Department of Energy. Although the reduction of oil prices was to render the design economically unfeasible, OTEC was a stirring idea, to put it mildly.

Oshiro quizzed Craven during an entire spring morning in his law office in the country town of Wahiawā. After Craven had talked through the broad outline of his thinking on marine design, Oshiro said, "John, there's a cause here."[18] Not only was Craven a big-picture visionary but, strangely more attractive, he was in an almost impossible political position. The reason was the immensely wealthy Cec Heftel, whose base in broadcasting had given him a high profile and a high probability of winning. In the course of the contest, Oshiro discovered that Dan Aoki, icon of the 442nd RCT and political right hand to Burns, was supporting Heftel, contrary to Ariyoshi's wishes, even though Aoki was still working in the governor's office. The second person who had most closely guarded Burns, press secretary Don Horio, also was supporting Heftel, and so—more or less—was Inouye.

Even starting with a huge lead and protected by a large expenditure of his own money, Heftel barely withstood the campaign that Craven mounted with the help of Oshiro and, behind him, Ariyoshi. It was the first clue (to be quickly forgotten by most people), that Heftel's political career, for all his executive ability, tenacity, ambition, and wealth—was based on broad but thin support.

More obviously, the congressional contest between Heftel and Craven reflected a division in the top levels of what had become the hyphenated Burns-Ariyoshi political camp. This division was actually about how Burns' several closest companions got along with Ariyoshi, which was none too well. An obviously frustrated Aoki made his own trip to Wahiawā, hoping that Oshiro might prevail on Ariyoshi to use him in grassroots party politics. Thereafter Oshiro believed that Aoki was going to run Ariyoshi's 1978 re-election campaign, as he once had run Burns'. In reality, the gentlemanly Ariyoshi and the warrior Aoki suffered, in Oshiro's words, from "a vacuum between them in terms of chemistry." Ariyoshi was not Burns. No one would ever be Burns. "They were two different people," Oshiro would say, "[and] even I had a hard time because George Ariyoshi was a different person."[19]

Prior to the campaign, Aoki suffered a heart attack, which meant that in 1978 Oshiro, for the third straight gubernatorial contest, was called upon to again run the campaign. His attempts to get out of politics had become part of his mystique. As the rescuer of campaigns, he became the undisputed boss of campaigns. Talking incessantly about everyone being sparrows, about everyone being coequal, he set a paradoxically autocratic standard of self-sacrifice that participants in the campaign were obviously expected to follow. He would become gaunt. His voice would turn hoarse. His idea of taking care of himself was to smoke his cigarettes through a filtered holder, which he would misplace. The breadth of his occasional smile would compete oddly with the possibility that, as in 1970, he might again collapse physically.

Across time, campaigns of Democratic governors became a kind of institution that floated around Oshiro, with each borrowing from the other. In 1970 a new mix of money, media, and manpower had been created. Money paid for the media, which created themes that were worked and reworked at the level of ordinary voters by door-to-door canvassing, telephoning, and coffee hours. While these are the common elements of campaigns, the smart, creative mobilization of resources by managers can be the key to victory. The nationally prominent political consultant, Joseph Napolitan, was so taken with Oshiro that he urged him to go national.

To ward off Fasi in 1978, Napolitan and Jack Seigle again turned to the production of a half-hour campaign film, *The Boy from Kalihi*, a successor to the *Catch A Wave* film of 1970. In the wake of Burns' million-dollar campaign, the legislature had enacted a ceiling on campaign spending, and as a result Ariyoshi had been elected to the governorship in 1974 on a modest campaign budget, $169,000. Thereafter the law was ruled to be a violation of the First Amendment guarantees on free expression (which is the root problem in campaign finance reform in America). With the spending restrictions lifted, Ariyoshi's campaign in 1978 spent $1.6 million to Fasi's one million.

The sources of such large sums of money further strengthened both the perception and actual working of machine politics. While candidates were fond of creating the impression that contributions misted onto them in small amounts, the fact was that the bulk of budgets cascaded in from people who did business with government—architects, engineers, planners, consultants, construction companies, bankers, public utilities, and so on.[20] Possibly no single factor so contributed to the perception of a Democratic machine. Ariyoshi himself would say that nothing "so negatively affected the quality of public life."[21] Not one to shrink from constitutional issues, he would urge from retirement that the legislature again take on the First Amendment protection of the campaign finance system.

Mike Tokunaga would denounce the campaigns of money and media as "selling apples." Oshiro was haunted by the fact that most of the campaign budgets went to media: "Your television time, your production, the consultant . . . all kinds of media experts that you need to put together a decent package . . . I've resented that."[22]

Although Ariyoshi's campaign was heavily funded, it maintained its claim to moral authority through a grassroots organization that was vastly superior to Fasi's individualistic efforts, to say nothing of the efforts of the Republican Party. In 1953 Aoki and Tokunaga had started with a Democratic Party list estimated at two thousand names.[23] If anyone on that list said they would like to help Burns, they were given a mimeographed sheet with space for the names of twenty-five people whose votes they solicited. If an individual on the sheet agreed to work on the campaign, his or her name went into the expanded card file, which grew from two thousand to six thousand. After 1970 Oshiro would say that Burns had thirty thousand unshakable supporters, and by the end of the combined Burns-Ariyoshi period this list had grown to forty-five thousand.[24] Accordingly, Oshiro was talking about a lot of sparrows, each with a name, address, and telephone number. In 1974 Oshiro had packed ten thousand people into McKinley High School to commune over plate lunches and help Ariyoshi to his margin of victory. In 1978, with Ariyoshi still trailing, Oshiro set his sights on filling the cavernous Aloha Stadium. The event alluded to the old-time campaign rally in which the modern Democratic Party had found its voice, but in reality it was an enormous logistical proposition.

The stadium itself was an underutilized monument to the idea that Hawai'i was on an equal footing with the rest of the United States. Despite the absence of major league franchises in Hawai'i, Aloha Stadium had fifty thousand seats, which made it larger than many of the major league stadiums of its time. Oshiro's rally was held two weeks before the election, on September 24, 1978, with a staggering gate count of 49,701. After hours of performance by Hawai'i's top entertainers, Ariyoshi appeared on stage, buried in a mound of leis, with a second bank of leis at his feet. He said, "I am what I am because of you." *Okage sama de.*

With a week until the primary election, *The Honolulu Advertiser* reported a poll showing Ariyoshi still trailing Fasi by a wide margin (44 percent to 34 percent). The political scientist Dan Tuttle, asked for his analysis, warned Ariyoshi's advisers to take the results seriously. Fasi, assuming victory, assigned Bob Dye to generate a list of five people to fill the cabinet and key staff positions of his new administration. In reaction to the poll, and to Tuttle's warning, Oshiro quickly set a campaign goal of making one hundred thousand telephone calls in the final week. The calling campaign was based on the organic image of a tree, in which one branch of calls created another that created another. Everyone called everyone about calling everyone. Some people received a half dozen calls, and some probably more.

AMONG SURVEY RESEARCHERS, voters of Japanese ancestry are known for their reluctance to say who they will vote for. It is the sort of thing on which a certain residual prejudice survives—the contention that Japanese live behind masks, that Japanese are inscrutable. In history they had been spied upon by the government and pried into by plantation supervisors who, like survey researchers, wanted to know how they would vote. Undoubtedly, a certain cultural reserve was at work. The undecided vote in the *Advertiser* poll was a surprising 20 percent.

Ariyoshi beat Fasi by 130,521 votes to 126,899 votes, or 50.3 percent to 48.9 percent. Although the undecideds almost surely were many fewer than they had seemed, it could be reasonably argued that the poll's publication tipped the scales. It mobilized Ariyoshi's side to a final, frenzied effort while reinforcing Fasi's tendency to savor victory before winning. The outcome also reflected the disciplined participation of Japanese Americans in the political process. Not only were Japanese Americans the largest group in the Democratic voter pool, but they turned out to vote at significantly higher rates than others, most notably Caucasians.[25]

Obviously, the campaign had aggregated people into ethnic patterns. Just prior to the election, four of five Caucasians said they favored Fasi, while Japanese voters said they favored Ariyoshi by nearly three to one (probably a conservative figure).[26] Eighty percent of Caucasians gave Fasi a positive approval rating, while two-thirds gave Ariyoshi a negative rating. In contrast, voters of Japanese ancestry were more inclined to see the value of both candidates, giving Ariyoshi a 61 percent approval rating and Fasi a 53 percent approval rating.

The conversation that obsessed campaign people—the managers, reporters, lobbyists, image-makers, and pollsters—was about "the Japanese vote," even though Japanese were prominently spread around all factions and both parties. In the most blatant play for Japanese votes in the campaign, Fasi had sent a mass mailing signed by eighteen Japanese American members of his cabinet, saying

> *As members of an ethnic group which fought long and hard against racial injustice, we feel that ethnic politics has no place in this campaign. The governor of Hawai'i should be selected not by the color of his skin but by the quality of his performance.*[27]

Fasi's wife, Joyce, was of Japanese ancestry, and Fasi generally enjoyed a certain hail-fellow rapport with many Japanese. Yet by a narrow margin he was a mismatch for the governorship. Voters who accepted Fasi as mayor rejected the idea of him being governor. While his job performance ratings soared over Ariyoshi's, his honesty numbers—related to community trust—were much lower than Ariyoshi's. Ron Amemiya believed that Kukui Plaza had stuck to Fasi and ultimately brought him down. Long afterward, Robert Dye would say, "It was all over for Frank after that." Fasi would try again and again, but the imagined arc that reached from City Hall through the governorship to the higher reaches of American politics had been broken.

Ariyoshi devoted the substance of his victory speech on general election night to an appeal for interracial harmony. "If we are going to lead," he said, "we are going to have to lead everybody."[28]

TO WHAT EXTENT were people divided by the campaign? By the standard of community tranquility and acceptance of the outcome, the answer is, not at all. But—there is always a but—in the post-statehood era a large majority of Japanese Americans repeatedly migrated in the course of campaigns to the candidate who most typified the story of 1954, 1959, and the Democratic Party. When the candidate was Ariyoshi—who was first elected in 1954—this happened more readily, but the pattern was to be repeated not only for Ariyoshi or candidates of Japanese ancestry, but across time for Democratic candidates—regardless of ancestry—for the rest of the century.

If the AJA were no longer such a tightly knit community, they shared a story and a heritage. History weighed heavily. If they favored Ariyoshi over

Fasi by three to one, it was remarked upon pointedly. In contrast, Caucasian voters in the Democratic primary could favor Fasi by an even wider margin, perhaps as much as five to one, and it went unremarked. The significance of that double standard became even greater in relationship to the essential character of the two opponents.

Ariyoshi was dignified and thoughtful. His sincerity of purpose and concern for community were never questioned. By comparison Fasi was unpredictable and manipulative. By almost any description, Ariyoshi was a unifying figure and Fasi a divisive one. That Caucasian voters would reject the incumbent Ariyoshi by such a margin in favor of Fasi raised a sobering question of how far Hawai'i had really come as an interracial community.

With all that said, perhaps the last line on 1978 was about how such tensions came and went, like clouds.

TWO YEARS LATER, in 1980, Ronald Reagan's election to the presidency on an antigovernment platform marked an enduring turn to the political right in American history. With a combination of Reagan's victory and Tom Gill's retreat from politics, Hawai'i's tradition of ideological liberalism somewhat waned, only to be replaced by a local blend of progressive, activist politics that had grown out of the constitutional convention. In addition to Waihe'e, delegates from Waihe'e's group who soon were elected to the legislature as Democrats included Carole Fukunaga, Anthony Chang, Tom Okamura, Gerald Hagino, and Anthony Takitani. From the independents of the convention, Jim Shon was elected to the House on O'ahu and Jeremy Harris continued his rise to prominence on Kaua'i—both as Democrats. Through the combined effect of the University of Hawai'i law school and the constitutional convention, the Democratic Party in essence had gained at least another generation of dominance in Hawai'i.

Ariyoshi held the broad center. In 1980 he backed an even more unlikely politician than himself, his budget director, Eileen Anderson, to run for mayor of Honolulu against Fasi, with an unlikely result: Anderson won. In many ways she was a female, Caucasian version of Ariyoshi. She was gentle, smiled warmly, spoke softly, liked numbers, and thought deeply about the administration of government. Like Ariyoshi, her apparent sincerity was her strongest asset. She had achieved a modest prominence as the legislative auditor's point person on planning and budgeting, played a central role with Ariyoshi, then surprisingly defeated the polished Fasi by a narrow margin in a Democratic primary election with a low voter turnout. Despite her lack of skills as a campaigner, talk began that she was Ariyoshi's heir apparent.

FRANK FASI DID NOT go away. Two years after his mayoral loss to Eileen Anderson, he ran for governor as an independent. The essence of his tactic was to avoid losing in the Democratic primary, then take on the Democratic candidate in the general election. He ran far behind Ariyoshi but, remarkably, got more votes than the Republican nominee, D. G. "Andy" Anderson of Windward Oʻahu. In the next Honolulu mayoral election, he enlisted D. G. Anderson's support and ran as a Republican against Eileen Anderson. Fasi defeated her much as she had defeated him—with an element of surprise. Fasi was back, unreconstructed. The most logical inference of his victory was that the voting public trusted him at the level of mayor and appreciated his achievements.

Although he talked about defending the interests of the "little man," Fasi was a ready-made Republican. He had begun his career by scrapping with the ILWU and engaging in Red-baiting. He had made money in business. He had a protectionist response to the growing investment of Japan in Hawaiʻi, repeatedly finding fault with the presence and influence of Japanese business.[29] He relished the role of chief executive officer and ran the city in a corporate way, eliciting commitments from his appointees, then measuring their performance accordingly. He had no lofty notions about social progress, liberalism, or the political left. In the words of Bob Dye, he liked to solve problems, not mysteries, "and didn't spend much time wondering if God is good or bad."[30] Fasi delivered political goods.

As part of his comeback, Fasi named D. G. Anderson his managing director. Anderson's determination to make government work in a businesslike way was much like Fasi's. Together they presented the possibility of seizing the political machinery of Hawaiʻi from the top down. Both were capable, with powerful personalities, egos, and desire to succeed. A longtime Republican, Jim Hall, became an executive assistant to Anderson and was assigned to work with a new city transportation director, a man named John Hirten, who had made a national reputation in San Francisco through the Bay Area Rapid Transit. They set plans in motion for further expanding Fasi's signature project, TheBus, rerouting city traffic on large, one-way thoroughfares, creating a one-way loop into and out of Waikīkī, new street signage, new street lights, and most importantly mounting a more effective push for mass fixed-rail transit. Hall was thrilled by the early accomplishments of the Fasi-Anderson regime, then watched in dismay as the two drifted away from one another.

Anderson resigned in the spring of 1986 after sixteen months as the city's number two executive, then ran unsuccessfully (and without Fasi's support) for governor. Their particular little story was not over. In 1994, as Fasi made his last, serious bid for the governorship, a popular state senator and U.S. congresswoman, Patricia Saiki, was assured the Republican nomination with Anderson's support. Fasi, having run out of parties through which to gain a nomination, created his own. He called it The Best Party and nearly succeeded in this desperate ploy, in defiance of all wisdom about the power of the two-party system in American political culture.

After two failed attempts to regain the mayor's office yet a second time, Fasi and Jim Hall set out to write a book about Fasi's amazing political career. He had spent sixteen years trying to become mayor, nearly twenty years as mayor, and more than a decade on various comebacks and failed campaigns for governor. In an introduction to the would-be book, the text alluded to *Catch A Wave.* "I'd rather make them," it said.

> *If you don't make waves, you get rolled over by them. Nothing ever gets accomplished in Hawai'i if you don't stir things up a bit.*[31]

It credited Fasi's accomplishments to being "outspoken, willing to take chances, mixed in with imagination and plain old fashioned guts, oh yes, and by being more than just a little bit controversial." The book project floundered on a disagreement between Fasi and Hall.

THAT FASI QUICKLY if briefly rose to the top of the Republican Party said something about the long, sad journey of the Republicans in post-statehood Hawai'i. After electing William Quinn as governor, Hiram Fong as a United States senator, and a majority in the new State senate, they gave way to the Burns coalition. Often Republicans posed no threat whatsoever. In 1974 the Republican candidate for governor, Randolph Crossley, was a spent force and after losing moved to the West Coast. In 1978 the Republican candidate was a young state senator, John Leopold, who complained publicly that the Republican Party did not provide him with financial backing. He further charged that influential Republicans belonged to an establishment "club" devoted to the status quo. He accurately stated that Fasi, and not the Republican Party, had become "the loyal opposition," adding: "As an entity, the party has abdicated its position."[32] After taking his defeat at the hands of Ariyoshi, Leopold also moved to the mainland.

The glimmer of life in the Republican Party came from a small circle of candidates who served first in the House and then in the Senate. The most energetic and engaging were D. G. Anderson, a successful self-made businessman; Patricia Saiki, a teacher; and Fred Rohlfing, an attorney. They were, respectively, of part-Hawaiian, Japanese, and Caucasian ancestry and were deeply attached to Hawai'i. Each was attractive, projected a sense of mainstream moderation, and had succeeded over and over in legislative campaigns. Among them they ran repeatedly for mayor of Honolulu, lieutenant governor, governor, the U.S. House, and the U.S. Senate. Had Saiki not won two terms in the U.S. House, they would have accumulated a collective record of undiluted frustration spanning four decades.

Their tactics could be faulted, but the essential problem lay with the irrelevance of their party to the major trends of life in Hawai'i. While the Democratic Party located new constituents (most prominently newcomer haoles, Hawaiians, Filipinos, and women), the Republican Party would periodically take a lurch to the political right, marginalizing itself. Its consistent gains were among the burgeoning movement of fundamentalist, born-again Christians. While the rise of fundamentalism undeniably had a strong, if difficult to quantify, effect on politics in Hawai'i, the fundamentalists projected a sense of self-righteousness and intolerance that drove voters away in races where the choices were well defined.

Reagan had lost to Jimmy Carter by a wide margin in Hawai'i, and his ensuing crusade against the size and reach of the federal government did not resonate well in Hawai'i. Such important initiatives as the search for alternative sources of energy were put to an end by Reagan. Many areas of federal spending were put in jeopardy. When air traffic controllers went on strike, Reagan crushed the strikers by hiring new controllers, reminding the nearly one-third of Hawai'i's union households why they had joined unions in the first place.

In a state that had legalized abortion first, right-wing elements were energized to crusade against its practice, causing a new constituency of female voters to become ardent Democrats. In 1990, Patricia Saiki seemed certain to move up from the U.S. House to fill an empty senate seat, but her momentum was slowed by her explanations of why she was not as close to the Republican President George Bush as she appeared to be. She lost to Democrat Daniel Akaka in a key moment, as a result of which native Hawaiian participation in the Democratic coalition grew stronger. In a test of party versus gender, politically active feminists lined up in droves for Akaka, despite Saiki's own record as a working mother and an articulate female politician. As late as 1992, in the year that Saiki could have won the governorship in Hawai'i, the fundamentalist Christian right exerted its influence in the local Republican Party and joined its fellows in making a scene at the Republican national convention, again alarming Hawai'i voters. It was the sort of thing that caused D. G. Anderson to resign from the Republican Party, caused Rohlfing to move to Maui, and caused Saiki to withdraw from public life.

The American political pendulum did not swing in Island Hawai'i. During the first half of the twentieth century it stuck on the Republican side and during the second half it stuck on the Democratic side. The statehood description of Hawai'i as a two-party state failed to materialize. Why this happened was so uncomfortably close to the quick of island life that it was not really discussed nor subjected to intellectual inquiry.

Beyond the self-defeating nature of the Republican Party, the Democratic Party's success had to do with the power of the governorship, the power of the State, incumbency, and the security of the mostly Democratic congressional delegation. It had to do with the pressures of living at close range in an island environment, and with the resulting pressure on the major elements of society to stay in step with one another.

The theme of Burns' administration was the Open Society. Ariyoshi was dedicated to opening up such institutions as the Democratic Party and to creating a level playing field for business. His successors promised fresh air. Nonetheless the centralization that Burns had decried in 1959 clung to the political and governmental creations of the post-statehood period. To what extent the endless negotiation of differences resulted in an open society is debatable. If openness is defined as freedom of expression and action, the Hawai'i of the seventies and eighties was not as open as society on the east and west coasts of America.

Ideally the plantation tradition of inhibition would have given way to an expanding civic dialogue. Political parties would have developed more reasoned positions and scenarios. The press would have developed a greater capacity to inform, educate, and involve the public. Instead the functioning of the daily newspapers was compromised by a joint operating agreement that required both federal and state exemptions from antitrust law. Meanwhile, mainland American chains began buying up the radio and television stations. In 1973, the gigantic Gannett Corporation bought the *Honolulu Star-Bulletin,* and eventually would buy the *Advertiser* in a two-step process aimed at ending competition in the daily market altogether.[33]

In contrast to the enthusiasm for public life brought on by statehood, the press in Hawai'i from the seventies onward—the press of the national economy—became if anything less informative, and certainly more sensationalized. Politics and government were downplayed. The mutual wariness of government and press became more akin to mutual animosity. The local political establishment projected a story of virtue rewarded, while newspapers, radio, and television projected a story of a self-serving, self-perpetuating political machine. It was yet another way in which the idealized narrative of statehood—the self-confident, progressive "one people, one Hawai'i," in Burns' words—gradually yielded to a multiplicity of views and multiple enclaves of influence.

THE 1982 ELECTION

As George Ariyoshi contemplated re-election in 1982, he turned fifty-six. He had spent half of his life in public office. His lieutenant governor for four years, Jean Sadako King, ran against him. King originally was a participant in the early union movement. She had eventually turned to elective politics, quickly rising to prominence in the House and Senate. Her expressed concerns were about the environment and planning, a realm that had been heavily worked, and she lost to Ariyoshi by a wide margin.

After serving only one term in the State House of Representatives, John D. Waiheʻe ran for lieutenant governor against a seemingly certain winner, State Senator Dennis O'Connor. With the support of the ILWU and a strong neighbor island vote, Waiheʻe won, in the process displaying an uncanny grasp of how to animate the Democratic coalition. In the general election, he was a good complement to Ariyoshi: young and respectful, dynamic and Hawaiian. They formed a credible team, and their victory by a wide margin was assured by having both Fasi as an independent and D. G. Anderson as a Republican in the race. (The numbers were 141,043 for Ariyoshi, 89,303 for Fasi, and 81,507 for Anderson.)

Burns had been elected to three four-year terms, and now so had Ariyoshi. By serving as acting governor during a year of Burns' last term, and because of the two-term limit imposed on his successors, Ariyoshi was to be the longest-serving governor in the history of Hawaiʻi.

JOHN WAIHEʻE AND THE GOVERNORSHIP

Although Ariyoshi did not have Burns' obsession with who would follow him in office, neither was he entirely disinterested. For four years, Eileen Anderson was an heir apparent, but then lost to Fasi. At one point Ariyoshi hoped Walter Dods would become governor, but Dods was ascending to the leadership of First Hawaiian Bank. No one—neither Ariyoshi nor Waiheʻe himself—assumed that Waiheʻe automatically would run for the governorship in 1986. He had served only one term in the State House before winning his term as lieutenant governor. In a political culture that had come to value experience in office, Waiheʻe had little. He looked young. His advisers agonized over his lapsing into the intonations of pidgin. His main identity was derived from the constitutional convention. He had moved up the political scale so quickly that no one understood the nature of the relationships he was forming, not even Waiheʻe himself. When Waiheʻe was elected to the legislature, Alvin Shim had said, "John was born under the right star."[34]

Shim knew things about Waiheʻe that others did not. Having grown up watching the ILWU's soup kitchen in Honokaʻa, Waiheʻe had a special touch with labor people. He felt he could walk into a roomful of union men and women and connect with them almost automatically. He had gone to work in Shim's firm, with all its labor clients, even before graduating from law school. Like Shim himself, a part of him lived in the uncharted journey of the Hawaiian movement, and a part lived in the conventions of unions, laws, government policies, and politics. In the mid-seventies, Shim and Waiheʻe had begun meeting with a group called together by Dan Inouye to talk about potential future candidates for governor. A sampling of participants suggests they represented a wide range of people and interests. Filipino American Chris Pablo was a young health care executive who was active in the Democratic Party. Chinese American Stuart Ho had served in the legislature and had come into the investment business through a famous father, Chinn Ho. Fred Trotter had been a plantation manager and—as an offspring of the royalists James and Kuaehelani Campbell—was the family representative on the board of trustees of the vast Campbell Estate. The influential part-Hawaiian Myron Thompson had led Queen Liliʻuokalani Children's Center, then served as Burns' administrative director. And then there were Shim and Inouye.

From the memory of various participants, it appears the committee first got together in the mid-1970s as ferment in the Hawaiian community was rising sharply. It continued through the participation of younger members, such as Waiheʻe and Pablo, which then led to a memorable gathering at Inouye's apartment in Waikīkī after the constitutional convention.[35]

The theme of these meetings was that the Democratic Party must put forward a native Hawaiian candidate and elect him to govern Hawaiʻi. Participants came to call themselves the Committee to Elect a Hawaiian Governor, although Inouye did not think of the committee as having a name.[36]

The discussion centered on the likelihood that Ariyoshi would serve at least one more term (he then was in his first elected term). After that, one of several Caucasians—Heftel or Fasi, for example—was most likely to win the governorship. So with careful preparation, a credible Hawaiian candidate might be ready for a serious run in fifteen or so years, either in 1990 or 1994. The meetings bogged down in a discussion of candidates. Walter Heen seemed the only likely possibility, but he had taken a judgeship appointment from Burns and was retired from politics.

One day in 1978 Inouye arrived from Washington and called the committee together at his Waikīkī apartment. Waiheʻe recalled him saying, "It's time to get serious about electing a Hawaiian governor, and I think it should be this guy," and he nodded at Waiheʻe. Inouye recalled walking through the door with Waiheʻe and saying that Waiheʻe was going to be the next governor. "And you should have seen Waiheʻe's face," Inouye recalled. "What? What? What? I don't think he was ever thinking of running for governor."[37]

It was not that this group plotted to achieve its ends, but the conversations with Inouye became part of how Waiheʻe thought of himself, and how a small handful of influential, active people thought of him. For example, when he won his legislative seat in 1980, it was with the help of Stuart Ho and Fred Trotter. When he ran for lieutenant governor in 1982, it was with a single-minded belief that he could win, even though his opponent was more experienced and better known.

In the campaign of 1982 for lieutenant governor, one of the keys to Waiheʻe's victory was the enigmatic Nadao Yoshinaga, a 442nd RCT veteran and also a labor lawyer. Yoshinaga was originally the brain of the ILWU in the Senate, but retired from the legislature in 1970. Thereafter he had become a mentor of younger political figures, with a far-reaching but unconventional sort of influence. He wore a baseball cap in the manner of a retired plantation worker. He often appeared to be by himself, but then would engage certain people he liked in intense bursts of conversation. Even then, he often spoke in a mocking, sarcastic way, and in the early stages of their acquaintance, Waiheʻe thought Yoshinaga was making fun of him. He then realized Yoshinaga was trying to challenge him with a question, which Waiheʻe would reduce to, "Are you going to be a Hawaiian leader, or are you going to be a Hawaiian leader of all the people?"[38]

The image of the retired guru talking with the young man may sound quaint, but it led to Yoshinaga supporting Waiheʻe with the ILWU, and on election night Waiheʻe reaped the neighbor island bulge of union votes that still made a difference. Waiheʻe liked problems. He liked to debate issues and formulate programs and policies. But at the end of the day, these conversations were about finding society's balance point and things of the heart. In conversation, he knew how to recall listening to his father, whom he revered, and the ILWU man, Yoshito Takamine, whom he admired.

FOR MOST OF A TWO-YEAR PERIOD, between 1984 and 1986, Waiheʻe seemed to have disappeared into the two-dimensional role of lieutenant governor. Almost inevitably, Cec Heftel was going to become governor. Heftel was smart, successful, aggressive, and rich. He owned Hawaiʻi's largest television and radio stations, as well as a mainland chain. As a broadcaster, he could say whatever he wanted, so he had created an image of being fiercely independent. In 1976 he had spent a million dollars of his own money to win a seat in Congress, where he had cultivated an image as a capable and caring person who got things done. An impressive scattering of Democrats had supported him in his congressional races, such as Dan Aoki, Don Horio, and, from the heart of Inouye's staff, Henry Giuni. He led by such a distance in various poll pairings for governor that other candidates were intimidated. When Ariyoshi looked around, he did not have a credible alternative, now that Eileen Anderson had been defeated by Fasi. Candidates for governor are not produced out of thin air.

Waihe'e was nervous in the face of challenging Heftel. He did not feel ready. He had accumulated a campaign debt in his race for lieutenant governor and had let four years pass without raising the money to pay it off. His political base seemed inadequate. In polls, he looked weak. Ariyoshi was not supporting him. If he had been born under a star, as Shim had said, his star was below the horizon. In this uncertain frame of mind he made a trip to Washington D.C. Inouye gave him words of encouragement, but Henry Giuni—who rightly had a reputation as a political genius—was telling Inouye, "The kid's going to lose."

Waihe'e then went to see Heftel on the floor of Congress. They linked up in the cloak room, then went off together. Waihe'e was open to the idea of staying put in the lieutenant governor's office, or otherwise being talked out of running. They went for a car ride. Heftel was impatient. He said he wanted to cut through the little stuff and get to the conversation. What would it take, he asked, to keep Waihe'e from running? He said he could help Waihe'e in a lot of ways. He could even help Waihe'e with his campaign debt. Waihe'e suddenly felt himself hanging way out on the edge of something, and he always found the edge to be exhilarating. In that moment, he decided to run for governor.[39]

THE CAMPAIGN OF 1986

By the spring of election year, Waihe'e thought he must be gaining ground. In strategy and schedule, he had attempted to do all the right things. Bill Paty astounded his erstwhile Republican associates by agreeing to serve as chairman of Waihe'e's campaign. Yoshinaga was playing a major role in his own way, and a cadre of young people was at work, many of them with experience under Ariyoshi.

The person Waihe'e needed most was Robert Oshiro, who by this time had managed four straight winning gubernatorial campaigns.[40] Waihe'e had driven to Wahiawā to talk with Oshiro, who asked why he wanted to be governor. Not satisfied with what he heard, Oshiro declined to help.[41] Waiheʻe went back a second and third time with the same result. Paty then called and asked Oshiro to listen in on a campaign meeting and give his advice. Oshiro thereafter told Waiheʻe that he was headed for a certain loss. Waiheʻe said that was why he needed Oshiro. Oshiro researched Waiheʻeʻs background as a student activist and a leader of the convention. He decided Waiheʻe was an agent of change who had displayed a willingness to work within the system.

Waiheʻe would come to represent many things for Oshiro, but one was simply the challenge of election politics. Waiheʻe offered an opportunity to prove that the difference in a winning campaign was not the money or media of the "Catch a Wave" or "Boy from Kalihi" campaigns, but the mystical grass roots. The difference was sparrows. It was the supporter list, which had grown from two thousand to six thousand in 1954, to thirty thousand in 1970, and by now was forty-five thousand. Where the big media campaign was like selling apples, Waiheʻe had to be sold person to person.

Perhaps most amazing of all was Waiheʻeʻs new relationship with Dan Aoki. As an upstart in the party in 1972, Waiheʻe had thought of Aoki as one of the most arrogant people who walked. He remembered winning votes on the floor of the State convention, only to have Aoki stride up—chomping on a cigar, his chest thrown out—and win the election by casting a fistful of proxy votes. In their first conversations about the governorship, Waiheʻe thought Aoki was asking, "Are you the one who will be the first Hawaiian governor?" As they talked, Waiheʻe discovered Aoki was at loose ends with Ariyoshi, and that he seemed alienated and lost without Burns. Waiheʻe was stunned to hear that Aoki wanted to teach campaign organization to Hawaiians. That became Aokiʻs job. Aoki spent all his time with native Hawaiians who knew little or nothing about conventional politics. Many of the nisei generation came in and worked quietly behind the scenes. Waiheʻe was to think, "It seemed like they all sat down one night and decided, ʻWe have to take care of the Hawaiians.ʻ"[42]

Among younger Democrats, the old factional lines that had partially dissolved with Ariyoshi were breached completely with Waiheʻe. Waiheʻe supporters ran across the old Burns-Gill spectrum. For example, Byron Baker had been a newsman, then a Gill supporter, then a liberal legislator. Bob Nakata had organized the battle of Waiāhole Valley. Rick Egged had run polls for Burns in 1970, then supported Gill in 1974. Walter Ritte had discovered politics at the constitutional convention. Carole Fukunaga had worked for Anson Chong and Tom Gill before serving in the constitutional convention, then in the legislature. Sandra Ebesu had been a Burns supporter first, then was close to Ariyoshi as a result of her father bringing him into the Democratic Party.

A cadre to animate the electorate was important, but the electorate had become an ever-larger universe. By late summer, Waihe‘e desperately needed a boost in the polls. The population of 683,513 in Burns' 1962 election had surpassed a million in 1986. In the new impersonality of top-level politics in Hawai‘i, a poll boost would give Waihe‘e a fundraising boost that would give him a media boost. On August 4, *The Honolulu Advertiser* ran the results of its institutional poll on the front page. Waihe‘e was so nervous that he refused to look, jumping instead to his horoscope, which said that today was not going to be a good day. The *Advertiser* had Heftel leading by 54 percent to 18 percent, with 10 percent for Patsy Mink and 15 percent undecided. The Hawaiian Government Employees Association was also running a poll, and its numbers were even worse. Numbers that bad can crush candidates. In the morning, Waihe‘e saw an image of himself as a fringe candidate, limping through two more months of desultory campaigning until the primary election mercifully brought an end to it.

Waihe‘e's wife, Lynne, was the first to catch fire. She announced they were just getting started, as did his children, his mother, and several in-laws who happened to be visiting. Paty assured him that the end had not arrived. Waihe‘e found Oshiro in his campaign office, glued to the telephone, turning people out for a rally of workers that afternoon. Oshiro said they had to generate an immediate answer to the poll with a strong grassroots campaign meeting. The meeting was held in the cafeteria of Farrington High School, the public school heart of Kalihi that is named, ironically, for the Wallace Farrington who had governed the territory in tails and *pince nez*. Where earlier such meetings had turned out several dozen workers, this one brought out several times that many. Oshiro, in a highly charged state, delivered a pep talk in such a fierce tone that it seemed more like a harangue of fighting troops as they went into battle. Paty spoke, and then Waihe‘e.

Waihe‘e had been trying to do the right things, set strategies and follow schedules. Now he decided to forget the polls and instill passion in the campaign. "Throw away the book," he said. "Talk with everyone."[43] He was in the crisis mode that he liked best. From that moment, the campaign was different, not in structure or strategy, but in tone and emotion. The campaign bumper sticker said, "Waihe‘e, Heart and Soul." In a big, sprawling political party that had become two parties—the party of the status quo and the party of change—Waihe‘e became the candidate of change who honored the keepers of the status quo.

On one level, his message was about a program—in fact, it was about almost everything the Democratic Party had ever imagined in the fields of education, health care, and subsidizing low- to moderate-income housing, plus what it was beginning to imagine for Hawaiians. This resulted partly from the fact that suddenly the state had revenue, thanks to Ariyoshi saving money, to the legislature passing a hotel room tax, and also to the investment capital pouring in from Japan.

More than anything the campaign was about Waiheʻeʻs being young, capable, and filled with energy. Where many candidates turn over their time to schedulers grudgingly, Waiheʻe was out shaking hands and talking to people day and night. His goal was three coffee hours a night. If he did not have three coffee hours on his schedule each night, he would go by headquarters to find out why. When he traveled the Big Island with his close friend and adviser, Chuck Freedman, he would try to shake every hand in a small town, jump back in the car and ward off exhaustion with a nap, then jump out in a new town and do it all again.

It was a long, rugged campaign, marked by allegations from Heftel of an unethical smear, the facts of which were never proven. Waiheʻeʻs outgoing personality was more and more in contrast to Heftelʻs studied demeanor.

That Waiheʻe could maintain his positive frame of mind over such a protracted, uphill battle was less surprising to Shim than to most people. Shim claimed to have once seen unpublished poll numbers in which Heftel led by 60 percent to Waiheʻeʻs 6 percent. When Waiheʻe came to him saying he nonetheless wanted to run, Shim had urged him not to. When Waiheʻe next called Shim, he said he was disturbed by cultural conflicts in his campaign. As a Hawaiian he wanted to promote harmony, but the process pressured him to engage Heftel in conflict. Shim took Waiheʻe to Roshi Tanouye, the master of a meditation zendo in upper Kalihi valley. Tanouye was a significant but unpublicized force in Hawaiʻi, operating at an unmapped intersection of cultural and spiritual issues. Among his followers, who included some of the communityʻs most influential people, he had acquired a reputation for seeing into people and events in ways that others could not. He was also a master of the martial art of kendo, which is practiced in Japanese *dojo* with sword-like sticks. No one ever doubted that Tanouye was the real thing.

Tanouye said Waiheʻe should go talk with a Hawaiian woman named Nana Veary. Mrs. Veary soon was to publish a book titled *Change We Must*, revealing an unconventional, lifelong spiritual journey that was rooted in the metaphysics of Hawaiian culture. Born in 1908, she had spent many of her childhood days with her grandparents, who lived in a grass house in the remnants of the Hawaiian fishing village at the entrance to Pearl Harbor. Her grandfather was a traditional canoe builder who prayed to a tree before cutting it down. Her grandmother fed strangers who passed by without ever learning their names. Asked by Nana why she had fed a particular man, she had replied in Hawaiian, "I was not feeding the man; I was entertaining the spirit of God within him." In describing her affirmation of change, Nana wrote, "I unloose the wellsprings of my being and make a complete deliverance of the self to Life. This I do with joy, withholding nothing."[44]

Waiheʻe set up a meeting with Mrs. Veary at a restaurant at the Colony Surf Hotel on the far end of Waikīkī Beach near Diamond Head. Shim remembered her advice to Waiheʻe as: "First, don't forget your culture. Second, don't put someone down to build yourself up." Waiheʻe remembered a discourse: "The essence of being Hawaiian is helping others. It is the meaning of aloha. It is not to become powerful for your own sake, but for others." In the course of a campaign that depended on "withholding nothing," Waiheʻe talked with her repeatedly.

Although Waiheʻe had gained ground, a reading of polls suggested even in the closing weeks that his campaign had fallen far short. In mid-September, the *Advertiser* poll had Heftel leading Waiheʻe by 49 percent to 28 percent, with 13 percent for Patsy Mink and another 11 percent undecided. Waiheʻe had moved up, but Heftel had not really moved down, and Heftel's lead was again widely interpreted as insurmountable.

Two months previously, Dan Aoki had been to a party with Hawaiian supporters of Waiheʻe. The next day he died of a heart attack. When Waiheʻe spoke at the funeral, he looked out into the crowd. In the back row was a group of homeless Hawaiians who were living on the beach in Waimānalo. They were Aoki's new friends. On election night, someone brought a lei from a flowering tree on Maui that had been dedicated as a memorial to the first sergeant from the 442nd who had stood with Burns in the old days. When the winning margin was announced, Waiheʻe grabbed the lei and the microphone and began to recount the story of the campaign. As the greatest come-from-behind victory story in the history of Hawaiʻi state politics, it was an instant legend. When Waiheʻe got to the part about Aoki, he violated the protocol that says leis are to be presented by the giver. Pulling the lei over his own head, he dedicated the victory to the memory of Dan Aoki.

The margin was 106,000 for Waiheʻe to 84,000 for Heftel. For once the winner had spent considerably less than the loser. The Republican candidate in the general election was D. G. Anderson. He was the best chance of the Republican Party since the near loss by Burns and Gill in 1966. For most of the campaign, Waiheʻe and Anderson ran nearly even. Remarkably, both were of Hawaiian ancestry. While Anderson was an attractive candidate in his way, he did not have the sprawling resources of the Democratic Party behind him. Waihe'e opened a lead late in the campaign and won by a margin of 174,000 to 160,000.

The alliance that had been forged by Burns as party chairman had now taken first an AJA then a Hawaiian to the governorship, just as Burns, in his last days, had imagined. Maybe, he had said, a Filipino would be next, and that would be the case as well. So far as the results of these gubernatorial elections were a healing process, they addressed the hurts of a century.

ARIYOSHI ON REFLECTION

When George Ariyoshi said his farewells to the 1986 Democratic Party convention, former House Speaker Elmer Cravalho predicted that he would become a Harry Truman, a chief executive who was more highly regarded in history than by his contemporaries. As Cravalho's comment implied, seemingly few of Ariyoshi's accomplishments attracted favorable attention, yet paradoxically he had been rewarded over and over by the voting public with re-election. When he retired at age fifty-nine, he had won twenty-four straight elections including three terms as governor.

Nonetheless, the image of caretaker clung to him. Before a more accurate sense of his accomplishments could set in, he, his wife, and his daughter were stopped for detailed questioning by U.S. Customs on their return from a trip to Japan. Initially challenged for failing to declare fully the value of items in their possession, they were subjected to a detailed investigation.[45] Press reports described a diamond-studded woman's watch that was valued variously at ten thousand and twenty-five thousand dollars, as well as a valuable pendant and a dress by a celebrated fashion designer, Hanae Mori.[46] Ariyoshi issued a statement saying that part of the jewelry in question belonged to his wife before its leaving the country, that most of the pieces were gifts to his wife on the trip, and that as gifts he had no idea the jewelry was so valuable.

The case dragged on without further statement on Ariyoshi's part. The actual settlement turned on a customs conclusion that Ariyoshi, having paid $1,700, should have made a declaration resulting in a payment of $2,700. For this discrepancy he was required to pay $11,389.[47] With that the case was closed, but damage had been done to the public perception of Ariyoshi. He had always been well-mannered and high-minded, and the incident at customs fulfilled people's conviction that Ariyoshi must surely be as flawed as other politicians.

He had led Hawai'i through the turbulence of the seventies. When the boom economy faded, he had kept government on a steady course and distributed the pain widely. His obsession with fairness and stewardship were constant guides in his dealings with people. His contribution to the environment was considerable. Just as he helped stabilize the natural environment, he had helped stabilize the social environment. His long administration was notably free of scandal. He had constantly innovated with new technologies, new economic possibilities, and new government systems. He had considerably expanded the real-world meaning of Hawai'i's role in the Pacific. He had so thoroughly met the challenge of being America's first nonwhite governor that the idea was no longer remarkable. Other people of color would readily follow him in Hawai'i and in other states.

In the 1994 survey that exalted Burns, 12 percent of the public identified Ariyoshi as the governor who did the most for Hawai'i. His mostly unpublicized but systematic service to educational, cultural, and international development projects throughout the 1990s elevated his public standing. Much of the rediscovery of Ariyoshi had to do with the decade-long stagnation of Hawai'i's economy. As government programs and services lurched from crisis to crisis in the 1990s, Ariyoshi's smooth, steady handling of the fiscal problems of the 1970s was favorably and even fondly recalled.

Waihe'e's spectacular rise to the governorship in 1986 was followed, after six successful years of rising affluence, by a spectacular decline in popularity. The most recurring criticism of Waihe'e was that he overspent relative to a declining economy, and he left office with only 5 percent of the public identifying him as the governor who had done the most for Hawai'i.

This scenario of step-by-step decline led many in the mass media to anticipate the election of a Republican governor following Waihe'e. A three-way race in which Frank Fasi again ran as an independent, splitting the opposition vote of Republican Patricia Saiki, led to a first-term victory for Democrat Ben Cayetano. A simple miscalculation by the Republican candidate (Linda Lingle)—letting up in the last two weeks of the campaign—handed Cayetano a second term.

Chapter 15

Conclusion

With America's 1898 annexation of Hawai'i, the struggle of Hawaiians to perpetuate themselves as a people and the struggle of Asian immigrants to make their way in America were set in motion simultaneously. These became the two most active forces in Hawai'i's contemporary political history, eventually playing themselves out in 1954, 1959, the 1978 constitutional convention, and many of the gubernatorial elections since statehood. In the "black hole" of Hawai'i's history, between annexation and World War II, a great deal more change occurred than is typically suggested. For this, much of the credit must be given to the settlers from Japan and even to Japan itself. If Americans would begin to agree with this observation, it would result in thinking of Japan much as we think of Britain and France—as a country that has fundamentally contributed to American culture and history.

The test of Japanese American community development was the crisis of December 7. While Hawai'i's resolution of that crisis was neither completely rational nor fair, it was at least not a racially based relocation and internment as occurred on the West Coast. That it was developed by undemocratic means—in darkness, guided by intelligence agencies and martial law—is perplexing, to put it mildly, but the survival of the Japanese American community in Hawai'i is a monumental legacy of the prewar period. If this aspect of the story is not a testimony to democracy, it is nonetheless testimony to relationships in which acquaintance, information, and practicality all played a part.

In the development of Hawai'i as a state of the United States, the avoidance of a mass internment was the overarching event of the twentieth century; it allowed all else to happen. An unbroken line connects December 7 to the formation of nisei military units, the revitalization of territorial politics, statehood, and finally to the succession of Caucasian, Japanese,

Hawaiian, and Filipino governors. This progression continued in a national context, in which Hawai'i has made unique contributions in Pacific relationships, in civil rights, in reform of immigration and naturalization, in abolition of the internal security law that allowed for the internment, in the national apology to World War II internees, and in reparation for the internment. The nisei of Hawai'i changed America.

To be sure, Japanese Americans did not do all this by themselves. Their success came not only from their own actions but from the support they received from others, their determination to work with others and, once they gained power, their fair treatment of others. This same determination led key nisei to give support—including political support—to both individuals and groups other than their own. The experiment of Hawai'i, in which Japanese Americans played such a catalytic role, has been proven to have a wide and inclusive base of beneficiaries.

In returning to 1954, it is useful to see that the founders of the modern Democratic Party around Burns were intimately connected with the circle around the most progressive Republican, Joe Farrington. They shared the goal of getting the Japanese community through the war. By then Hawai'i had set itself on being a multiracial society in which labor was organized and bargained collectively, forming an essential center of political gravity from which margins of victory were built. The Democratic revolution, as it was called, was a way of accelerating a previously defined direction and institutionalizing a set of simple ideals to pursue greater openness, opportunity, and equality.

In this broad and complex revisiting of the past, the whipping boys of history—the Republican Party, the missionary descendants, the Big Five, and the American military—require revisiting as well. Although less effectively than the Democrats, the Republicans sought statehood. Almost all the early-day AJA candidates were Republican. The Republican Party passed a collective bargaining law for the territory in 1945. The haole elements who were trying to keep nonwhites down on the plantation with one hand were paradoxically opening doors of educational opportunity with the other. In much the same way, the prewar military that produced such hideous schemes as George Patton's hostage plan must also be credited with systematically revising its estimate of the nisei. Their views were far better informed than Washington's. As the war approached, more and more testimony for the nisei was being generated in Hawai'i, and virtually all the progressive thinking regarding the nisei mobilization came from Hawai'i. From Frank Atherton and Charles Hemenway to General Emmons and Robert Shivers, the multiracial experience of Hawai'i produced some of the more enlightened Caucasians in America. It is from this perspective that the process of change can be seen as less a matter of partisanship, as it so often has been made to appear, and more a matter of societal development, particularly the development of a multiracial ethic.

THE ISLAND PARTY SYSTEM

The fact that Burns, as the founding figure, helped the Japanese community survive the war was essential to his success and to his being elevated to mythic heights in the public memory. Paradoxically, what he set in motion, the succession of Democratic political figures in the postwar period, is proof of an unseen hand—a political machine endlessly at work. The governorship passing from Democrat to Democrat vividly reinforced this impression. Clearly, there has been an aggregation of forces—banks, architects, engineers, contractors, and labor unions—that has understood the power of the governorship and has concentrated on maintaining entrée and influence, much as occurs in national politics with the presidency. This is a bipartisan combination of special interests, the influence of which has been constantly reinforced by the ever-rising cost of campaigning in the era of mass media.

With that said, there is not more but less to the image of a ruling Democratic machine than meets the eye. Partisan accounts of Hawai'i's history (including my *Catch A Wave*), have exaggerated the importance of political parties because they relied heavily on the partisan views of a handful of Democrats (Burns, Gill, Aoki, and so on). However mysterious or poetic, the succession of Democratic governors was haphazard and idiosyncratic. Burns nearly gave the governorship away in 1966; Ariyoshi barely won in 1974 and 1978; Waihe'e worked a miracle in 1986; and Cayetano won his two terms in large measure because of tactical mistakes by opponents. More objectively, the Democratic hold should be put in context of Hawai'i's contribution to civil rights and equal opportunity. This shift was reinforced by the evolving identities of the national Democratic and Republican parties in the last half of the twentieth century which, because of race relations if for no other reason, favored the Democrats of Hawai'i. The grassroots Democratic Party organization in Hawai'i became the keeper of a powerful mythology about equality that not only Hawai'i but America desperately needed. Otherwise the Democratic Party has served as a mechanism of acculturation as much as anything else. It brings people of differing backgrounds to a table in the center, increasingly including Caucasians after Ariyoshi's opening of the party in 1974. Haoles who want to contribute to the group are embraced, and those who seek to dominate in the old way, by virtue of their race, are shunted aside. Otherwise, the major shifts of the twentieth century (such as the resurgence of native Hawaiian life) are too subtle and subterranean to be adequately reflected in narratives of conventional politics, most particularly in the essentially single- or island-party environment of Hawai'i.

In regard to the one-party pattern that dominated the twentieth century, the posture of the Democratic Party as both the keeper of the status quo and the proponent of change in Hawai'i has become too clever and confusing. The argumentation, analysis, and development of programs that occurred from statehood into the 1970s have been gradually displaced by posturing. The extent of power constitutionally vested in the governorship—the governor who is more nearly a president—is a self-perpetuating part of this problem. All paths lead not merely to the State capitol, but to the governor's office on the fifth floor.

A HAWAIIAN NATION

In simplest terms, Hawai'i's political history has been about control. Overrun by America, the nation of Hawai'i lost control of its government, resources, and ability to shape its future. With statehood, Hawai'i regained a measure of control. The 1960s were about celebrating control. The 1970s and well into the 1980s were about maintaining control and about expanding control if possible through such devices as the Hawai'i State Plan, the revised Hawai'i constitution, and challenges to the U.S. Constitution. The story since then has been progressively about loss of control, most obviously for economic reasons. The exception to this trend has been the inconclusive attempt by native Hawaiians to regain greater autonomy, which has been romantically described as sovereignty.

Although the Democratic Party has served as a sympathetic environment for Hawaiians, neither the Democratic governors nor the Democratic congressional delegation have resolved the issues of dispossession resulting from annexation. While the formation of OHA and the elections of Waihe'e and Akaka have reflected concern and commitment, these steps have been undertaken as coalition-building in an American political context, when the underlying issues of Hawaiians are about nationality and nation. Thus far neither native Hawaiians nor the U.S. government have defined a new relationship. Yet, that which is re-emerging, an indigenous Hawaiian nation, was in historic terms only recently submerged. What will ultimately be resurrected will force a redefinition of the State of Hawai'i, with ramifications for the federal government, particularly the military. It will also have ramifications for other indigenous people in America and around the world, many of whom are watching the sovereignty debate in Hawai'i with interest.

The resurgence of Hawaiians, interrelated with the dramatic achievements of Asian immigrants in America, underscores the existence of not only a multiethnic history in Hawai'i but a multilayered transnational history. As the island edge of America, Hawai'i begins the twenty-first century as both the fiftieth state and a submerged nation, as a passageway of Pacific cultures and peoples, and as a semiseparate, mixed society that functions somewhere beyond conventional definition, the possibilities of which have only been glimpsed.

Notes

CHAPTER 1

1. Fuchs, *Hawai'i Pono,* vii.
2. Statehood and Hawai'i's People by John A Burns, Congressional Record, House, 1959; 14564–66.
3. Gov 13-85, Archives of Hawai'i, letter, Lyndon B. Johnson to John A. Burns dated May 1, 1968. Files of governors are preceded by "Gov."

CHAPTER 2

1. For a detailed account of academic and general audience nonfiction sources, see Tamura, "Using the Past to Inform the Future: An Historiography of Hawai'i's Asian and Pacific Islander Americans."
2. Tamura, "Using the Past to Inform the Future," 57.
3. Hearing Transcript, May 10, 1898, House Committee on Foreign Affairs, National Archives, as described in Coffman, *Nation Within,* 304–305.
4. Coffman, *Nation Within,* 102–106.
5. Coffman, *Nation Within,* 69–70.
6. The treatment of Farrington draws on Hardy, *Wallace R. Farrington.*
7. Information about Wilson draws from Krauss, *Johnny Wilson: First Hawaiian Democrat.* This is one of the few books to shed light on the territorial period.
8. Krauss, *Johnny Wilson,* 45–46.

CHAPTER 3

1. See Iriye, *Pacific Estrangement,* and Moriyama, *Imingaisha.*
2. Moriyama, *Imingaisha,* 18.
3. The pattern of Japanese immigration fluctuated widely over time, in response to such factors as annexation, the Gentlemen's Agreement of 1907, the introduction of picture brides, and the strikes of 1909 and 1920. Neither Beechert in *Working in Hawai'i: A Labor History,* nor Tamura in *Americanization, Acculturation, and Ethnic Identity: The Nisei Generation in Hawai'i,* venture definitive numbers or percentages.

4. The treatment of Sokabe is drawn from Nakano, *Samurai Missionary: The Reverend Shiro Sokabe*.

5. Duus, Masayo, *Unlikely Liberators*, Preface.

6. Coffman, *Nation Within*, 199–202. The main document to which the Republic of Hawai'i's provocation of Japan refers is a report by Hatch dated February 17, 1896. This document, either overlooked or ignored by other writers, is essential to understanding the Republic's role in beginning the alienation of Japan. It can be found in the Foreign Office and Executive (F.O. and Ex.) file of the Republic in the archives of Hawai'i.

7. Coffman, *Nation Within*, 213, again based on F.O. and Ex. files. See February and March, 1897.

8. Coffman, *Nation Within*, 274–275.

9. Robinson, *By Order of the President: FDR and the Internment of Japanese Americans*, 16.

10. Robinson, 16–19.

11. A leading historian of American expansion, Walter LaFeber sketches an outstanding account of the San Francisco school incident. His writing repeatedly interrelates the shoddy treatment of Japanese immigrants with the deterioration of U.S.-Japan relations. See LaFeber, *The Clash: A History of U.S.-Japan Relations*, 87–89.

12. An invaluable reconstruction of Japanese business history can be found in Honolulu Japanese Chamber of Commerce, *The Rainbow: A Bridge from East to West, Past to Future*. See especially the material about Ozaki on pages 48, 53.

13. Regarding plague and origins of the Chinatown fire, see Honolulu Japanese Chamber of Commerce, 40–50.

14. Honolulu Japanese Chamber of Commerce, 47.

15. Honolulu Japanese Chamber of Commerce, 127.

16. Honolulu Japanese Chamber of Commerce, tables compiled by the Japanese Merchants Association, 110.

17. Honolulu Japanese Chamber of Commerce, 114.

18. Honolulu Japanese Chamber of Commerce, 111.

19. Honolulu Japanese Chamber of Commerce, 127–128.

20. Takashi Tsutsumi was all but unknown until publication of Duus' *The Japanese Conspiracy: The Oahu Sugar Strike of 1920*.

21. Duus, *The Japanese Conspiracy*, 67. Chapter 4 describes development of the conspiracy theory. Chapter 5 describes the conspiracy trial.

22. Gusukuma. "Nisei Daimyo: The Life of Shunzo Sakamaki."

23. Duus' book was originally published in Japanese as *Nihon no inbō*.

24. Tamura, *Americanization, Acculturation, and Ethnic Identity*, 52.

25. Tamura, *Americanization, Acculturation, and Ethnic Identity*, 56.

26. Shibusawa's meeting in Tokyo and the situation surrounding it was developed by Noriko Shimada, in "Eiichi Shibusawa and Takie Okumura: Americanization of Japanese in Hawai'i During the 1920s," and also by Monobe, in "Invisible Thread: The Japanese Government and the Americanization Movement among the Issei and Nisei in Hawai'i During the 1920s and the 1930s."

27. Monobe, "Invisible Thread," 1.
28. Shimada, "Eiichi Shibusawa and Takie Okumura," 1.
29. Shimada, 8.
30. Shimada, 10.
31. Shimada, 14.
32. Shimada, 16.
33. Shimada, 17.
34. Monobe reported the Japanese Foreign Ministry, at Shibusawa's request, committed $6,000 in 1921 for a "campaign of education intended for the Japanese" (30) and also paid for bilingual printing of brochures and pamphlets. According to Monobe, other payments were made to influence the press and support community education through Japanese studies.
35. Monobe, 16.
36. Hardy, 135.
37. Hardy, 136.
38. Robinson, 16.
39. Robinson, 22.
40. Tamura, *Americanization, Acculturation, and Ethnic Identity,* 130. Descriptions of the New American Conference rely on Tamura.
41. Nishimura interview, 1994.
42. Ota and Oshiro, "Mediator between Cultures: Tasuku Harada."
43. Ota and Oshiro, 179–180.
44. Monobe, 11, 12.
45. Duus, *The Japanese Conspiracy,* 268.
46. Duus, *The Japanese Conspiracy,* 300.
47. Shimada, 20.
48. Belief that the Japanese Exclusion Act was the last step toward the downward spiral leading to the Pacific War has been embraced by many writers, most prominently Walter LaFeber of Cornell in *The Clash* and Akira Iriye in *Pacific Estrangement.*
49. Hooper, *Elusive Destiny: The Internationalist Movement in Modern Hawai'i,* 70.
50. The widely used phrase *Wilsonian internationalism* is used here to refer to Wilson's call for a League of Nations and a world made safe for democracy.
51. Hooper, 106.
52. Shimamura, "Hawaiian Japanese Civic Association," 29–31.
53. For a list of Japanese associations, see Tetsuo Oi's essay in Honolulu Japanese Chamber of Commerce, *The Rainbow: A Bridge from East to West, Past to Future,* 212–214.
54. Clissold, "Influence of Lionism," 31–32.
55. Monobe, 16.
56. Harada, "The Social Status of the Japanese in Hawaii," 10.
57. Harada, 13.
58. Gusukuma, "Nisei Daimyo," 29.
59. Gusukuma, 30.

CHAPTER 4

1. Kawano interview, the John A. Burns Oral History Project (BOHP).
2. Zalburg, *A Spark Is Struck: Jack Hall and the ILWU in Hawai'i*.
3. Zalburg, 4.
4. Quin, *The Big Strike*.
5. People who knew Shivers intimately included Hung Wai Ching (interview), Sue Isonaga (interview), and Mrs. Masaji Marumoto (interview).
6. Inazo Nitobe's seminal work on *bushidō* was originally published in 1905. It is still widely republished in the West under slightly varying titles (and therefore is not cited in the bibliography).
7. Robinson, *By Order of the President*, 14.
8. For details on this strategically based analysis, see Linn, *Guardians of Empire: The U.S. Army and the Pacific, 1902–1940*.
9. Linn, 88.
10. Linn, 104.
11. Linn, 105.
12. Linn, 110.
13. Linn, 155.
14. Linn, 88.
15. Linn, 152.
16. Linn, 156.
17. "Gen. Short Says No Racial Lines in Reserve Call," *Honolulu Star-Bulletin*, 20 February 1941.
18. Kawakami, *From Japan to Hawai'i, My Journey*, 42.
19. Coggins interview, 1985. The size of the ONI group is based on the recollection of Cecil Coggins. The range seems credible, because Coggins' memory was generally in harmony with other verifiable records.
20. Kido interview, BOHP.
21. Yoshida papers, Hawai'i War Records Depository, Hamilton Research Library, University of Hawai'i.
22. Burns interview, BOHP, 1975.
23. Boylan and Holmes, 33–34.
24. The detail of Shivers weeping is in BOHP. In the interview, Burns reflected a somewhat ambivalent attitude toward Shivers.

CHAPTER 5

1. This account was derived from Coffman, *Catch A Wave*; Burns repeated this description in his oral history, which then was republished in his biography. Coggins described a comparable process (apparently within ONI) of prioritizing arrests, in which the cards were given to regional police stations for execution in the event of an attack. How these two relate is not known.
2. Coffman, *Catch A Wave*, 16.

3. Personal conversation among friends.

4. An exception to the general pattern of ignoring the Justice Department arrests in Hawai'i is in Saiki, *Ganbare.*

5. Yoshida interview, 2001.

6. Kanazawa interview, 2001.

7. People who knew Marumoto described a "clubbed foot," implicitly congenital in origin. His son, Wendell, corrected this misimpression by describing an injury from riding a mule as a young child.

8. Marumoto's life has been extensively documented, including an oral history taken in 1985, when he was 79, by the Oral History Project of the Watumull Foundation.

9. This photograph is in the Marumoto family collection. Another photograph taken at a Japanese Chamber of Commerce teahouse party around this time shows the two men sitting at a distance from one another.

10. Yoshida papers, Hawai'i War Records Depository, Hamilton Research Library, University of Hawai'i.

11. Kimura, "Some Effects of the War Situation upon the Alien Japanese in Hawai'i."

12. Hooper, *Elusive Destiny,* 111.

13. *Honolulu Advertiser,* "Service Group, Civic Club Merge," 24 July 1942, 7.

14. Names of officers, past presidents, and committee members and directors were reported in the *Honolulu Star-Bulletin* on 8 August 1939, 27 June 1940, 21 July 1941, and 11 July 1942.

15. *Honolulu Star-Bulletin,* "Civic Club Is Planning Active Year," 8 August 1939, 9.

16. Murphy, *Ambassadors in Arms: The Story of Hawaii's 100th Battalion,* 23. The numbers apparently came from Japanese consulate records.

17. Murphy, 22.

18. Murphy, 22.

19. *Honolulu Advertiser,* "Hawai'i Educators Endorse Expatriation," 26 October 1940, 2.

20. *Honolulu Advertiser,* "Service Group, Civic Club Merge," 24 July 1942.

21. Okihiro, *Cane Fires: The Anti-Japanese Movement in Hawai'i, 1865–1945,* 274.

22. Neither the author, in his 1971 interview of Burns, nor the historians who took his oral account in 1975 were prepared to ask him informed and detailed questions about 1941.

23. Burns, BOHP.

24. The account of the evacuation and internment relies mainly on Grodzins, *Americans Betrayed: Politics and the Japanese Evacuation.* Appeals made in California for fair treatment of Japanese-ancestry people are on pages 62–63.

25. Grodzins, 64, quoting Congressional Record, 77th Cong., 1st sess., 10 December 1941, A5554.

26. Grodzins, 32.

27. A proposal of the Pacific League. Grodzins, 38.

28. Grodzins, 195.

29. Grodzins, 196, reporting testimony to the Tolan Committee, a congressional inquiry.
30. Grodzins, 206.
31. Ching interview, 1994.
32. Grodzins, 132, quoting from Knox's letter to the Tolan Committee.
33. National Archives, Box 1131, Folder 7, Item 1, Memorandum to the secretary of the navy, written by Franklin D. Roosevelt, 26 February 1942, from National Archives, courtesy Ted T. Tsukiyama.
34. Kaneko, interview, 2001.
35. Emmons, *Brief Personal History from Memory*, 11.
36. Honolulu attorney Ted T. Tsukiyama has played a key role in developing a deeper understanding of the nisei's military experience.
37. Ellen Godbey Carson and Ted T. Tsukiyama, "Tale of Two Generals," *Honolulu Star-Bulletin*, 2 December 1991, A-15.
38. Carson and Tsukiyama, "Tale of Two Generals."
39. Emmons, *Brief Personal History from Memory*.
40. This conclusion was based on congratulatory notes from such key figures as Gen. "Hap" Arnold and others, found in Emmons' papers at the Hoover Institute.
41. The figures are derived from the Coggins interview, a newspaper account of the Police Contact Group, and the obvious checking and cross-checking of Shivers. Edwards, in *Spy Catchers of the U.S. Army in the War with Japan*, 26, claims 700 "nisei informants" worked with the FBI. I gradually became skeptical of the high-side figures.
42. Memorandum for John J. McCloy, written by Colonel Moses Pettigrew, 17 November 1942, National Archives, courtesy of Tsukiyama.
43. Coggins interview, 1985, 25. Subsequent quotes from Coggins are from this long interview unless otherwise indicated.
44. Zacharias, *Secret Missions*, 63.
45. Coggins, "The Japanese-Americans in Hawaii," 78.
46. Coggins interview, 1985, 81–83.
47. Coggins, "The Japanese-Americans in Hawaii."
48. National Archives, RG 407-360, Box 17, Folder 1, Item 16, 3.
49. National Archives, RG 407-360, Box 17, Folder 1, Item 17, 1, R. W. Crawford, acting assistant chief of staff, to Admiral R. J. King, 29 May 1942.
50. Nosaka, "Brother in War and Peace: The 100th Infantry Story," 58.
51. Duus, *The Japanese Conspiracy*, 42.
52. Eric Yamamoto, conversation with the author, 15 June 2001. Yamamoto is an expert on legal cases relating to internment at the University of Hawai'i Law School.
53. RG 165, Box 1131, Folder 7, Item 11, 9, Gen. Thomas T. Handy to Gen. Marshall, 9 July 1942.
54. Allen, *Hawaii's War Years*, 134.
55. Tsukiyama, "Origins of the 442nd," 12, citing report on "The Military Utilization of United States Citizens of Japanese Ancestry," 14 September 1942.

56. Reischauer's views of Japan shaped a generation of Americans, but have been criticized as Cold War orthodoxy. His paper linking AJA to postwar Japan is in RG 407-360, Box 147, Folder 5, Item 24, 1, entitled "Memorandum on Policy Towards Japan," written by Milton Eisenhower to John J. McCloy.

57. RG 407-360, Box 147, Folder 5, Item 17, 1.

58. RG 407-360, Box 147, Folder 5, Item 22, which is a draft of a letter from Stimson to Roosevelt.

59. Memorandum by Colonel W. E. Crist, Conference re: Use of Japanese in Army, 4 January 1943, to General Strong, declassified 3 June 1993. This revealing five-page document was provided by Ted T. Tsukiyama, who coordinated research in the National Archives. It substantially corroborates the oral history of Coggins.

60. RG 407, MID 291.2 Japanese, Col. W. E. Christ, Asst. Ex. O., Military Intelligence Service (MIS), (291.2) to Lt. Col. K. S. Gibson, 8 January 1943.

61. Myers to Col. E. M. Wilson, 28 February 1943.

62. RG 107, Box 22, Folder 2, Item 22.

63. This is described by Cpt. John M. Hall, who was on Marshall's staff, in a memorandum to OWI.

64. Allen, *Hawaii's War Years*, 135.

65. Emergency Service Committee (ESC), Report Covering Period 1 January 1943 to 31 March 1943, located in Hawai'i War Records Depository, Hawai'i-Pacific room, Hamilton Research Library, University of Hawai'i.

66. Oba and Yoshida interview, 2001.

67. I have interviewed veterans who dispute the importance of conflict with mainland nisei and accordingly discount the importance of the trip to Jerome.

68. Tokunaga interview, 1208–1209.

69. The military population of Hawai'i during World War II changed constantly and was classified. The military figures are drawn from Allen (284, 349, 366), as further synthesized by Bailey and Farber, 27–29. The sole focus of both works is wartime Hawai'i.

70. Testimony to House Naval Affairs Committee, 13 April 1943.

71. Murphy, *Ambassadors in Arms*, 292.

72. Nosaka, "Brother in War and Peace," 59.

73. Soga, *Poets Behind Barbed Wire*, 57.

74. Kido, presentation to 1944 conference of Territory of Hawai'i Social Workers, ESC, Hawai'i War Records Depository.

75. Extensive minutes and records were kept by the ESC, O'ahu Conference of Americans of Japanese Ancestry. The conference referred to was held 28 January 1945. Hawai'i War Records Depository (HWRD), Hamilton Research Library, University of Hawai'i.

76. Shigeo Yoshida, "The Job Ahead," O'ahu Conference of Americans of Japanese Ancestry, 28 January 1945. HWRD.

77. Stanley Miyamoto, O'ahu Conference of Americans of Japanese Ancestry, 28 January 1945. HWRD.

CHAPTER 6

1. Young Oak Kim told this story in May 2001, eulogizing Sakae Takahashi. It echoes Duus' *Unlikely Liberators*. Takahashi modestly confirmed Duus' story in a 1994 interview for the Japanese Cultural Center of Hawai'i.
2. Young Oak Kim, correspondence with author, 15 November 2001.
3. Hooper, *Elusive Destiny*, 109.
4. Kido interview, BOHP.
5. That Kawano met with, worked with, and believed himself to be a member of the ESC is clear. ESC records conflict as to his membership on the committee. My sense is that he was asked to join the committee but that there was some unease within the group because of his radical background.
6. Kido interview, BOHP.
7. Ibid.
8. Zalburg, *A Spark Is Struck*, 62.
9. Kido interview, BOHP.
10. Itagaki's correspondence with Hemenway dwelled on the problems of the dispossessed mainland AJA and contrasted the relative good fortune of AJA in Hawai'i. For more information see Tendai Educational Foundation, *Japanese Eyes, American Heart*, 351–358.
11. Zalburg, 122–129.
12. Boylan and Holmes, *John A. Burns*, 73.
13. BOHP, Mau, the source of all biography on him.
14. Dr. Franklin Kometani, son of Katsumi "Doc" Kometani, conversation with the author, 18 May 2001.
15. For extensive accounts of the 1948–1950 Democratic conventions, see Boylan and Holmes, *John A. Burns.*
16. Holmes, *The Specter of Communism in Hawaii,* 123.
17. Holmes, 148.
18. Boylan and Holmes, 88–89.
19. Holmes, 188.
20. Zalburg, 187.
21. Holmes, 170.

CHAPTER 7

1. Burns, BOHP.
2. The information that follows draws on Boylan and Holmes, *John A. Burns: The Man and His Times,* and Burns, "Jack Burns: A Daughter's Portrait."
3. Boylan and Holmes, 143.
4. Boylan and Holmes, 21.
5. Boylan interviews.
6. Congressional Record, 86th Cong., 1st Sess., 28 July 1959, 14564.
7. The date 1948 is an estimate.
8. This is an imperfect list. Neither a file nor newspaper record could be located. It is derived from various accounts that have been cross-checked. The mem-

ory of Katsugo Miho, as a founding member of the 442 Club, seems most accurate. Inouye said he was in law school but remained generally informed of the effort to thank people who had parented the unit.

9. Tokunaga interview, 1215.
10. Holmes, *The Specter of Communism in Hawaii,* 125–126.
11. ESC, 30 March 1943, to Robert L. Shivers, signed by Masaji Marumoto, Shigeo Yoshida, Masa Katagiri, Shunzo Sakamaki, Stanley Miyamoto, Robert Komenaka, Mitsuyuki Kido, Earnest Murai, Iwao Miyake, Katsuo Miho, and two persons whose signatures cannot be deciphered. Shivers papers, courtesy of Sue Isonaga.
12. "Shivers Claims He'll Not Seek Governorship," *The Honolulu Advertiser,* 5 August 1949.
13. Boylan and Holmes, 92.
14. Personal papers of Robert Shivers; these are not archived.
15. Kai interview, 11 May 1988.
16. Kido interview, BOHP.
17. Kido interview, BOHP.
18. This interpretation comes from Walter Heen. It refers to a mass of literature, like that found in Fuchs's *Hawai'i Pono.*
19. Tuttle interview, 2001.
20. Personal correspondence with author.
21. Masato Doi and Katsugo Miho interviews, 2001.
22. Daniels, *Coming to America,* 329.
23. Tokunaga interview, 12 September 1989.
24. Boylan and Holmes, 30, which also says "None held significant appointive office in county or territorial governments," overlooking Wilfred Tsukiyama's job as city and county attorney of Honolulu.
25. Bell, *Last Among Equals,* 233.
26. Bell, 253.
27. Bell, 238.
28. Boylan and Holmes, 146.
29. Bell, 244; Boylan and Holmes, 150.
30. Unger and Unger, *LBJ: A Life,* 225–226.
31. For greater detail, see Bell, 273–276.
32. Congressional Record, 86th Cong., 1st sess., 28 July 1959, 14565.
33. Bell, 337.
34. For greater detail, see Bell, 273–276.

CHAPTER 8

1. Edward P. Dole, quoted in U.S. Congress, Report of Subcommittee on Pacific Islands and Puerto Rico on General Conditions in Hawai'i, vol. 1, 10, quoted by Bell, *Last Among Equals,* 43.
2. Congressional Record, 28 July 1959, 14566.
3. Fuchs, in *Hawai'i Pono,* deals at length with this event.

4. Heen interview, 2001, 2002.
5. Miho interview, 2001.
6. Summary of General Conclusions, Governor's Ad Hoc Commission on Operations, Revenues and Expenditures (CORE), State of Hawai'i, November 1974.
7. Hitch, *Islands in Transition,* 170.
8. Hitch, 181.
9. Hitch, 265.
10. Burns, First Inaugural Address, 1962.
11. Miho interview, 20–21 May 1997, 71.
12. Miho interview, 74.
13. Brown interview, 1999.
14. Brown interview, 1999.
15. The generalization is derived from Edward Burns' descriptions of his older brother made to the BOHP. The specific is from a conversation I had with Edward Burns during this period.
16. Oshiro interview, 1988, 1372.
17. Takabuki, *An Unlikely Revolutionary,* 73.
18. Daws is best known in Hawai'i for his general history, *Shoal of Time.* His observation was made in conversation with the author circa 1974.
19. I was sitting beside Carmelo Fasi at the time.
20. Heen interview, 1999.

CHAPTER 9

1. Biographical material on Ariyoshi relies primarily on this autobiography, *With Obligation to All,* unless otherwise noted.
2. Fuchs, *Hawai'i Pono,* 340.
3. Fuchs, 341.
4. Ariyoshi, 48–49.
5. Takushi interview, 1999.
6. Hitch, 161.
7. MacNaughton interview.
8. Takabuki, *An Unlikely Revolutionary,* 75.
9. Ige, *Boy from Kahaluu,* 161–162.
10. Cooper and Daws, *Land and Power in Hawaii,* 89.
11. Ibid., 97.
12. Coffman, *Catch A Wave,* 114.
13. Dannemiller interview.
14. A more complete account of this campaign launch dinner is in *Catch A Wave,* 95. It is recounted here because it summarizes the retrieval and reinterpretation of history.
15. Ariyoshi, 78.

CHAPTER 10

1. Commission on Operations, Revenues, and Expenditures, State of Hawai'i, Report to the Governor, 1973 (known as CORE), 1.

2. CORE, xii.
3. This is such a complex, pervasive subject as to defy references. Interested researchers might begin looking at groups such as Waiāhole-Waikāne, Third Arm, Ota Camp, and activities such as opposition to construction of H-3 highway, and internecine battles within the Protect Kahoʻolawe ʻOhana.
4. Gov 13-85, Archives of Hawaiʻi, letter dated May 1, 1968.
5. The manner in which Hamilton was brought down by the campus demonstrations, and the political reaction to his handling of those demonstrations, has never been detailed, nor do I attempt it here. My level of certainty is derived from repeated conversations with one of the regents, the late George McPherson.
6. *Hawaiʻi Observer,* 18 May 1974.
7. Phillips, *Hawaiʻi's Democrats,* 145.
8. Attributed by Dator to Robert Brumbaugh in *American Behavioral Scientist* 42, no. 3 (November/December 1998), 300.
9. Oshiro interview, 1372.
10. Oshiro was influenced by Harold Roberts, an NLRB economist.
11. Oshiro interview, 1384.
12. Oshiro interview, 1387.
13. Boswell, "An Old Pro Reflects on Ariyoshi's Victory," *The Honolulu Star-Bulletin,* 2 December 1974, 2.
14. Coffman, *Catch A Wave,* 59.
15. The speech was reprinted in *The Honolulu Advertiser,* 21 September 1974.
16. Phillips, *Hawaiʻi's Democrats,* 164, drawing from *The Honolulu Advertiser,* 21 September 1974, A3.
17. Takushi interview, 1999.
18. Oshiro interview, 1385.
19. Shim interview, including entire following vignette.
20. Shim interview.
21. Takushi interview, 1999.
22. Yokouchi told this story on the 25th anniversary of Burns' death at a Washington Place commemoration.
23. Sheenagh Burns, correspondence with the author, 3 May 2000.
24. Sheenagh Burns interview.
25. Shim interview.
26. Waiheʻe interview, 1994.
27. Sheenagh Burns, 182, 183.

CHAPTER 11

1. Kent, *Hawaiʻi: Islands Under the Influence,* 155.
2. Cooper and Daws, *Land and Power,* 447.
3. Ariyoshi, *With Obligation to All,* 53.
4. Ariyoshi, 55.
5. Historically this large estate was known as Bishop Estate for its founder, Bernice Pauahi Bishop. It was subsequently named Kamehameha Schools/Bishop Estate, then the words Bishop Estate were dropped, partly in an attempt to refocus

the work of its trustees, partly for public relations purposes. It is called Bishop Estate throughout this text.

6. Since the exercise of eminent domain lay at the end of a failed negotiation, the idea of "fair market value," although relying on identifiable comparable pieces of real estate, should be used advisedly.

7. The number 6,781 as of 30 June 1985 was cited in "A Report of the Governor 1974–1985," Hawai'i State Library.

8. Cooper and Daws, 413.

9. Cooper and Daws, 402.

10. Cooper and Daws, 463.

11. Cooper and Daws, 393.

12. Toffler, *Powershift*, xix. In the personal introduction Toffler looked back over twenty years at the impact of *Future Shock*.

13. Hoyt, "Who Are the 'Transients' on Welfare?" *The Honolulu Advertiser,* 15 April 1971, E1.

14. Keir, "Antihippie Move in the Senate," 3 April 1971, A1.

15. Boswell, "Ariyoshi Wants Newcomers Off Rolls," *The Honolulu Advertiser,* 4 June 1971.

16. Keir, "Ariyoshi Attacks Money Cost," *The Honolulu Advertiser,* 4 June 1971, A1. Ariyoshi spoke at the high school graduation in Pāhoa, Hawai'i, a declining plantation town that would became a strangely boutiqued settlement for the new migrants.

17. The welfare program administrator was Edwin Tam; his remark was reported in the 28 May 1978 *Honolulu Advertiser*.

18. "Urges Slowed Growth Policy," *The Honolulu Advertiser*, 3 May 1974, A5.

19. Ariyoshi, 1977 State of the State Address to Hawai'i Legislature.

20. "Ariyoshi Wants U.S. Funds to Help Support Immigrants," *Honolulu Star-Bulletin,* 27 April 1978, A2.

21. "Growth Management Issues in Hawai'i. Problems, Perspectives, Policy Implications." State of Hawai'i, Hubert S. Kimura, project coordinator, December 1977.

22. Ibid., 6.

23. Cooper and Daws, 190–191.

24. Biographical information and opinions in this section are from Kono interview, August 2000.

25. Kono, email to the author, 25 August 2000.

26. State of the State Address to the Ninth State Legislature, 23 January 1978.

27. Ibid.

28. Senator Francis Wong on final reading of HB 2173–78, HD 3, SD 3, CD1; 1978 Legislature.

29. Keith, "The Hawai'i State Plan Revisited," 56–59.

30. I produced a series of presentations on the plan designed to increase public participation. I also observed public participation workshops through which hundreds of people became involved. It seemed impossible either to cover the breadth of the plan or for groups of people to focus on such a large number of variables.

31. DeLeon, Dave. Unpublished manuscript about activism in Hawai'i, 36. The thought that H-3 could fill a book has occurred to several writers, the foremost being Gavan Daws on the night he shared a drink with George Cooper. They decided to write a case study of the highway, only to have Cooper lead them off into his open-ended inquiry into land and power. DeLeon wrote an as yet unpublished account of the 1970s, prominently including H-3, and historian and teacher, Rick Ziegler, wrote a personal account, also unpublished, of his opposition to H-3 in the 1980s. Material on opposition to H-3 draws mainly on three sources: DeLeon, Ziegler, and an extensive interview with Robert Nakata.
32. Frances Damon later married the Hawaiian writer John Dominis Holt and took his name.
33. DeLeon, 7.
34. Kawaguchi's firm was Parsons Brinckerhoff Inc.
35. Kawaguchi, *Infrastructure for Urban Growth,* 129.
36. The exemption story relies primarily on Kawaguchi and secondarily on Yamasaki. Their recollections essentially agree.
37. Keir, "Most Oahuans want new Koolau freeway," *The Honolulu Advertiser,* 24 January 1978, A1. The *Advertiser's* Hawai'i poll reported O'ahu voters favoring the freeway by a margin of 53 to 36 percent and statewide voters by 49 to 35 percent.
38. Robert Dye was on Heftel's staff and represented Heftel in the meetings. Interview, Dye.
39. Kawaguchi, 129.
40. The remarks of Inouye and Stafford were transcribed from a videotape of the floor debate. These could also be found in the congressional record.
41. After Ariyoshi left office, Yamasaki framed a copy of Ariyoshi's letter and put it on his wall.
42. Kawaguchi interview, 2000.
43. http://www.tfhrc.gov/pubrds/may98/h3.html.

CHAPTER 12

1. All references to Expo '70 are from a personal interview with Tom Sakata and from Burns' voluminous Expo '70 file in the Archives of Hawai'i (Gov 13-43).
2. Kuhaulua, *Takamiyama: The World of Sumo,* 171.
3. State Data Book of 1978, Honolulu Department of Business, Economic Development and Tourism, 416. The baseline 1960 Japanese visitor count was 14,800, rising to 131,500 in 1970.
4. Sakata to Don Horio, apparently relayed to Burns, 14 June 1970.
5. Hawai'i's contractor was Obayashi-Gumi.
6. Gov 13-43, Archives of Hawai'i. The quotes are from a memorandum written by George Kanahele 28 August 1970 after speaking with Burns, 2.
7. Carl Wright, "1st Japan-Hawaii Economic Council Meeting to Convene," *Honolulu Star-Bulletin,* 31 October 1972, D10.
8. Ariyoshi, *With Obligation to All,* 181–182.

9. Ibid., 182.

10. "Japanese Investment: The Golf Course Invasion." *Hawai'i Observer*, 22 January 1974, No. 24.

11. Hikaru Kerns, "Japanese Investment in Hawai'i." *The Hawai'i Observer*, 11 June 1974.

12. In 1999, addressing the Japan-Hawai'i Economic Council, Governor Cayetano said, "Looking back . . . it is clear that Hawai'i's economy was wed so strongly to Japanese investment that as Japan's economy declined, as Japanese tourism and investment declined—so did Hawai'i's economy."

13. Greg Wiles, "Survey: Japan not Losing Appetite," Adv 5 July 1989, quoting Kenneth Leventhal & Associates survey. Leventhal consistently tracked Japanese investment in America.

14. Ibid., quoting Harry Harnett, Leventhal & Associates.

15. Greg Wiles, "The Japanese Way: Seeing Hawai'i on $586 a Day," Adv 14 April 1989.

16. *The Third Attitudinal Survey of Honolulu Residents, 1983.* The Institute of Statistical Mathematics, Tokyo, in collaboration with the Research Committee on the Study of Honolulu Residents, Monograph 1, University of Hawai'i Press, February 1980.

17. *The Third Additudinal Survey,* 5.

18. Ibid., 35.

19. Ibid., 51.

20. Kono interview, August 2000.

21. Albert Miyasato's story is from Knaefler, *Our House Divided,* 97–106.

22. Ibid., 104.

23. Hazama and Komeiji, *Okage Sama De: The Japanese in Hawai'i,* quoting Department of Health Statistical Report 1982, 51, Table 61.

24. Congressional Record, 28 July 1959, 14564.

25. Ariyoshi, 171.

26. Hazama and Komeiji, *Okage Sama De,* 102.

27. This is quoted from a video produced by KHET/Honolulu, Joy Chong-Stannard, director, for Mō'ili'ili Community Center in 1995.

28. Yoshida papers, Hawai'i War Records Depository, Hawai'i Pacific Room, Hamilton Library, University of Hawai'i.

29. Ariyoshi, 170.

30. Along with several professional designers, I participated in this discussion of Japanese values in relationship to an overall design concept and story line.

31. A file containing unsigned "think" pieces was provided to me confidentially by a participant in this process. It included a remarkable piece that almost certainly was written by Ariyoshi himself.

32. This piece is organized and written in Ariyoshi's style and has such phrases as "when I called for authority to control the rate of growth. . . ."

33. This is from the same four-page document cited previously.

34. For a more detailed description of Ariyoshi's interactions with national governments, including his controversial relationship with Ferdinand Marcos of the Philippines, see Ariyoshi, 189–191.

35. Hong interview, 2001.
36. For detail on Pacific International Center for High Technology Research see Ariyoshi, *With Obligation to All,* 188–189.
37. Norris and Kiste interviews, 2001.
38. Ariyoshi, 185.
39. Ariyoshi, 185. Confirmed in interviews with Norris and Kiste, 2001.
40. Final Report, Economic Growth and Development through Unity, Pacific Basic Development Conference, 17 February 1980, introduction.
41. Final Report, Economic Growth and Development through Unity, 3.
42. For a description of the strategic and security issues of decolonization, see Howe, Kiste, and Lal, *Tides of History,* Chapter 13.
43. See Howe, Kiste, and Lal, 229, for a discussion of denial in context of the decolonization movement from 1962 to 1980 in the Pacific; for a far-reaching historiography of American denial of imperialism, see Crapol, *James G. Blaine, Architect of Empire;* for details of American annexation of Hawai'i, see Coffman, *Nation Within,* particularly Chapters 6, 9, and 15.
44. For an account of decolonization with brief references to Kiribati see Howe, Kiste, and Lal, Part 2 and Chapter 8.
45. Ariyoshi, 186.
46. All quotes in this paragraph are from Howe, Kiste, and Lal, 236.
47. Vitousek interview, 1998.

CHAPTER 13

1. Lawrence Fuchs, conversation with the author, 1997. He acknowledged Kekuni Blaisdell as one of many readers of his draft manuscript.
2. See repeated references to Kuaehelani Campbell in Coffman, *Nation Within;* also Silva, "Kū'ē! Hawaiian Women's Resistance to Annexation," 2–15.
3. Bell, *Last Among Equals,* 257.
4. Part of this generalization arises from a documentary I wrote and produced called *O Hawai'i: From Settlement to Kingdom.* The drift of this thinking has not been challenged, and the film is considerably used by classroom educators. A great deal of work needs to be done on how Hawaiians survived during this period.
5. Holt interview, 28 July 1983.
6. For entirely different reasons, overlapping narratives on anthropology accord Boas much the same role in history: Baker, *From Savage to Negro: Anthropology and the Construction of Race, 1896–1954,* and D'Souza, *The End of Racism: Principles for a Multiracial Society.*
7. In Coffman, *Nation Within,* see references to Professor John Burgess of Columbia and his relationships with Roosevelt, Dole, and Thurston.
8. Quoted by Baker, 122, from W. E. B. DuBois, *Black Folk Then and Now,* vii.
9. Benedict, *Race: Science and Politics,* 192.
10. Ibid., 51; Benedict credited University of Hawai'i sociologist Romanzo Adams for this observation.
11. Tennant McWilliams of the University of Alabama was a principal scholar of the documentary *The Last Queen,* a coproduction of *The American Experience.*

12. Holt interview, 1983.

13. Holt, *On Being Hawaiian,* 9.

14. Holt, 8.

15. Richard Pagliniwan, conversation with Tom Coffman, 2000.

16. Haertig, Lee, and Pukui, *Nana I Ke Kumu.*

17. I originally wrote this story in 1975 in a booklet "Ten Years of Community Action," recounting the Community Action Program. It survives in a few libraries.

18. Coffman, "Ten Years of Community Action."

19. Myron Thompson, trained as a social worker, originally directed the Queen Lili'uokalani Children's Center, then served as Burns' administrative director (chief of staff), and subsequently head of two State departments (Social Services and Hawaiian Homes) before becoming a trustee of Bishop Estate.

20. Rubin interview, 2001.

21. Rubin interview, 2001.

22. Wong interview, 2000.

23. DeSoto, Rubin, Waihee, and Wong interviews.

24. Inouye interview, 2001.

25. I interviewed Mrs. Ne in 1983 and was stunned by her powers of memory. For her writings see *Tales of Molokai,* with Gloria L. Cronin, Lā'ie, Hawai'i: The Institute for Polynesian Studies, 1992

26. Ritte, *Na Mana'o O Kaho'olawe,* 17.

27. Ritte, 43.

28. Ritte, 38.

29. Ritte, 27.

30. Ritte, 36.

31. Ritte, xii.

32. Aluli, *Kaho'olawe: Na Leo o Kanaloa,* xiv.

33. Daniel K. Inouye to Jimmy Carter, 20 December 1977, reprinted in Ritte, 95.

34. In my first conversation with Waihe'e, about 1975, I suggested that he run for office; he said he planned to follow Shim's example and work for political causes behind the scenes.

35. This is a simplified explanation. Delegate Jim Shon, an advocate, provided an expanded version: "Initiative does not always result in a public vote, as it is often used to force the legislature to act. And Referendum is not always a vote on an initiative for a new law, but can be used to ask the electorate its view on an issue."

36. "Tom Gill Looks At Today's Hawai'i," *Honolulu Star-Bulletin,* 5 January 1978, A15.

37. For example, Waihe'e was aware that the leadership of both First Hawaiian Bank and the Hawaiian Government Employees Association was opposed to initiative, referendum, and recall.

38. DeSoto interview, 2001.

39. This is Waihe'e's interpretation of how he became informally designated as majority leader. Interview.

40. Hawaiian Education Program Standing Committee Report 57.
41. Carol Fukunaga, conversation with the author, May 2001. Fukunaga, who managed the amendment, thought of it as a palatable way of sating the independents' appetite for slicing into the powers of government.

CHAPTER 14

1. This was an unsolicited opinion expressed by several Ariyoshi cabinet members in several interviews.
2. Pratt, *Hawai'i Politics and Government,* 13.
3. Dye interview, 2000.
4. Ariyoshi, *With Obligation to All,* 144.
5. Ariyoshi, 147.
6. Pratt, 125.
7. Ariyoshi, 93.
8. Pratt, 63.
9. Dye interview, 2000.
10. Ariyoshi interview, 1996.
11. Jerry Burris, "4 Year Battle Narrows to 1 Week," *The Honolulu Advertiser,* 2 October 1978, A1.
12. Thomas P. Gill, "Looks at Politics Today in Hawai'i," *Honolulu Star-Bulletin,* 5 January 1978, A15.
13. Jerry Burris, "Admits Savings Is Costly Politically," *The Honolulu Advertiser,* 10 December 1976, A5.
14. Doug Boswell, "Gov. Ariyoshi, 20 Months into Term, Feels He's Finally Pulling It Together," *Honolulu Star-Bulletin,* 3 August 1976, A1.
15. Doug Boswell, "State Tax Collectors Set Straight," *Honolulu Star-Bulletin,* 14 June 1978, A2.
16. Gregg Kakesako, "Ariyoshi vs. Fasi on Isles' Growth," *Honolulu Star-Bulletin,* 2 October 1978, in which Ariyoshi referred to a quote of Fasi by the 6 March 1978 *U.S. News and World Report,* later the subject of an Ariyoshi television spot assailing Fasi.
17. Oshiro interview, 1387.
18. Ibid., 1387.
19. Ibid., 1386.
20. Without publicly available reports, I painstakingly documented this pattern in a 1973 series in the *Honolulu Star-Bulletin.* One of the subsequent reforms that survived First Amendment challenges was a requirement of reporting expenditures, which enabled reporters to readily document contribution patterns many times throughout subsequent elections.
21. Ariyoshi, 161.
22. Oshiro interview, 1390.
23. Tokunaga interview, 1223.
24. Tokunaga interview, 1223.
25. Pratt, 245.

26. Gerry Kier, "Fasi Surges into Strong Lead," *The Honolulu Advertiser,* 30 September 1978, A1.

27. Greg Kakesako, "Mayor's Cabinet Officers Make a Pitch for AJA Vote," *Honolulu Star Bulletin,* 9 September 1978, A2.

28. Greg Kakesako, "Winners Vow to Heal Racial Rift: Ariyoshi Appeals for Unity," *Honolulu Star-Bulletin,* 8 November 1978, A1.

29. For example, he was to describe Japanese investment as "alarming" and advocate an end to foreign investment. When Emperor Hirohito died, he refused to lower the flags at City Hall to half mast.

30. Dye interview, 2000.

31. Quoted from a two-page draft titled "The Mayor of Paradise," by Jim Hall, 2.

32. Jerry Burris, "Leopold: GOP Powers Trying to Beat Me," *The Honolulu Advertiser,* 21 June 1978, A1.

33. As of 2001, the *Honolulu Star-Bulletin* was apparently saved by public intervention and the joint operating agreement was dissolved.

34. Shim conversation about 1977.

35. Waihe'e was interviewed three times on this subject, once in 1994, twice in 2001. All interviews were internally consistent. In the absence of a paper record, the only clouded issue is the time frame and the membership over time. I accept Waihe'e's recollection as described in the text. The unearthing of notes would be welcome and could shift the story modestly but not, I think, decisively.

36. Inouye interview, 2001. Inouye readily confirmed the existence of the group and particularly remembered announcing his choice of Waihe'e, but shrank from the idea of a name.

37. Inouye interview, 2001.

38. Waihe'e interview, 2002, quoting Yoshinaga.

39. Waihe'e interview, 2002.

40. Waihe'e interview. Waihe'e, like Oshiro, described repeated meetings between the two.

41. Oshiro interview, 1391.

42. Waihe'e interview.

43. Waihe'e interview.

44. Veary, *Change We Must,* 98. See 22, metaphysics; 44, traditional canoe-building; 98, change.

45. The incident at Customs occurred May 26, 1987. "Ariyoshi, Wife Detained in Dispute with Customs," *The Honolulu Advertiser,* 28 May 1987.

46. Nina Berglund, in "Ariyoshi Resigns from First Hawaiian," *The Honolulu Advertiser,* 19 June 1987, reported the high-side figure of $25,000.

47. "Ariyoshi Pays $11,389 Fine for Failing to Declare Presents," *Honolulu Star Bulletin,* 28 November 1987.

Bibliography

Allen, Gwenfread. *Hawaii's War Years*. Honolulu: University of Hawai'i Press, 1950.

Aluli, Emmett. *Kaho'olawe: Na Leo O Kanaloa*. Honolulu: Ai Pōhaku Press, 1995.

Ariyoshi, George. *With Obligation to All*. Honolulu: Ariyoshi Foundation, 1997.

Bailey, Beth, and Farber, David. *The First Strange Place*. New York: The Free Press, 1992.

Baker, Lee D. *From Savage to Negro: Anthropology and the Construction of Race, 1896–1954*. Berkeley: University of California Press, 1998.

Beechert, Edward. *Working in Hawai'i: A Labor History*. Honolulu: University of Hawai'i Press, 1985.

Bell, Roger. *Last Among Equals: Hawaiian Statehood and American Politics*. Honolulu: University of Hawai'i Press, 1984.

Benedict, Ruth. *Race: Science and Politics*. New York: Viking Press, 1945.

Boylan, Dan, and Holmes, T. Michael. *John A. Burns: The Man and His Times*. Honolulu: University of Hawai'i Press, 2000.

Burns, Sheenagh. "Jack Burns: A Daughter's Portrait." *The Hawaiian Journal of History* 24 (1990): 163–184.

Clissold, Edward L. "Influence of Lionism." *Pan-Pacific*. January–March (1940): 31–32.

Coffman, Tom. *Catch A Wave: A Case Study of Hawaii's New Politics*. Honolulu: University of Hawai'i Press, 1973.

———. *Nation Within: The Story of America's Annexation of the Nation of Hawai'i*. Honolulu: EpiCenter, 1998.

———. *May Earth Live*. Television program. Honolulu: Hawaii Public Television, 2000.

———. *O Hawai'i: From Settlement to Kingdom*. Television program. Honolulu: Hawaii Public Television, 2000.

Coggins, Cecil H. "The Japanese-Americans in Hawaii." *Harper's Magazine*. June (1943): 75–83.

Commission on Operations, Revenues, and Expenditures. State of Hawai'i, Report to Governor, 1973.

Congressional Record. Washington D.C., 28 July 1959.

Cooper, George, and Daws, Gavan. *Land and Power in Hawaii: The Democratic Years*. Honolulu: Benchmark Books, 1985.

Crapol, Edward. *James G. Blaine: Architect of Empire.* Wilmington: Scholarly Resources Inc., 2000.

Daniels, Roger. *Coming to America: A History of Immigration and Ethnicity in American Life.* New York: Harper Collins, 1990.

Daws, Gavan. *Shoal of Time: A History of the Hawaiian Islands.* Honolulu: University of Hawai'i Press, 1974.

DeLeon, Dave. Unpublished manuscript.

D'Souza, Dinesh. *The End of Racism: Principles for a Multiracial Society.* New York: The Free Press/Simon & Schuster, 1995.

DuBois, W. E. B. *Black Folk Then and Now.* New York: Henry Holt, 1939.

Duus, Masayo. *The Japanese Conspiracy: The Oahu Sugar Strike of 1920.* Berkeley: University of California Press, 1999.

———. *Unlikely Liberators.* Honolulu: University of Hawai'i Press, 1983.

"Economic Growth and Development through Unity." Final report. Pacific Basin Development Conference. 17 February 1980.

Edwards, Duval A. *Spy Catchers of the U.S. Army in the War with Japan.* Gig Harbor: Red Apple Publishing, 1994.

Emmons, Delos. *Brief Personal History from Memory.* Palo Alto: Hoover Institute, undated.

Fuchs, Lawrence S. *Hawai'i Pono.* Vol. 2. New York: Harcourt Brace & World, 1961.

Fujiwara, Vicky, and Rochford, Jerry. *Two Green Valleys.* Videocassette. Windward Video, 1977.

Grodzins, Morton. *Americans Betrayed: Politics and the Japanese Evacuation.* Chicago: University of Chicago Press, 1949.

Gusukuma, Chance. "Nisei Daimyo: The Life of Shunzo Sakamaki." Master's thesis. University of Hawai'i, 1999.

Haertig M.D., E. W.; Lee, Catherine A.; and Pukui, Mary Kawena. *Nana I Ke Kumu.* Honolulu: Hui Hanai, 1972.

Harada, Tasuku. "The Social Status of the Japanese in Hawaii." *Institute of Pacific Relations Preliminary Paper.* July (1927): 10.

Hardy, Thornton Sherburne. *Wallace R. Farrington.* Honolulu: Honolulu Star-Bulletin Ltd., 1935.

Hatch, Francis. *Report of the Republic of Hawaii's Ambassador to the United States.* 17 February 1986. Foreign Office and Executive File of the Republic. Archives of Hawai'i.

Hawaii Observer. 1974.

Hawai'i War Records Depository. University of Hawai'i.

Hazama, Dorothy Ochiai, and Komeiji, Jane Okamoto. *Okage Sama De: The Japanese in Hawai'i.* Honolulu: Bess Press, 1986.

Hitch, Thomas K. *Islands in Transition.* Honolulu: First Hawaiian Bank, 1992.

Holmes, T. Michael. *The Specter of Communism in Hawaii.* Honolulu: University of Hawai'i Press, 1994.

Holt, John Dominis. *On Being Hawaiian.* Honolulu: Topgallant Press, 1964.

Honolulu Advertiser, The. 1940–1978.

Honolulu Japanese Chamber of Commerce. *The Rainbow: A Bridge from East to West, Past to Future*. Honolulu: Honolulu Japanese Chamber of Commerce, 1970.

Honolulu Star-Bulletin. 1939–1978.

Hooper, Paul F. *Elusive Destiny: The Internationalist Movement in Modern Hawai'i*. Honolulu: University of Hawai'i Press, 1980.

Howe, K. R.; Kiste, Robert; and Lal, Brij V., eds. *Tides of History: The Pacific Islands in the Twentieth Century*. Honolulu: University of Hawai'i Press, 1994.

Hosokawa, Bill. *Nisei*. New York: William Morrow and Co. Inc., 1969.

Ige, Thomas. *Boy from Kahaluu*. Honolulu: Kin Cho Jin Kai, 1984.

Iriye, Akira. *Pacific Estrangement*. New York: Harcourt Brace Jovanovich, 1967.

———. *Power and Culture*. Cambridge, MA: Harvard University Press, 1981.

Kawaguchi, Stanley. *Infrastructure for Urban Growth*. New York: American Society of Civil Engineers, 1985.

Kawakani, H. S. *From Japan to Hawaii: My Journey*. Honolulu, 1976.

Keith, Kent M. "The Hawai'i State Plan Revisited." *University of Hawai'i Law Review* 7, no. 1 (Spring 1985).

Kent, Noel J. *Hawai'i: Islands Under the Influence*. Honolulu: University of Hawai'i Press, 1983.

Kimura, Yukiko. "Some Effects of the War Situation upon the Alien Japanese in Hawaii." *Social Process in Hawai'i*. 1943: 18–28.

Knaefler, Tomi Kaizawa. *Our House Divided: Seven Japanese American Families in World War II*. Honolulu: University of Hawai'i Press, 1991.

Krauss, Bob. *Johnny Wilson: First Hawaiian Democrat*. Honolulu: University of Hawai'i Press, 1994.

Kuhaulua, Jesse, with Wheeler, John. *Takamiyama: The World of Sumo*. New York: Kodansha International, 1973.

LaFeber, Walter. *The Clash: A History of U.S.-Japan Relations*. New York: W. W. Norton & Company, 1997.

Linn, Brian McCallister. *Guardians of Empire: The U.S. Army and the Pacific, 1902–1940*. Chapel Hill: University of North Carolina Press, 1997.

McWilliams, Tennant. *The Last Queen: American Experience*. Documentary. Public Broadcast System.

Monobe, Hiromi. "Invisible Thread: The Japanese Government and the Americanization Movement among the Issei and Nisei in Hawai'i During the 1920s and the 1930s." Paper presented at Crossroads Conference, Honolulu, University of Hawai'i, August 2001.

Moriyama, Alan Takeo. *Imingaisha*. Honolulu: University of Hawai'i Press, 1985.

Murphy, Thomas D. *Ambassadors in Arms: The Story of Hawaii's 100th Battalion*. Honolulu: University of Hawai'i Press, 1954.

Nakano, Jiro. *Samurai Missionary: The Reverend Shiro Sokabe*. Honolulu: Hawai'i Conference of the United Church of Christ, 1984.

Nosaka, Raymond. "Brother in War and Peace: The 100th Infantry Story." *Go For Broke, 1943–1993*. Honolulu: Veterans of 442nd Regiment, 1993.

O'ahu Conference of Americans of Japanese Ancestry. Honolulu, 28 January 1945.

Okihiro, Gary Y. *Cane Fires: The Anti-Japanese Movement in Hawai'i, 1865–1945.* Philadelphia: Temple University Press, 1984.

Ota, Masao, and Oshiro, George. "Mediator between Cultures: Tasuku Harada." *The Hawaiian Journal of History* 33 (1990): 174–175.

Phillips, Paul C. *Hawaii's Democrats.* Washington D.C.: University Press of America, 1982.

Pratt, Richard C. *Hawai'i Politics and Government.* Lincoln: University of Nebraska Press, 2000.

Quin, Mike. *The Big Strike.* Olema, CA: Olema Publishing Company, 1949.

Ritte, Walter. *Na Mana'o O Kaho'olawe.* Honolulu: Aloha 'Āina O Na Kūpuna, 1977.

Robinson, Greg. *By Order of the President: FDR and the Internment of Japanese Americans.* Cambridge: Harvard University Press, 2001.

Saiki, Patsy Sumie. *Ganbare.* Honolulu: Kisaku, Inc., 1982.

Shimada, Noriko. "Eiichi Shibusawa and Takie Okumura: Americanization of Japanese in Hawai'i During the 1920s." Paper presented at Crossroads Conference, Honolulu, University of Hawai'i, August 2001.

Shimamura, Clarence Y. "Hawaiian Japanese Civic Association." *Pan-Pacific.* January–March (1940): 29–31.

Silva, Noenoe. "Kū'ē! Hawaiian Women's Resistance to Annexation," *Social Process in Hawai'i* Vol. 38, 1997.

Soga, Keiho, and Takei, Sojin. *Poets Behind Barbed Wire.* Honolulu: Bamboo Ridge Press, 1983.

State of Hawai'i, Herbert S. Kimura, project coordinator. "Growth Management Issues in Hawai'i: Problems, Perspectives, Policy Implications." December 1977.

Takabuki, Matsuo. *An Unlikely Revolutionary: Matsuo Takabuki and the Making of Modern Hawai'i.* Honolulu: University of Hawai'i Press, 1998.

Tamura, Eileen H. *Americanization, Acculturation, and Ethnic Identity: The Nisei Generation in Hawaii.* Urbana and Chicago: University of Illinois Press, 1994.

———. "Using the Past to Inform the Future: An Historiography of Hawai'i's Asian and Pacific Islander Americans." *Amerasia Journal* 26:1 (2000): 55–85.

Tendai Educational Foundation. *Japanese Eyes, American Heart.* Honolulu: Tendai Educational Foundation, 1998.

The Third Attitudinal Survey of Honolulu Residents, 1983. Institute of Statistical Mathematics, Tokyo, in collaboration with the Research Committee on the Study of Honolulu Residents, Monograph 1, University of Hawai'i Press, February 1980.

Toffler, Alvin. *Powershift.* New York: Bantam Books, 1990.

Tsukiyama, Ted T. "Origins of the 442nd." *Go For Broke, 1943–1993.* Honolulu: Veterans of 442nd Regiment, 1993.

Tsukiyama, Ted T., and Carson, Ellen Goodbey, "Tale of Two Generals," *Honolulu Star-Bulletin*, 2 December 1991, A-15.

Unger, Irwin, and Unger, Debi. *LBJ: A Life.* New York: John Wiley & Sons, 1999.

Veary, Nana. *Change We Must.* Honolulu: Institute of Zen Studies, 1989.

Zacharias, Ellis M. *Secret Missions: The Story of an Intelligence Officer.* New York: G. P. Putnam's Sons, 1946.

Zalburg, Sanford. *A Spark Is Struck: Jack Hall and the ILWU in Hawaii.* Honolulu: University of Hawaiʻi Press, 1979.

Ziegler, Richard. "Hawaii's Road to Ruin." Unpublished manuscript.

INTERVIEWS

Unless otherwise noted the interviews were conducted by the author. BOHP refers to the John A. Burns Oral History Project. The interviews were conducted in the years 1975 and 1976 by a team of three people: Stewart Gerry Brown, Daniel Boylan, and Paul Hoopers. The tapes and transcripts are housed in the Hawaiʻi Collection of the Hamilton Library at the University of Hawaiʻi.

Ariyoshi, George R. 1994, 1995, 2000, 2001.

Boylan, Dan. 1999, 2000, 2001.

Brown, Kenneth. 1999.

Burns, John A. BOHP.

Burns, Sheenagh. 2000, 2001.

Ching, Hung Wai. 1994.

Coggins, Cecil. Interview by Katherine Herbig. 9 August 1985.

Dannemiller, James. 1999.

Dator, James. 2000.

DeSoto, A. Frenchy. 2001.

Doi, Masato.

Dye, Robert. 2000.

Ebesu, Sandra. 1999.

Fukunaga, Carol. 1999.

Heen, Walter. 1999, 2001, 2002.

Ho, Stuart. 2002.

Holt, John Dominis. 1983.

Hong, Stanley. 2001.

Inouye, Daniel K. 2001.

Isonaga, Sue. 1994.

Kai, Ernest. Interview by Chris Conybeare and Daniel W. Tuttle, Jr. 11 May 1988. Hawaiʻi Political History Documentation Project, Volume III, Center for Oral History, Social Science Research Institute, University of Hawaiʻi, 1996, p. 1277.

Kanazawa, Kenji. 2001.

Kanazawa, Shimeiji (Ryusaki). 2001.

Kaneko, William. 2001

Kawaguchi, Stanley. 2000.

Kawano, Jack. BOHP. 21 August 1975.

Kido, Mitsuyuki. BOHP. 17 July 1975; 31 July 1975.

Kim, Young Oak. 2001.

Kiste, Robert. 2001.

Kono, Hideto. 2000.

Kuroda, Yasumasa. 2001.

Marumoto, Masaji. The Watumull Foundation Oral History Project. 1987.

Marumoto, Shigeko. 1999.

Marumoto, Wendell. 2001.

Mau, Chuck. BOHP. 21 September 1975.

MacNaughton, Malcolm. BOHP. 11 May 1983.

Miho, Katsugo. Interview by Katherine Collins. 20–21 May 1997. Oral History Project of 442 Club.

Miho, Katsugo. 2001.

Nishimura, Earl. JCCH. 1994.

Ne, Harriet. 1983.

Norris, Jerry. 2001

Oba, Ron, and Yoshida, Yoshiaki. 2001.

Oshiro, Robert C. Interview by Chris Conybeare and Daniel W. Tuttle, Jr. 7 April 1988. Hawai'i Political History Documentation Project, Volume III, Center for Oral History, Social Science Research Institute, University of Hawai'i.

Paglininawan, Richard. 1999.

Rubin, Winona. 2001.

Sakata, Tom. 2000.

Shim, Alvin. 2000.

Shon, James. 2000.

Takahashi, Sakae. JCCH. 1994.

Takushi, James. 1999.

Tokunaga, Mike. Interview by Larry Meacham and Daniel W. Tuttle, Jr. 12 September 1989. Hawai'i Political History Documentation Project. Volume III, Center for Oral History, Social Science Research Institute, University of Hawai'i, 1996.

Trotter, Fred. 2002.

Tuttle, Daniel W. 2001.

Vitousek, Peter. 1998.

Waihe'e, John D., III. 1994, 1995, 2002.

Wong, Norma. 2000.

Yamasaki, Wayne. 2001.

Yim, John. 1992.

Yoshida, Yutaka K. 2001.

Index

About the Author

Tom Coffman traveled America as a college student writing about the civil rights movement. At twenty-three he began writing about government and politics in Hawaiʻi, first for the *Honolulu Advertiser* and then the *Honolulu Star-Bulletin*. From this experience he wrote his widely read, widely quoted study of campaign politics, *Catch A Wave*. Thereafter he left daily journalism and won numerous awards as a professional media and documentary producer.

In 1998 he returned to print in *Nation Within*, the history of America's annexation of Hawaiʻi, which attracted the Hawaiʻi publishers' Poʻokela award for nonfiction in 1999. In the same year he received the Hawaiʻi Award for Literature.

As a journalist who researches history, his grasp of Hawaiʻi's political culture is both firsthand and archival. He is at once a careful analyst and a readable storyteller, delivering fine fragments and sweeping trends.

He is married to Lois Lee, a social worker. They have three children.

Production Notes for Coffman/THE ISLAND EDGE OF AMERICA

Cover and Interior designed by Argosy in Adobe Berkeley, with display type in ITC Franklin Gothic.

Composition by Argosy.

Printing and binding by Thomson-Shore, Inc.

Printed on 60 lb. Joy White.